Urban Housing, Livelihoods and Environmental Challenges in Emerging Economies

Urban Housing, Livelihoods and Environmental Challenges in Emerging Economies

Edited By

Rajesh Bhattacharya
Annapurna Shaw

Orient BlackSwan

URBAN HOUSING, LIVELIHOODS AND ENVIRONMENTAL CHALLENGES IN EMERGING ECONOMIES

ORIENT BLACKSWAN PRIVATE LIMITED

Registered Office
3-6-752 Himayatnagar, Hyderabad 500 029, Telangana, India
e-mail: centraloffice@orientblackswan.com

Other Offices
Bengaluru, Chennai, Guwahati, Hyderabad,
Kolkata, Mumbai, New Delhi,
Noida, Patna

First published by Orient Blackswan Private Limited 2021

ISBN 978-93-5442-233-1

Typeset in
Goudy Old Style 11/13
by Le Studio Graphique, Gurgaon 122 007

Printed in India at
Kensington Printing & Packaging, Noida 201 301

Published by
Orient Blackswan Private Limited
3-6-752 Himayatnagar, Hyderabad 500 029, Telangana, India
e-mail: info@orientblackswan.com

Contents

Abbreviations

AAP	Aam Aadmi Party
ACCA	Asian Coalition for Community Action
ACHR	Asian Coalition for Housing Rights
ADBI	Asian Development Bank Institute
AEIS	Special Areas of Social Interest
AMRUT	Atal Mission for Rejuvenation and Urban Transformation
ANC	African National Congress
ANPUR	Associação Nacional de Pós-graduação e Pesquisaem Planejamento Urbano e Regional (National Association of Graduation and Research in Urban and Regional Planning)
BBKC	Bhule Bisre Kalakar Co-operative
BEE	Black Economic Empowerment
BNH	Banco Nacional De Habitação/National Housing Bank
BMC	Bhubaneswar Municipal Corporation
BNG	Breaking New Ground Policy
BPL	Below Poverty Line
BRICS	Brazil–Russia–India–China–South Africa
BSUP	Basic Services for the Urban Poor
CDF	City-based Development Funds/Community Development Fund
CDM	Clean Development Mechanism
CEF	Caixa Econômica Federal
CEH	Conselho Estadual de Habitaçao/State Housing Council
CEM	Centre for Metropolitan Studies
CEO	Chief Executive Officer

CIT	Calcutta Improvement Trust
CMP	Community Mortgage Programme, Philippines
CODI	Community Organisations Development Institute, Thailand
COPROMO	Cooperativa Pró Moradia de Osasco/Osasco Pro-housing Cooperative
CPF	Central Provident Fund (Singapore)
CRA	Contingent Reserve Arrangement
CUEM	Concessão de Uso Especial para Fins de Moradia
DBSA	Development Bank of Southern Africa
DDA	Delhi Development Authority
DIPP	Department of Industrial Policy and Promotion
DPR	Detailed Project Report
DUSIB	Delhi Urban Slum Improvement Board
EBRD	European Bank for Reconstruction and Development
EBTU	Brazilian Urban Transportation Company
EIA	Environmental Impact Assessment
EIUS	Environmental Improvement of Urban Slums, 1972
ENANPUR	Encontro Nacionalda Associação Nacional de Pós-graduação e Pesquisaem Planejamento Urbano e Regional (National Meeting of the National Association of Graduation and Research in Urban and Regional Planning)
EWS	Economically Weaker Section
FCP	Popular Housing Foundation
FDI	Foreign Direct Investment
FGD	Flue-gas Desulphurisation
FGTS	Fundo de Garantiapor Tempo de Serviço
FIFA	Fédération Internationale de Football Association
FNDU	National Fund for the Development of Transports
FPHIS	Fundo Paulista de Habitaçao de Interesse Social/Sao Paulo State Fund for Social Housing

FSI	Floor Space Index
GDP	Gross Domestic Product
GHG	Greenhouse Gas
GIS	Geographic Information System
GoI	Government of India
GPMA	Gian P. Mathur & Associates Pvt. Ltd. (architects and planners)
HABI	Office of Housing (Brazil)
HC	Hazards Centre
HDB	Housing and Development Board (Singapore)
HFIs	Housing Finance Institutions
HIG	Higher Income Group
HIS	Habitação de Interesse Social/Social Interest Housing
HUDCO	Housing and Urban Development Corporation
IAPs	Retirement and Pensions Institutes
IB	Intelligence Bureau
IBGE	Instituto Brasileiro de Geografia e Estatística/ Brazilian Institute of Geography and Statistics
ICMS	Imposto Sobre Circulação de Mercadorias e Serviços
ICRIER	Indian Council for Research on International Economic Relations
IDB	International Development Bank
IDP	Integrated Development Plan, eThekwini Municipality
IFP	Inkatha Freedom Party
IHSDP	Integrated Housing and Slum Development Programme
IIED	International Institute for Environment and Development (UN)
IIM	Indian Institute of Management
ILO	International Labour Organization
IMC	Indore Municipal Corporation
IMF	International Monetary Fund

IPPs	Independent Power Producers
IPT-FUPAM	Institute of Technological Research and Foundation for Architectural and Environmental Research
JNNURM	Jawaharlal Nehru National Urban Renewal Mission
KC	Kathputli Colony
KIP	Kampung Improvement Programme
KZN	KwaZulu-Natal, a coastal South African province
Lao PDR	Lao People's Democratic Republic
LHWP	Lesotho Highlands Water Project
LIG	Lower/Low Income Group
MCMV	Minha Casa Minha Vida/My Home (or House) My Life
MCS	Mahila Co-operative Society
MDGs	Millennium Development Goals
MIG	Middle Income Group
MHUPA	Ministry of Housing and Urban Poverty Alleviation
MoHURD	Ministry of Housing and Urban-Rural Development of the People's Republic of China
MoUD	Ministry of Urban Development
MUP	Main Upgrading Programme (Singapore)
MP	Madhya Pradesh
MPUSP	Madhya Pradesh Urban Services for the Poor
NBSC	National Bureau of Statistics of China
NCU	National Commission on Urbanization
NDA	National Democratic Alliance
NDB	New Development Bank
NDHS	National Department of Human Settlements (South Africa)
NGO	Non-governmental Organisations
NWCMC	Nanded Waghala City Municipal Corporation
NSS	National Sample Survey
OBC	Other Backward Classes

OPP	Orangi Pilot Project, Pakistan
OUTA	Organisation Undoing Tax Abuse
PAC	Growth Acceleration Programme/Programa de Aceleração do Crescimento Urbanização de Assentamentos Precários
PAR	Plano de Arrendamento Residencial
PFL	Partido da Frente Liberal (Party of the Liberal Front)
PIL	Public Interest Litigation
PL	Partido Liberal (Liberal Party)
PLANASA	National Plan for Sanitation
PMAY- HFA 22	Pradhan Mantri Awas Yojana-Housing for All by 2022
PMCMV	Programa Minha Casa Minha Vida
PNDU	Urban Development National Policy
PNH	National Housing Policy
PPE	Personal Protective Equipment
PPP	Public-Private Partnership
2011 PPP	At 2011 international prices (Purchasing Power Parity)
PPSA	Pocket Poverty Situation Analysis
PREZEIS	Plano de Regularização das Zonas Especiais de Interesse Social/Plan of Regularisation for Special Zones of Social Interest
PRIA	Participatory Research in Asia
PRI	Programa de Recuperação Integrada/Integrated Recovery Programme
PROVER	Projeto de Urbanização de Favelas com Verticalização/Project of Squatter Settlement Upgrading with Verticalisation
PSDB	Partido da Social Democracia Brasileira (Party of the Brazilian Social Democracy)
PT	Partido dos Trabalhadores (Workers' Party)
PWD	Public Works Department
R&R	Resettlement and Rehabilitation Project

RAY	Rajiv Awas Yojana
RDP	Redevelopment Project Housing
RESOLO	Departamentode Regularização de Loteamentos/ Land Tenure Department
ROSCA	Rotating Savings and Credit Association
S&S	Sites and Services
SANRAL	South Africa National Roads Agency
SARS-CoV-2	Severe Acute Respiratory Syndrome Coronavirus 2
S.E.	Standard Error of the Regression Coefficient
SA	South Africa
SBA	Swachh Bharat Abhiyan
SC	Scheduled Castes
SCM	Smart Cities Mission
SDCEA	South Durban Community Environmental Alliance
SDF	Spatial Development Framework
SDG	Sustainable Development Goals
SECC	Soweto Electricity Crisis Committee
SIPs	Strategic Investment Projects
SNHIS	National System of Social Housing
SNTU	National System of Urban Transports
SPA	School of Planning and Architecture
SPARC	Society for the Promotion of Area Resource Centres (India)
SRA	Slum Redevelopment Authority; also Slum Rehabilitation Authority (Chapter 4)
SRP	Slum Rehabilitation Programme
ST	Scheduled Tribes
STDs	Sexually Transmitted Diseases
STPs	Sewage Treatment Plants
TAP	Training and Advisory Programme (under ACHR)
TB	Tuberculosis
TCTA	Trans-Caledon Tunnel Authority
TDR	Transfer of Development Rights

TISS	Tata Institute of Social Sciences
UBS	Urban Basic Services
UBSP	Urban Basic Services for the Poor
UDPFI	Urban Development Plans Formulation and Implementation
UK	United Kingdom
UKZN	University of KwaZulu-Natal
ULBs	Urban Local Bodies
ULCRA	Urban Land Ceiling and Regulation Act, 1976
UN	United Nations
UNCHS	United Nations Commission on Human Settlements
UNDESA	United Nations Department of Economic and Social Affairs
UN-Habitat	United Nations Human Settlements Programme
UNFCC	United Nations Framework Convention on Climate Change
UPP	Pacifying Police Units
US	United States
USAID	United States Agency for International Development
VAMBAY	Valmiki Ambedkar Awas Yojana
WASH	Water, Sanitation and Hygiene programme
WB	World Bank
WD	West Division
WHO	World Health Organization
ZEIS	Zonas de Especial Interesse Social/Special Zones of Social Interest

Tables, Figures and Images

Tables

Figures

Images

Acknowledgements

The COVID-19 pandemic of 2020–2021 and the lockdowns that have followed have delayed the publication of this volume, the planning of which began well before these events. The edited volume was initially undertaken to publish several papers presented at an international workshop held on 6–8 February 2017 at the Indian Institute of Management (IIM), Calcutta on urban housing, livelihood and environmental challenges in Brazil and India. Apart from researchers from India, and government officials and activists from Kolkata, there were participants from Brazil, UK and Thailand. The workshop was an initiative of the Institute's Centre for Development and Environment Policy (CDEP). We take this opportunity to express our thanks to the CDEP for its financial and logistical support. We would also like to thank our faculty colleagues and doctoral students at IIM-Calcutta, who contributed to the lively discussions and debates at the workshop.

During the course of its publication, the scope of this volume was expanded to include other large emerging economies and thereby add to its reach and relevance. We thank all the contributors to the volume, both the paper presenters at the workshop as well as those who enthusiastically responded to our call for papers post the workshop. Without the co-operation and patience of all contributors, this volume would not have been possible. We also thank the editorial team at Orient BlackSwan for their valuable expertise and advice in transforming our manuscript into a book. Finally, we thank both our families for their wholehearted support and belief in the success of this endeavour.

Introduction

Rajesh Bhattacharya and Annapurna Shaw

INTRODUCTION

In the first decade of the twenty-first century, for the first time in history, the world's urban population exceeded its rural population. It is expected that by the middle of the century, more than two-thirds of humanity will live in towns and cities. Much of this urbanisation will take place in emerging economies, particularly in Asia and Africa. Currently, cities occupy a mere 3 per cent of the Earth's land, but account for more than 80 per cent of global GDP, two-thirds of the world's energy consumption, more than 70 per cent of global greenhouse gas emissions and a disproportionate share of governments' revenues (UNDESA 2014, 2016).

In September 2015, 193 member countries of the United Nations adopted the 2030 Agenda for Sustainable Development, with a commitment to working towards achieving no less than seventeen Sustainable Development Goals (SDGs)—one of which is to make cities inclusive, safe, resilient and sustainable. In 2016, at the UN Habitat III conference, one of the goals of the 'New Urban Agenda' was to

> meet the challenges and opportunities of present and future sustained, inclusive and sustainable economic growth, leveraging urbanisation for structural transformation, high productivity, value-added activities and resource efficiency, harnessing local economies and taking note of the contribution of the informal economy while supporting a sustainable transition to the formal economy (United Nations 2017: 7).

It is interesting to note that while the statement talks about leveraging urbanisation for 'structural transformation', it also talks about a parallel 'transition to the formal economy'. One of the stylised facts of development derived from the experience of Western economies is that in the process of economic development, a country that starts out with primarily an agrarian economy first sees industries overtaking agriculture in national output and employment; at a certain stage of development, services overtake industry in terms of both output and employment. Agriculture's shares in output and employment decline continuously throughout this process. Needless to say, structural transformation is central to the process of urbanisation as it drives people from rural to urban areas, which develop on the basis of industries and services.

However, for more than four decades now, it has been recognised that rural-urban migration in developing countries has resulted in the burgeoning of an informal sector and informal settlements, and not in the smooth transition from field to factory or from village dwellings to working-class housing in the cities, as expected in the dominant narrative. This has resulted in dystopian visions evident in terms like 'planet of slums' (Davis 2006) or 'planet of the wageless' (Watts 2011). The problem with informality, as famously captured in the 1991 report to the International Labour Conference by the Director-General of the International Labour Organization (ILO), is the following:

> The dilemma, put simply, is whether to promote the informal sector as a provider of employment and incomes; or to seek to extend regulation and social protection to it and thereby possibly reduce its capacity to provide jobs and income for an ever-expanding labor force (Schlyter 2002: 2).

This dilemma is at the heart of the challenge of policy-making for urban areas in emerging economies. If urban informality is indeed the dominant process driving their rural-urban transformation, then how do we design policies for sustainable cities? If much of what is happening in the cities in developing countries is outside the formal, regulatory reach of governmental authorities, how do we align our traditional policy objectives of urban housing and urban livelihoods with the pressing need for sustainable development? This volume is an attempt to understand the issues of urban livelihoods, housing and environment in their connectedness. While the issues are global and general, the motivation behind the volume is to bring together perspectives from several emerging economies—Brazil, China, India, Russia, South Africa and Thailand—where, despite significant differences in country-level experiences, concerns similar to those raised above have animated debates on public policies for several decades now. The idea is to benefit from harnessing the histories of different societies to throw light on common contemporary challenges.

This volume has taken its final shape as the COVID-19 pandemic cast its long shadow over humanity, destroying lives and livelihoods. As lockdowns, quarantines, social distancing and self-isolation measures become routine or turn into recurrent features of social, familial and individual lives, the need to rebuild the social fabric during and after the pandemic assumes critical importance. Nowhere is this need felt more urgently and acutely than in the cities—which have been the hotspots of the pandemic in different countries.

Studies on the impact of the pandemic on urban areas have focussed on (*i*) environmental aspects; (*ii*) the socio-economic aspects, including livelihoods, poverty and inequality; (*iii*) management and governance; and (*iv*) housing, mobility and other aspects of urban design (Lai et al. 2020; Sharifi and Khavarian-Garmsir 2020). As a result of the public health measures aimed at combating the pandemic, now observed across many countries simultaneously, economies have plunged into recessions, businesses have shut down or laid off workers, and workers have lost livelihoods in the formal as well as the vast informal economies, thus pushing millions into poverty (ILO 2021). Studies have explored the connection between air pollution levels in cities and infection and death due to the novel coronavirus SARS-CoV-2 (Coccia 2021). Similarly, the pandemic has generated debates on the quality of housing, design of transportation and public places, access to amenities, and public health infrastructure—thereby presenting a more complex picture than what had been predicted at the beginning of the pandemic

(Sharifi and Khavarian-Garmsir 2020). The planning of this volume began before the onset of the pandemic and yet, looking at the evolving debates on its impact, we find that the chapters address issues that have currently become critical. While these issues—housing, livelihoods and environment—are not specifically presented in the context of the pandemic, they are analysed from regional, comparative and historical perspectives, thus providing a breadth of ideas and experiences that would help scholars, practitioners and policy-makers think of appropriate responses to the unprecedented urban crises unleashed by the pandemic.

COMPARATIVE DEVELOPMENTAL TRAJECTORIES

The six countries on which we have contributions in this volume—Brazil, China, India, Russia, South Africa and Thailand—are 'emerging economies' in the sense that in terms of per capita income levels, they are not yet at the same level as richer economies, but their faster growth rates compared to the latter place them in a transitional stage of developmental catch-up. Emerging countries typically experience a host of challenges that accompany fast growth—structural change in the economy, releasing labour from agriculture, rapid urbanisation, rising environmental pollution and demographic changes. These changes are often accompanied by significant ongoing economic reforms in international trade, financial systems and the regulatory environment, which present their own political challenges.

The six countries vary significantly among themselves in terms of ethnic or cultural diversity, social disparities and income inequalities. Brazil, South Africa, India and Thailand are ethnically more diverse than the others, while income inequality is particularly high in Brazil, China and South Africa. They still face many developmental challenges, at the forefront of which is the need to break out of historically determined structures of social and economic privileges, and bestow equal opportunities on all citizens. Russia and China are countries where attempts to break out of such social structures of privilege were made during the socialist revolutions of 1917 and 1949, respectively. But with the turn towards market reforms and globalisation, since 1979 in China and 1991 in Russia, new forms of economic and social stratification have emerged. In the other countries, concerns over social discrimination and economic exclusion have often fuelled social movements and reforms, in the past and the present, and continue to animate contemporary popular politics. In the urban context of today, ensuring social inclusion through the provision of decent housing and livelihoods, keeping in mind environmental sustainability, is as much a challenge in these post-socialist or socialist market economies as it is in Thailand, Brazil, South Africa and India.

Of the six countries, China, India, Brazil and Russia are among the largest countries by size of population and area. The differences in population size and population densities among the countries in the set are considerable, with India and China having more than six times the population of the next most populous country, Brazil, and about twenty times the population of the least populous country, Thailand. Within our set of countries, population densities vary considerably—from 8.8 people per sq. km. of land area in Russia to 454.9 people per sq. km. of land area in India. Among the three most densely populated countries in our set, India has more than three times and nine times the population densities of China and Thailand, respectively. All the countries in the set, except India, are classified as upper middle-income, while India is a lower middle-income country (according to World Bank classification based on per capita incomes of countries) (see World Bank Blogs 2018).

Economic differences between the countries also show up in poverty rates. At $1.90 per day (in terms of 2011 international prices, using PPP or purchasing power parity exchange rates for conversion), three countries had zero or near-zero poverty—China, Russia and Thailand—in 2016, 2018 and 2019, respectively. Brazil had less than 5 per cent of its population in poverty in 2019, while South Africa had a little less and India had a little more than one-fifth of its population in poverty in 2014 and 2011, respectively. However, the $1.90 per day poverty line measures extreme poverty. The relevant

Table I.1: Some Key Socio-economic Indicators

Country	GDP in 2019 (in billion, current US$)	Population in 2019 (in million)	Population density in 2018 (number of people per sq. km. of land area)	GDP per capita in 2019 (current US$)	Poverty headcount ratio (2011 PPP) (% of population) at $1.90 a day	Poverty headcount ratio (2011 PPP) (% of population) at $3.20 a day	Poverty headcount ratio (2011 PPP) (% of population) at $5.50 a day	Gini Index (World Bank estimate)	Ethnic fractionalisation
(1)	(2)	(3)	(4)	(5)	(6)	(7)	(8)	(9)	(10)
Brazil	1,839.8	211.1	25.1	8,717.2	4.6	9.1	19.6	53.4	0.55
China	14,279.9	1,397.7	147.8	10,216.6	0.5	5.4	24	38.5	0.15
India	2,868.9	1,366.4	454.9	2,099.6	22.5	61.7	87.4	35.7	0.81
Russian Federation	1,699.9	144.4	8.8	11,585.0	0	0.4	3.7	37.5	0.33
South Africa	351.4	58.6	47.6	6,001.4	18.7	37.3	56.9	63	0.88
Thailand	543.5	69.6	135.9	7,806.7	0.1	0.3	6.2	34.9	0.43

Notes:

1) Poverty headcount ratio is the number of people with income below $1.90/$3.20/$5.50 a day (2011 PPP) as percentage of the total population.
2) The years corresponding to the figures in columns (6)–(9) are: Brazil and Thailand (2019), Russian Federation (2018), China (2016), South Africa (2014) and India (2011).

Source: The figures in column (6) are from Fearon (2003). For the rest of the columns, the figures are from World Bank Open Data, https://data.worldbank.org/.

poverty lines for lower middle-income and upper middle-income countries are $3.20 per day and $5.50 per day (World Bank 2018). By the former measure, in those same years, Russia and Thailand had near-zero poverty, while China and Brazil had 5.4 and 9.1 per cent of their populations in poverty, respectively. For India and South Africa, as per the World Bank, the corresponding figures were 61.7 per cent and 37.3 per cent, respectively. At $5.50 per day, in those same years, the figures for Brazil, China, South Africa and India are 19.6 per cent, 24 per cent, 56.9 per cent and 87.4 per cent, respectively, while for Russia and Thailand, the figures are low at 3.7 per cent and 6.2 per cent, respectively.

Due to the COVID-19 pandemic, however, most countries in the world have seen rising unemployment and poverty. Among the countries we consider in this volume, only China's economy grew in 2019–2020 by 2.3 per cent as per World Bank estimates (World Bank 2021). Each of the other five economies contracted, with the GDP of India, South Africa, Thailand, Brazil and Russian Federation, falling by 7.3, 7.0, 6.1, 4.1 and 3 per cent, respectively (ibid.). It has been estimated that in 2020, 8.8 per cent of total working hours were lost and the global shortfall in employment increased by 144 million (ILO 2021).This has led to a fall in labour income, halting the progress and wiping out the gains made in the eradication of poverty since 2015. It is estimated that an additional 108 million working people are now living in extreme or moderate poverty (that is, on income less than $3.20 per day), relative to 2019 (ibid.).

When it comes to inequality of incomes as measured by the Gini Index (estimated by World Bank), Brazil and South Africa (53.4 and 63, respectively) are significantly more unequal compared to Thailand (34.9), India (35.7), Russia (37.5) and China (38.5). But in terms of inequality measured by the share of the top 10 per cent income-earners in national income, inequality is high in all the countries in our set (Alvaredo et al. 2018). Thus, all the countries selected for study in this volume face the challenge of making economic growth more egalitarian. The challenge is, however, more for some countries as compared to others.

It has been argued by some economists that ethnic divisions or fragmentations lower a country's economic growth rate or public goods provision (Alesina et al. 1999; Easterly and Levine 1997). Whatever the connection between economic variables and ethnic diversity, the latter surely poses challenges for achieving social equality by adding complexity to the development process through the existence of disparities that have evolved historically between social groups. In Table I.1, column (10) presents a measure of aggregate ethnic diversity called 'ethnic fractionalisation', which is calculated as the probability that two individuals selected at random from a country will be from different ethnic groups. South Africa and India have the highest levels of ethnic fractionalisation, followed by Brazil. China has the lowest score and Russia and Thailand fall in between China and Brazil.

Given this comparative picture, it is not surprising that these emerging countries have mostly been studied separately, their differences looked upon as more significant than their similarities. This volume is not an attempt to downplay those differences and force thematic commonalities on country-level experiences and challenges. Rather, its objective is to showcase how diverse societies experience certain common challenges, and address common concerns. The diverse national contexts offer a rich platter of social experiments and policy innovations in the urban sphere to the interested reader, eager to look beyond the immediate national context for solutions to large-scale complex problems. We now turn to the broad trends in urbanisation in the six countries.

URBANISATION: LEVELS AND TRENDS

Urbanisation is closely linked to the structural transformation of the economy and, as noted before, one of the strategies for achieving the SDGs is to leverage urbanisation for such structural transformation. Table I.2 presents shares of GDP accounted for by agriculture (including forestry and fishing), industry (including construction) and services for the six countries in 2019.

Table I.2: Sectoral Shares in Value-added (percentage of GDP), 2019

Country	Agriculture, forestry and fishing	Industry, including construction	Services
Brazil	4.4	17.9	63.3
China	7.1	38.6	54.3
India	16.0	24.8	49.4
Russian Federation	3.5	32.2	54.0
South Africa	1.9	26	61.2
Thailand	8.0	33.4	58.6

Note: The figures may not add up to 100 row-wise because of definitions of each sector used in the database.

Source: World Bank Open data, https://data.worldbank.org/.

All the countries are in an advanced stage of structural transformation, as evident in the low contribution of agriculture (including forestry and fishing) to national GDP, with India having the highest share of agriculture at 16 per cent of GDP. However, there are significant differences between these countries when it comes to levels and trends of urbanisation, as shown in Table I.3.

Table I.3: Urban Population in 2018

Country	Total urban population (in millions)	Urban population as percentage of total population	Average annual rate of growth of the urban population, 2015–2020 (per cent)
Brazil	182.6	86.6	1.05
China	837.0	59.2	2.42
India	460.8	34.0	2.37
Russian Federation	107.2	74.4	0.18
South Africa	38.1	66.4	1.97
Thailand	34.6	49.9	1.73

Source: UNDESA 2018, 'World Urbanisation Prospects 2018'.

The three Asian countries are less urbanised than the rest. Brazil has 86.6 per cent of its population living in urban areas, followed by Russia (74.4 per cent) and South Africa (66.4 per cent). With frenetic urbanisation in the last two decades, China is 59.2 per cent urbanised today, with more than 800 million people living in urban areas. About one-third of India's population (34.0 per cent) and half of Thailand's (49.9 per cent) population live in urban areas. Despite being the least urbanised among these six countries, India has the second largest urban population (460.8 million) in the world.

Further, as can be seen from Table I.3, India and China have the highest average annual growth rates of urban population as estimated for the period 2015–2020, with China (2.42 per cent) slightly ahead of India (2.37 per cent). But China's rate of growth of urban population is expected to slow down markedly in the next two decades while India's, though declining, is expected to remain high—in fact, at the highest level—among these six countries. By 2050, India will add 416 million urban dwellers while China will add 255 million (UNDESA 2018). It is estimated that between 2015 and 2035, the number of cities with population over ten million will increase from six to ten in China and from four to eight in India. Brazil with two cities and Russia with one city with population over ten million will not add any more to the list by 2035, while Thailand will add Bangkok to the list and South Africa will add none. China will have eighteen cities in 2035 with population between five and ten million compared to eleven cities in 2015, while the number of such cities in India will remain unchanged at five over the same period. If we look at cities with population between one and five million, the difference between China and India is greater—China will increase the number of cities from ninety-two to 155 between 2015 and 2035, while India is expected to see only a modest increase from fifty to sixty-five such cities over the same period. South Africa and Thailand have relatively high growth rates of urban population at 1.97 per cent and 1.73 per cent, respectively, at present, with the rates expected to fall gradually till 2050. Despite its already advanced levels of urbanisation, Brazil's urban growth is expected to continue, albeit at a slower pace in the future. Russia, though less urbanised than Brazil, is expected to urbanise at a slower pace than Brazil in the future.

The pattern of urbanisation in each country is uniquely shaped by its specific national history (McGranahan and Martine 2012). Brazil's 'precocious' urbanisation is explained by the combination of demographic growth and import-substitution industrialisation that fuelled rapid urbanisation between 1930 and 1980, despite political resistance to it at the governmental level (ibid.). Its urban growth rate has declined sharply since 1980, due to slower demographic growth and economic crises faced in the 1980s and 1990s. China, too, had officially resisted urbanisation and valourised agrarian societies till the end of the 1970s. Unlike Brazil, however, industrialisation and urbanisation in China had rural roots. It was rural industrialisation, rather than city-based industrialisation, that led to population concentration and the development of rural townships into towns and cities. Increased decentralisation of power to governments at town and city levels helped to merge townships into cities and rural industrialisation fuelled the growth of towns. In the 1990s, coastal cities became engines of growth, with hundreds of millions of rural migrants moving to cities. Currently, China has a policy of actively promoting the urbanisation of economic activities; however, it has historically been and continues to be less keen to give rural migrants the status of permanent residents in cities—creating, as a result, a huge 'floating population'.

Russia, at the time of the Socialist Revolution in 1917, was less urbanised than Europe and even Latin America. Russia, however, experienced early urbanisation compared to China, and was more urbanised at the time of the unravelling of the Soviet Union than China is today. Hence, rapid urbanisation in Russia (akin to Brazil) occurred during the era of central economic planning—from the 1920s to the 1970s—with urban growth slowing down since the 1980s. This is unlike China, where rapid urbanisation occurred in the post-reforms period. Russia's rapid urbanisation was part of a broader socialist model of industrialisation, coupled with a focus on regional balance. This process of urbanisation came to an abrupt halt with the fall of Soviet Russia, leaving existing cities exposed to market forces, and resulting in spatial restructuring and relocation.

Like Brazil, the development of urban centres was stunted in India under colonial rule, with enclave-type urban developments in port cities and key towns (Shaw 2012). Post-colonial India experimented with planned development aimed at rapid industrialisation between 1950 and 1980, together with regional balance. Indian planning was inspired by Soviet five-year planning and, like Brazil, followed an import-substitution industrialisation strategy. The growth of urban population was highest during the decades of planning—that is, between the 1940s and the 1980s—and has been slowing down since the 1990s. India's urbanisation has traditionally been characterised as 'top-heavy', that is, dominated by large cities, which keep growing due to both in-migration and spatial expansion. However, according to recent studies, India's degree of urbanisation remains largely hidden in official census data, and alternative measurements using different sources show a higher degree of urbanisation (Onda et al. 2019; van Duijne 2019) Moreover, it has been argued that India's recent urbanisation has been led by small towns and 'vibrant smaller settlements—spaces outside the metropolitan shadow', which may not be even classified as urban in official statistics (Mukhopadhyay et al. 2020: 582). Urban growth in India is also largely fuelled by an informal economy, as we will see later, and presents special challenges for inclusive development, given anti-migrant sentiments and the political power of urban elites in Indian cities.

Although more urbanised than India, South Africa faces the same challenge of social exclusion due to its peculiar history of racially segregated urban development, which began with the mining boom of the late nineteenth and early twentieth century and its follow-up industrialisation. Apartheid policies led to the spatial segregation of white and black residents in the cities, causing a spatial mismatch between jobs and residence and uneven provision of public services. This has resulted in distorted or fractured cities (McGranahan and Martine 2012). The rate of urbanisation slowed down between 1951 and 1991 due to apartheid policies and has recovered in the post-apartheid regime since 1994. South Africa still faces serious challenges in eliminating apartheid-era distortions.

Post-1960s, Thailand's economy has grown rapidly, based on exports, foreign direct investment (FDI) and tourism. Thailand's urban population is slightly less than South Africa's, but is dominated by the Bangkok urban area. Thailand's urban population grew rapidly since 2000, but Bangkok remains a primate city; the economic development of Thailand revolves around the expansion of both industries and services in the Bangkok urban area, which also makes it one of the most visited and, at the same time, most congested cities of the world.

The very different patterns of urbanisation in these six countries, however, present certain common challenges for inclusive growth—housing for the poor, providing decent livelihoods and ensuring environmental sustainability.

HOUSING, LIVELIHOODS AND ENVIRONMENT: A CRITICAL TRIAD IN THE TWENTY-FIRST CENTURY

Since the 1950s and 1960s, when rapidly urbanising and industrialising Third World countries first experienced waves of rural–urban migration, it has become clear that much of the urban labour force works in the informal economy (Sanyal and Bhattacharya 2009). To the dismay of 'modernisation' theorists, the informal economy did not dissolve, but over time became an enduring and, in many cases, an expanding part of the urban economy (Bhattacharya 2014; Bhattacharya and Sanyal 2011). When the SDGs were formulated in 2015, the development agenda indicated some recognition of the contribution of the informal economy with calls for a 'sustainable transition to the formal economy'. Informality, so characteristic of urban growth in emerging countries, has implications for the triple challenges of providing decent work and decent housing for the cities' poor labour force, while reducing the urban carbon footprint.

From Table I.2, we have argued that structural transformation in terms of the share of agriculture (and allied activities) in GDP had advanced significantly in all six countries. In terms of the structural transformation of labour, however, there are significant differences between them. For example, we can see from Table I.4

that in India and Thailand, only 57.4 per cent and 68.6 per cent, respectively, of the labour force is employed outside agriculture. In South Africa, Russia and Brazil, the share of the labour force in the non-agricultural sector is close to that of the developed or rich economies, at 94.7, 94.2 and 90.9 per cent, respectively. China is inching towards the levels of the developed countries, with 74.7 per cent of its labour force employed outside agriculture. In India, the process of urbanisation might appear to be retarded to the extent that labour continues to remain in agriculture—with agriculture accounting for 42.6 per cent of total employment. However, there is evidence to show that many rural households have significantly diversified their sources of income, with greater dependence on

Table I.4: Informality and Urbanisation

Country	Non-agricultural employment (as percentage of total employment)	Informal employment (as percentage of total employment)	Population living in slums (as percentage of urban population)
(1)	(2)	(3)	(4)
Brazil	90.9	47.1	16.3
China	74.7	N.A.	24.6
India	57.4	88.1	35.2
Russian Federation	94.2	N.A.	N.A.
South Africa	94.7	31.5	25.6
Thailand	68.6	64.4	23.7

Notes:
1) The figures in column (2) are for the year 2019.
2) The years corresponding to the figures in column (3) are: Brazil and South Africa (2020), India (2019) and Thailand (2018).
3) The figures in column (4) are for the year 2018.

Source:
1) For columns (2) and (4), World Bank Open Data, https://data.worldbank.org/.
2) For column (3), ILOSTAT, https://ilostat.ilo.org/topics/informality/.

local non-agricultural earnings or remittances sent by migrant members. This has led to villages being transformed into small towns, whether classified as such in official statistics or not (van Duijne 2019).

Most importantly, much of the employment in emerging economies is informal in nature—that is, employment without the protection of labour legislations, social security and other benefits. Available official data shows that 88.1 per cent of the total employment in India in 2019 was informal in nature. The corresponding figures for Thailand in 2018 and Brazil and South Africa in 2020 were 64.4, 47.1 and 31.5 per cent, respectively. No official data on informal employment in China and Russia is available. However, unofficial estimates present high and rising informal employment in these countries too. For example, Park et al. (2012) argue that based on three alternative definitions, informal employment in urban China may range from 19.9 per cent to 37.2 per cent of total employment. According to the estimates in Charmes (2012), informal employment constituted 12.1 per cent of total employment in Russia during the 2005–2010 period.

It is estimated that about a quarter of the world's urban population lives in informal settlements. In Table I.4, we see that despite very different levels of economic development and diverse patterns of urbanisation, in all countries except Russia, a significant proportion of the urban population lives in slums—ranging from 16.3 per cent in Brazil to 35.4 per cent in India, while China, South Africa and Thailand have around a quarter of their urban population living in slums. Slums have traditionally presented the most difficult challenges for urban planners—the difficulty arising from the fact that slums are residences of the urban poor, but also the location for the informal manufacturing and service enterprises, operated often in violation of environmental and public health laws.

We now turn to the third dimension of concern in this volume, namely the urban environment. In part, we have already covered it in our discussion of urban housing and livelihoods. Urban sustainability encompasses both the 'green agenda' issues of resource efficiency, mitigation and adaptation to climate change, and the broader concerns of preserving the global commons, as well as the micro-level 'brown agenda' issues of housing and access to basic services in the city (Satterthwaite 2004; Shaw 2018). In fact, the first objective under Goal 11 of the UN's Agenda for Sustainable Development (which deals with cities and human settlements) is to '[b]y 2030, ensure access for all to adequate, safe and affordable housing and basic services and upgrade slums.' Our discussion of urbanisation and informality has provided the context within which such 'brown agenda' issues need to be understood and tackled. It is necessary to now turn to some of the explicit 'green agenda' aspects of development, as indicated in Table I.5.

Table I.5: Greenhouse Gas (GHG) Emissions by Country

Country	**Total greenhouse gas emissions (kilotonne or Kt of CO_2 equivalent)**	**Total greenhouse gas emissions (% change from 1990)**
(1)	(2)	(3)
Brazil	2,989,418.0	86.1
China	12,454,710.6	220.0
India	3,002,894.9	116.5
Russian Federation	2,803,398.5	–22.0
South Africa	502,130.3	43.8
Thailand	440,411.7	111.7

Note: The figures for all countries in columns (2) and (3), except South Africa, are for the year 2012. For South Africa, the figure is for 2007.

Source: World Bank Open Data, https://data.worldbank.org/.

Table I.5 shows country-wise contributions to greenhouse gas or GHG emissions and percentage change in emissions from 1990. Unsurprisingly, given China's frenetic industrialisation and urbanisation, it is the largest emitter of GHG in the world and its emissions have increased by 220 per cent since 1990. India contributes less than one-fourth of China's GHG emissions, and its emissions have grown by 116.4 per cent since 1990. But in the event of faster industrialisation and accelerated urbanisation in the future, India will have a similar impact on global GHG emissions as China, unless a greener mode of urbanisation and cleaner energy is adopted. The emission levels of Brazil and Russia are not very far behind India's levels, even though these countries are much smaller in population, indicating a higher degree of industrialisation and urbanisation in the former. However, unlike Brazil, which has seen an 86.1 per cent increase in emissions since 1990, Russia has actually seen a reduction of 22 per cent, mainly due to the decline of the heavy polluting industry after the collapse of the Soviet Union. Thailand and South Africa, both smaller economies compared to the rest, have seen increases in GHG emissions, with the increase being more than 100 per cent for Thailand.

AIM OF THE VOLUME

This volume aims to bring together researchers and practitioners working on critical research, policy formulation, delivery and grassroots activities around the issue of housing, livelihoods and environment in urban Brazil, China, India, the Russian Federation, South Africa and Thailand. The different chapters will shed light on where these countries are placed in terms of providing opportunities to improve housing for the low-income; housing policies currently in place; how these policies are being impacted by economic liberalisation and globalisation; livelihoods of the urban poor in the changing city; informal processes of shelter and livelihood-building; and environmental concerns in urban infrastructure financing and planning. The fourteen chapters that comprise this volume are largely a product of a three-day workshop on 'Housing, livelihoods and environmental challenges in urban India and Brazil', held at the Indian Institute of Management, Calcutta during 6–8 February 2017. Apart from researchers from India, there were participants from Brazil, UK and Thailand at the workshop.

While thinking about bringing out a volume of the workshop's papers, the editors decided to extend the coverage to a few other emerging economies in order to understand the issues raised in the workshop within a larger global context. What we have noted is that lately, there has been a growing interest in comparative studies of emerging countries; however, to the best of our knowledge, there are few volumes examining these countries on the topic of urban housing, livelihoods and environment. The great physical distance between some of the countries has possibly come in the way of comparative field work, and scholarly interchange and output in these areas have been restricted. The proposed volume could be regarded as an effort to bring together the writings of scholars on Brazil, China, the Russian Federation, South Africa and Thailand, located in their countries of origin or in other parts of the world, as well as Indian scholars from different parts of the country. This could be the beginning of greater South–South exchange in the future.

Such an exchange could prove valuable for these countries as they have much to learn from each other. For instance, post the 1960s, and particularly since 2000, the Brazilian central government has involved itself more and more in local issues, and provided both regulatory and funding support for the improvement of low-income housing in its cities. Compared to the piecemeal efforts of the Indian state, Brazil's performance in this as well as in the improvement of other basic services, including health and education of its urban poor, is way ahead of India's. However, the crime and violence associated with low-income housing remains a challenge for the Brazilian state, with greater militarisation of inner-city neighbourhoods often proving to be counter-productive and with high social costs. Low-income areas in Indian cities, though more deprived in terms of physical infrastructure, have not been characterised by such violence, although petty theft and insecurity of tenure make life in such neighbourhoods precarious. Many of the institutions, both regulatory and funding, that Brazil has created for the improvement of low-income housing and for the facilitation of participation from the grassroots, are pointers to the path India can take to solve its urban housing and basic services problems. On the other hand, why and how poor areas in Indian cities continue to support the fairly peaceful co-existence of a diverse population could be of interest to Brazil.[1]

These and other such cross-country experiences in urban development remain to be examined and deliberated through more comparative research on the countries selected here. This volume is a small endeavour in this regard. One of the first volumes of its kind to compare urban housing, livelihoods and environment in six diverse emerging economies, the chapters in the volume provide a mix of case studies and macro policies for a more comprehensive understanding of complex issues, while the diverse disciplinary backgrounds of the authors bring a variety of perspectives with which the issues at hand can be grappled with.

STRUCTURE OF THE VOLUME

The volume is arranged in four parts: Part 1 is about the role of the central state in housing provision, Part 2 is on the redevelopment of slums, Part 3 covers informal housing and right to the city, and Part 4 is on the environmental re/configurations of urban infrastructure, housing and livelihoods. Four chapters comprise the first part, showing interesting contrasts in the role of the state in housing provision in Brazil, India and Russia. Chapter 1 by Marques traces the evolution of housing policies for the poor in Brazil, starting from the 1930s when the building of affordable housing by the federal state began. Overall, he finds that there has been an improvement in the housing conditions of the poor due to stronger redistributive policies and favourable demographic conditions. Chapter 2 by Shaw is on low-income housing in urban India, examining government policy from after independence in 1947 to the present. It highlights the problems of public-sector housing provision and its gradual privatisation. Yet, if properly implemented, following the suggestions of the target population, public housing programmes could provide satisfactory housing to the low-income population and therefore should remain an important contributor to housing supply, which is increasingly being provided by other means. In Chapter 3, Hazra and Norkina examine Soviet housing policy and the production of mass housing for industrial workers in Russia in the 1950s and 1960s. Based on a detailed case study of a 'Kruschyovka' residential complex in Moscow, they show the impacts of such centralised provision on quality of life and on current thinking on urbanisation. Although very satisfactory in its heyday, today such housing faces obsolescence unless it can be recycled and reused.

In Chapter 4, Sengupta compares the recent housing policy of urban India and Brazil and finds that governments in both countries seem to be experimenting with alternative ways of complementing the market provision of affordable housing along with strong state intervention, reflecting a unique blend of both enabler and provider roles for the state. This is in contrast to the early 1990s, when 'enabling strategies' had dominated. This mix of both market and state intervention highlights the reality that a correct housing policy stance for the urban poor in the global South is still debatable, and cannot be 'a benign handover to the market or the private sector'.

Part 2 turns to an issue that has become central to plans to restructure and modernise/post-modernise the largest cities of the global South, whether via central government funding for smartening cities or via state/local government projects to remove slums. This issue is the redevelopment of slums/squatter settlements which continue to occupy a significant presence in the cities of the emerging economies. D'Ottaviano, in Chapter 5, reviews the history of favelas in Brazil and changes in public policy towards them over the last two decades. Her chapter highlights the positive impacts of greater funding from the federal government for the favelas post the 2000s, as well as the negative impacts of mega events like the World Cup in 2014 and the Olympics in 2016, which led to their removal and/or dislocation. In Chapter 6, Bhide observes that a closer examination of the Smart Cities Mission, launched in 2015 by the present NDA (National Democratic Alliance) government of India, has unleashed changes that are not confined to displacement alone. The reach of the changes is much larger and an entire way of life, of settlement and of urbanisation is sought to be changed, posing threats to the sheer modes by which settlements could survive and develop in cities. Taking the case of two smaller metropolitan cities, Indore and Bhubaneswar, this chapter argues that the current path of 'smartmentality' comprises a new determination to discipline the 'undisciplined' informal settlements and the poor through punitive means and a recasting of the political. In Chapter 7, Boonyabancha and Kerr turn to people's initiatives and community networks in solving the problem of housing for the urban poor in Asian cities. Existing formal systems of housing development privilege either traditional government-led models of intervention or private-sector/contractor-led market models that bypass and exclude the urban poor. This chapter discusses the community networks, organisations and institutions that enable popular initiatives from below in matters of finance and credit for housing, sharing of information and negotiating with more powerful elites.

This leads us to Part 3 of the volume, with three chapters that further explore the situation of informal housing and the rights of their residents to the city. In Chapter 8, Raman delves into one of these rights, the right to property, and how it eludes the powerless. Based on ethnographic research carried out in a squatter settlement called Kathputli Colony (KC) in Delhi, it narrates the politics of creating in-situ property rights under the central government programme, RAY (Rajiv Awas Yojana). While the institutional and legal framework governing RAY constricted the political spaces that poor groups have to claim their property rights in urban land, KC residents nevertheless, via prolonged negotiation and struggle, managed to influence the project implementing authority to alter its contracts and procedures. However, the project is yet to be implemented and the promise of rights to land is as yet unrealised. In Chapter 9, Saharan looks at informal settlements and livelihood processes in Durban, South Africa and its surrounding municipalities. She shows the disconnect between the city's focus on improving the physical conditions of the settlements and the multi-dimensional survival logic of the marginalised population. Such conflict in rationalities between the state and its poor residents has slowed down the process of spatial integration in the post-apartheid city. In the following chapter, Fernandes et al. argue that the improvement in livelihoods of the poor and the marginalised in the city is 'very much dependent on changes in their symbolic capital' and that of their neighbourhoods or where they live. For this to happen, the 'pedagogies of monsterisation' that are at the heart of the othering processes that create an underclass must be abandoned for a more open and tolerant world view, where knowledge systems and ways of living outside the dominant systems of knowing and doing are accepted. They examine the context of urban violence in Brazil and Rio de Janeiro where marginalised youth are seen as the face of danger, disorder and crime.

The final part of the volume, on the environmental re/configurations of urban infrastructure, housing and livelihoods, brings together four chapters that reflect different scales of analysis for understanding environmental issues in the cities of emerging countries. They range from a country-level analysis, to that of a region within a country, to the city-level, the latter examined over historical time and space. In Chapter 11, Bond examines the contradictions between the rhetoric and reality of the New Development Bank (NDB) set up by the BRICS (Brazil–Russia–India–China–South Africa) bloc of countries and the three loans given to South Africa for urban infrastructure development. While NDB's original mandate had stressed environment-oriented infrastructure lending, in reality it has enabled South Africa to continue along a path of unsustainable minerals-energy extraction, with many of the country's basic needs still unmet. Such a policy has also resulted in high levels of air pollution, greater levels of corruption, and a more uneven urban structure. Chapter 12 by Sharan is on location, livelihoods and the environment in contemporary Delhi, India. In reviewing the environmental concerns of Delhi from its colonial past to the present, he notes that slums, economic activity, air and water pollution have been conjoined historically, but now there is a strong emphasis on their (il)legality rather than on the poverty of their residents. In the case of the pollution of the Yamuna river, it has resulted in the demolition of thousands of hutments on the banks of the river, with the courts taking 'an aggressive stance against the illegal poor, coupled with highly capital-intensive, even if largely ineffective, technological solutions'. In Chapter 13, Ma and Chen look at the role of small towns in China as an alternative to the large city for absorbing migrants and providing a more liveable environment, in the context of that country's rapid urbanisation. Taking the case of twelve small towns in northwest China, they use a binary logistic regression model to identify those factors influencing small-town development and suggest ways to strengthen the attractiveness of such towns. Concerns over children's education, travel convenience, the need for a sense of belonging and time patterns of work emerge as the most significant variables explaining the probability of moving out of the small towns.

In the final chapter, Bandyopadhyay and Ghosh, using a 'micro-history' approach, provide a glimpse into class and tenancy relations in Kolkata during 1914–1926, when an ambitious street scheme of the Calcutta Improvement Trust recycled more than 200 acres of prime land in the city, and dis-housed at least 50,000 individuals living in densely populated, ethnically mixed neighbourhoods in the core of the old Black town. There was dislocation of the everyday life of the working population and acute housing shortage. The authors point out that writings on contemporary transformations in the urban order often fail to appreciate the traces of the city's connection with the imperial globalisation of the nineteenth and early twentieth centuries. Their chapter projects a much longer history of continuity and rupture in India's urban developments.

CONCLUSION

This volume brings together a collection of fourteen chapters that offer multidisciplinary perspectives on the housing-livelihood-environment triad. Together, they bring to centre-stage many of the continuing debates on how best to house the urban poor and ensure livelihoods keeping in mind environmental impacts. They highlight important questions: What should be the role of the state, what should be the role of the market and what role can the community and civil society play? At the backdrop of these universally relevant questions is the particular condition of the world's emerging economies with their continuing and fairly rapid demographic growth, urbanisation and industrialisation processes, and unfulfilled basic needs of a section of the population. What path should these countries follow to ensure both growth and equity with minimum adverse impact on the environment?

Considering the role of the state in housing the poor, the first four chapters of the volume provide a diversity of perspectives gleaned from the experiences of three countries, Brazil, India and Russia. The Kruschyovka housing of Moscow, built during the socialist, pre-liberalisation era, represents the beneficial aspects of housing provision by the state, namely access by ordinary working people to good quality subsidised housing in central locations of the city. This was possible because the government owned the land and was the builder, and basic needs rather than profits from real estate determined housing construction and location. Prefabrication of parts and co-ordination between processes of production and assembly at site, both under state control, ensured the rapid completion of units. From this almost ideal situation (which has changed post the 1990s), we have more mixed outcomes from Brazil and India, both of which have used state and market to fill in gaps in housing supply, but with some significant differences. By the time the private sector became an important player in the delivery of housing in Brazil in the 2000s, the federal state, during the period of military rule from 1965 to 1985, had scaled up its efforts for massive housing delivery. Post-1985, with the return to democracy, local governments took the lead until the 2000s, when federal policies once again became important, as did the role of the private sector, simultaneously. Thus, much of the housing transformation at the micro level in low-income urban neighbourhoods had already occurred before the entry of the private sector. This is in contrast to India, where a huge deficit in low-income housing existed prior to the entry of the private sector in the mid-1990s, which continues to exist three decades after economic liberalisation was officially started in 1991. Earlier, the state's piecemeal attempts were plagued by inefficiencies, including the slow production of completed units. Since the 1990s, the central government's flagship housing programmes have involved both private players and local/city/state governments to create more housing supply. However, the private sector has shown willingness to build housing for the poor only when granted a slew of incentives, including constriction and densification of the built-up area for low-income housing, and subsequent development and sale of the extra buildable area by the developers at market rates. Slum upgrading or redevelopment by the private sector has thus meant squeezing in many more households in a given area of land by building standardised units in vertical buildings, regardless of the consequences of this on the way of life and livelihoods of the poor.

Parts 2 and 3 of the volume, however, show how it is not always a simple case of state versus market, with an ostensibly welfare-oriented state in contrast to a profiteering and unrestrained market. For mega events, such as the World Cup 2014 and the Olympics in 2016, both held in Rio de Janeiro, the state was active in the removal/dislocation of informal housing. In Kathputli Colony, a squatter settlement in Delhi, despite the central government's programme (RAY) to bestow in-situ property rights, ultimately such rights continue to elude the powerless. In eThekwini, South Africa, the city government's focus on improving the physical condition of the squatter settlements clashes with the multi-dimensional survival logic of the squatters, slowing down plans for their integration with the wider city.

This brings the need for more active involvement of the community to solve housing and livelihood problems, and the aligning of these goals with a lower carbon footprint. In fact, according to Boonyabancha and Kerr (Chapter 7), community or people-driven actions at the grassroots to improve housing access are possibly the 'only realistic, reasonable and scaleable models' for inclusive housing in situations where neither the state nor the market is doing a satisfactory job. However, the poor cannot act alone but require partnerships and alliances with local government and/or NGOs, as well as networking with other low-income groups to ensure success on a larger scale. A good example of this is the country-wide slum upgradation underway in Thailand, which is supported by CODI, a government organisation, which disburses funds to co-operatives of slum dwellers who take all the decisions about where to live, including searching for land plots and selecting the type of housing unit. Community networking is essential to the sustainability of this people-driven model, as the poor from different parts of the city discuss and exchange information on land prices, housing designs, construction costs, etc., thereby minimising the overall costs of the upgrading project for their co-operative.

Community networking is vital for another reason as well. As raised in the chapters by Bhide (Chapter 6), Saharan (Chapter 9) and Fernandes et al. (Chapter 10), the informal settlements of the urban poor represent a 'living style' that is not in consonance with the dominant/hegemonic style of living that characterises the middle- and upper-income areas of the modernist/post-modernist city. Thus, improving the physical conditions of the settlements without considering what this does to their ways of living and earning, and thereby surviving, will be of limited benefit. Their living style needs to be acknowledged for its differences from the mainstream, based as it is on the use of limited resources, co-habited spaces for work and living, multi-generational families and much higher population densities. This living style, rather than being denigrated and reviled, must be recognised for its contribution to lowering the carbon footprint of the city, as noted by Brand (2009). It must also be acknowledged on its own terms to enable what Fernandes et al. call a 'paradigm of potency' for the marginalised in the city. Here, community networking would enable mutual support to such groups in their endeavour to hold on to their ways of living, while seeking to improve their prospects in the city.

Finally, we turn to the question of the path/s the six emerging countries discussed in this volume could follow to ensure both growth and equity along with low carbon emissions. Here, it is important to keep in mind the macro-structures of global governance that can exert influence on national-level policies via loans and/or aid, along with advice/conditionalities that are pro-market and unaccepting of any other knowledge and practice systems other than their own. Bond's analysis of the functioning of the BRIC's New Development Bank and the loans it has made to South Africa shows how difficult it is for a global lending agency to break out of the Bretton Woods frame. The loans are for the privatised supply of services with little community consultation or genuine green concerns, and have been made to the country's 'most notoriously corrupt institutions'

(Chapter 11). In a similar vein, at the national level, the choice of pathway has been influenced by past understandings and the attitudes of urban elites towards the poor and their livelihood activities, which are seen as causing environmental pollution. Sharan's study of Delhi (Chapter 12) illustrates this, highlighting the deeply class-biased nature of the judiciary. Ma and Chen, in their study of small towns in China, suggest an alternative pathway to manage the country's rapid urbanisation, namely by focussing on small towns and promoting their growth. However, this will mean reversing existing national funding policies favouring the large city, policies which have resulted in them having far better infrastructure and educational facilities that continue to attract migrants. Bandyopadhyay and Ghosh (Chapter 14), through their study of Kolkata's restructuring during 1914–1926 and its echoes in contemporary urban transformations, reiterate the importance of looking at the city's past to understand the contours of its present development.

Thus, the pathways open to the countries under study are partly circumscribed by their own particular histories. But this element of 'path dependency' should not blind us to the possibility of forging new visions and changing underlying structures. A great deal will depend on community and civil society to form the kinds of bonds and networks to articulate alternate visions based on equity, inclusiveness and environmental sustainability. Rising secondary and higher education among the lower-middle class and the poor, growing consciousness of their political rights and power as a voting bloc, together with their aspirations for a better life could be drivers in this direction, enabling them to demand from the political system greater accountability in the delivery of public goods and environmental justice.

End Note

1. However, recent studies have brought to light the increase in hate crimes against religious minorities in India, including communal violence in cities, in recent years (Basu 2021).

References

Alesina, Alberto, R. Baqir and W. Easterly. 1999. 'Public goods and ethnic divisions'.*The Quarterly Journal of Economics* 114(4): 1243–1284.

Alvaredo, Facundo, L. Chancel, T. Piketty, E. Saez and G. Zucman (eds). 2018. *World Inequality Report 2018*. Cambridge, MA: Belknap Press of Harvard University Press.

Basu, Deepankar. 2021. 'Majoritarian politics and hate crimes against religious minorities: Evidence from India, 2009–2018'. *World Development* 146, Article No. 105540.

Bhattacharya, Rajesh. 2014. 'The Informal Sector: The Role of Urban Commons'. *Yojana* 58: 46–49.

Bhattacharya, Rajesh and K. Sanyal. 2011. 'Bypassing the squalor: New towns, immaterial labour and exclusion in post-colonial urbanisation'. *Economic and Political Weekly* 46(31): 41–48.

Brand, Stewart. 2009. *Whole Earth Discipline: An Ecopragmatist Manifesto.* New York: Viking Penguin.

Charmes, Jacques. 2012. 'The informal economy worldwide: Trends and characteristics'. *Margin: The Journal of Applied Economic Research* 6(2): 103–132.

Coccia, M. 2021. 'Effects of the spread of COVID-19 on public health of polluted cities: Results of the first wave for explaining the *dejà vu* in the second wave of COVID-19 pandemic and epidemics of future vital agents'. *Environmental Science and Pollution Research* 28: 19147–19154.

Davis, Mike. 2006. *Planet of Slums*. London: Verso.

Easterly, William and R. Levine. 1997. 'Africa's growth tragedy: Policies and ethnic divisions'. *The Quarterly Journal of Economics* 112(4): 1203–1250.

Fearon, James D. 2003. 'Ethnic and cultural diversity by country'. *Journal of Economic Growth* 8(2): 195–222.

ILO. 2021. *World Employment and Social Outlook: Trends 2021*. Geneva: International Labour Office, ILO. Available at https://www.ilo.org/wcmsp5/groups/public/---dgreports/---dcomm/---publ/documents/publication/wcms_795453.pdf (accessed June 2021).

Lai, K. Y., C. Webster, S. Kumari and C. Sarkar. 2020. 'The nature of cities and the Covid-19 pandemic'. *Current Opinion in Environmental Sustainability* 46: 27–31.

McGranahan, Gordon and G. Martine. 2012. 'Urbanisation and development: Policy lessons from the BRICS experience'. IIED Discussion Paper, International Institute for Environment and Development, London. Available at http://pubs.iied.org/pdfs/10622IIED.pdf (accessed April 2021).

Mukhopadhyay, P., M. H. Zérah and E. Denis. 2020. 'Subaltern Urbanization: Indian Insights for Urban Theory'. *International Journal of Urban and Regional Research* 44(4): 582–598.

Onda, K., P. Sinha, A. E. Gaughan, F. R. Stevens and N. Kaza. 2019. 'Missing millions: Undercounting urbanization in India'. *Population and Environment* 41(2): 126–150.

Park, Albert, Y. Wu and Y. Du. 2012. 'Informal Employment in Urban China: Measurement and Implications'. Washington, D.C.: World Bank Group. Available at https://documents1.worldbank.org/curated/en/383331468220789675/pdf/777370WP0Infor00Box377299B00PUBLIC0.pdf (accessed April 2021).

Sanyal, Kalyan and R. Bhattacharya. 2009. 'Beyond the factory: Globalisation, informalisation of production and the new locations of labour'. *Economic and Political Weekly* 44(22): 35–44.

Satterthwaite, David. 2004. 'Sustainable Cities or Cities that Contribute to Sustainable Development?' In David Satterthwaite (ed.), *The Earthscan Reader in Sustainable Cities*, 80–106. Sterling, VA and London: Earthscan.

Schlyter, Charlotta. 2002. 'International Labour Standards and the Informal Sector: Developments and Dilemmas', Working paper. Geneva: Employment Sector, International Labour Organization.

Sharifi, A. and A. R. Khavarian-Garmsir. 2020. 'The COVID-19 pandemic: Impacts on cities and major lessons for urban planning design and management'. *Science of the Total Environment* 749, Article No. 142391.

Shaw, Annapurna. 2012. *Indian Cities*, Oxford India Short Introductions. New Delhi: Oxford University Press.

———. 2018. 'Towards Sustainable Cities in India'. In J. Mukherjee (ed.), *Sustainable Urbanization in India*, 23–37. Singapore: Springer.

UNDESA. 2014. 'World Urbanisation Prospects: The 2014 Revision, Highlights' (ST/ESA/SER.A/352). New York: United Nations Department of Economic and Social Affairs. Available at https://esa.un.org/unpd/wup/publications/files/wup2014-highlights.Pdf (accessed April 2021).

———. 2016. 'The World's Cities in 2016—Data Booklet (ST/ESA/SER.A/392)'. New York: United Nations Department of Economic and Social Affairs. Available at http://www.un.org/en/development/desa/population/publications/pdf/urbanization/the_worlds_cities_in_2016_data_booklet.pdf (accessed June 2021).

UNDESA. 2018. '2018 Revision of World Urbanisation Prospects'. New York: United Nations Department of Economic and Social Affairs. Available at https://population.un.org/wup/Download/Last (accessed April 2021).

United Nations. 2017. 'New Urban Agenda. New York?' Available at http://habitat3.org/wp-content/uploads/NUA-English.pdf (accessed April 2021).

van Duijne, R. J. 2019. 'Why India's urbanization is hidden: Observations from "rural" Bihar'. *World Development* 123, Article No. 104610.

Watts, Michael J. 2011. 'Planet of the Wageless'. *Identities* 18(1): 69–80.

World Bank. 2018. *Poverty and Shared Prosperity 2018: Piecing Together the Poverty Puzzle*. Washington, D.C.: World Bank. Available at https://openknowledge.worldbank.org/bitstream/handle/10986/30418/9781464813306.pdf (accessed April 2021).

______. 2021. *Global Economic Prospects*. Washington, D.C.: World Bank.

World Bank Blogs. 2018. 'New country classifications by income level: 2018–19', 1 July. Available at https://blogs.worldbank.org/opendata/new-country-classifications-income-level-2018-2019 (accessed April 2021).

Part 1

Changing Contexts and the Role of the State in Housing Provision

1

Housing Policies in Recent Brazil

Eduardo Cesar Leão Marques

INTRODUCTION

This chapter discusses housing policies for the poor in Brazil in recent times. The 2000s and the 2010s have brought significant transformations in urban policies, changing the historical legacies of the country. Considering the recent political and economic crisis, which has had the country in its grip since 2015, it is easier to review the past than forecast the future, although some trends can and will be discussed.

Considering the parallel trajectories of state construction, urbanisation and living conditions that mark many countries of the global South, the chapter may contribute to the discussion of state policies in Southern countries, instead of being focussed on one single country. Higher-income groups solve their housing demands through market mechanisms, but the low-middle classes and the poor depend on state policies, which traditionally were associated with the construction of new housing units for sale. In recent years, public policies have been diversified, both with policies designed to face precarity, and 'demand-side' programmes associated with market production for the low-middle classes.

The housing conditions of the poor have been a problem in Brazil at least since the end of the nineteenth century. The first state policies for the provision of affordable housing started only in the 1930s. These state actions, still on a very small scale, are aimed at producing new units for financed[1] sale for very specific social groups, which are elected by the state as a strategy for national development. During this same period, Brazilian cities grew demographically and territorially, with intense migration from the countryside that accelerated after the 1940s. The process consolidated an extensive urban network with several dozen large cities and metropolitan areas. Only during the military period were housing policies for the poor massified, once again focussed almost exclusively on the construction and sale of new housing units located in large projects at the urban peripheries. Since housing policies did not even come close to satisfying the increasing demand produced by migration, the large majority of the new urban inhabitants mobilised self-built strategies for shelter, creating a large stock of housing precarity, notably in locations with high residential segregation and very bad sanitary and sheltering conditions.

When the country returned to democracy in the 1980s, this was the urban heritage it had to deal with. In the absence of federal policies, local governments took the lead in the 1990s to create a wider range of policy alternatives, including programmes against precarity, such as slum upgrading and the regularisation of irregular settlements, as well as social rent, social zoning and self-help housing projects. In the 2000s, several of these policies migrated to the federal level, bringing national policies back to the realm of urban planning, regulation, and direct financing and investments. At the same time, besides federalising the new and more diversified policy agenda, recent decades have seen an increase in the presence of and tasks performed by private companies in the delivery of housing and urban policies. The goal of this chapter is to present these processes in broad terms.

The chapter has two sections, in addition to this introduction and the conclusion. In the first section, I briefly reconstruct the historical legacies that gave form to urban and housing policies. In the next section, I discuss the transformations that have occurred since the return to democracy, characterised first by a retraction of the federal government and by the policy activism of local governments, but later by the return of national initiatives, especially after 2003. The period under consideration shows more diversified urban policies and important efforts towards institution-building by several agencies in multiple government levels of the Brazilian federal system. At the end, I discuss the changes introduced by the governments that have been in power since 2016 and by the present fiscal and political crisis, all of which pose important risks for the advancements made in the past two decades. These processes are still unfolding, considering not only the strong right-wing turn of the 2018 presidential election, but also the absence of an urban agenda, and the instability of the government that took office.

CITIES, URBAN SPACES AND STATE POLICIES

The majority of the urban network in Brazil until the end of the nineteenth century was located on the coast and associated with exporting mineral and agricultural materials–Rio de Janeiro, Salvador, Recife, Santos, among others. The size of the cities, however, was very small. In 1872, for example, the two largest cities in the country, which had been colonial capitals during Portuguese domination–Rio de Janeiro and Salvador–had 275,000 and 130,000 inhabitants, respectively (less than 4 per cent of the country's population). São Paulo would become the largest Brazilian city only in the 1940s, and had just 30,000 inhabitants (0.3 per cent of the country's population) in 1872. In fact, until 1920, the six largest cities concentrated less than 10 per cent of the country's population.[2]

Industrialisation during the twentieth century, and especially since the 1930s, increased migration to cities such as São Paulo and Belo Horizonte. These migration flows led the urban population to increase between 3.9 and 5.2 per cent per year in the next four decades, while the rural population grew between 1.6 and -0.7 per cent per year (Martine and McGranahan 2014). The net balance of rural migration to cities would reach seven million and 13.6 million people between 1950–1960 and 1960–1970, respectively. As a result, the Brazilian urban population jumped from 12.9 million in 1940 to 31.3 million in 1960 (Baeninger 2011).

In the 1960s, the country developed its first national housing policies. These were part of a broader effort towards state formation, which began with the 1930 civilian *coup d'état* that ended the long-standing control of the agricultural and rural elites over both local and federal politics (Nunes 1997). The period was marked by the authoritarian but modernising governments of Getúlio Vargas, which lasted until 1945.[3] In what concerns our subject here, the Vargas government started a strong effort at economic modernisation that included the construction of a Brazilian state corporatism, in Schmitter's (1979) terms: formatting an (politically controlled) interest intermediation system for both labour and business, including several labour regulations, as well as social policies. These were all subordinated to a broader project of urban and industrial development that privileged some (strategic) urban occupations as protected and entitled to rights and state policies. This system subordinated citizens' rights to the individual's position in the occupation structure in what Santos (1979) called 'regulated citizenship'.

Among these policies were the first national housing initiatives, focussed solely on the construction of new housing units for financed sale, inaugurating a choice for housing property that lasts (and structures policy choices) until today. The housing policies were produced by the IAPs (Retirement and Pensions Institutes), structured by professional category (state, industry, ports, transportation, commerce and banking workers), each with different levels of rights and contributions. The rest of the labour force (its majority) remained unprotected, including the largest groups—rural, domestic and urban informal workers. As their names indicate, the IAPs were focussed on other goals, but the acquisition of land and the production of houses for sale became part of their strategy for investment of the new pension system's assets, considering the weakness of the Brazilian financial system at the time. This obviously also provided political support from the beneficiary groups (Azevedo and Andrade 1981; Bonduki 1998). Even with restricted coverage, the IAPs created several services for their constituents, in addition to pensions and retirement plans—housing, sanitation around the projects and the first federal health assistance initiatives—inaugurating the Brazilian social protection system (Santos 1979).

Federal urban policies would be mainly restricted to the IAPs' production in the following decades, except for the formation of the Popular Housing Foundation (FCP) in 1945. This new agency, however, produced less than 17,000 housing units until the 1960s, when it was made extinct (Azevedo and Andrade 1981), while the IAPs built around 124,000 new housing units between 1937 and 1964 (Bonduki 1998). Therefore, the total federal production between 1930 and 1964 was around 140,000 units, housing at most 900,000 people,[4] while the cities received 23.6 million new inhabitants between 1940 and 1970 (Martine and McGranahan 2014). The federal government tried to manage the housing crisis by regulating rent and rent prices by law in 1942, but this froze market production for rent, worsening the situation (Bonduki 1998). Until the 1960s, other urban policies such as planning, water, sanitation, electricity, garbage collection and transportation would stay with almost no federal regulation or investments (Marques 2016b).

It is obvious that the recently arrived migrants found ways of solving their shelter problem. Given the absence of strong state policies and the prohibitive costs of market solutions, different precarious solutions were disseminated in Brazilian cities, mainly cortiços, favelas and irregular settlements. The cortiços are the oldest precarious housing solution, dating from the end of the nineteenth century. They are collective houses where each family occupies only one room, usually sharing bathrooms, kitchens and laundry areas with other families. They were historically located at city centres, but are also spread nowadays inside favelas, or even in housing projects produced by the state.

Favelas are settlements in which land was occupied, individually or collectively, by the population. The inhabitants, therefore, are not land owners, although they own the constructions, since they have self-constructed them. However, depending on the status of the land and the length of time of occupation, they may have gained the right to stay, according to Brazilian law.[5] Tenure conditions are much better in favelas located on public land because, by Brazilian law, they cannot be evicted, contrary to private land. In their origin, favelas lacked infrastructure completely, but several of them have received equipment and services since the 1980s, creating a quite heterogeneous situation nowadays. Although the famous Rio de Janeiro favelas are located in high slope areas, favelas may also be located in flat regions by river banks (as they are mainly in São Paulo), or in other kinds of locations.

Finally, in irregular settlements, the inhabitants have bought plots (paid in full or only partially), but the developers failed to complete the legal and administrative processes of land parcelling, hampering the issuing of individual titles to the buyers. Therefore, the inhabitants own the land and have land tenure in this case, although they do not have legal titles. These settlements have different infrastructure conditions, ranging from a complete absence even of well-defined streets, to having almost all facilities and services, albeit of lower quality.

These precarious solutions are disseminated in different combinations in Brazilian cities, depending on their histories, topography and availability of vacant land. In any case, however, all of them have a typical urban form created from 1940 to 1980, with richer social groups in central areas (with amenities and infrastructure), and large and extensive peripheral regions on their outskirts, usually known as *periferia*. These fringes of the metropolitan areas grew at population rates higher than 5 per cent per year until the 1990s, mainly with the expansion of self-constructed houses in irregular settlements and favelas, and almost no state infrastructure and services. Considering the topography and the history of the city, there were also, in some cases, critical pockets of poverty inside the richer areas, such as in Rio de Janeiro.

The first massive urban policies began after the 1964 *coup d'état* as part of the large restructuring of the Brazilian state undertaken by the military governments. After imposing a strong fiscal centralisation that hampered the formulation of policy alternative by local administrations, the federal government created a new institutional architecture for housing and sanitation. Among the several new agencies, the most important was the National Housing Bank (BNH) created in 1964, with the incorporation of previous agencies (housing sections of the IAPs and the FCP). In 1968, the BNH launched the National Housing System and the National Sanitation System, and in 1971, the National Plan for Sanitation (PLANASA). In 1969, the BNH was authorised to use resources from the FGTS (*Fundo de Garantia por Tempo de Serviço*), a public fund fed with compulsory deposits from the payroll accountings of workers and employers. The housing and sanitation systems were organised with similar logic, associated with federal funds under the umbrella of the BNH, state-level funds and funds associated with state- or metropolitan-level housing and sanitation companies. As a result, each state created its own agencies and funds to be able to receive the BNH resources (Maricato 1987)—Cohabs and Cehabs (state- or metropolitan-level housing public companies) for housing and state sanitation companies (CES). Although very centralised in decision-making, this system expanded the services substantially, and contributed to the formation of housing and sanitation policy communities nationwide (Rezende and Heller 2002). In terms of housing, this model continued with the production of one single housing product—new housing units for financed sale, produced by private constructors in large-scale housing projects, located at the extreme peripheries of cities, where land was cheaper (in fact, bought as rural land and converted into urban land by local authorities).

Regardless of all its faults, this system introduced massive-scale housing production for the first time in the country. Between 1967 and 1986, approximately 2,300,000 housing units for low and lower middle-income families were produced (Azevedo 1988). This production was characterised by low quality, usually quite segregated locations, not to mention widespread corruption in private construction contracts (Maricato 1987). The location of the housing projects contributed to and reinforced the already strong trend of residential segregation of Brazilian cities. As a social policy, additionally, the system had serious problems of targeting, since it also produced 2,200,000 housing units for the middle classes, who could easily access houses in the market (Azevedo 1988).

In terms of sanitation, services also improved, but in a very unequal way. There was a substantial increase in the availability of treated water, but a much smaller improvement in sewage services. In water, the availability of public systems for the urban population increased from 41.8 per cent in 1960 to 79.2 per cent in 1980. On the other hand, sewage systems were present in 26 per cent of urban homes in 1960, but the figure increased to only 37 per cent in 1980. The coverage of treated sewage was substantially lower, but there were no reliable numbers available. Garbage collection and urban drainage remained entirely in the hands of the sub-financed local governments and without a federal policy during this period. In all of these services, the advancement of the system was paralleled by an increase in inequalities, both among regions of the country and social groups inside each city (Arretche 2019).

The 1960s and the 1970s were also the golden era of territorial planning in Brazil, with the creation of large regional development plans and agencies, as well as urban and metropolitan plans. In 1973, the federal government created by law (Law 14/73) nine official metropolitan regions, which received new agencies for planning the services of common use, but with almost no efficacy. The BNH incentivised the production of local Master Plans for the municipalities through a specific financial arrangement, but although many plans were produced, much less planning occurred. The Gegran in São Paulo and the PUB Rio in Rio de Janeiro are examples of these, produced not only by local architects such as Lúcio Costa (author of the 1969 Rio de Janeiro plan) but also international consultants, such as the Greek architect Constantinos A. Doxiadis (also author of the original plan for Islamabad, capital of Pakistan).

In this period, metropolitan trains—suburban trains and subway—entered the national agenda for the first time. In 1975, the federal government created the Brazilian Urban Transportation Company (EBTU) and its federal financial system—the National System of Urban Transports (SNTU) and the National Fund for the Development of Transports (FNDU). As in the cases of housing and sanitation, these institutions should contribute to state-level funds and companies, allowing the construction of large metropolitan infrastructures. The results were poor, although the initial phases of the Rio de Janeiro and the São Paulo subways were made possible by this institutional arrangement. In fact, with the decay of this federal system in the 1980s, the rhythms of subway construction declined almost to zero since the state governments did not have the financial capacities necessary for the expansion of the systems.

The military regime and its policies declined economically and politically through the 1970s, hit by the oil shocks and the economic crisis of the 1970s and the explosion of foreign debt by the early 1980s, as well as by internal political pressures from below demanding democracy. As a result, regardless of the survival of several of the regime's institutions in the 1980s, their policies declined continuously. The closure of BNH in 1986 represented a key moment in this decay.

In demographic terms, a wide network of large cities had already been formed by 1980 as a product of an urbanisation process that increased the urban growth rate from 31.2 per cent in 1940 to 67.6 per cent in 1980. This network had several large cities, but also a relatively low urban primacy. In contrast to other Latin American countries, in 1980, the largest metropolises–São Paulo and Rio de Janeiro–had only 15.3 per cent and 10.6 per cent of the country's urban population, respectively (Cunha 2016).

In fact, the nine largest metropolitan regions concentrated 29.8 per cent of the Brazilian population, and between 1960 and 1980, the urban population had jumped from thirty-two million to eighty-two million. The large majority of these fifty million new urban residents went to live in precarious housing in favelas and irregular settlements in the metropolitan *periferias*. The National Bureau of Statistics estimated that 3.5 per cent of the urban households were in favelas, but many studies suggested that this figure was largely underestimated (Maricato 1987). In terms of basic sanitation, regardless of the general improvement in previous decades, only 79.5 per cent of the 40 per cent poorer households in 1991 had access to water, 18 per cent to sewage systems, 64.4 per cent to garbage collection, and 22.5 per cent of them did not even have a bathroom (Marques 2019).

To sum up, the scale of housing and urban policies in Brazil changed considerably during the military period, substantially enlarging state presence. The policies, however, still lacked the design, the quality and the scale of production necessary to face the problems accumulated through time.

THE RETURN TO DEMOCRACY IN THE 1980s AND 1990s

The decline of the military regime had contradictory effects on urban policies. On the one hand, it reduced strongly the available resources for policies in the 1980s, creating major challenges for the cities and making social conditions even more difficult to face. Most analysts expected a worsening of urban conditions, but the 1991 Census showed that the indicators continue to improve (Faria 1992). This apparent paradox was explained by the joint effect of the very active social movements of the period, the return of electoral competition and inertia of the state organisations, and local technical communities created during the military period in several policy fields (Marques and Bichir 2003).

On the other hand, the reduction in federal programmes and regulation opened up an important window for policy innovation by local governments. This was the moment of the first free state and municipal elections (in large cities) in twenty years. As a result, several local (mainly municipal) governments started innovating urban policies to face the difficult urban conditions (and the absence of resources) and, of course, to compete electorally. A key element in this process was the slow but steady expansion of left-wing political parties in local governments between the end of the 1980s and the early years of the 2000s, when the Workers' Party (PT) was elected for the presidency for the first time. Several local governments created new policy alternatives, targeted to face housing and urban precarity, instead of just insisting on small-scale production of new housing units.

Among these new policies, the following must be cited—slum upgrading, irregular settlement regularisation, social rent initiatives, self-help housing controlled by community associations (*mutirão autogestionário*), among others. Innovations in planning policies reinforced this tendency, as in the case of social purpose zoning (*Zonas de Especial Interesse Social* or ZEIS), which reserved plots in central locations of the city for social housing or for priority urbanisation. The new institutions and technologies of social participation that became famous worldwide as a Brazilian product, such as participatory budgeting, are part of this same wave and local dissemination of policy innovations (Abbers 2000). These policies were created as innovations and circulated intensely among local governments, fuelled by the mobility of ideas but also by the circulation of these ideas by technicians, activists and advocates of more distributive and participatory policies among municipalities and governments. By the mid-1990s, therefore, the field of urban policies had already been transformed by the presence of (already tested) alternative policies to the traditional programmes of new housing units for financed sale in the *periferias*. This wave of innovation reached the whole country and the federal level only in the 2000s, as we will see in a moment.

After the closure of BNH in 1986, there was no specific federal institution for urban and housing policies. Another federal bank–the Caixa Econômica Federal (CEF)–incorporated the assets of the housing bank, but CEF is a commercial bank with no expertise in urban policy formulation, resulting in a strong demobilisation of federal urban policies. In fact, urban issues and the urban agenda circulated among more than ten federal institutions only between 1986 and 1994 (Arretche 1995). During the late 1990s, the priority of fiscal adjustment of the Cardoso administrations (PSDB/PFL,[6] centre-right) led the federal government to reduce investments in housing and sanitation to a minimum level and to concentrate them on housing vouchers, which was around 85 per cent of the expenditures of the period (Bonduki 2008). The emphasis on economic stabilisation was so strong that another federal priority was to pressure the local agencies of housing and sanitation to restructure themselves or close their doors. However, the federal government also introduced improvements by implementing a series of microeconomic reforms for market regulation and risk reduction, involving mortgages, warranties, and land and housing registrations. These changes contributed to unlocking market production, bringing in a smooth return of housing construction after 1996 that later turned into a construction boom after 2005 (Dias 2012), during the Workers' Party federal administrations (PT/PL,[7] centre-left).

It is important to add that crucial demographic processes also had positive consequences on Brazilian cities during this same period. Since 1980, Brazil experienced a very strong decline in fertility rates—the average fertility rate in 1960 was 6.2 children per woman, but it fell to 4.4 in 1980 and 1.8 in 2010. A similar reduction happened in migration, with the estimated net balance of migration (i.e., net absolute number of migrants) to cities dropping from 17.4 million in 1970–1980 to 9.2 million in 1980–1991, and to just 6.0 million in 2000–2010 (Martine and McGranahan 2014). As a result, the urban growth rates changed substantially, dropping from 4.7 per cent and 4.2 per cent yearly between 1960–1970 and 1970–1980, to 2.6 per cent, 2.5 per cent and 1.6 per cent per year in 1980–1991, 1991–2000 and 2000–2010, respectively (ibid.). Even with this slower pace, the urban population reached 84.4 per cent of the country's population in 2010, 31.9 per cent of which was in the ten largest metropolitan areas.

Regardless of that, the spatial structure of Brazilian metropolises was not substantially altered, and the peripheral municipalities continued to grow more than central areas, although less and less as time went by. In fact, in the ten largest metropolitan regions, while the central municipalities grew at 3.0 per cent, 1.8 per cent and 0.9 per cent per year in 1980–1991, 1991–2000 and 2000–2010, respectively, the peripheral municipalities grew at 4.3 per cent, 3.6 per cent and 1.8 per cent per year in the same decades (Cunha 2016). Therefore, urban growth dropped generally, but the processes that structured the metropolises were not substantially changed.

In terms of access to services and policies, there has been a long-term trend of improvement, although there are still inequalities among social groups, regions of the country and cities (Marques 2019). This improvement apparently took place even in the most precarious areas (Ministério das Cidades/CEM 2008), although in this case the evidence is not so easy to interpret. Brazil developed nationally comparable data on precarity only recently, in the 2000s, and even so problems of comparability remain. For 2000, estimates of the Ministry of Cities developed by the Centre for Metropolitan Studies (CEM) suggest that the country had around 12.4 million people and 3.1 million households in precarious areas, which corresponded to 14.3 per cent of the country's population. There are no figures for the whole country for 2010, but the presence of precarity in the four metropolitan regions of the state of São Paulo increased from 13.5 per cent to 14.3 per cent between 2000 and 2010, while it decreased from 15 per cent to 14.5 per cent of the population in the metropolitan region of São Paulo alone (Emplasa/CEM 2013). The average social indicators of precarious areas over time suggest continuous improvement.

A different measure of housing precarity is provided by the estimation of the housing deficit, or the amount of housing units necessary for replacing not only precarity in terms of construction and infrastructure, but also housing density, cohabitation and excessive burden with rent payments. Considering these elements, Brazil would need 5.01 million urban housing units, or 9 per cent of the urban housing stock in 2014 (Fundação João Pinheiro 2016). The most important component of this deficit would be associated with an excessive burden of rents (56.2 per cent), followed by cohabitation (32 per cent), and precarity and excessive density (6 per cent each). In the case of this estimate, houses may be needed inside or outside precarious areas, and houses inside areas like favelas may or may not be part of the deficit.

The federal government returned to the picture strongly only in the 2000s. The first important event of this new period was the approval of the City Statute by Congress in 2001. This law detailed the session of the 1988 Constitution associated with cities, establishing mainly the so-called 'social function of property'. The Constitution included strong measures against land speculation—increasingly progressive land tax, compulsory construction and expropriation paid with state bonds; however, it postponed the establishment of the details of these instruments for ordinary regulation. These provisions should be applied progressively, although they have to be described and spatially delimited in each municipal Master Plan. Before the Statute of Cities, they could not be applied even by the most politically motivated local administration.

The real momentum of urban policy production, however, was provided by the creation of the Ministry of Cities in 2003, a clear political choice of the newly elected PT government, close to the urban agenda and its associated social movements. The formation of the Ministry itself was part of the above-mentioned process of policy innovation and dissemination, since its first generations of decision-makers were part of the network of technicians and activists that had circulated previously at the local level. While starting from scratch, the Ministry gradually expanded its structure and constructed a relatively capable technical apparatus (Klintowitz 2015), although it was not very insulated from the broader political environment (Rolnik 2009). In financial terms, its budget jumped from R$ 290 million in 2005 to R$ 21.5 billion in 2014 (Proni and Faustino 2016).

In the following years, a new system of urban and housing policies of considerable complexity began to be structured. In 2005, the Ministry created the National System of Social Housing (SNHIS), with a national fund and a representative Council. In the following years, several sectoral policies gained national plans, and some of them represented their first national regulations—housing in 2007, solid waste in 2011, urban mobility in 2012, and sanitation in 2013. Together, they formed a national system—the Urban Development National Policy (PNDU)—thereby regulating policies traditionally formulated and implemented by local governments. This not only promoted the urban local policy agenda of the 1990s at the national level, but also contributed to enhancing cohesion between policies and reducing territorial and regional inequalities.

In terms of political participation, six National City Conferences were held between 2003 and 2016, and a National Council of Cities (Con Cidades) was structured with eighty-six participants, forty-nine of them from civil society organisations. Besides that, new National Funds per policy sector were created for policy financing, all associated with representative Councils (Klintowitz 2015).

The process also contributed to the improvement of administrative and technical capacities at the local governments. This involved mainly new dedicated agencies with specific bureaucracies, institutionalised participation, local funds and councils, and local plans. A study comparing these housing and urban policy instruments between 2004 and 2009 suggested that they are still low and uneven among the 5,557 municipalities. However, it also showed an important expansion of these municipal capacities, in great part as local responses to federal policies, financing and incentives (Ministério das Cidades/CEM 2012).

Federal investments to urban policies also returned during this period. The financing of the upgrading of precarious areas was gathered under the umbrella of the Growth Acceleration Programme (PAC). Between 2007 and 2014, the PAC spent US$ 15.7 billion in slum upgrading programmes in several metropolitan areas–road construction, drainage, sanitation, stabilisation of geotechnical or flooding risks, and (in some cases) the construction of cable cars.[8] These public works benefitted 1,282 communities, with an estimated 2.5 and 7.6 million households and persons, respectively (D'Ávila 2015). Some of the largest favelas in the country received massive investments, such as Alemão, Pavão/Pavanzinho/Cantagalo and Rocinha in Rio de Janeiro, and Paraisólis and Heliópolis in São Paulo, but many others still wait for interventions. In any case, the promotion of integrated and complete urbanisation was given central place in the federal policy urban agenda, instead of the evictions typical of the 1970s and the localised interventions of the 1980s and 1990s.

In terms of financial credit for housing, the effects of the new policies, including the changes in regulation implemented during the Cardoso administration in the 1990s, were astonishing. Credit provided by private companies for housing production remained steady around US$ 15 billion per year between 1994 and 2000, but grew continuously from 2003 onwards, reaching US$ 50 billion in 2010. In the same direction, credit provided by the public housing financial schemes jumped from only around US$ 3.5 billion in 2005 to US$ 25 billion in 2010 (Dias 2012). Finally, the FGTS expenditures for housing increased from R$ 2.6 billion in 2001 to R$ 58.6 billion in 2014 (Proni and Faustino 2016).

These figures still do not account completely for the effects of the main federal housing project–the My House, My Life (MCMV) programme. The first phase of the programme started in 2009, less as a housing programme and more as one of the anti-cyclical measures to prevent the effects of the 2008 international economic crisis from reaching Brazil. In fact, although quite innovative institutionally and very well-financed, the programme was contrary to the spirit of the policy system in formation at the federal level since 2003, and was severely criticised by some of the proponents of that system (Krause et al. 2013). A second phase of the programme was launched in 2011 (activities were planned till 2014), with some of the previous problems at least mitigated. The main issues included the low quality of the houses, the isolated location of the projects (and, therefore, their effects on urban segregation) and the low availability of good infrastructure. Some of these problems were solved through time incrementally, but others persisted and stayed as challenges for the third phase launched in 2015. The future of this programme has been uncertain since the contested impeachment of President Dilma Rousseff in 2016. The two following federal administrations—Temer's and Bolsonaro's—drastically reduced investments, but did not halt the programme.

In previous Brazilian housing policies, the federal government lent financial resources to local state funds and companies who hired private constructors to build the houses, which had been previously designed by other private companies. In the new scheme, the federal bank (CEF) directly hired the private companies in two different formats: (*i*) buying their products with no intermediation of local agencies (in the first of the three income brackets of the programme, for the very low-income group); (*ii*) lending money to finance the final buyers of projects constructed by private companies directly (in the second and third income brackets, for low and lower-middle class families). The first bracket included families with a monthly family income of less than US$ 455 and the second up to US$ 935 originally (the values were recalculated several times later). Project, price and housing characteristics were established by the federal government, but the construction process was entirely the responsibility of the private companies. This scheme was adopted to speed up the process, which was very important considering the macroeconomic goals of the policy. Another major policy innovation involved the concession of up to 90 per cent of subsidies for the first bracket and up to 30 per cent in the second, directly from the federal budget. This was a very important feature of the programme, since only with this degree of subsidies could families with almost no income make a demand for housing policies. In fact, the population included in the first income bracket of the programme had never been reached by any policy previously. Local governments participated in the system, providing land for the projects of the first income bracket, as well as organising the demand based on the registries they maintain on housing demand.[9]

As a result of the fast implementation design and the strong political priority of the programme,[10] the volume of production reached new scales in a short period of time. Between 2009 and 2015, the programme commissioned the construction of 3.8 million housing units. Some 2.1 million of them had already been delivered by the end of 2015 and the rest were still under construction (Proni and Faustino 2016). Among the delivered units, around 700,000 corresponded to the first bracket and the other 1.2 million to the second. In terms of investment, this production corresponded to US$ 74.9 billion (D'Ávila 2015) and the subsidies reached around US$ 39 million until February 2015, US$ 28 billion of which was provided to the first bracket (Proni and Faustino 2016).

On the other hand, the programme brought back to the centre of urban policies the traditional product in the country—new units for financed sale in peripheral projects. By doing so, the programme subverted the logic of the urban policy system under construction, aimed first and foremost at enhancing the production of the city and at reducing precarity, with a secondary focus on housing production itself. The emphasis on planning and on an integrated approach to urban problems (with the production of urbanity and the reduction of precarity as goals) was also replaced by a targeted preoccupation with the production of new (and more) units. Additionally, the programme also created incentives for the construction of housing projects in urban peripheries, with potential negative effects on residential segregation. These elements tend to be more important (and dangerous) in large cities, which already have fragmented governments, highly segregated urban structures, and where well-located land is likely to be very expensive.

The future of all these programmes, however, is highly uncertain at the moment. In August 2016, the President of the Republic, Dilma Rousseff, was impeached in a highly contested process.

The vice-president who took office, Michel Temer, belonged to a different political party and dedicated his two years in office to the development of a quite conservative agenda. In the general election of 2018, the political turn was intensified with the victory of an extreme right-wing candidate, Jair Bolsonaro. He has radicalised the liberal economic turn of his predecessor, but with a very unstable base of support and no visible urban agenda. At the same time, in the years since 2015, the Brazilian economy has been experiencing an intense economic crisis with one of the largest recessions in three decades, reducing the available resources for investment at all levels of government.[11] The MCMV, however, was not extinguished and, in fact, a third phase of the programme was launched in March 2016 with the goal of producing one million housing units till 2018. The pace of this programme after that, as well as the investments of PAC, however, has been close to zero. Considering the (private sector) interests this policy awakened, it is probable that this policy (or something of its kind) will return with speed as soon as public finances improve, although disconnected from urban planning and with reduced subsidies and fewer redistributive contents.

Finally—although not directly related to housing—it is important to mention two associated trends in local (municipal) policies and governments. On the one hand, in recent years, several experiences of private participation in policy provision were disseminated through the country. These include the development of many forms of public-private partnerships (PPP) for service delivery or for the production of large-scale urban renovation projects in several cities, regulated by a federal law from 2004. In many cases, these partnerships are launched but do not become effective,[12] but in large cities such as São Paulo and Rio de Janeiro, they are increasingly common. These have been enhanced with the introduction and dissemination of air rights in the form of 'bonus of additional construction potential' (Cepacs), created for the first time in São Paulo in 2002 (Sarue and Pagin 2018). These were especially relevant in the production of recent large urban projects, the most important of which is the Porto Maravilha project in Rio de Janeiro, associated with the Olympic Games and the football World Cup (Sarue 2016).

At the same time, and complementarily, local governments have been developing increasing local capacities for regulation of the services hired with private companies in several policy areas, such as bus transportation, the regulation of private development and garbage collection (Marques 2016a). This involved the construction of new agencies and bureaucracies, as well as information systems and policy instruments, although the efficacy of these is still to be tested (Campos 2015; Hoyler 2018; Ralize 2018; Requena 2018). Therefore, in the recent period, local governments in Brazilian cities are more dependent on private companies, but also more able to regulate their activities and suggest a transformation in the roles of private and public agents with the mutual enhancement of both (Marques 2016a), somewhat similar to the MCMV programme.

CONCLUSION

As we have seen, the recent decades, and especially the 2000s, represented an important moment for the creation and diversification of new urban policies in Brazil, as well as for the construction of administrative and technical capacities, both at the local and the federal levels. In some of these new policies, the private sector occupied a new and empowered role, although it was surrounded by new regulatory tools whose efficacy will be tested in the near future. This coincided with a favourable moment in urbanisation and demographic processes. All these elements contributed to the promotion of services and the construction of better housing and urban conditions, although they were still incapable of facing the large stock of precarity and the intense inequalities that mark Brazilian cities.

The future of these trends became uncertain due to not only the economic and fiscal crisis experienced since 2016, but also the political crisis that started with the president's impeachment in 2016 and persists today under the extreme right-wing presidency inaugurated in 2019. These elements suggest that the direct continuation of the projects and policies discussed previously is improbable. However, a complete reversal of the policy trends of recent decades is also improbable, for at least two reasons: First, the production of a broader set of policies for housing and for cities was not just a product of one specific government. This was caused by a dislocation of the policy agenda and by the dissemination of new policy alternatives inside the policy community since the 1990s, with slum upgrading standing as one of the most important examples of this process. Second, programmes such as the MCMV and the PPPs for local service delivery have mobilised broad coalitions involving private contractors and politicians who will lobby for more policies of this kind in the near future. Therefore, it is reasonable to consider that these two important policy trends in Brazil—the presence of a broader set of national housing and urban policies, and the key role given to private actors in housing and urban policies—will tend to continue in the future, once the recent crisis is overcome. Their integration with local urban planning and their redistributive content, however, depend basically on the urban struggles that unfold in the near future, as well as on the reversion of the recent right-wing political shift.

End Notes

1. 'Financed sale' refers to the sale of housing units through public financial arrangements. This differs from subsidised sale, social rent schemes, and so on.

2. The source of the demographic data used in this chapter is the Brazilian Institute of Geography and Statistics (IBGE), except when explicitly stated otherwise. Available at http://seriesestatisticas.ibge.gov.br (accessed May 2021).

3. Vargas would return to power in 1950 as an elected president and stay in office until his suicide in 1954, which postponed for ten years another *coup d'état* in formation, until 1964 (Neto 2014).

4. Considering an average housing density of 6.5 persons per household. Although very high, this estimate is reasonable for the family structure and the housing density prevalent in the period.

5. According to the 1988 Constitution, one who occupies a small parcel of land (less than 250 sq. m.) for her/his own use for more than five years, without contestation, is entitled to tenure (but not property). It is also important to highlight that land in Brazil is private or public.

The 1988 Constitution created forms of communal land for indigenous peoples, and for descendants of slaves who occupied certain locations, but these are almost non-existent in cities and metropolises.

6. PSDB stands for Partido da Social Democracia Brasileira (Party of the Brazilian Social Democracy), and PFL is Partido da Frente Liberal (Party of the Liberal Front).

7. PT stands for Partido dos Trabalhadores (Workers' Party), and PL is Partido Liberal (Liberal Party).

8. This last case was an intensely contested technical solution, considering their very high maintenance costs. After some years, several of them were discontinued, confirming early criticisms. See http://g1.globo.com/rio-de-janeiro/noticia/2016/10/teleferico-do-alemao-no-rio-e-fechado-por-falta-de-pagamento.html (accessed June 2021).

9. In fact, this is a simplification. The rules of the programme were very complex, detailed and changed substantially through time as an answer to the many criticisms suffered by the programme. For a detailed discussion, see Rodrigues (2015).

10. The Ministry of Cities estimated that the programme created 912,000 direct and indirect jobs annually (D'Ávila 2015).

11. http://www1.folha.uol.com.br/mercado/2017/12/1940049-novos-dados-indicam-que-recente-recessao-nao-foi-a-pior-da-historia.shtml (accessed January 2021).

12. http://m.folha.uol.com.br/mercado/2017/12/1946003-cresce-procura-de-prefeituras-por-parceria-com-empresas.shtml (accessed January 2021).

References

Abbers, Rebecca. 2000. *Inventing Local Democracy: Grassroots Politics in Brazil*. Boulder: Lynne Rienner.

Arretche, Marta. 1995. 'Políticas de desenvolvimento urbano na crise: Descentralização ou crise no modelo do BNH?' In Elisa Reis, Maria Hermínia Almeida and Peter Fry (eds), *Pluralismo, Espaço Social e Pesquisa*. São Paulo: Hucitec/ANPOCS.

______. 2019. 'Territorial inequalities and citizenship'. In Marta Arretche (ed.), *Paths of Inequality in Brazil: A Half-Century of Changes*. New York: Springer/Ed. Unesp/Fapesp.

Azevedo, Sérgio. 1988. 'Vinte e dois anos de política de habitação popular 1964–86: Criação, trajetória e extinção do BNH'. *Revista de Administração Pública* 224: 107–119.

Azevedo, Sérgio and Luis Andrade. 1981. *Habitação e Poder: Da Fundação da Casa Popular ao Banco Nacional da Habitação*. Rio de Janeiro: Zahar.

Baeninger, Rossana. 2011. 'Crescimento da população da região metropolitana de São Paulo: Desconstruindo mitos do século XX'. In Lúcio Kowarick and Eduardo Marques (eds), *São Paulo: Novos Percursos e Atores*. São Paulo: Ed. 34.

Bonduki, Nabil. 1998. *Origens da Habitação Social no Brasil: Arquitetura Moderna, Lei do Inquilinato e Difusão da Casa Própria*. São Paulo: Estação Liberdade.

______. 2008. 'Política habitacional e inclusão social no Brasil: Revisão histórica e novas perspectivas no governo Lula'. *Arq.urb - Revista de Arquitetura e Urbanismo* 1(1).

Campos, Marcos. 2015. 'O mercado de viagens e as disputas em torno das linhas de ônibus'. *Novos Estudos Cebrap* 105: 35.

Cunha, José. 2016. 'Population dynamics and migration: 1991–2010'. In Eduardo Marques (ed.), *São Paulo, XXI Century: Spaces, Heterogeneities and Inequalities*. New York: Routledge.

D'Ávila, Adriana. 2015. 'PAC - Urbanização de assentamentos precários'. Paper presented at the 29th World Congress of the International Union of Housing Finance, Rio de Janeiro.

Dias, Edney. 2012. 'Do Plano Real ao Programa Minha Casa, Minha Vida: negócios, votos e as reformas da habitação'. MSc. dissertation, DCP/University of São Paulo. Available at www.teses.usp.br/teses/disponiveis/8/8131/tde-08012013-145204/pt-br.php (accessed January 2021).

Emplasa/CEM. 2013.*Diagnosis of Precarity in the Cities of São Paulo Macrometropolis*. São Paulo: CEM. Available at http://centrodametropole.fflch.usp.br/en/pesquisa/precarious-settlements-diagnosis-slums-cities-sao-paulo-macrometropolis-2013 (accessed March 2021).

Faria, Vilmar. 1992. 'A Conjuntura Social Brasileira: Dilemas e Perspectivas'. *Novos Estudos Cebrap* 33.

Fundação João Pinheiro. 2016. *Déficit Habitacional no Brasil 2013–2014*. Belo Horizonte: Fundação João Pinheiro.

Hoyler, Telma. 2018. 'O cotidiano esquecido da regulação na produção habitacional privada'. In Eduardo Marques (ed.), *As Políticas do Urbano em São Paulo*. São Paulo: Ed. Unesp/CEM.

Klintowitz, Danielle. 2015. 'Entre a reforma urbana e a reforma imobiliária: a coordenação de interesses na política habitacional brasileira nos anos 2000'. PhD thesis, Fundação Getúlio Vargas, São Paulo. Available at http://bibliotecadigital.fgv.br/dspace/handle/10438/13791 (accessed January 2021).

Krause, Cleandro, Vicente Correia Lima Neto and Renato Balbim. 2013. 'Minha casa minha vida, nosso crescimento: Como fica a política habitacional?' *Revista Brasileira de Estudos Urbanos* 15.

Maricato, Ermínia. 1987. *Política Habitacional no Regime Militar*. Petrópolis: Vozes.

Marques, Eduardo. 2016a. 'De volta aos capitais para melhor entender as políticas urbanas'. *Novos Estudos Cebrap* 35(2): 15–33. Available at https://www.scielo.br/pdf/nec/v35n2/1980-5403-nec-35-02-15.pdf (accessed March 2021).

______ (ed.). 2016b. *São Paulo, XXI Century: Spaces, Heterogeneities and Inequalities*. New York: Routledge.

______. 2019. 'Housing and Urban Conditions in Brazil'. In Marta Arretche (ed.), *Paths of Inequality in Brazil: A Half-Century of Changes*. New York: Springer/Ed.

Marques, Eduardo and Renata Bichir. 2003. 'Public policies, political cleavages and urban space: State infra-structure policies in São Paulo, Brazil—1975–2000'. *International Journal of Urban and Regional Research* 27(4): 811–827.

Martine, George and Gordon McGranahan. 2014. 'Brazil's negligent urban transition and its legacy of divided cities'. In George Martine and Gordon McGranahan (eds), *Urban Growth in Emerging Economies: Lessons from the BRICS*. London: Routledge.

Ministério das Cidades/CEM. 2008. *Assentamentos Precários no Brasil Urbano*. Brasília: Ministério das Cidades. Available at http://centrodametropole.fflch.usp.br/en/books/assentamentos-precarios-no-brasil-urbano (accessed March 2021).

______. 2012. *Capacidades administrativas dos municípios brasileiros para a política habitacional*. Brasília: Ministério das Cidades/CEM. Available at http://centrodametropole.fflch.usp.br/en/books/capacidades-administrativas-dos-municipios-brasileiros-para-politica-habitacional (accessed March 2021).

Neto, Lira. 2014. *Getúlio – 1945–1954: Da Volta Pela Consagração Popular Ao Suicídio*. São Paulo: Companhia das Letras.

Nunes, Edson. 1997. *As gramáticas políticas do Brasil*. Rio de Janeiro: FGV.

Proni, Marcelo and Raphael Faustino. 2016. 'Avanços e limites da política dde desenvolvimento urbano no Brasil (2001–2014)'. *Planejamento e Políticas Públicas* 46. Brasília: IPEA.

Ralize, Samuel. 2018. 'Limpeza urbana: política, modelos institucionais e os limites do Estado'. In Eduardo Marques (ed.), *As políticas do urbano em São Paulo*. São Paulo: Ed. Unesp/CEM.

Requena, Carolina. 2018. 'Paradigma e mudança na mobilidade urbana'. In Eduardo Marques (ed.), *As políticas do urbano em São Paulo*. São Paulo: Ed. Unesp/CEM.

Rezende, Sonaly and Léo Heller. 2002. *O saneamento no Brasil: políticas e interfaces*. Belo Horizonte: Ed. UFMG.

Rodrigues, Leandro. 2015. 'A produção habitacional o Programa Minha Casa Minha Vida na Região Metropolitana de São Paulo'. MSc. dissertation, DCP/University of São Paulo. Available at http://www.teses.usp.br/teses/disponiveis/8/8131/tde-29072015-144127/pt-br.php (accessed January 2021).

Rolnik, Raquel. 2009. 'Democracia no fio da navalha limites e possibilidades para a implementação de uma agenda de reforma urbana no Brasil'. *Revista Brasileira de Estudos Urbanos* 21(2): 30–50.

Santos, Wanderley G. dos. 1979. *Cidadania e justiça*. Rio de Janeiro: Ed. Campus.

Sarue, Betina. 2016. 'Grandes projetos urbanos e a governança das cidades: O caso do Porto Maravilha'. *Novos Estudos Cebrap* 105: 56.

Sarue, Betina and Stephano Pagin. 2018. 'Renovação Urbana: Conflitos, instrumentos e gradualismo'. In Eduardo Marques (ed.), *As Políticas do Urbano em São Paulo*. São Paulo: Ed. Unesp/CEM.

Schmitter, Philip. 1979. 'Still the Century of Corporatism?' In Philip Schmitter (ed.), *Trends toward Corporatist Intermediation*. London: Sage Publications.

II

Towards a More Humane Urbanism

*Low-Income Housing in Urban India**

Annapurna Shaw

INTRODUCTION

The world is becoming increasingly urban with more than half its population living in urban areas in 2017, up from 30 per cent in 1950. By 2050, 66 per cent of the world's population will be urban. In view of this, there has been an urgent call for 'people-centered, sustainable urban development' by global organisations such as the UN (UN-Habitat 2012) to enhance the quality of life of a majority of the earth's population and to do it in the most sustainable way. On the one hand are optimists such as the former Secretary General of the UN, Ban Ki-moon, who believe that 'as the world seeks a more people-centered, sustainable approach to development, cities can lead the way with local solutions to global problems' (ibid.: Preface). But others see the future as dark, namely the earth becoming, more and more, 'a planet of slums' (Davis 2007 [2006]). India, in particular, must take heed of these alternate scenarios as it will be the largest contributor to the world's urban growth between 2014 and 2050. It is projected to add 416 million

---

*This is a revised version of a paper presented at a conference on 'Political Economy of Emerging Market Countries: The Challenges of Developing More Humane Societies', organised by Niehaus Center for Globalization and Governance, Princeton University, Georgetown University India Initiative and Indian Institute of Management Calcutta, 30 December–3 January 2017, Kolkata and Santiniketan, West Bengal.

urban dwellers by 2050, exceeding China's 255 million and Nigeria's 189 million (United Nations 2018).

What path is India taking in its urban transition and how can it be made 'people-centered and sustainable'? How can it be made more humane? This larger question is examined in this chapter, with a closer look at public policy choices in one aspect of the country's urban transition challenge, namely low-income housing. The term 'humane', as used here, implies a broader sense of compassion and tolerance for diverse and sentient life forms, human and non-human. It is closely associated with people-centric and green solutions.

Humane urbanism is not a widely used term in existing academic literature or policy documents on the Indian city, but is increasingly appearing in important discussions in other countries. It has been associated with the work of Rutherford Platt (2006, 2014), a historical geographer, to refer to the gradual switch from top-down urban policies that served a small elite for most of the past century in America, to citizen involvement and popular initiatives to make American cities more green, equitable, efficient and people-friendly, which began to take shape from the 1990s. Humane urbanism, in the context of American cities, took several forms, such as creating affordable housing, networks of bike paths, grassroots efforts to bring nature back to the city, and other low-tech, self-sustaining programmes. In a more recent book, Rose (2016) lists 'compassion' as one of the five qualities of a 'well-tempered city' that is inclusive of all its residents and provides a high quality of life. Interestingly, such ideas of humanity and compassion as necessary attributes to a good city, germinating in the context of an advanced capitalist country, are also echoed in China's post-2007 policy documents, where there has been a call for 'human-being urbanization' (Chen 2018) or urbanisation that is focussed on people and their needs.

What can be surmised from these examples is that the fallout of two decades of single-minded market-oriented reforms, followed by the financial crisis of 2007, has revealed many vulnerabilities within the cities of both developed and developing countries, and the need for a re-look at the usefulness of a purely market or commercial paradigm to solving urban problems. In India, it has echoes in N. R. Narayana Murthy's call for a more 'compassionate capitalism' (*The Indian Express* 2017) and the social activist Harsh Mander's 'egalitarian compassion' (Mander 2015). However, such ideas are yet to resonate within the policy discourse of Indian cities. This chapter nevertheless shows how implementation of policy at the ground level can be greatly improved when humaneness or compassion become the key drivers.

The next section is on low-income housing provision by the Indian state from the early plan years to the present, and its failures rooted in its views on housing and the poor. The third section takes the case of successful implementation of a central government housing programme in the city of Nanded, Maharashtra to highlight the positive results when municipal authorities take a humane view and incorporate local people's concerns during the process of programme implementation. The last section concludes the chapter with a discussion of the idea of a 'humane urbanism' in the context of Indian cities and with observations on the possibilities and limitations of achieving it under the existing political and economic framework.

HOUSING FOR THE URBAN POOR

I now turn to one specific issue, which in many ways epitomises the challenges of developing more humane societies in developing countries, and that is the issue of housing for the urban poor. In 1988, in a first of its kind, the central government under Rajiv Gandhi set up a National Commission on Urbanization (NCU) to study in detail the challenges of urban transition in the country and to recommend solutions. The Commission had made the following observation (NCU 1988: 475): 'The most visible and dehumanising manifestation of India's urbanisation is the large number of squatters and shanty dwellers so ubiquitous in all our major cities.' Despite the Commission's recommendations, more than two decades since its report, the numbers of squatters and shanty dwellers have only increased, although absolute levels of poverty in urban India have declined. In the last decade, India's slum population increased from fifty-two million in 2001 to sixty-five million in 2011 (Census of India 2011). Out of the 4,041 statutory towns, slums were found in 2,613 of them, or in more than half. Another fact to be noted is that during the last decade, the concentration of Scheduled Castes (SCs) in slums has increased. In absolute numbers, the SC population increased from 9.6 million to 13.3 million by 2011, while their percentage in the total slum population increased from 18.5 per cent to 20.4 per cent. In the urban slums of Tamil Nadu (39.8 per cent) and Punjab (32.0 per cent), it exceeded 30 per cent. Both these trends, the first of increasing numbers of slum dwellers and the second of a rising concentration of SCs in slums, are evidence of increasing inequalities in Indian cities and the failure of existing land and housing policies. In fact, the government's own review committee, the Working Group on Urban Poverty, Slums and Service Delivery System of the Planning Commission's 2011 Steering Committee on Urbanization, has acknowledged that the 'proliferation of slums, as much of the evidence both in-country and international suggest, is not so much a manifestation of demographic shifts, but the result of the failure of the land and housing policies, and legal and delivery systems' (Planning Commission 2011: 8).

Such failure is rooted in the character of the state, which in the pre-liberalisation era lacked the 'relative autonomy' to resist the pulls of its dominant proprietary classes (industrial capitalists, rich farmers, civil and military bureaucracy and white-collar professionals), who had ensured that the gains of development went primarily to themselves (Bardhan 1984).[1] In the post-liberalisation period, the state's close relationship with a diversified private sector continues in reconstituted ways, marked by its increasing role as discretionary facilitator to resources in demand by the private sector, by means such as the control of entry into formerly reserved sectors of the economy, influence over the supply of inputs such as land, coal, other raw materials, and credit, and by the creation of new legislation while abolishing old ones (Chandra 2015; Nair 2019). Despite the rhetoric of inclusive development, the patronage-based relationship between the private sector and the state overshadows other developmental concerns, and redistribution through better housing for the poor is not very high on the political agenda, as housing shortage among the poor in Indian cities becomes more acute, particularly when compared to that in the middle- and upper-income groups. According to the Ministry of Housing and Urban Poverty Alleviation's Technical Group on Urban Housing Shortage (MHUPA 2012), the nation's urban housing shortage dropped from twenty-six million units in 2007 to 18.78 million in 2012.[2] But, as shown in Table 2.1, for the Economically Weaker Section (EWS) with household incomes of Rs 5,000 and less a month, the shortage was around ten million, or over half the total. For the Lower Income Group (LIG) with household monthly incomes between Rs 5,001 and 10,000, it was 7.4 million, around 39 per cent of the total. The balance of the shortage of around 4 per cent comes from the Middle Income Group (MIG). There is no shortage in the Higher Income Group (HIG).

Table 2.1: Composition of Urban Housing Deficit, 2012

Household monthly income	Income class	Number in millions	Number in percentage
(1)	(2)	(3)	(4)
Rs 5,000 & less	Economically Weaker Section (EWS)	10.55	56.18
Rs 5,001 to 10,000	Lower Income Group (LIG)	7.41	39.44
Above Rs 10,000	Middle Income Group (MIG)	0.82	4.38
Total		18.78	100.00

Source: Report of the Technical Urban Group on Urban Housing Shortage (MHUPA 2012).

Table 2.1 itself reveals a great deal about the failures of public policy in solving the housing problem of those at the bottom end, while having reduced housing shortage for the middle class and making it disappear for the rich. Housing activists would surmise that it has been more a case of a lack of sincere intent to solve this problem than that of ever-growing numbers and shortage of finances. As in the case of the delivery of basic public services such as sanitation, school education and health, the most affected population is the poor, who must buy substitutes for these services from the private sector at much higher prices. In the case of housing, it can mean homelessness or living in poor, makeshift housing arrangements with a lack of basic facilities and a low quality of life. Yet, without improving the quality of life of the bottom end of the urban population, Indian cities cannot become more humane.

One question that needs to be further examined is: Why has the housing shortage grown so severely among the urban poor, and what has been the role of the state, market, non-governmental agencies and the slum dwellers themselves? A second question is the state's approach to housing in its development policy. To understand both of these issues, it is necessary to briefly look at the history of low-income housing policy in India. In the first two decades post-independence, following the partition of the subcontinent and the entry of 7.5 million refugees, the state was an active provider of housing, observing that 'private enterprise is not in a position to do the job so far as low-income groups are concerned' (Planning Commission 1951). However, funding for housing under the first three Five-Year Plans and the Annual Plans (1966–1967 to 1968–1969) as a proportion of the total plan outlay was 'quite meagre', and investment in public housing was 'token investment' (Sivaramakrishnan 1969: 1433). Moreover, unlike East Asia, in the initial decades after independence in India, housing was treated not as an economic good, but solely 'as a welfare measure or some kind of social service programme subservient to other economic development programmes' (ibid.: 1444). Given the scarcity of resources, the state sought to reduce its investment burden on this non-productive sector by delivering housing that was the cheapest possible and of the smallest size. This mindset of providing the smallest possible dwelling unit to the poor with the cheapest materials to cut the size of government subsidy has continued to the present time, despite high levels of dissatisfaction from end users. In contrast, in Japan and much of East Asia, housing was regarded as both a driver of economic growth and a welfare good, and housing quality was not compromised to save resources (Ronald and Druta 2018).

The housing programmes of the 1950s and 1960s were 'disjointed' and had a wide range of beneficiaries: for instance, the 1952 Subsidised Housing Scheme for Industrial Workers and Economically Weaker Sections, the 1956 Slum Clearance and Improvement Scheme and the 1959 Rental Housing for State Government Employees (Hingorani 2011). Outcomes for the urban poor were disappointing as the housing delivered was either unaffordable or located too far away, and it was generally sold off to upper-income groups. At the same time, new construction could not keep up with slum clearance and there was a net loss of housing stock. The poor had no option than to seek housing in slums which, though illegal, were well-located (ibid.).

By the 1970s, global thinking on slums had changed and policy shifted from slum clearance to slum improvement. Slums began to be regarded as housing solutions and poverty alleviation was made an integral part of shelter schemes, as it began to be increasingly realised that an integrated approach to shelter provision was needed, focussing on land, materials, finance, technology, as well as poverty alleviation. Important schemes were the 1972 Environmental Improvement of Urban Slums (EIUS), the 1980 Sites and Services (S&S) and the 1986 Urban Basic Services (UBS). There was, however, a gradual shift in responsibility for social housing from the central government to state governments and their housing boards. Changes were also occurring in the mode of financing, from complete government subsidy to targeted subsidies and cross-subsidies (Wadhwa 1988). Housing outcomes for the middle and upper classes improved during the 1970s and 1980s mainly due to housing credit expansion, but for the poor, there was no relief, although an opportunity to address their housing problem did present itself in the drafting of the first National Housing Policy in 1987. In the March 1987 preamble to the draft, the need for shelter was for the first time recognised as a basic human need, next to food and clothing, marking a preliminary step towards its acceptance as a fundamental right (Kumar 1989). But this preamble was removed in the final version of the policy, and while the policy put forward an integrated approach to housing, it was not geared to alleviate the housing problems of the urban poor (ibid.). In fact, going by the policy, the state's direct role in housing provision was reduced to that of a facilitator and enabler of housing, which was expected to come from the private sector, with more financial responsibility from individual households.

Post-1991, the private sector continued to be given a much larger role in housing provision, while further deepening of the housing finance market enabled middle- and upper-income groups to buy their own homes and provided credit to the private construction industry (Hingorani 2011). However, the Ninth Plan (1997–2002) stated that it would focus on households at the lower end of the housing market, for instance, on those households below the poverty line, headed by women and SC/STs. For them, there would be direct state intervention and subsidies via programmes such as VAMBAY (Valmiki Ambedkar Awas Yojana), launched in 2001, and targeted at Below Poverty Line (BPL) households. Other major initiatives during the time included an expansion of the UBS (Urban Basic Services) to UBSP (Urban Basic Services for the Poor) and the 1997 National Slum Development Programme. However, despite these programmes, progress was limited due to institutional and governance weaknesses. Since the passage of the 74th Amendment Act of 1992, devolution of responsibility for slums and poverty alleviation had been passed on to urban local bodies (ULBs), but there were, as yet, no specific provisions in municipal law for dealing with such issues, and ULBs' capacity to deal with this new function was still weak. The process of town planning in the ULBs, moreover, did not provide for the poor (Mathur 2009).

This is the context in which the big-ticket urban housing programmes of recent times have been launched, with the objective of creating 'slum-free cities' and based on a new integrated approach to slum redevelopment that combined housing, infrastructure and titling. The JNNURM (Jawaharlal Nehru National Urban Renewal Mission) provided central funding for improving urban infrastructure and service from 2005 till 2014, and attempted to strengthen urban institutions and governance by modifying the laws that have come in the way of functioning of the land and housing markets, community participation and improved fiscal situation of urban local bodies. Its housing components, BSUP (Basic

Services for the Urban Poor) and IHSDP (Integrated Housing and Slum Development Programme), had a central government funding component of 50 per cent to 90 per cent (for sixty-five mission cities) and 80 to 90 per cent (for any other selected cities/towns). But despite the large budget and focussed attention, its outcomes have been limited in impact, partly because of the long time taken to complete construction with small yearly additions of new units. Taken together, under both these programmes, 1,250,691 dwelling units were sanctioned, of which 988,308 have been constructed and 783,029 occupied as of 31 December 2015 (MHUPA 2016: 26). There are 262,433 units still being constructed under these programmes. In 2011, RAY (Rajiv Awas Yojana), a housing programme directed at slum upgradation and tenure security, was launched, with 50 per cent to 75 per cent of the project cost borne by the central government. The construction/upgradation of 141,848 units was approved under RAY (ibid.: 25). Thus, under JNNURM and RAY, only 1,392,539 dwelling units have been sanctioned, which hardly makes a dent in the huge shortage, as estimated in 2012, of 17.96 million LIG and EWS units. In fact, housing supply from these programmes constitutes only 7.7 per cent of the shortage, as estimated in 2012, and has taken a decade to build, with many projects still incomplete. Both JNNURM and RAY have been discontinued since the new government came to power in May 2014 and have been replaced by AMRUT (Atal Mission for Rejuvenation and Urban Transformation) and PMAY-HFA 22 (Pradhan Mantri Awas Yojana-Housing for All by 2022), respectively, which were started in 2015. While AMRUT, unlike JNNURM, does not have any housing component, PMAY is a massive urban housing programme to build twenty million dwelling units, largely through the private sector, and thereby provide housing for all by 2022. Have these more recent programmes made any dent in improving housing conditions for the urban poor? Do they have any scope for doing so?

Here, it is important to distinguish between the thinking driving such programmes and their delivery systems. One flaw pointed out by both academics and housing activists has been the government's focus on the construction of 'new' housing rather than on the upgradation of existing dwellings, despite the fact that international best practices for housing the urban poor encourage the latter as the least disruptive way of improving housing (Patel 2013; Satterthwaite 2010). Both the BSUP and IHSDP, as components of JNNURM, emphasised new construction, although in-situ redevelopment was the solution of choice under the programme. As noted by the government's Working Group (Planning Commission 2011), new construction comes with the attendant problems of delays in implementation and cost escalation, which can make such housing unaffordable for the urban poor. Along with 'fresh housing construction', incremental housing, rental housing, together with 'accessible credit options' for the urban poor need to be explored (ibid.: 22–23). RAY, regarded as pro-poor and inclusive, has had mixed outcomes. While most projects under RAY have been in-situ rather than relocation, land optimisation has been a prime driver of project design, particularly in more urbanised states such as Maharashtra, with multi-storeyed dwellings being the dominant choice of project implementers. In many cases, this was despite the slum dwellers wanting single-storey structures (Sampreet and Bhise 2014). Housing for All by 2022 or Pradhan Mantri Awas Yojana, an ongoing programme, launched in 2015, has already faced criticism as being 'singularly unimaginative and poorly thought-through' (Patel 2016: 38). With little learning from past experiences, its future outcomes are already being regarded as limited and its ambitious goal of removing the urban housing deficit is unlikely to be achieved, as only 19,255 houses have been constructed between 2015–2016 when the annual target rate should be around three million (Nair 2016; Singh 2016).

According to housing studies experts, the shortcomings are hardly surprising as these newer programmes, even the more carefully thought-out ones such as RAY, are just 'old wine in new bottles' (Bhide 2014). In her examination of BSUP housing projects in Bengaluru, Kamath (2012) observes that the so-called newer programmes still follow the conventional practice of public housing built by contractors where the ULBs have little control over the building process which has been outsourced to private agents. This has caused a lack of co-ordination and accountability on the one hand, while on the other, has not resulted in better delivery, either in numbers of units or in quality. Second, there is little feedback from the ground-up on what the people want and no attempt to enter these into the design process. In fact, lack of genuine participation of slum dwellers in any planning prior to project implementation has been noted even in programmes such as RAY, which were based on the premise of inclusion of local-level inputs (Sampreet and Bhise 2014).

A third feature of the newer programmes is the emphasis on using land as a resource in building for the poor. In this method, first used in Mumbai's slum redevelopment by the SRA (Slum Redevelopment Authority) in the mid-1990s, private developers built *pucca* dwellings on a fraction of the slum land to house the slum inhabitants 'for free', and then with extra FSI (Floor Space Index), granted by the government as an incentive, built on the remaining land for sale in the market. Regarded as a win-win for all stakeholders, this method has now become the norm for redevelopment in Mumbai for both private and public land. However, critics have warned that it results in greatly increased population densities in already crowded areas of the city and does not contribute to an improvement in the living conditions of the poor, who are confined in high-rises covering less than half the plot area with no change in supporting infrastructure (Patel 2016). Moreover, individual flat sizes, around 250 sq. ft. under BSUP, increased to 300 sq. ft. under PMAY, are insufficient for larger families.

Overall, in the past ten years, there has been too much reliance on the private sector to build for the poor and too little monitoring by the state to see that it satisfactorily fulfils its end of the agreement. In the specific case of PMAY, the slowness of its take-off has largely been due to an over-reliance on the private sector (Nair 2016). The central government's subsidy has been small, just Rs 1 lakh (100,000) to Rs 1.5 lakh (150,000) per unit, while the cost of even a low-income unit could be around Rs 8 lakh in the larger metropolitan areas. This had discouraged state governments from taking up the programme more enthusiastically, and the private sector was not forthcoming either (Kumar 2016; Sahu 2017). After modifying the credit-linked subsidy scheme, one of the verticals within PMAY, to further incentivise the private sector by raising the income limits for eligibility loans, increasing the amount of subsidised loans, relaxing the norms for built-up area and including the middle-income group (Kundu 2017), the programme has picked up. As of 8 June 2021, it involves all states and union territories in the country with a total of 11.2 million dwelling units sanctioned and 4.83 million completed.[3]

HOUSING OF THE URBAN POOR

With state attempts at mass housing having had a poor record, both in the past and in ongoing programmes, the solution, according to many housing activists and experts, lies in accepting housing built in the informal economy and supporting its upgradation and improvement. While this is the path suggested increasingly by international best practice, in the Indian case, given the huge size of low-income housing requirement, it will also need to be supplemented by other sources of provision because in actual practice, demolitions and removal of slum populations have gone on as per the needs of the state for urban land; or the state has enacted legislation, seeking to formalise informal layouts and housing, but in the process has set in motion forces that are making housing availability even scarcer for the poor (Bhide 2014). State-led housing supply for the poor, despite its failings, can add to low-income housing stock, and there are also cases of satisfactory housing provision by the state, although they are not very numerous. One defining characteristic of the successful cases is the greater interaction with the affected population and adjusting aspects of a pre-fixed programme to suit local needs. Here, housing provision is marked by a more humane approach, with the state helping to upgrade informal housing on the basis of suggestions from the people themselves, so that it is 'housing of the poor' rather than a one way, top-down, 'housing for the poor', where the poor are passive recipients, not consulted during the process of house-building. When central government-sponsored housing programmes are implemented in this way by the sub-national state, there is a greater chance of it making a difference in the living conditions of the urban poor. This is illustrated through a more detailed look at Nanded, Maharashtra, a city of 5.5 lakhs (550,000) in 2011, and the way the Nanded Waghala City Municipal Corporation (NWCMC) implemented the central government's BSUP programme (Desai 2015) during the years 2009–2013.

To start with, the NWCMC used an expanded definition of slum to cover any settlement with more than twenty-five houses and having inadequate infrastructure, rather than the census definition which applies to 300 households and above. This enlarged the coverage of the programme to include both squatter settlements and unauthorised layouts (*gunthewaris*) as slums. The NWCMC also did not follow the Government of Maharashtra's cut-off date of 1 January 1995 to determine the eligibility of individual families for housing under BSUP and considered a range of documents, not just the electoral list, to determine eligibility. Thus, a larger number of settlements were identified as slums and a larger number of people were to be benefitted. By the end of 2012, 132 settlements with 27,985 dwellings were to be covered by the BSUP programme. Most of the settlements were to be redeveloped in-situ, with some relocation where it was unavoidable.

Under the BSUP programme, cities had to prepare DPRs (Detailed Project Reports), which had to be sanctioned by the state government and the central government to avail of central funding. In the case of Nanded, after the first DPR had been sanctioned and implementation was to begin, it was found that people were unwilling to vacate their houses. Using an NGO to build trust and starting the building of four houses led to a turn-around. But it was then found that people were opposed to the new layouts proposed in the DPR, which would result in medium-rise clusters, and they could not be persuaded otherwise. Following this impasse, NWCMC 'developed a new approach to try and take into account people's concerns and demands' (Desai 2015: 273), and this involved in-situ development on the existing plot footprint. Ultimately, this is what was done for most of the settlements. Thus, in the implementation phase, NWCMC had to deviate from what had been proposed in the sanctioned DPRs of many settlements. What is also noteworthy is that thirteen design models were prepared for the reconstruction of *kuchha* houses to *pucca*. Thus, those eligible to a house under BSUP had a wide choice of house types, rather than one fixed type imposed from above.

During the process of implementation, other concerns were expressed by people, such as large family size and overcrowding in the mandated 269 sq. ft. structure. The NWCMC responded by providing two BSUP units for such families, the second unit being built as a first-floor addition to the ground-floor BSUP unit. Another complaint that surfaced was the quality of construction by the contractor appointed by the NWCMC. In 2012, municipal officials created a sub-approach to in-situ redevelopment on the existing plot footprint, in which people had the option of constructing the houses themselves. More than one-third or 10,551 dwelling units were approved for self-construction. Here, they were not required to follow any of the thirteen design models, but could build as they wished.

Not surprisingly, the degree of satisfaction among BSUP beneficiaries has been high and the NWCMC's approach of engaging with the residents of informal settlements and 'modifying and evolving its BSUP approach to address people's concerns, demands and desires' (Desai 2015: 275) is what is needed to make government mass housing projects work on the ground. While the Nanded approach needs to be replicated in other Indian cities, its one drawback is that although the quality of individual homes improved to the satisfaction of their owners, there was not much improvement at the settlement level, as in-situ redevelopment on existing plot footprints did not leave much space for other amenities or new infrastructure development. Thus, an approach that allows for both settlement-level planning and peoples' concerns is required and can be attempted in the future.

However, what the Nanded case clearly highlights is that a humane approach by government officials towards the urban poor and their housing needs, responding to their emerging concerns as the construction process was ongoing, and having the ability to modify their approach to suit ground realities, even adding new features to it, is what distinguishes it from the usual story of a failed project. The case is important as it shows that government policy per se, despite its often rigid framework and implementation requirements, can be implemented at ground level in a nuanced manner that caters to the actual needs of the target group. But this requires that officials listen to the local people and incorporate their views in planning and plan implementation.

CONCLUDING OBSERVATIONS

In the Indian context, a humane urbanism would have to include giving people greater say in the planning of cities, and placing people-centred and human-scale policies at the forefront of urban development (Shaw 2012). But first and foremost, a humane urbanism in the Indian context must assure an improvement in the living conditions of its poor, and ensure that slum and squatter settlements are provided with water and sanitation and slum dwellers are not evicted from their homes, unless they are provided with alternate housing. Given the history of public housing in India, and its inability to meet the current housing demand among the poor, informal housing has to be upgraded rather than destroyed. These suggestions have already been made to the government by its own Working Committee (Planning Commission 2011) under proposed initiatives for the Twelfth Five-Year Plan, and they include: the provision of security of tenure to slum dwellers, slum upgradation as a solution of choice, universalisation of water and sanitation to all urban areas and a non-eviction strategy. The Committee has urged that 'basic minimum civic facilities to the urban poor should be guaranteed', and this should include safe drinking water, a clean toilet, sewerage, storm-water drainage and solid waste management. The provision of these services should not be linked to the legal status of the slum or squatter settlement. Currently, public services are provided to notified slums only. Upgrading essential services in informal settlements can be a long-term saving for the state, as this would reach more people and be less resource-intensive. It has also been suggested by the United Nations as well as the World Resources Institute.

Some of the advice from various agencies and experts has finally been accepted by the government, and in the recently published India Habitat III National Report (MHUPA 2016b), the 'new urban agenda' to be adopted by the country aims to promote 'inclusive urban development' via a mix of the following strategies: universalisation of basic services, including education and health; governability of cities focussed on social cohesion, especially among classes that stand excluded from the development mainstream and civic engagement; access to housing as a tool for alleviating poverty and as a growth escalator; and putting in place a strategy for reducing 'working poverty' (ibid.: 137). Slum upgradation has not been directly mentioned, but is possibly covered under 'ensuring better living conditions for the slum population' (ibid.: 138). The details of how these goals will be implemented are not present in the report, but the acknowledgement of their critical importance in India's urban transition is a starting point.

However, given the existing political and economic framework, what are the possibilities and limitations of achieving these goals? While this chapter has listed many limitations, seen through the history of India's public housing policy, are there still possibilities of better outcomes, as shown in the case of Nanded? For the country as a whole, possibilities lie in broader changes, such as rising literacy and educational aspirations among the poor themselves and a greater awareness of their rights. Demanding better services from the state, either directly or through political representatives at the local level, could be the best way of obtaining these services. Some possibilities also lie in the non-government sector and in civil society with small organisations, such as Rotary and Lions clubs, working at the grassroots to fill in the gaps between the government and the urban poor. But much will also depend on the willingness of the state and urban middle classes to share scarce resources such as urban land. Will the pro-business interests of the state, in particular, the central state, and its preoccupation with facilitating corporate-sector advancement, leave any room for a genuine effort to improve housing conditions of the urban poor? The case of Nanded shows that the sub-national state and the local state still have some leeway to interpret laws and regulations to suit the local context, and through this, implement policies in a more humane way.

End Notes

1. Following Chandra (2015), the 'state' refers to any branch of government (appointed or elected) at any level (national, state or local).

2. Based on a similar methodology, an ICRIER (Indian Council for Research on International Economic Relations) report has estimated the shortage to be twenty-nine million in 2018. Employing a broader approach, urban housing shortage is estimated to be fifty million, and more than 99 per cent of the shortage is confined to low-income groups. See Roy and Meera ML 2020.

3. Available at https://pmay-urban.gov.in/storage/pdf/PMAY-U-National-review-8-6-2021.pdf (accessed 3 July 2021).

References

Bardhan, Pranab. 1984. *The Political Economy of Development in India.* Oxford: Basil Blackwell.

Bhide, Amita. 2014. 'Foreword'. In Chandana Das Sampreet and Raju Bhise, *Slum Free India: Myths and Realities–A Status Report on Rajiv Awas Yojana 2014*. New Delhi: YUVA.

Census of India. 2011. 'Primary Census Abstract for Slum'. New Delhi: Office of the Registrar General & Census Commissioner, India. Available at http://www.censusindia.gov.in/2011-Documents/Slum-26-09-13.pdf (accessed March 2021).

Chandra, Kanchan. 2015. 'The New Indian State: The Relocation of Patronage in the Post-Liberalization Economy'. *Economic and Political Weekly* 50(41): 46–58.

Chen, Jie. 2018. 'The Transformations of Housing Regime and its Impacts on Urbanisation in China'. In Urmi Sengupta and Annapurna Shaw (eds), *Trends and Issues in Housing in Asia: Coming of an Age*. Abingdon, Oxon, UK: Routledge.

Davis, Mike. 2007[2006]. *Planet of Slums.* London and New York: Verso.

Desai, Renu. 2015. 'Informality and State-led Intervention for Slum Improvement in a Mid-sized City: The Case of Nanded'. In Darshini Mahadevia (ed.), *Shelter Security in Urban India: Pathways, Barriers and Outcomes*, 261–281. New Delhi: Concept Publishing Co.

Hingorani, Pritika. 2011. 'Revisiting Low Income Housing: A Review of Policies and Perspectives'. Paper prepared for a discussion on 'Revisiting Upgrading: Low-income Housing and Infrastructure' at the India Urban Conference, Mysore, 17 November. Bangalore: Indian Institute of Human Settlements.

Kamath, Lalitha. 2012. 'New Policy Paradigms and Actual Practices in Slum Housing: The Case of Housing Projects in Bengaluru'. *Economic and Political Weekly* 47(47 & 48): 76–86.

Kumar, Arun. 1989. 'National Housing Policy: The Implications'. *Economic and Political Weekly* 24(23): 1285–1294.

Kumar, Vickram. 2016. 'PM's "Housing for All Scheme" is going nowhere in 20 States a year after its launch'. *The Daily Mail (UK)*, 5 June. Available at http://www.dailymail.co.uk/indiahome/article-3626479/Pradhan-Mantri-Awas-Yojana-PM-s-Housing-scheme-going-20-states-year-launch.html (accessed January 2021).

Kundu, Amitabh. 2017. 'Housing for the Urban Poor? Changes in Credit-Linked Subsidy'. *Economic and Political Weekly* 52(52): 105–110.

Mander, Harsh. 2015. 'Forgotten Brethren'. *Outlook*, 20 April. Available at www.outlookindia.com/magazine/story/forgotten_brethren/293980 (accessed January 2021).

Mathur, Om Prakash. 2009. 'Slum-Free Cities: A new deal for the urban poor'. The National Institute of Public Finance and Policy (NIPFP). Available at www.indiaenvironmentalportal.org.in/files/Final%20Poverty%20Rep.pdf (accessed June 2021).

Ministry of Housing and Urban Poverty Alleviation (MHUPA). 2009. *Urban Poverty Report, 2009*. New Delhi: Oxford University Press.

———. 2012. 'Report of the Technical Group on Urban Housing Shortage'. New Delhi: Government of India.

———. 2016a. 'Annual Report 2015–2016'. New Delhi: Government of India.

———. 2016b. 'India Habitat III: National Report'. New Delhi: Government of India.

Nair, Ravi. 2019. 'How Modi Bypassed Norms to Try and Enable Adani's Entry into Airport Business'. *Newsclick*, 27 March. Available at: https://www.newsclick.in/Modi-Adani-Privatisation-of-Airports (accessed March 2021).

Nair, Shalini. 2016. 'One Year of Housing for All: At this Pace it's Indeed a Dream by 2022'. *The Indian Express* (New Delhi), 25 June. Available at http://indianexpress.com/article/business/economy/

one-year-of-housing-for-all-pradhan-mantri-awas-yojana-a-dream-by-2022-2874246/ (accessed January 2021).

NCU (National Commission on Urbanisation). 1988. 'Report of the National Commission on Urbanisation', Vol. 2, Part 4. New Delhi: NCU, Government of India.

Patel, Sheela. 2013. 'Upgrade, rehouse or resettle? An assessment of the Indian government's Basic Services for the Urban Poor (BSUP) programme'. *Environment and Urbanization* 25(1): 177–188.

Patel, Shirish B. 2016. 'Housing for All by 2022: Assignment Delivered, Accountability Nil'. *Economic and Political Weekly* 51(10): 38–42.

Planning Commission. 1951. *First Five Year Plan*. New Delhi: Planning Commission, Government of India.

______. 2011. 'Report of the Working Group on Urban Poverty, Slums and Service Delivery System'. New Delhi: Steering Committee on Urbanisation, Planning Commission, Government of India.

Platt, Rutherford. 2014. *Reclaiming American Cities: The Struggles for People, Place and Nature since the 1900s*. Amherst: University of Massachusetts Press.

______ (ed.). 2006. *The Humane Metropolis: People and Nature in the Twenty First Century City*. Amherst: University of Massachusetts Press.

Ronald, Richard and Oana Druta. 2018. 'Housing and Urban Transformations in Japan'. In Urmi Sengupta and Annapurna Shaw (eds), *Trends and Issues in Housing in Asia: Coming of an Age*. London: Routledge.

Rose, Jonathan F. P. 2016. *The Well-Tempered City*. New York: Harper Wave.

Roy, Debarpita and Meera ML. 2020. 'Housing for India's Low-Income Urban Households: A Demand Perspective', Working Paper 402. ICRIER. Available at: icrier.org/pdf/Working_Paper_402.pdf (accessed March 2021).

Sahu, Prasanta. 2017. 'Pradhan Mantri Awas Yojna: Progress of Modi government's ambitious project to build pucca houses by 2022 is tepid'. *Financial Express*, 31 May. Available at http://www.financialexpress.com/economy/pradhan-mantri-awas-yojana-progress-of-modi-governments-ambitious-project-to-build-pucca-houses-by-2022-is-tepid/693818/ (accessed January 2021).

Sampreet, Chandana and Raju Bhise. 2014. 'Slum Free India: Myths and Realities: A Status Report on Rajiv Awas Yojana 2014'. New Delhi: YUVA.

Satterthwaite, David. 2010. 'Upgrading slums: With and for slum dwellers'. *Economic and Political Weekly* 45(10): 12–16.

Shaw, Annapurna. 2012. *Indian Cities*, Oxford India Short Introductions. New Delhi: Oxford University Press.

Singh, Sandeep. 2016. '"Housing for All by 2022" First Year Report: Room for improvement'. *The Indian Express* (Delhi), 23 July. Available at http://indianexpress.com/article/india/india-news-india/housing-for-all-by-2022-first-year-report-room-for-improvement-2930619/ (accessed January 2021).

Sivaramakrishnan, K. C. 1969. 'Urban Housing: Challenge and Response'. *Economic and Political Weekly* 4(36): 1443–1445.

The Indian Express. 2017. 'NR Narayana Murthy lambastes Infosys COO's salary hike', 3 April. Available at https://indianexpress.com/article/business/companies/n-r-narayana-murthy-lambastes-infosys-coos-salary-hike-4596928/ (accessed March 2021).

UN-Habitat. 2012. *State of the World Cities Report 2012/2013: Prosperity of Cities*. New York: UN-Habitat.

United Nations. 2018. *World Urbanization Prospects: The 2018 Revision*. New York: United Nations Department of Economic and Social Affairs, Population Division. Available at: https://population.un.org/wup/Publications/Files/WUP2018-Report.pdf (accessed January 2021).

Wadhwa, Kiran. 1988. 'Housing programmes for urban poor: Shifting priorities'. *Economic and Political Weekly* 23(34): 1762–1767.

III

The Kruschyovka Kalashnikov

Sourav Hazra and Ekaterina Norkina

INTRODUCTION

After the Industrial Revolution[1] of the eighteenth and nineteenth century, and subsequent expansion of the global urban population[2] (primarily led by exponential economic in-migrations into major international cities), the need for planned public housing was established as a core area of focus for governments.[3] The key objective of such programmes was not so much to do with the reduction of housing inequality (as is typically the popular perspective in the Indian context), as it was to primarily provide affordable, safe, clean, healthy and environmentally sustainable housing[4] for the millions of people who emerged as residents in these new industrial towns/cities.

RUSSIAN CONTEXT

The Socialist Revolutions of 1917[5] transformed urban and housing development parameters in post-Tsarist Russia. The Soviet government was now in complete control of economic and social development (primarily through multiple five-year economic plans[6]), and an impetus to the provision of housing as a social guarantee[7] for the population emerged as a focal point to support and deliver this strict growth agenda.

Central planning programmes, first announced in 1924 by Joseph Stalin,[8] led to the creation of heavy industry/manufacturing-based economic nodes, resulting in rapid urbanisation and the creation of new urban centres across Russia.[9] Citizens relocated from the agrarian countryside to engage in work in these new cities, resulting in a burgeoning need for public housing. The Soviet system therefore did achieve a high rate of urbanisation,[10] and what we find interesting are the methods they utilised to collectively support this urbanisation through the provision of housing policies and infrastructure.

With this study of the Soviet public housing model and associated ideas, we can hope to understand and adapt solutions to mass housing needs[11] in other emerging economies, where public housing, primarily as accommodation for low to middle-income groups, is a key issue in fighting sporadic slum development and the mushrooming of unauthorised housing colonies across urban agglomerations. This chapter is positioned to study both the success and the failure in the Soviet housing push, and determine how such strategies can be analysed, improved upon and (with customisation) applied to the problems we are facing in other parts of the developing world.

The discussion in the next few sections of the chapter is organised around the following key issues:

1. **The Soviet approach towards provision of housing for all its citizens and its success[12] in meeting housing needs, in the wake of the hyper-urbanisation of the Soviet era.** We show the importance of mass housing/public housing/affordable housing (terms used interchangeably) as a critical tool for scaling up residential infrastructure for migrating population clusters. In addition, we also focus on the policies and strategies adopted by the Soviet government, which effectively recognised the rudimentary needs of the incoming populace and drove institutional support for such interventions.

   We argue that a study of these strategies becomes significant as the role of public institutions in mass housing needs to be strengthened across cities in the global South, along with an urgent need to concentrate on supporting country-level housing policies and prioritisation.

2. **Discussion on the Russian 'Kruschyovka'[13] model of housing, which successfully delivered volume in mass housing along with economic value through innovation in design and construction.** We highlight the success of Kruschyovka housing due to its simplicity of focus, basic amenities, efficient design, and the use of innovative construction models and building development methods to achieve the rapid delivery of housing projects. An important takeaway coupled with the time aspect of this example is the detailed market-based approach adopted by Russian housing planners to understand the key needs of the migrating families, and then integrate the same in the design and construction.
3. **The importance of choosing suitable locations for mass housing, typically within the city municipal boundaries and within primary urban agglomeration areas, and its benefits highlighted through the Kruschyovka example.** Location served as a key success factor in both attracting and sustaining the population that initially moved into such projects in Soviet Russia. Locating Kruschyovka houses closer to the urban centre of Moscow and planning for families led to the development of the provision of support facilities such as schools, healthcare, play areas, etc.
4. **Maintenance and operation of public housing as a long-term asset, with periodic infrastructure upgrades to sustain the market value of assets.** In this section, we discuss the inability of Soviet housing concepts to implement long-term maintenance and development, along with the consequent degradation of assets over the longer term, especially around the districts of primary city areas, and the resultant issues that have originated from this systemic failure. The discussion highlights the importance of factors which lead to the long-term sustainability of such social projects (such as public housing) to enable impactful change and their seamless integration into an economic model.

5. **Replacement of public housing, which needs to be strategically integrated into the development of modern private developer townships, as residences slowly transform into a private enterprise on a longer time scale.** We discuss the need to balance economic profits and the delivery of social needs in the context of the redevelopment of Kruschyovka housing into private townships[14] in today's Moscow. The economic and social costs of such replacement, and the achievable methods of undertaking such redevelopment projects are highlighted.

SOVIET PARTY PROPOSES, RUSSIA DISPOSES

All you have to do to get a house is to be born in the Soviet Union. You are entitled to housing. I was born in the Soviet Union. So I have a right to a house.

Nikita Khrushchev

Migration, in Soviet times, was mostly a result of economic planning and the industrialisation of cities, identified by the central party. The growth of urban agglomerations followed the new hubs of industrialisation and was kept in line with industrial policy. Cities were developed to cater to industrial enterprises, and their population increased as the industrial enterprises expanded their manufacturing and production. Most of these new cities,[15] which organically grew into large agglomerations, were fuelled by out-migration of labour from the rural areas of Russia. There was a shortage of urban housing in the initial years of this labour migration from the 1920s to the 1950s, and access to a real-estate sales market was almost non-existent.

Post the initial urbanisation period of the 1920s, housing became a priority for the Soviet government from the mid-1950s, after Nikita Khrushchev was appointed the leader of the Russian Communist Party. Realising and recognising the need to sustain the development of new industrial nodes, and envisaging the importance of public housing to enable the relocation of citizens over the next two decades, a construction blitzkrieg was announced.

Over the period of 1940–1970, housing construction developed at a significantly fast pace, with area per capita nearly doubling across key Russian cities.[16]

To lay the foundation of this residential expansion, a considerable amount of thought was put into policy parameters that would ensure the successful implementation of the projects. In addition, initial support for the development of public housing was made possible through specific guarantees. Key amongst them were the following ideas which were the building blocks of this programme:

Provision of 'Right to housing' in the Constitution was an important tool for creating an overarching environment in which to provide housing to all citizens. In Soviet Russia, 'Right to housing' was ensured by the state. As per the Constitution of the Russian Federation, 1977, Article 44: 'The citizens of the USSR have the right to housing'. This right therefore gave the urban administration the necessary licence and charter to implement affordable housing projects for the in-migrating labour and their families (typically low-income in character) in the newly agglomerated urban areas. Through this fundamental right, the production and distribution of houses served as a backbone to reduce the chronic shortage of residential stock during rapid urbanisation. A necessary corollary to this right also gave public authorities and regional governments the power and encouragement for housing construction, and the creation of suitable conditions for the realisation of the right to housing.

Ironing out the issues of landownership in Russia, especially in key industrial cities, was the most effective trait in Russian mass housing. The nature of landownership in Soviet times, all of which primarily belonged to the state, reduced land acquisition and prohibitive pricing bottlenecks for low-income residential projects. However, the key distinction of importance here is that private property was not acknowledged by the state, although personal ownership usage and control rights were accepted. But the right of personal ownership of housing areas did not allow their use for rentals or profit through sale, and thus the development of these projects over the mid-1950s in Russia witnessed minimal involvement of the private sector. This absence of private profiteering on social goals discouraged experimentation on design and price, and ensured that affordability was maintained even during supply shortages.

The Russian state being the developer, buyer and seller, another key aspect of the background policy to support mass housing was financing support. With 100 per cent state budget financing provided for projects, both land development and construction timelines were maintained without compromising any key social objectives. Scaling up and the use of innovative construction techniques, irrespective of cost and deployment, were put through for best results. This kind of financing support also made planning significantly more effective for town planners, as they issued decrees which identified locations or micro-regions where housing projects were built along with public services such as education, retail and other socio-cultural facilities, planned as a co-ordinated and integrated ecosystem.

These rights or guarantees set the platform for the development of mass housing in Russia, and provide a valuable insight into the policy and strategy environment that needs to exist even before such transformational changes are implemented in a country. Our work is not to question the morality or long-term social effects of such policies, but to highlight the lessons from this experiment to ensure that certain pre-conditions or non-negotiables are established to achieve mass housing, specifically for countries going through a rapid process of urbanisation.

In India, delivery of public housing projects hinges on critical issues such as land acquisition, land pricing, financing gaps, etc., and whether policies from the government on these key matters can be passed swiftly to form a beneficial launchpad for low-income group housing. Also, we need to ask the question: If mass housing projects are turned over to private developers (to a large extent through PPP or Public-Private Partnership projects), does their profit motive skew the basic social tenets of providing housing to the masses?

THE KRUSCHYOVKA KALASHNIKOV

What the Russians have done is to develop the only technology in the world to produce acceptable, low-cost housing on a large scale.

An official from the US National Bureau of Standards, as quoted in the *Chicago Tribune*, 1967 (*Bloomberg CityLab* 2017)

An urgent requirement for housing in Soviet Russia led to the initial push towards mass production (of houses). The demand for residential stock was almost immediate, and a solution was urgently required as a response to economic adjustment and rapid urbanisation due to in-migration to the newly industrialised cities of Russia. Innovation came in the form of industrialisation of the building industry and application of mass production concepts to residential projects. Further, with the market completely controlled by the state (the buyer, the seller and the developer being the Soviet government, as mentioned earlier), this inherent need forced the leap towards industrialisation. The first models of such prefabricated residential buildings, which were primarily cheap and easily-erected apartment blocks, came up in Moscow in the 1940s, but large-scale development took place primarily under Soviet leader Nikita Khrushchev from the mid-1950s (and hence the term Kruschyovka for such forms of Russian housing).

'The Soviet must create modern and comfortable family housing as the material basis for communism. These accommodations will provide material and cultural abundance for the entire population. Every proletarian family should have its own fully-equipped flat,' held Khrushchev (Varga-Harris 2008). A Kruschyovka was a Russian public housing designed and erected by the Soviet government, typically according to a standardised format (characterised by similar planning elements across two to three types of categories) for ease of use of mass construction materials, plug-and-play fittings to reduce on-ground construction timelines, and for development at a minimal cost.

Most of the buildings had five storeys, typically the maximum number of floors allowed by building regulations of the time, and usually without an elevator. Smaller, three to four storey

Kruschyovka blocks were sometimes built as well, but were much fewer in number. In the years ahead, Kruschyovka buildings also diversified into nine to fifteen storeys, but typically retained the standardised design principle. In 1968, using these construction techniques, the Soviet government was able to deliver 1.4 billion sq. ft. of residential living space. In contrast, the United States—a far more industrialised country at that time—built about 1.5 billion sq. ft. of housing across America.

The success of the Kruschyovka in the initial phases of the housing expansion not only lies in the adoption of new construction techniques, but much of the credit also goes to the concept of planning based on the determination of user needs and the choice of micro-location of these apartment blocks that is best suited to integrate work and play. In the initial run-up to this type of housing, the officials of the Soviet Economic Planning and Housing Construction wing conducted personal interviews and mailed questionnaires on all aspects of housing. Respondents were asked questions on their lifestyles, such as time spent in staying indoors and studying, attendance at socio-cultural events at theatres/restaurants, ideal time spent on outdoor activity, on walks and sports, and choice of places to go to for the same.

The results were carefully recorded and used to analyse tenant needs and wants, and incorporate the same from the perspective of the location of the apartment block in the city, rather than the size and design of the micro-apartments themselves. Based on these interviews as well as the need for central planning to populate specific cities and regions/locations within them, micro-districts within municipal areas of the city were chosen to develop the Kruschyovka apartments. Typically, these new residential districts were built in inner-city areas with transportation access to work, urban facilities and entertainment/social infrastructure. Also, in terms of outdoor facilities, care was taken to integrate the housing with parks, play areas and gardens. Land pricing was not a cause for concern in the development of the Kruschyovka in the Soviet system as all land in its entirety belonged to the state, as discussed earlier, and therefore it was the administration's prerogative to choose the nature of land use for any specific region, this time for locating residential apartment blocks.

Careful planning of the Kruschyovka by the administration and its ability to attract residents (despite its standardised and plain design elements) is a key learning from this example. In fact, Russian migrants preferred to take up lower-category jobs in the city so they could choose to stay in the available Kruschyovka housing accommodations. The relative connectivity and access to the city's urban amenities, as well as retail, cultural and higher education centres lured newcomers with promises of exclusivity and a sense of prestige.

If we are to summarise the effective implementation of the Kruschyovka in the Russian housing market, it primarily filters down to several key learnings from the approach to achieve similar results in the twenty-first century, either across India or other countries with significant housing shortages.

1. **Commitment and Cost:** Justification for industrialisation or mass housing in Russia and its dedicated drive towards implementation by the highest administrative authority was one of the primary tools for success. The industrial nature of Russian public housing construction is evident from the emphasis on lower labour consumption, reduced construction time and the ability to undertake year-round construction for the development of Kruschyovka buildings. The use of prefabricated components did offer real savings on the cost of construction, but more important is the larger indirect time and cost savings for the entire process due to the priority status accorded to the housing industry by the Soviet government. Through the same, building products were standardised with minimal changes in specifications. Large manufacturing plants and construction complexes operated through the entire year, production was guaranteed, and the industry was blessed by the administration with high priority labour allocation. As per Soviet claims, the net result of both innovations in construction and incentivising the industry was a total

of 40–50 per cent cost savings on factory output and construction labour. This is not counting the additional notional savings on the erection of such prefabricated units at faster speeds—at least 30–45 per cent faster than the usual brick construction.

2. **Design:** Design for industrialisation through a standardised approach to housing apartments, keeping in mind user needs and lifestyle, as well as usage of outdoor infrastructure. The apartment blocks are typically clustered around nurseries, kindergartens and schools, so that as per optimum planning, children do not have to cross busy thoroughfares. Support amenities such as general stores and service shops are also included, sometimes within the ground floors of the houses or in separate buildings. Size of an apartment was a key area of discussion and debate in the initial planning years, and there was the use of the concept of 'net living space', which was used to measure the practical need for residential areas for each person, in terms of their usage of only the living room and bedrooms. Thus, the focus of this public housing was centred more on functionality rather than luxury in order to rapidly build up scale, and not lose the objective of housing the millions moving into Russian industrial cities.
3. **Construction:** For the first time, the industrialised building construction process witnessed the use of prefabrication in housing construction and the use of precast concrete components such as boxes, panels and pieces so that they could be assembled on site. These would require less labour inputs and reduce time for construction, proving to be the suitable answer for shorter delivery time frames for residential housing projects. Rapid construction was also achieved through modular construction techniques, which were championed by Gosstroy, the Soviet State Construction Committee, which also carried out significant research through their institutes to improve building development techniques and promote the use of new building material. In addition, efficiency in construction was also achieved

through the deployment of a non-negotiable Building Standards or National Code. Once adopted, these codes had the full support of the Soviet administration, and were religiously followed through regular quality checks by the Gosstroy, and disseminated to regional areas of Russia during visits of state officials.

4. **Turnkey Delivery:** Combining both the construction of building materials in factories and the erection and finishing of the apartment blocks under one management led to significant synergies in time and efficiency, especially as housing character was standardised and did not use specialised designs. Precasting plants and building trusts worked seamlessly together under Soviet administration in one given area. Tasks were divided into specific activities and completed by different teams, with typical work distribution as per the following guidelines:
   - Production and erection of panels and bathroom elements for housing.
   - Production and erection of panels for support infrastructure, such as schools and nurseries.
   - Erection of brick and cast-in-place concrete buildings for housing.
   - Site clearing, excavation, foundations for micro-districts.
   - Sanitary, electrical, mechanical, special and finishing work for entire neighbourhoods.

   A testament to the efficacy of construction are the delivery magnitudes; for example, in 1969, these teams combined to complete 50,000 apartments, twenty schools, thirty kindergartens and nurseries, five movie houses, shopping centres, a hotel and a sports palace—an impressive array in an entire housing ecosystem for the migrant population. A single authority for construction and a lean internal communication system meant fewer delays and maximisation of labour downtime.

LIFE AND AFTERLIFE

> *Even if you are willing to overhaul this entire apartment, it still will not be a comfortable place to live today....If I was offered a resettlement package to move away to newer apartments in close vicinity, I would without hesitation pack my things and move the same day.*
>
> Third-floor resident of a Kruschyovka apartment in current Moscow

In early 2017, Sergey Sobyanin, the Mayor of Moscow, announced that the Russian capital would launch an ambitious effort to demolish 8,000 Soviet-era public housing blocks comprising 25 million sq. m. of residential space, almost 10 per cent of Moscow's total residential real estate. Almost sixty years after its initial development, the iconic Kruschyovka will make way for modern private developer apartments through a resettlement programme.

Public opinion is divided, with some residents defending their right to stay in the Kruschyovka neighbourhoods, where they have spent most of their childhoods and adult lives, while many others profess to be happy to bid goodbye to the obsolete housing of the 1950s. People staying in these Soviet housing buildings inform us that they are mostly in a derelict state, with complaints of small living and bedroom areas, absence of lofts and luggage spaces, little or no insulation, no elevators, lack of sound insulation, and a general lack of maintenance, which has made the buildings unsafe and non-upgradeable.

The current state of Soviet housing in Russia today and the vital need to replace them after over half a century, throws up questions concerning the long-term sustainability of public housing. It also foretells the need to integrate and align mass housing with trends of the time, allowing for adjustments both on the physical side of the construction, viz., professional maintenance and upgradation, and taking into account the transformation of public ownership into private possession.

It is important to note that the average life expectancy of a Kruschyovka block, originally built in the 1950s and 1960s, was not anticipated to be more than twenty-five to thirty years, after which an integrated round of capital maintenance was envisaged to upgrade and lengthen the life of these houses. The failure of communism and the tumultuous transition of the Russian state from a planned to a market economy led to a systemic failure, primarily with regard to the maintenance of public housing. By the 1980s and 1990s, much of the Soviet prefabricated housing required infrastructural renovation; not only did such overhaul not take place, but in the early years of the free market economy, housing stock and supply of good quality urban housing also actually declined in number, making the Kruschyovka a precious commodity even without their due maintenance upgrade.

With the introduction of the free market economy post-1991, housing in Russia changed from a rationed commodity (independent of a person's purchasing power) to a market good that can be freely bought and sold. To make matters worse, as a rule to bring in private ownership into the country, sudden legislation allowed all tenants of state-leased individual housing to claim legal ownership of their apartments without payment of any consideration money. But this forced privatisation did not solve the problem of long-term sustainability of public housing in Russia and merely led to a hyperinflation in the housing market. Amidst the collapse of the Russian economy in the 1990s, the cost of average-sized public housing rose alarmingly, making market-led sale and purchase unviable. This absence of a real-estate sales market further led to greater material depreciation of the housing stock, and without any machinery or financial support in place for physical maintenance and upkeep of the asset, it eventually turned into a bad-asset high-cost downward spiral.

This is a keen lesson from the Russian example, where the initial development of public housing was successful in reducing housing shortages brought about by migratory urbanisation, but the long-term structural adjustments of the economy were too disruptive to bring in a natural transformation to private ownership and sustainability. Typically, the long-term sustainability of public housing is an organic transformation. Built into the core of its development model, ownership is slowly passed onto the tenants over time, who form Resident Welfare Associations and maintain the value and usability of the asset (through a paid co-operative maintenance model) post its life expectancy. In certain cases, replacement of the entire asset is also undertaken by demolishing old public housing and bringing in private developers to redevelop such housing into modern townships. The value and appreciation in the older asset through the years makes this a profitable exercise for private stakeholders.

The Singapore Story

Although a digression of sorts, it does make sense to briefly bring in the example of Singapore and its public housing initiatives through the government-administered Housing and Development Board (HDB). The country houses the majority of the Singapore resident population[17] through this hugely successful mass housing scheme. In short, post the 1950s and through the current era, Singapore has been a beacon in presenting to the world a number of solutions with regard to the provision of public housing, enabling it to sustain

Image 3.1: Singapore Public Housing

Photograph: needpix.com.

the effectiveness of HDB housing through the decades. Like the Russian example, Lee Kuan Yew, Singapore's Prime Minister from 1959 to 1990, was keen to deliver home ownership to every citizen in Singapore, thereby promoting a distinct identity for the island nation, which wove together a mixed population of ethnic Chinese, Indians and Malays in the initial years of its formation.

In the next few paragraphs, we discuss the key factors behind the true success of Singapore's HDB initiative, which other countries (specifically Russia) failed to adopt, thus making Kruschyovka housing mostly a non-sustainable mass housing development initiative, which was successful only in the short term.

1. **Ensuring planning control** is a key imperative towards long-term sustainability of public housing projects. This is why the Singaporean model of offering the flats for a lease term of ninety-nine years makes more sense than an outright sale. Current Prime Minister Lee Hsien Loong explains the logic behind this strategy:

   > HDB sells the flat to Singaporeans for 99 years. They own it and can pass it on for maximum one/two generations. After that, the flat returns to the state, the government redevelops the land, and builds new flats with modern techniques for living needs of future generations. This is the only way to recycle the land and ensure that all our descendants can buy new flats of their own (adapted from *Channel News Asia* 2018).

2. **Focus has been on maintenance and facilities management** of the HDB flats from the 1950s, along with the appointment of professional Towns Councils to undertake repair, renovation and upgradation of the HDB assets. Large-scale improvement works on existing public housing projects have been undertaken since 1990 at regular intervals, through programmes under the Estate Renewal Strategy, such as the Main Upgrading Programme (MUP). These help to bring common and core facilities up to par with newer HDB developments, and in some cases, can ensure full life expectancy and value of the public asset, thus making a viable case for a replacement strategy.

3. **Long-term political commitment** is a keen choice of the Singaporean government, especially when it comes to housing. Through the last few decades, support to HDB projects across Singapore has not wavered/reduced in priority, but on the contrary, has increased with the government's focus on the development of new HDB towns. Stronger than ever is the willingness of the administration to ensure that all Singaporean citizens can afford to own HDB apartments, and low-interest housing loans along with CPF (Central Provident Fund) schemes help to move closer to the goal of housing for all.

CONCLUSION AND KEY LEARNINGS

In conclusion, we have tried to ideate some of the crucial focus areas that have been instrumental in delivering success to the great housing push of Soviet times, as well as some learnings from their shortcomings, with the objective of delivering some broad-brush solutions to the situation we face in most developing countries today.

1. It is imperative that the government be wholly involved in the entire development value chain of mass housing, at least till the initial shortages are met, specifically as the target population is the Lower Income Group (LIG) and Economically Weaker Sections (EWS) of the Indian population, for whom housing is a life need rather than an investment option.
2. Developing countries ought to clearly look at public housing to alleviate shortages in the LIG segment and view the same from a social angle rather than an economic one. Bringing in private partnership for the first push towards mass housing might be beneficial in some cases, but may dilute the social objective and tip the scales towards profit-driven motives.
3. A strict policy environment should be set for the growth of mass housing developments and to give a priority sector

push for low-cost housing through various mechanisms that support the factors of production, such as construction, labour availability, design, financing and delivery.

4. Research, application and the use of innovative technologies for both construction of mass housing at lower costs and, more importantly, fast-track timelines of delivery should be encouraged. Sustained efforts at bringing in technology will reap large benefits for scaling up the construction of housing projects, especially when the shortages are in such high numbers and in-migration to Indian cities is rapidly increasing.
5. Standardise the product offered for housing to lower-income groups after considerable research into user needs. As a corollary to this, aim to bring in public housing construction companies, which will follow these guiding principles and building standards to ensure the quick replication of similar models across India.
6. View mass housing as a short- to medium-term objective to address needs in the wake of mass migration and urbanisation, with the general assumption that these residential projects will be replaced organically by private developer townships after the end of their lifecycle.
7. Combine delivery of public housing projects with asset management and maintenance so that the underlying value of the asset is maintained and capital appreciation is achieved. Care should be taken to ensure that capital upgrades to the public housing projects are made mandatory through a public mechanism to ensure longer-term sustainability.

We conclude by observing that the key concepts that ensure the success and delivery of social housing projects are primarily bigger-picture innovation strategies and consumer-driven solutions. The success of delivering effective mass housing to citizens does not depend on the type of state-governing model, viz., a socialist or a capitalist one. What really works is simply initiatives focussed towards creating underlying value and delivering a quality experience of living to low-income group residents, rather than driving housing proposition as an investment/capital gains asset.

End Notes

1. During this period, it was mostly the agrarian and rural societies of Europe and the US that became industrial and urban in character.

2. *The Guardian* quotes: 'Between 1714 and 1840, London's population swelled from around 630,000 to nearly 2 million'. Available at https://www.theguardian.com/cities/2014/may/15/the-evolution-of-london-the-citys-near-2000-year-history-mapped (accessed March 2021).

3. Primarily the governments of the UK and the US.

4. British authorities formulated policies to solve the severe problems of slums that occupied large areas of Britain's industrial cities at the end of the nineteenth century. The conservative government introduced measures such as reduced stamp duty, as well as providing financial incentives for home ownership.

5. Both the February and October revolutions of 1917, which dismantled the Tsarist autocracy and led to the rise of the Soviet Union.

6. Refers to the series of nationwide centralised economic plans in the Soviet Union, beginning in the late 1920s, of which the initial five-year plans were primarily aimed to achieve rapid industrialisation.

7. 'Right to Housing' is provided by the Constitution of Russian Federation, 1977, as per Article 44.

8. Joseph Stalin was a Soviet revolutionary and politician, who led the Soviet Union from the mid-1920s until 1953 as General Secretary of the Communist Party of the Soviet Union.

9. Urbanisation exhibited across Moscow and Saint Petersburg, as well as Russia's peripheral regions of Siberia, Far East, Urals and the Northwest.

10. Cities were created in the Soviet planning system primarily to serve industries (such as mining, steel, power production, etc.), and expanded organically into administrative centres for population, with industrial output burgeoning from these locations.

11. 'Mass housing' has been used alternately with 'public housing' to denote social housing managed and operated by the government, as a means to provide affordable living spaces in cases of hyper-urbanisation.

12. Such was the success of the initial housing push in the Soviet Union that a delegation of eight experts from the US travelled to Russia from 23 August to 9 September 1969 for a better understanding of the housing programme with the objective of carrying back lessons through a technical exchange programme.

13. Mass housing named after Nikita Khrushchev, Soviet statesman and First Secretary of the Communist Party.

14. Available at https://www.themoscowtimes.com/2017/05/04/moscow-housing-demolitions-from-rubble-to-riot-op-ed-a57898 (accessed March 2021).

15. Besides Moscow and Saint Petersburg, other cities with maximum urbanisation were the Northwest, Siberian, Volga, Chernozem and Volga-Vyatka regions (Tolyatti, Bratsk, Novogrod, Saransk, Lipetsk, etc.).

16. As per a US Department of Commerce publication, in 1968 housing production in Russia was in the range of 1.4 billion sq. ft. compared to approximately 1.5 billion sq. ft. in the US, exhibiting the pace at which housing was being constructed in the Soviet Union.

17. Available at https://data.gov.sg/dataset/estimated-resident-population-living-in-hdb-flats?resource_id=a7d9516f-b193-4f9b-8bbf-9c85a4c9b61b (accessed March 2021).

References

Becker, Charles, S. Joshua Mendelsohn and Kseniya Benderskaya. 2012. 'Russian urbanization in the Soviet and post-Soviet eras', Working Paper. United Kingdom: International Institute for Environment and Development, United Nations Population Fund.

Bloomberg CityLab. 2017. 'The Disappearing Mass Housing of the Soviet Union', 9 March. Available at https://www.bloomberg.com/news/articles/2017-03-08/the-disappearing-mass-housing-of-the-soviet-union (accessed July 2021).

Channel News Asia. 2018. 'NDR 2018: Why are HDB leases 99 years long? PM Lee explains', 19 August. Available at https://www.channelnewsasia.com/news/singapore/ndr-2018-hdb-lease-99-years-flat-national-day-rally-10631442 (accessed June 2021).

Durmanov, Volodymyr. 2010. 'Housing development in Ukraine and Russia in past and in future'. *Architecturae et Artibus* 2(2): 12–18.

Kosareva, Nadezhda and Raymond Struyk. 1993. 'Housing Privatization in the Russian Federation'. *Housing Policy Debate* 4(1).

Krasheninnikov, Alexey. 2013. Case studies for the *The Challenge of Slums: Global Report on Human Settlements 2003*, United Nations Human Settlements Programme (UN-Habitat). United Kingdom: Earthscan Publications Ltd.

Meuser, Philipp and Dimitrij Zadorin. 2016. *Towards a Typology of Soviet Mass Housing: Prefabrication in the USSR 1955–1991*. Berlin: DOM Publishers.

United Nations. 2004. *Country Profiles on the Housing Sector: Russian Federation*. Geneva, Switzerland: United Nations Economic Commission for Europe.

United States Department of Commerce. 1970. *Industrialized Building in the Soviet Union*. Washington, D.C.: National Bureau of Standards.

Varga-Harris, C. 2008. 'Homemaking and the Aesthetic and Moral Perimeters of the Soviet Home during the Khrushchev Era'. *Journal of Social History* 41(3): 561–589. Available at http://www.jstor.org/stable/25096523 (accessed June 2021).

———. 2015. *Stories of House and Home: Soviet Apartment Life during the Khrushchev Years*. Ithaca, NY: Cornell University Press.

Zavisca, Jane R. 2012. *Housing the New Russia*. Ithaca, NY: Cornell University Press.

IV

(De) Embracing 'Enabling' Housing Strategies?

Evidence from Southern Countries

Urmi Sengupta

INTRODUCTION

The need to scale up housing production by all possible means is accepted and acknowledged by all scholars and commentators in the field. According to the United Nation's estimate, one in eight people in the world live in slums today, equating to a population of over one billion, and this figure is likely to double by the year 2030 (UN-Habitat 2016). Governments around the world sought to address the growing slum population through direct provision of housing, which has turned out to be too expensive and unwieldy. Since the early 1990s, the UN and the World Bank (WB) have started deploying the language of 'enabling strategy', which represents an apparent reversal of the 'provider approach', to address the housing challenges of the global South. Both Brazil and India have been at the forefront of the enabling paradigm in the 1990s; however, in recent decades, they have introduced a series of national housing programmes that sing from a slightly different rhyme sheet. For their magnitude, scale and amount of subsidies involved, these programmes are not only considered important milestones in reasserting 'housing' as an issue of national importance for government policy and action, but also signal an apparent departure from the enabling paradigm. This chapter revisits some of the flagship government programmes in the two countries within the broad context of UN-Habitat's enabling housing strategies to explore, first, how far enabling strategies have been followed, and second, whether there are empirical similarities in terms of programmes and processes. It traces earlier accounts of enabling strategies, where the priority was to establish market provision of housing and economic development, up to a new phase of housing provision, involving large-scale state-led housing development (popularly known as affordable housing) that shows a hybrid approach, rather than the popular market-based housing approach.

The next section presents an overview of the enabling housing paradigm, followed by a review of government housing programmes in Brazil and India, with an aim to identifying the conceptual contradictions that obscure the international housing policy debate today. The material presented here is derived from a mixture of interviews, an extensive review of the literature, and official statistics focussed on plans and programmes in Brazil and India.

DECODING THE ENABLING HOUSING PARADIGM

The World Bank and UN-Habitat have been persistent advocates of the enabling housing paradigm in response to the endemic housing shortage of the last few decades, which peaked in the 1990s (Sengupta 2006; Yap 2015). The enabling strategy was first articulated in the General Assembly of the United Nations in 1998, and was simultaneously emphasised in several UN and World Bank reports (UN-Habitat 1988, 2001, 2003, 2006, 2016; World Bank 1993) and reiterated by Agenda 21, Millennium Development Goals (MDGs) and recently in the Sustainable Development Goals (SDGs), lending more credence to an inclusive approach to sustainability. The advice dispensed by the World Bank and UN-Habitat in the 1990s was rooted in the twin framework of rescaling the state and enabling the market. The thrust of this framework was to encourage private-sector involvement in housing provision, leaving the state to engage in financial, legislative and regulatory reforms that would boost housing supply, including low-income housing. The policy was a direct transfer from leading industrialised countries such as Britain, Canada, France, Germany, Italy, Japan and the United

States (the G7 countries and now G10[1]), which were getting rid of 'social housing' in the 1980s, following a period of sustained progress in addressing key housing challenges in their respective countries through a successful 'welfare system'. This follows a large and successful council or municipal housing, which had been a distinctive feature of these industrialised countries between the World Wars and the 1980s, and which had undoubtedly helped them in shaping their economy and society. However, similar 'liberal policies' were proposed in the developing countries, irrespective of their local housing needs, consequences and, more importantly, irrespective of their financial, legislative or regulatory capacity to address the housing crisis through private housing development. The policy prescription also ignored the lack of housing provision in the previous decades, which means that enabling strategies were being implemented in a vacuum of strategic policy and ground infrastructure. According to Foch (2013), this apparent heavy-handedness is due to industrialised countries being the main donors of the World Bank, and thus exerting (always) a strong voice in the World Bank's policy regime, governance and preferences on development aid. As a result, governments in developing countries gradually started moving away from their social objectives to meet the World Bank's loan conditions.

International politics aside, scholarship over the years has assessed the performance and limitations of the enabling housing framework, highlighting issues in both principle and implementation, and questioning its relevance for continuity into the next decade (Ahmed 1998; Choguill 1997; Datta and Jones 1999; Islam 1996; Jones and Ward 1995; Ogu and Ogbuozobe 2001; Rahman 2001; Rolnik 2013; Sengupta 2006; Smets 1997; Tipple et al. 1999). These criticisms, when pieced together, offer a coherent portrayal of under-performance of the policy and under-achievement on the ground (see Sengupta 2019 for further discussion). After thirty-five years of policy experimentation, it is now evident that the enabling housing strategy was a premature policy transfer from international organisations to the developing countries. In a crude sense, enabling housing was meant to address 'urban' housing challenges through private housing supply (Bradlow et al. 2011; Choguill

1997; Datta and Jones 1999; Islam 1996; Jones and Ward 1995; Ogu and Ogbuozobe 2001; Rahman 2001; Rolnik 2013; Sengupta 2006; Smets 1997; Yap 2015) in the rapidly urbanising developing countries. In particular, population growth in cities in the global South fuelled demands for new housing units, triggering a change in approach that would better link housing to the wider capital market. Key urban agencies managing housing (and land) in these developing countries started exploring how this demand from urban households could be captured to improve their overall economic performance. More formal housing also meant increasing the level of taxation and borrowing in the financial market. Economic rationalities became dominant and a large number of public agencies found the enabling strategy exceedingly compelling and attractive. So did the World Bank, with the potential for growth of their housing finance portfolio.

Undoubtedly, Southern countries are huge markets for the Bank, and tapping these markets had become the Bank's core focus in the past decades. Young (2016) observed that housing finance comprised roughly 50 per cent of the WB Group's housing commitments in India, during the 1990s and beyond. In sharp contrast to the previous decades that witnessed the Bank investing in housing programmes, slum upgrading, sites and services, or developing housing policy, in recent decades it has changed direction to focus on bringing housing finance in line with the pervasive neoliberal principles of economic development. In the Bank's own admission, in its thirty-two years of shelter lending review, it was found that a much smaller share of lending now goes to support low-income housing (10 per cent of total shelter lending since the mid-1990s, versus more than 90 per cent from the mid-1970s to the mid-1980s) and to support low-income countries (20 per cent, down from about 40 per cent from the mid-1970s to the mid-1980s). So efforts were concentrated mainly on 'middle- and high-income housing' as a target market through commodification of all housing—its production, consumption and even the management for profit. Clearly, it was led by the idea that there is a mutually reinforcing relationship between the production of housing and the accumulation of capital, which was witnessed in the established countries of the global North. So the creation of private housing estates at the outskirts of Sao Paolo or Kolkata is considered analogous to private housing development on the outskirts of San Diego or London, which emerges from very different circumstances, times and places. But the compelling and stereotyping tendency assumes that policies that worked for developed countries would work well in the poorer countries of the global South as well. For example, home ownership became a central concept, irrespective of the fact that low-income people in these cities do not have enough income to meet the loan conditions of these newly formed financial institutions, and they perhaps need more 'rental' units or interim shelter provision. Though it was argued that the priorities of the government should be to establish the conditions for individuals to accrue wealth and housing, most government agencies provided opportunities for the private sector to secure a foothold in the activities of government service provision, including housing. In many ways, key agencies from the national to the municipal level became partners, and 'institutional arrangements were dedicated to enabling the private sector, encouraging housing-for-profit approach no matter how deeply the state is committed to the urban poor and how much funding goes to the housing subsidy programme' (Bradlow et al. 2011; Yap 2015).

The latest review of enabling strategies and other literature has identified a number of issues that relate to the inability of the private sector to address the housing requirements of the poor: targeting has been poor, lack of participation, and piecemeal and project-based programmes were perhaps not very effective. Whilst these criticisms did not prompt any slowdown in the implementation of these 'enabling strategies' due to their close alliance with widespread neoliberalism, privatisation and economic efficiency, they were seen as being much more important than housing the poor. A great deal of persuasive writing has, however, emerged that does not just highlight failures, but makes a case for the return of stronger state intervention in housing (Angel 2000; Cao and Keivani 2014; Mukhija 2001, 2004; Yap 2015). Increasingly, it is recognised that market-oriented economic reforms have obfuscated the real problems faced by the urban poor as they have failed to address the core principles of enablement–transparency, participation, and access to housing and basic services for all. In response, the past decade has seen a sudden surge in state-administered large-scale housing programmes in many developing countries, involving multibillion-dollar investments disbursing sophisticated subsidy packages (Sengupta and Tipple 2007; UN-Habitat 2016; Wang and Shao 2010). Recently, countries such as Brazil and India have been seen to be adopting a variety of enabling strategies with a strong 'urban' (read formal) housing focus, with closely intertwined strategies of crisis management through state-administered, large-scale housing programmes targeting the urban poor. In many ways, this displays a predisposition towards the earlier provider approach. In particular, while the policy has moved away from the enabling orientation that was for many years the core focus, as this chapter will show, it is still reliant on the private sector to deliver state plans and programmes.

The next section will review key Indian and Brazilian housing policies and programmes. The chapter does not intend to evaluate these programmes or their outcomes, but rather to capture how different national housing programmes are moving within the broad policy architecture.

GOVERNMENT INTERVENTION IN BRAZIL AND INDIA

Brazil and India reveal similarities and differences in housing policy reforms due to a specific 'path-dependent' process inherent to their rapidly liberalising economies, and their respective demographic, socio-economic, institutional and cultural contexts of policy development, and how they approached the policy transition from provider to enabler or market-based housing provision. The housing shortage in Brazil currently stands at 5.45 million, corresponding to 10 per cent of the national housing stock. The 2010 national census reported 11.4 million favela inhabitants, constituting 7 per cent of the urban population. This is a significant number, which includes the accumulated deficit of 7.9 million units. These projections subscribe to the wider view across Latin America that although informal settlements have been a housing solution during the decades of rapid urbanisation, it was during the dismantling of the housing welfare system that favelas condensed, leading to the perverse convergence of precarious living conditions and violence (Rolnik 2013: 1061).

In India, according to the Twelfth Five-Year Plan (2012–2017), urban housing shortage stands at 18.78 million units, which is expected to grow at a compound annual rate of 6.6 per cent up to the year 2022. India is 33 per cent urban today, although several independent studies have projected different figures on urban housing deficits. According to the 'White Paper—Indian Housing Industry',[2] the urban housing shortage is expected to reach 34.1 million units by the year 2022. The housing industry in India suggests that around thirty million units in all categories will be needed to house every Indian, which requires 300,000 acres of land and half-a-trillion dollars of investment for 15 billion sq. ft. of floor space to be built. By this account, India needs a manifold increase in its housing supply.

Brazil—Re-emergence of State-centric Policies: Back to Basics?

The housing crisis, as popularly manifested by the favelas in Brazil, has a long history of existence, expansion and unbridled growth. Early interventions (up until the 1990s), especially in cities such as Rio de Janeiro and São Paulo,[3] were marked by a highly centralised clearance policy that relocated squatters on the outskirts of the city. Programmes such as PRÓ-LUZ, PROFAVELA and PROMORAR were focussed on urban infrastructure and the construction of housing units through direct government subsidy. The 1990s, termed as the 'lost decade' by Valença (1999), saw the rapid withdrawal of the national government from housing, in tandem with the transfer of the social housing obligation to the local governments. Plans and programmes were dominated by two principal aspects of low-income housing delivery: return of squatter upgrading and the back-to-the-city movement. The former intended to build self-managed and community-built homes as a way to reduce costs and reinforce citizenship.[4] The latter was an ideological response, mainly from the social democratic and left-leaning parties, to empty buildings in the city centre. The argument was that even the poor, working-class population has rights to the city and should be integrated into the urban culture. In 2000, the country had nearly a million empty homes, half of which were in São Paulo alone. Empty buildings have continued to provide a viable opportunity to house the urban poor in cities in Brazil, whilst the benevolent state acted as a facilitator in the process by altering legislations and constitutions, suggesting that all properties have some social purpose. In São Paulo, the municipality policy focussed on PROVER (Projeto de Urbanização de Favelas com Verticalização/Project of Squatter Settlement Upgrading with Verticalisation), also known as the 'Cingapura Project', promoting apartment-style vertical units (generally five- to eleven-storeyed, with small units of 42 sq. m.) constructed by private developers. Local municipalities such as Diadema proactively identified vacant properties and allocated them for the construction of HIS (Habitação de Interesse Social/Social Interest Housing) through Special Areas of Social Interest (AEIS) I and II in their master plans. However, despite its intellectual and inclusive origin, it had the hallmark of a classic top-down approach without any room for public consultation, and the government appeared to be cherry-picking projects based on political indoctrination.

The next decade of Brazilian housing continued to exhibit a state-centric, pro-people regeneration (of vacant buildings) alongside settlement upgrading policies. Between 2001 and 2004, the Workers' Party once again took over the administration of São Paulo, reigniting the discourse on the revitalisation of empty buildings and participation of the population as a way to build citizenship. Programmes such as PRI (Programa de Recuperação Integrada/Integrated Recovery Programme) defined areas for urban intervention through the demarcation of ZEIS (Zonas de Especial Interesse Social/Special Zones of Social Interest). A part of the interventions were also made by the state government through the PAC (Programa de Aceleração do Crescimento Urbanização de Assentamentos Precários/Growth Acceleration Programme), in part supported by the federal government through a comprehensive Home Lease Plan—PAR (Plano de Arrendamento Residencial). As a result of these initiatives, the number of takeovers of vacant buildings in the inner city increased. The municipal administration used the Bairro Legal (Cool Neighborhood) Programme as a tool to implement a set of integrated actions in run-down neighbourhoods occupied predominantly by the low-income population,[5] in order to improve access to public services, greenery and amenities. It differs from the programmes of the previous administrations due to its strong emphasis on integrated action among different municipal agencies and stakeholders, including the non-governmental organisations and civil society. This bottom-up approach enabled low-income people to an extent.

As of April 2002, there were approximately 2,866 recorded projects running nationwide. Upgrading projects aimed at basic sanitation but found it difficult to match the urban standards of the formal city, whereas resettlement into the city centre was criticised for being fragmentary and inhibitory to both participation and investments from the dwellers, thus generating new debts, whilst the deregularised finance system rarely reached the poor. Some state and municipal housing initiatives gained visibility, especially with the dismantling of the BNH system in 1986, but with the exception of São Paulo state—which set up a housing fund based on a 1 per cent increase in value-added tax (ICMS or Imposto Sobre Circulação de Mercadorias e Serviços)—most other schemes were short-lived and targeted urgent housing situations (Valença and Bonates 2009). The enabling housing approach was not capable of achieving a rebalancing of the housing order. Instead, it saw a reassertion of the social class division.

Minha Casa Minha Vida (MCMV) marks a milestone in the history of Brazilian housing by conceptualising an emphatic return to the direct provision of social housing for the urban poor. Launched by President Lula da Silva in 2009, the programme aimed to build millions of homes for low-income Brazilians, making it effectively an affordable housing scheme on a national scale, based on home ownership. The programme, which translates to 'My

Home My Life', had an outlay of R$ 34 billion (US$ 18 billion), delivering more than two million homes by 2014, with 1.6 million more under construction. The federal government expected more than twenty-five million people to be covered by the programme by 2019. Interestingly, amidst the hyper drive for home ownership and in an apparent fusion of ideas, the Epiringa and Rizkallah Jorge buildings[6] in São Paulo became the first two vacant properties developed under the MCMV programme, and a rare example of rental subsidy. The Epiringa building (constructed in 1968 for the Federal Labour Court) has been converted into a social housing facility with 120 one-bedroom and studio units. The total cost of refurbishment would be in the order of R$ 11 million (US$ 5.5 million). It has been envisaged that beneficiaries would pay R$ 15 (US$ 7.5) per month, which reflects a subsidy of one-tenth of the market rent.

Neither the ideological underpinnings of the government's intervention nor the level of subsidies was questioned, despite the fact that the programme was launched during the financial crisis of 2008. Justified as government correction to market failure, its initial impetus sprang, at least directly, from the need to keep Brazil's economy, employment and wages stable during the recession. However, the programme remained quintessentially one of social housing and heralded a return to the state-run public housing of the previous era. There were criticisms for steering the subsidy from beneficiaries to developers, which not only manifested in poor design quality, but also reduced options. It is almost entirely (97 per cent) in the hands of private promoters (housing construction companies), a measure justified to speed up the process, avoiding the endless procedures adopted by government institutions (Valença and Bonates 2009). Since financing limits are pre-established, the values for calculating profits and sales revolve around: (*i*) land value, which is lower in peripheral neighbourhoods; (*ii*) lower cost of design achieved using standardised and repetitive designs, in addition to promoting large complexes, in order to maximise economies of scale; and (*iii*) production costs, minimised by using second-rate materials. This resulted in rather small (of around 32 sq. m.), poor quality housing units at peripheral locations, missing the critical link between affordability, design, access and mobility. In Rio, for example, 53 per cent of MCMV units delivered before 2013 were located in the remote West Zone (up to four hours from the city and employment opportunities). Despite operational challenges in programmes such as MCMV, the emerging trend suggests that housing policy in Brazil is showing an increasing and demonstrable predisposition towards social housing for those who cannot afford 'housing' built by private developers. The persistent housing shortage has influenced this trend. According to the 2010 census, housing shortage in Brazil stood at 5.45 million. A further 11.4 million people lived in favelas that, whilst providing a housing solution during the decades of rapid urbanisation, have condensed, leading to 'precarious living conditions and violence during the dismantling of housing welfare system' (Rolnik 2013: 1061).

India: Rebalancing State and Market Actions

Government intervention in housing in India during the pre-1990 period was characterised by the object of its emphasis rather than the degree of government involvement (Sengupta and Tipple 2007). Slum or *bustee* improvement projects took primacy in the period immediately following independence from British rule. The First Five-Year Plan called slums a 'national problem', suggesting clearance, but the government soon realised that it had neither the monetary nor the institutional capacity to achieve those goals. Hence, the second Plan recognised upgrading and improvements. The period is also marked by new legislative/institutional building processes[7] that included an internationally maverick approach to tenure regularisation, such as the Calcutta *Thika* Tenancy Act in Kolkata and *chawls*[8] in Mumbai that benefited thousands among the poor. The period between the 1970s and 1990 saw the state acting as a *de facto* developer to build public housing alongside upgrading, and implementing Sites and Services schemes to address the problem of slums.

The 1990s witnessed the emergence of the twin pillars of the present governance architecture: decentralisation and liberalisation. Consistent with global trends of democratisation, the dramatic declaration in the Ninth Plan, 'Housing is State [Government's] subject', was abandoned with the Seventy-Fourth Constitutional Amendment, which made Urban Local Bodies (ULBs) responsible for housing and services. This turn towards 'decentralisation' marks a major departure from the provider regime, which predominantly consisted of hierarchical relations. The devolved responsibility has led to the emergence of a particular kind of housing schemes for the poorer section, which were designed by the Centre but required matching funds from state and local governments and were supposed to be implemented by ULBs. The Urban Basic Services Scheme (1986), later renamed as Urban Basic Services for Poor (1991), the Nehru Rozgar Yojana's Scheme of Housing and Shelter Upgradation (1990) and the National Slum Development Programme (1996) were among these. Housing decentralisation did not manifest in the same way as observed in Brazil, however, the centrality of the regional level grew stronger in the case of mega-cities such as Mumbai, Kolkata and Delhi, where the regional governments designed welfare models with their own strong identities.[9]

Across the nation, a liberalisation policy was introduced with significant fanfare that led to a paradigmatic shift in the housing delivery process. Public-private partnership and regulatory reforms, coupled with a deregulated finance sector, firmly established the government's role as an enabler of housing, with a focus on all-income housing. The National Housing Policy,[10] 1994 made an explicit recognition of the economic contribution of the housing and construction sector in generating employment. Around twenty-five new housing finance institutions (HFIs) were set up between 1990 and 2000 (Sahu et al. 2009) to boost lending and construction activities targeted at middle- and high-income households. By 2001, 100 per cent FDI (Foreign Direct Investment) was allowed in integrated township development. FDI in housing construction brought scale into the housing industry; however, the relationship between FDI and low-income homes is not clear. Prior to reform, India mostly relied on bi- and multilateral ties for longer-term investment. The government was reluctant to allow 100 per cent FDI until 2005. According to DIPP (Department of Industrial Policy and Promotion), FDI in housing and construction accounted for 10 per cent in 2006. Further, neoliberal adjustments continued through to slum programmes in mega-cities such as Mumbai. For instance, the SRP (Slum Rehabilitation Programme) implemented by the Slum Rehabilitation Authority (SRA), first in 1997, can be described as the precursor of the current slum redevelopment programmes. Nijman (2008) describes SRP as marking a critical shift in the state's role, from a provider of public housing to that of a facilitator of the construction of low-income housing by optimising on Mumbai's complex zoning and density regimes, to ensure development rights and assure maximum profits for private builders at virtually no cost to the exchequer. However, the slum population continued to soar, putting an upward pressure on urban housing shortage. By 2012, urban housing shortage stood at 18.78 million units, and was expected to grow at a compound annual rate of 6.6 per cent up to the year 2022.

The first decade of the enabling regime has raised three interrelated concerns: first, there was a lack of coherence in applying the enabling approach across different states that varied greatly in terms of their economic development, political willingness and the consequent need for its re-examination. Second, the economic power of the enabling framework was doubted, given that the trickle-down effect as envisaged never materialised; and third, the applicability and suitability of enabling principles were not conducive to the concept of decentralisation, and the delivery of low-income housing at the local level became increasingly questionable. As a result, and in a seeming reversal of its role, the central government reverted to direct provision by initiating a series of pro-poor focussed housing programmes for the next fifteen years or so. The approach focussed on the centrality of the cities, which was reinforced by the wider forces of macroeconomic environment and economic globalisation. Against this background, various major urban-focussed capital investment and urban reform programmes were launched, some with ambitious goals to modify laws that had distorted the functioning of land and housing markets, to formalise the property rights system and to put in place efficient governance structures at the local level.

Perhaps the first post-neoliberal and conceptually important intervention in housing materialised through the Jawaharlal Nehru National Urban Renewal Mission (JNNURM), launched in 2005. As an integrated programme, it was based on three strands of policy—alignment of urban housing, infrastructure and services; developing urban governance through decentralisation; and development of new models of low-income housing in sixty-five major cities.[11] Despite putting the right foot forward, JNNURM buckled under the weight of its own goals, mainly those that are unabashedly neoliberal—securing economic reforms and a 'private-sector first' approach. The former is evident from the central government making JNNURM grants conditional on state governments reducing stamp duty rates. The latter has been actively pursued by the funding agencies. For instance, the World Bank, which partly finances the Urban Reform and Management Project in Karnataka (as part of JNNURM), threatened to pull out due to the lack of an enabling environment, which resulted in the introduction of a number of enabling environment reforms, including the amendment of legislations (Baindur and Kamath 2009). In sum, JNNURM reflects a top-down approach with limited participation from the states, resulting in just 22 per cent of the target being achieved. Most interestingly, the Government of India provided financial assistance to identified cities, ranging from 35 per cent to 90 per cent of their requirement, to facilitate states in promoting sustainable urban development. In terms of government subsidy, as noted by Singh (2016) during 2005–2014, projects worth Rs 1,100 billion were sanctioned under JNNURM with central government assistance of Rs 507 billion. In principle, JNNURM meant to facilitate effective private-sector participation in infrastructure development; however, the contradictory approach of the government at the micro and macro levels sent out confusing signals. Perhaps the government needed to set some ground rules regarding keeping subsidy standard at both levels.

Government intervention in slum settlements continued with another ambitious scheme—Rajiv Awas Yojana (RAY), launched in 2013 with the aim of creating slum-free cities. The objective of the programme was to bring existing slums into the formal economic circuit, with access to basic amenities and to develop institutional and market mechanisms to tackle shortages in land and housing (Tiwari and Rao 2016). Quintessentially a slum rehabilitation scheme with a neoliberal twist, RAY could not take off due to overlaps with other schemes and a lack of willingness on the part of state governments to secure land for relocation of slum dwellers. In 2015, RAY was replaced by the NDA-II government's flagship programme, dubbed 'Housing for All by 2022'. This mission aims to provide central assistance to ULBs and other implementing agencies through states and/or union territories for in-situ rehabilitation of existing slum dwellers using land as a resource through private participation, and interest rate subsidies on loans[12] for housing EWS and LIG households. Under this programme, the government has pledged to construct up to twenty million houses by the year 2022 and, according to preliminary estimates, an outlay of Rs 3 trillion (approximately US$ 44 billion) has been allocated which is to be spread over the next seven years. While it is too early to critique the programme, its deliveries remain questionable due to supply-side and demand-side challenges. Availability of land will be a major challenge to ensure the construction of ten million houses in urban areas for EWS, which will require 57,000 acres of urban land (roughly 50 per cent of the total land in Mumbai). This, when placed in the context of the additional urban land for competing uses, becomes even more unrealistic. For instance, it has been projected that urbanisation will eventually double the land requirement from 3 per cent to 6 per cent, which means that land is needed not just for housing but for industries and infrastructure. Finding additional land in a sustainable urban location will prove difficult, while encroaching upon the agricultural hinterland will be even more difficult due to livelihood issues, as made blatantly clear by the Singur[13] (West Bengal) example. On the other hand, regulatory infrastructural reforms that address land issues are still outstanding. Furthermore, the capacity of the construction and building materials industry to construct three million-plus units per annum is seriously doubted, as the delivery in the past five years has not exceeded one million. India thus needs to increase its building output by ten-fold in the next seven to eight years to achieve the new goal.

More crucially, the programme designed under enabling principles has an excessive reliance on its partners. Banks and civil society are under-prepared to disburse the volumes of loans planned for the programme. Demand-side challenges include a lack of affordable housing finance for EWS as the government grant of Rs 100,000 (US$ 1,490) per dwelling, whilst being higher than previous programmes, is a poor reflection of the needs of the poor. It is imperative that the government design an institutional arrangement for more effective targeting, before injecting massive subsidies between Rs 100,000 to Rs 325,000 per household.

In the 2000s and 2010s, the housing policy dynamic in India has become multilayered at best and paradoxical and self-defeating at worst. The rural–urban debate has now moved to a big city–small city debate. Critics have claimed that the fund disbursal pattern of JNNURM brought out a big-city bias and a move towards polarised development (Kundu and Samanta 2011). This is despite the fact that metropolitan cities are known to have better access to civic amenities like safe drinking water and sanitation, as compared to non-metropolitan cities. There are also issues around second homes and speculative purchases that leave a significant proportion of new housing catering to effectively no one. As per the Census of India 2011, around eleven million houses are lying vacant in urban areas, which would address 60 per cent of the total housing deficit. Decentralisation remains just rhetoric, as the institutional infrastructure to foster decentralisation and the ability of the urban local bodies to implement centrally-designed programmes are seriously questionable. The government, however, continues to announce new subsidies with every budget opportunity to address the national goal of 'Affordable Housing for All', without fully realising their ramifications. It announced the Pradhan Mantri Awas Yojana (PMAY) in 2015, which is essentially a 'Housing for All' scheme. Under this programme, as already mentioned, the government has pledged to construct up to twenty million houses by the year 2022. It has recently announced that 2,508 cities in twenty-six states have been selected for PMAY. In many ways, PMAY could be compared with the 'My Home My Life' (*Minha Casa Minha Vida*) programme in Brazil which aims to build one million new units, and 'is entirely (97 per cent) in the hands of private promoters to speed up the process' (Valença and Bonates 2009). In the 'My Home My Life' programme, subsidies are given directly to private developers and flats up to a minimum of 32 sq. m. are proposed, whereas PMAY aims to provide affordable homes using four delivery approaches covering both supply-side and demand-side subsidies.[14] The programme aims to match the current housing deficit of 18.2 million units. The Union Budget of 2016–2017 made provisions for 100 per cent deduction from profits to an undertaking from a housing project for flats up to 30 sq. m. in metro cities and 60 sq. m. in other cities. The budget also mentions an exemption of service tax on the construction of affordable houses up to 60 sq. m. under any scheme of the central or state government, including PPP (Public-Private Partnership) schemes, to incentivise developers to build affordable housing. Whilst the goal is noble, the increased thresholds will make it easier for middle-class encroachment into the heavily subsidised segment of the housing market, in which the poor will lose out. NSS (National Sample Survey) data revealed that the bottom 30 per cent of urban households cannot pay an instalment more than Rs 1,200 per month.

To summarise, despite being replete with welfare rhetoric, the centrally-designed programmes have held on to neoliberal qualities, especially in creating opportunities for the private sector, thus blurring the lines between the enabling and provider approaches. It can be argued that these programmes have introduced an increasingly commercial and speculative element into urban management and aim at engineering investment-oriented markets in land, services and municipal debt.

INTERNATIONAL HOUSING POLICY AND SOME POLICY CONTRADICTIONS

The previous sections discussed housing approaches in Brazil and India, which emphasise global trends and resistance to the wholesale acceptance of an enabling housing framework. Both countries have initiated state-administered large-scale housing programmes within diverse institutional contexts, as observed by Buckley et al. (2016). There are interesting similarities and contrasts in the approaches to low-income housing delivery in Brazil, which can be distilled to understand the international trend in low-income housing delivery in Southern countries. In India, the government has adopted a rather arrogant and highly centralised approach to social housing delivery, excluding the urban local bodies and civic organisations, including end users, from participation in decision-making. Blinded by the notion of gaining speed and efficiency, it fails to understand that without the active participation of state and local partners to carry out the wider reforms considered pivotal to success, it will be unable to achieve its goal. Moreover, very few urban local bodies have the capacity to carry out these well-intentioned structural reforms, or oversee City Development Plans, or manage and influence the private sector for the implementation of the projects. This holds true in the Brazilian case as well, where institutional capacity—both at state and municipal levels—is less developed (Valença and Bonates 2009). However, Brazilian federalism is considered one of the most decentralised in the world in conferring autonomy to municipalities, one that is rarely seen anywhere else. But it too faces challenges in implementation. At the local level, very few cities have been able to employ mechanisms to control land speculation and improve access to secure, serviced and well-located land for social housing, as revealed in the experience of the MCMV Programme. This is partly due to a lack of technical capacity, but more significantly, such challenges remain at the political level, although legal and institutional reforms have been stepped up to some extent. According to Campos and Guilhoto (2017), housing supply and financing of low-income housing at the state level faced a return of public housing development policies in Brazil, mainly through programmes related to the PNH (National Housing Policy) and MCMV. The creation of the Conselho Estadual de Habitaçao (CEH)/State Housing Council and Fundo Paulista de Habitaçao de Interesse Social (FPHIS), which is the Sao Paulo State Fund for Social Housing, are particularly relevant here for taking the low-income housing agenda forward.

To sum up, perhaps our clearest finding is that governments both in Brazil and India are united in adopting mixed models of housing provision, reflecting a unique collaboration of the enabler and provider roles of the state. This not only implies a re-engagement of the respective governments in low-income/public housing delivery, but also suggests that, while still adhering to enabling principles or the market approach to housing in general, the state is taking onto itself the responsibility of providing for the poor. Thus, as one policy approach follows another, the discursive space for government policy doctrine acquires a layered structure that contains elements of both approaches. A combination of both supply-side and demand-side subsidy, cash and loan subsidy further suggests a middle path. Whilst these developments are still evolutionary, they constitute an important basis for the eventual transition from an enabler approach back to a provider approach. At the least, this finding changes the presumption that a correct housing policy stance for the urban poor in the global South should be one of benign handover to the market or private sector. Arguably, on this basis, considerably more, not less, attention should be given to providing housing to the poor in these countries and structuring solid subsidy programmes to do so. Governments in both countries retain a strong role in housing provision, and there are renewed attempts to provide housing beyond those provided by the private market, shaped by the wider welfare concerns of the government.

Such a policy reversal is not confined to the cities of the global South. In the UK and Europe, many governments have initiated brick-and-mortar investment over individual subsidies. In a poignant advice to governments around the world, UN-Habitat (2016) imparts a clear message to start rebuilding public housing where needs are critical. In line with national and international trends, the World Bank shelter policy has also evolved. For the Bank, the form of shelter assistance most in demand, in recent years, has been the one that is directed towards improving the financing and targeting of housing subsidies. Large, fiscally-oriented loans have been approved in countries such as Brazil, the Islamic Republic of Iran, Mexico, Morocco and Russia, which show signs of changing times.

Nevertheless, the pursuit of policy changes confronts many challenges within the complex dynamics of both supply- and demand-side environments that did not exist in the provider era of the 1980s. There are now twice as many democratic governments in the world compared to two decades ago, and they are overwhelmingly more decentralised. Over time, the low-income housing market has seen phenomenal growth, is no longer a marginal investment and is an economy of scale capable of giving profitable returns. The former requires the plans and programmes to be inclusive, process-driven and responsive to the diverse local needs, for which the government's role remains critical. The latter requires the government to organise the supply chain around delivering low-income housing, enabling procurement of building material at scale to facilitate the construction industry, and design the right delivery models to encourage private-sector participation at scale. Designing acceptable credit risk for housing financing and devising integrated programmes that bring everything together will be the lynchpins of its success. In terms of policy, the chapter suggests that a new phase of policy involves a distinctive hybrid approach rather than a convergence with an 'enabling' or 'provider' approach. Southern countries such as India and Brazil are yet to arrive at a static position and conform to a particular model; rather, they seem to be experimenting with alternative ways of complementing market provision through strong state interventions.

End Notes

1. The Group of Ten (G10) is made up of eleven industrial countries (Belgium, Canada, France, Germany, Italy, Japan, the Netherlands, Sweden, Switzerland, the United Kingdom and the United States), which form the consortium to decide on global economic, monetary and financial matters.
2. This is based on the recent report by the research and consultancy firm RNCOS.
3. See Pasternak (1995) and Pasternak and D'Ottaviano (2014) for details.

4. For instance, in Osasco, COPROMO (Cooperativa Pró Moradia de Osasco/Osasco Pro-housing Cooperative) occupied and negotiated a large area of the city and built a housing project with 2,000 units through a community-built housing initiative financed by the São Paulo State Housing and Urban Development Company.

5. The priority areas for intervention were chosen according to a social exclusion criterion (defined as a situation of collective deprivation, which includes poverty, discrimination, subservience, inequity, non-accessibility, lack of public representation). The Bairro Legal was implemented in the first phase in Capão Redondo, Brasilândia, Lajeado, Jardim Ângela and Grajaú, since they had a higher percentage of low-income families (15 per cent or more). In phase two, it was extended to the districts of Campo Limpo, Guaianazes, Iguatemi and Anhanguera.

6. The Rizkallah Jorge building in the city centre was built in the 1940s and was intended as a luxury hotel; instead, it became a company head office. Sixty years on, under the private initiative option of the Residential Leasing Programme, it has been converted into 167 studio apartments measuring 30–40 sq. m., each with a bed-sitting room, kitchen, bathroom and utility area. The new occupants are low-income families (see Budds et al. 2005).

7. The National Building Organisation was created in 1954 to facilitate research in building construction activity, and the Town and Country Planning Organisation in 1962, to facilitate spatial planning activities across the country. At the state level, various Housing Boards were created during the same period.

8. *Chawls* are public or private rental housing built in the nineteenth and twentieth century by the government or private landlords to accommodate the migrants who came from villages to take up employment in the growing cotton industry. *Chawls* are buildings with one-room or two-room units of not more than 200 sq. ft., attached to a common corridor with shared toilets on each floor.

9. However, it should also be noted that these cities have not always promoted welfare interventions as real priorities for the city, despite the considerable budget at their disposal. This reflects their attitudes and approach towards city development. For instance, Delhi's approach has been rather heavy-handed towards low-income housing, whilst Mumbai has made great efforts to address the problems by way of integration of transfer of development rights, etc.

10. The policy aimed to: (*i*) prevent luxury housing (for which the residential plot size was reduced from 2,000 sq. m. to 120 sq. m.); (*ii*) enable

self-help housing through fiscal and monetary measures for HIGs and MIGs; (*iii*) make the state directly responsible for providing housing for the poor; (*iv*) amend ULCRA (Urban Land Ceiling and Regulation Act) to bring about better supply of urban residential land; (*v*) strengthen both formal and informal sources of financing; and (*vi*) encourage rental housing (Sivam and Karuppannan 2002).

11. Under the JNNURM, the central government gives grants covering 50 per cent of the project cost for cities with population between one million and four million. For cities with a population higher than four million, the central grant is 35 per cent of the project cost. The remaining funding comes from the state's kitty and the urban local bodies or parastatals. At present, there are 523 projects related to urban infrastructure development that are being implemented in sixty-five cities across the country.

12. Under this programme, all eligible households are provided with a central grant between Rs 100,000–Rs 230,000 (US$ 1,483–US$ 3,412), depending on locational factors, and the loan with interest subsidy of 6.5 per cent payable in fifteen years. The amount disbursed through the loan is usually matched by the grant amount.

13. The Singur case came to the national spotlight in 2006–2007 with the controversy surrounding the acquisition of 997 acres of farmland for an automobile factory in Singur, 40 kms away from Kolkata, and located next to an important expressway in the state of West Bengal (India). The incumbent Left Front government had been accused of subsidising Tata Motors' small car factory at Singur and forcefully acquiring land from unwilling farmers. The farmers' protest, which ran for months, was brutally suppressed, initially using police forces. Eventually, under pressure, Tata Motors withdrew from West Bengal and went to Gujarat, where the plant is now under operation. It was a classic example of state–farmers conflict around neoliberal land acquisition, which ignored issues such as loss of land, adequate rehabilitation packages, and livelihood issues of farmers.

14. According to MHUPA (2015), the first approach relates to in-situ improvements, undertaken using a developer-led redevelopment process selected through an open bidding process. The developer is incentivised through FSI (Floor Space Index) relaxation and Transfer of Development Rights (TDR). The second approach relates to enabling EWS and LIG households through a credit-linked subsidy programme. Quintessentially a demand-driven approach, the government sits as a guarantor for the disbursement of low-interest loans. The third approach relates to direct subsidy from the central government, offered as grant assistance to the

public and private sectors, including parastatal agencies, for constructing a minimum of 35 per cent EWS units. The fourth approach is about providing loans for building individual homes for the EWS population. Collectively, these approaches prioritise women, economically backward groups in the Indian society, and the Scheduled Castes and Scheduled Tribes. Principally, eligible beneficiaries, most of them slum dwellers, are classified into the Economically Weaker Section (EWS) and Low-Income Groups (LIG).

References

Ahmed, I. 1998. 'Crisis of natural building materials and institutionalised self-help housing: The case of Grameen Bank in Bangladesh'. *Habitat International* 22(4): 355–374.

Angel, S. 2000. *Housing Policy Matters: A Global Analysis*. New York: Oxford University Press.

Baindur, V. and Lalitha Kamath. 2009. 'Reengineering urban infrastructure: How the World Bank and Asian Development Bank shape urban infrastructure finance and governance in India', Research report. New Delhi: Bank Information Centre.

Bradlow, B., Joel Bolnick and Clifford Shearing. 2011. 'Housing, institutions, money: The failures and promise of human settlements policy and practice in South Africa'. *Environment and Urbanization* 23(1): 267–275.

Buckley, R. M., Achilles Kallergis and Laura Wainer. 2016. 'The emergence of large-scale housing programs: Beyond a public finance perspective'. *Habitat International* 54: 199–209.

Budds, Jessica, P. Teixeira and Sehab. 2005. 'Ensuring the right to the city: Pro-poor housing, urban development and tenure legalization in São Paulo'. *Environment & Urbanization* 17(1).

Campos, Rodger Barros Antunes and Joaquim J. M. Guilhoto. 2017. 'The socioeconomic impact of low-income housing programs: An interregional input-output model for the state of Sao Paulo and the rest of Brazil'. *Habitat International* 65(July): 59–69.

Cao, J. A. and R. Keivani. 2014. 'The limits and potentials of the housing market enabling paradigm: An evaluation of China's housing policies from 1998 to 2011'. *Housing Studies* 29(1): 44–68.

Choguill, C. L. 1997. 'Ten steps to sustainable urban infrastructure'. *The Urban Age* 5(2): 22–23.

Datta, K. and G. Jones (eds). 1999. *Housing and Finance in Developing Countries*. London: Routledge.

Foch, Arthur. 2013. 'Explaining the G7 and G10's influence on World Bank decisions: The role of formal and informal rules of governance', Working Paper. Documents de Travail du Centre d'Economie de la Sorbonne 2013.35. Available at https://halshs.archives-ouvertes.fr/halshs-00824678/document (accessed March 2021).

IBGE. 1991, 2000, 2010. Census Demographico. Sao Paulo, Brazil: IBGE.

Islam, N. 1996. 'Sustainability issues in urban housing in a low-income country: Bangladesh'. *Habitat International* 20(3): 377–388.

Jones, G. A. and P. M. Ward. 1995. 'The World Bank's new urban management programs: Paradigm shift or policy continuity?' *Habitat International* 18(3): 33–51.

Kundu, Debolina and Dibyendu Samanta. 2011. 'Redefining the Inclusive Urban Agenda in India'. *Economic and Political Weekly* 46(5): 55–63.

MHUPA. 2015. 'Housing for All (Urban): Scheme Guidelines'. MHUPA, GoI. Available at https://pmaymis.gov.in/PDF/HFA_Guidelines/hfa_Guidelines.pdf (accessed June 2021).

Mukhija, V. 2001. 'Enabling slum redevelopment in Mumbai: Policy paradox in practice'. *Housing Studies* 16(6): 791–806.

———. 2004. 'The contradictions in enabling private developers of affordable housing: A cautionary case from Ahmedabad, India'. *Urban Studies* 41(11): 2231–2244.

Nijman, J. 2008. 'Against the odds: Slum Rehabilitation in Neoliberal Mumbai'. *Cities* 25(2): 73–85.

Ogu, V. I. and J. E. Ogbuozobe. 2001. 'Housing policy in Nigeria: Towards enablement of private housing development'. *Habitat International* 25: 473–492.

Pasternak, S. and C. D'Ottaviano. 2014. 'Half a century of self-help in Brazil'. In J. Bredenoord, P. V. Lindert and P. Smets (eds), *Affordable Housing in the Urban Global South: Seeking Sustainable Solutions*, 242–255. London: Earthscan.

Pasternak, T. S. 1995. 'Squatter Settlements and Slums in Brazil: Twenty Years of Research and Policy'. In B. Aldrich and R. Sandhu (eds), *Housing the Urban Poor*. London: Zed Books.

Rahman, M. M. 2001. 'Bastee eviction and housing rights: A case of Dhaka, Bangladesh'. *Habitat International* 25: 49–67.

Rolnik, R. 2013. 'Late neoliberalism: The financialization of homeownership and housing rights'. *International Journal of Urban and Regional Research* 37: 1058–1066.

Sahu, Geetanjoy, Yacoub Zachariah and Sandipan Baksi. 2009. 'National level background document on urban issues and concerns'. Mumbai: Urban India Reforms Facility (UIRF), School of Habitat Studies, Tata Institute of Social Sciences. Available at https://urk.tiss.edu/wp-content/uploads/2020/08/National-Leval-Background-Document.pdf (accessed June 2021).

Sengupta, U. 2006. 'Government intervention in public private partnership in housing in Kolkata'. *Habitat International* 30(3): 448–461.

______. 2019. 'The State-led Housing Development in Brazil and India: A machinery for Enabling Strategy?' *International Journal of Housing Policy* 19(4): 509–535.

Sengupta, U. and A. G. Tipple. 2007. 'Performance of public sector housing in Kolkata in the post reform milieu'. *Urban Studies* 44(10): 2009–2027.

Singh, M. 2016. 'Planning for Smart Cities in the Indian Context'. *Shelter* 17(1): 47–50.

Sivam, A. and A. Karuppannan. 2002. 'Role of state and market in housing delivery for low-income groups in India'. *Journal of Housing and the Built Environment* 17(1): 69–88.

Smets, P. 1997. 'Private housing finance in India: reaching down market?' *Habitat International* 21(1): 1–15.

Tipple, A. G., D. Korboe, G. Garrod and K. Willis. 1999. 'Housing supply in Ghana: A study of Accra, Kumasi and Berekum'. *Progress in Planning* 51(4): 253–324.

Tiwari, P. and J. Rao. 2016. 'Housing Markets and Housing Policies in India', ADBI Working Paper Series 565. Tokyo: Asian Development Bank Institute.

UN-Habitat. 1988. *The Global Strategy for Shelter to the Year 2000*. Nairobi: UNCHS (Habitat).

______. 2001. 'The implications of globalization and privatization for the provision of and access to housing and urban development in the transition economies'. In *Cities in a Globalizing World: Global Report on Human Settlements 2001*, 88–93. London: Earthscan.

______. 2003. *The Challenge of Slums: Global Report on Human Settlements 2003*. Nairobi: UN-Habitat.

______. 2006. *Enabling Shelter Strategies: Review of Experience from Two Decades of Implementation*. Nairobi: UN-Habitat.

______. 2016. *World Cities Report*. Nairobi: UN Publications.

Valença, M. M. 1999. 'The lost decade and the Brazilian government's response in the 1990s'. *Journal of Developing Areas* 33(1): 1–52.

Valença, M.M. and M. F. Bonates. 2009. 'The Trajectory of Social Housing Policy in Brazil: From the National Housing Bank to the Ministry of the Cities'. *Habitat International* 34(2): 165–173.

Wang, Y. P. and L. Shao. 2010. 'Urban housing policy changes and challenges in China'. In J. Doling and R. Ronald (eds), *Housing East Asia: Socioeconomic and Demographic Challenges*, 40–70. London: Palgrave.

World Bank. 1993. *Public/Private Partnerships in Enabling Shelter Strategies.* Nairobi: UNCHS.

Yap, K. S. 2015. 'The enabling strategy and its discontent: Low-income housing policies and practices in Asia'. *Habitat International* 54(3): 166–172.

Young, Cheryl K. 2016. 'Accommodating Housing in India: Lessons from Development Capital, Policy Frames, and Slums', PhD Dissertation, University of California.

Part 2

Redevelopment of Slums

V

Brazilian Favelas

Two Decades of Public Policies

Camila D'Ottaviano

CONCEPT AND ORIGIN OF 'FAVELAS' IN BRAZIL

The favelas (inner-city slums), alongside tenement housing and peripheral irregular settlements (characterised by home ownership and self-construction), have historically been one of

Image 5.1: Favela, Jardim Jaqueline (Jaqueline Garden District), São Paulo, Brazil

Photograph: Camila D'Ottaviano.

the main forms of accessible housing for the low-income Brazilian population. Although they were born as a brand of the city of Rio de Janeiro during the early twentieth century, in the last decades of the twentieth century, favelas were spread all over Brazilian metropolises, large- and medium-sized cities.

During the era of slavery, until the year 1888, *senzalas* (slave quarters) were the prevalent form of housing for the farm workers. During the first phase of industrialisation, *cortiços* (tenement houses) became the spontaneous solution and *vilasoperárias* (villages with boarding for factory workers) was the private initiative supported by public authorities. Rent was the predominant form of access to housing for the poor. After 1930, substantial growth in the manufacturing industry, higher than 5 per cent, led to vast migration from rural to urban areas, resulting in larger cities, mostly in the southeast region of Brazil. Since then, state interventions to mediate landlord–tenant relationships have discouraged the construction of rental housing units. After the 1950s, urban settlement patterns have been supported by three pillars: low-cost land developments, home ownership and private home construction. Urban housing areas for the poor have spread horizontally, consolidating what came to be known as the 'peripheral area'.

Until almost the 1950s, the favelas were a typical phenomenon in Rio de Janeiro city, the national capital. In 1998, Zaluar and Alvito published a book named *Um Século de Favela* (A Century of Favelas), which provides testimony to the long-term presence of the favelas in the Brazilian urban fabric. Supposedly, the word 'favela' comes from a shrub of the same name, which is prevalent in the northeast region of Canudos, Bahia. After battling Antônio Conselheiro and his followers, the Brazilian army's soldiers did not find places to live in Rio de Janeiro upon their return in 1897. They decided to occupy the Morro da Providência (a hill close to the city centre), building makeshift shelters that ended up spreading to the hills in much the same way that the favela shrubs spread in Canudos. After that, the term 'favela' was used to designate any precarious housing cluster built in the hills of Rio de Janeiro. According to Abreu (1994: 35), it was only during the second decade of the twentieth century that the word 'favela' took on the meaning it has today, referring not exclusively to Morro da Favela (formerly, Morro da Providência) but to impoverished, unauthorised and illegal settlements in the hills.

According to Leeds and Leeds (1978: 12), 'the only feature that differentiates squatters from other types of residents is the fact that they are illegally occupying the land, since their occupation is based on neither ownership nor rental from legal owners'. Pereira Passos's urban reform in Rio de Janeiro (1902–1906) changed the city's design and the urban structure of Avenida Central (now Presidente Vargas Avenue), demolishing several tenement houses and consolidating the city's peripheral growth; this forced the poor to seek shelter in the hills, where construction was not regulated. Over the first half of the twentieth century, no specific measures were taken to curb the expansion into the Rio de Janeiro hills.

For the past three decades, there has been a continuous improvement of the housing units in favelas. Wooden shacks with sheet metal roofs have been gradually replaced by brick-and-cement houses with tile or concrete roofs. Just like in urban infrastructures, many favelas—especially those located in the southeast regions—are already equipped with electricity, water supply, garbage collection and even sewage systems (Pasternak and D'Ottaviano 2015).

Another important issue is the official statistics on favelas. Not until 1948 was the first survey conducted on favelas in Rio de Janeiro, which in those days was the federal capital. In 1950, the Brazilian Institute of Geography and Statistics (IBGE) decided, for the first time, to include favelas when estimating the population, using the federal district as a specific case study. The study, 'The favelas in the federal district', was published in 1953. Nevertheless, surveys were still very unequal from a geographic perspective.

At first, the concept of favelas was based on a group of dwellings with at least one of the following characteristics:

- minimal proportions—groups of buildings or residences with more than fifty units;
- type of housing—predominance of shacks or very basic shelters, made out of tin, sheet metal or similar materials;
- legal status of occupation—construction without permits or inspection, on lands belonging to third or unknown parties;

- public utilities–the lack, in whole or in part, of a sewage system, power, telephone service or water;
- urbanization–non-urbanized area, without roads, house numbers or street names (Guimarães 2000: 353).

Historically, there have been efforts from both public authorities and the academia to enhance the definition of favelas. We believe that the most appropriate variable for describing a favela is the legal status of the land. In the case of the city of São Paulo, all of the research conducted by the local government since the 1970s, as well as the 1980 study carried out by the Institute of Technological Research and Foundation for Architectural and Environmental Research (IPT-FUPAM), considers that the term 'favela' designates any set of housing units built with wood, sheet metal, tin, cardboard or brick and mortar, usually spread in an unorganised manner over plots of land not legally provided to those occupying the area (São Paulo 1992: 5).

The census criterion dictating that only groupings of fifty or more housing units may be called favelas does explain, in part, why favelas' populations have been underestimated in the national census. In São Paulo, for example, where local surveys were conducted, it is known that there are many favelas with fewer than fifty dwellings. A 1987 local government survey showed that 21.93 per cent of favela residents in São Paulo lived in settlements with fewer than fifty-one units. A 1991 study showed that 21.2 per cent of the houses in favelas were in settlements that did not meet the census criterion (Pasternak 2006).

The size of the clusters is directly related to the topography of the city and the type of terrain available for occupancy. In São Paulo, favelas are usually found in common lots, which are smaller areas when compared to the favelas in the Rio de Janeiro hills, or the ones in Salvador, which sometimes stretch all the way into the sea.

Starting in 1991, the IBGE began to adopt the concept of 'subnormal agglomerates'. Although quite generic, the concept sought to encompass the diversity of the irregular settlements existing in Brazil. Subnormal agglomerates cover favelas, occupied properties, caves, lowlands, impoverished communities, shanty towns, backwaters, *mocambos* (types of shacks), stilted houses and other precarious units. The last national census, taken in 2010, has further identified subnormal agglomerates by using a specific morphological survey, with geo-referenced identification and preparatory field visits to the agglomerates. Given previous underestimations and the 2010 advances in surveying, the favela count from the 2010 census proved more reliable, resulting in a substantial numerical jump in the number of favelas, especially in the northern area of Brazil, as we will see below.

According to the Manual of Sector Delineation, the 2010 census considers a subnormal agglomerate to be any settlement with at least fifty-one household units, mostly in need of essential public services, occupying or having occupied until recently a third party property—public or private—and generally arranged in a disorderly and dense manner. This definition must meet the following criteria:

> a) Illegal occupation of land or construction on land owned by others—public or private—either now or in recent years (having obtained the title of the property within the last ten years);
>
> b) Not within the legal standards of urbanisation—reflected by narrow and irregular pathways, plots of different shapes and sizes and building not legally approved by public offices—or the inadequate provision of essential public services (water supply, sewage system, garbage collection and electrical power) (IBGE 2011: 18).

Brazilian favelas have improved a lot over the past twenty years. In addition to urban development programmes and other improvements, some land tenure regularisation programmes, especially with the enforcement of the City Statute in 2001, have changed access to housing in favelas.

It is not a coincidence that the 2010 census in Brazil defined favela housing as a residence occupying, or until recently having occupied, a property belonging to a third party (IBGE 2011). After more than three decades of intervention in favelas, one must revisit the very concept of a favela: Should we include the urban/regularised occupied sites, that is, those with land tenure somehow recognised by the public authorities in the official statistics? Will the occupied sites that have now effectively been legalised no longer be considered favelas? If illegal occupancy previously meant a risk of eviction, does it mean the same thing today, when public policy largely seeks to urbanise settlements and allow people to stay? The empirical data available show that the physical infrastructure in favelas today is very similar to that found in urban housing. Favela units now have water supply, sewage, garbage collection and electricity. The predominant form of favela housing, at least in the less impoverished areas of São Paulo and Rio de Janeiro, is no longer the wooden shack. Street construction and layout may be different from the formal areas, but there are often street names and numbers. A new question has to be answered: What does it mean to live in a favela today?

As previously mentioned, the IBGE considers subnormal agglomerates to be 'the census sectors holding fifty or more contiguous favela houses' (Guimarães 2000: 353). If an agglomerate has twenty houses in one sector and twenty in another, these sectors will not be considered favelas, and this will result in an underestimation of the actual figures. On the other hand, with fifty-one favela houses, the entire sector will be considered a subnormal agglomerate, even if some of the houses in the area are not favela houses.

In São Paulo, an area, public or private, will be classified as a favela if it is illegally occupied by inhabitants. The defining element of a favela is the illegality of residency on the property. In the case of a public area, the process of favela classification starts with filing an administrative process in the local government administration, which in turn notifies the Secretary of Housing and the Department of Property. This information is forwarded to the Office of Housing (HABI). In the case of a private area, the responsible public sector is called to proceed with evictions, following a motion for repossession. Another way in which favelas are identified is through routine inspections, such as when an inspector becomes aware of an occupied area and notifies HABI. In the case of São Paulo, the consolidation of information on favelas led to an interesting registry of favelas, which is available from the Municipal Secretariat of Housing (http://www.habisp.inf.br).

Table 5.1 shows the principal characteristics of the three principal types of precarious housing in Brazil—favelas (squatter settlements), *cortiços* (low-income slum tenement housing) and peripheral irregular settlements.

Image 5.2: Favela Jaguaré—Inner Street, São Paulo, Brazil

Photograph: Camila D'Ottaviano.

Table 5.1: Brazil: Favelas, *Cortiços* and Irregular Settlements Characteristics

Type of settlement/ characteristics	Favelas—squatter settlements	Cortiços—low-income slum tenement housing	Irregular settlements
Type of access to land	Invasion	Rent	Ownership by purchase of the land
Location within the city	Usually peripheral	Usually central	Always peripheral
Housing characteristics	Individual houses, usually with two floors, self-built, brick, small dimensions, bad ventilation and/ or lighting conditions. Growing real estate market inside.	Single room shared by the whole family, common (collective) toilet/bathroom, kitchen and washboard. (Moura Municipal Law 1991)	Individual houses, usually in isolated plots, self-built, brick, medium dimensions. Without register or building permit. (Federal Law 6766)
Population characteristics	Younger than the municipal average, Black and migrant (NE[northeast region]). Industrial workers and service workers (growing) with regular register. Low income and low scholarship.	Older, with small families, usually without children, long-term, informal workers in services in the city centre, migrants. Many Latin Americans (Bolivia, Peru and Paraguay), Africans (Angola) and Haitians.	Younger than the municipal average, Black and migrant (NE). Industrial workers and service workers (growing) with regular register. Low income and low scholarship.
Infrastructure access	São Paulo: good access to water and electricity; 50% access to sewage	Good access to infrastructure (central area)	São Paulo: good access to water and electricity; 50% access to sewage

Source: Pasternak and D'Ottaviano 2015.

Image 5.3: Jardim Lapenna, Irregular Settlement, São Paulo, Brazil

Photograph: Camila D'Ottaviano.

FAVELA POPULATION IN BRAZIL

Today, the issue of favelas has reached an unprecedented magnitude in Brazilian history. Data from the 2010 census shows that the number of Brazilians living in these conditions rose from 6.5 million in 2000 to 11.4 million in 2010, with residents distributed throughout 6,329 'subnormal agglomerates' in 323 municipalities; 88 per cent of this type of dwellings are in the twenty largest Brazilian cities.

Favelas are prevalent in all regions of Brazil, albeit with different levels of concentration. According to the national demographic census, in 1991, there were 3,187 subnormal agglomerates; in 1996 this number rose to 3,348; in 2000 there were 3,906 settlements; and the 2010 census registered 6,329 subnormal agglomerates (see Table 5.2). Also, see Table 5.3 for a comparison of total households and favela households per region in Brazil from 1980–2010.

Table 5.2: Favelas by Major Regions in Brazil—1991, 2000 and 2010

Region	1991	2000	2010	Increase 1991–2000	Increase 2000–2010
North (N)	59	185	467	126	282
Northeast (NE)	517	674	1,349	157	675
Southeast (SE)	2,225	2,621	3,954	396	1,333
South (S)	327	392	489	65	97
Midwest (CO)	59	34	70	–25	36
Brazil	3,187	3,906	6,329	719	2,423

Source: National Censuses 1980, 1991, 2000 and 2010.

Similar to the agglomerates, favela dwellings and populations have been growing since 1980 and increasing at higher rates than the total population. According to Table 5.5, from 1980 to 1991, the number of total households grew by 3.08 per cent per year, while the number of favela households grew by 8.21 per cent per year. During the following census period–1991 to 2000–the number of total households grew by 3.05 per cent per year, while favela households had an annual increase rate of 4.15 per cent. From 2000 to 2010, the annual growth rate of Brazilian households was 0.57 per cent, while favela households increased 6.93 per cent per year. In 1980, the favela population was 2.25 million people; by 1991, it had hit more than five million; and in 2010, a total of 3,224,529 households in subnormal agglomerates housed fourteen million residents (National Census 1980, 1991). While the population in favelas accounted for 1.62 per cent of the total Brazilian population in 1980, it climbed to 2.76 per cent in 1991, to 3.04 per cent in 2000 and by 2010 had reached 5.61 per cent (see Table 5.4).

Favelas in Brazil have been a predominantly metropolitan phenomenon. In 1980, 79.16 per cent of favela households could be found in nine metropolitan regions throughout the country (Belém, Fortaleza, Recife, Salvador, Belo Horizonte, Rio de Janeiro, São Paulo, Curitiba and Porto Alegre). In 1991, there were 2,391 favelas (74 per cent) and 817,000 favela households (78 per cent) in these metropolitan areas, while in 2000, the percentage of people

Table 5.3: Total Households and Favela Households per Region in Brazil, 1980–2010

Region	Total households				Favela households			
	1980	1991	2000	2010	1980	1991	2000	2010
North	1,219,496	2,376,607	3,353,764	3,988,832	12,721	97,760	178,326	463,444
Northeast	8,036,803	10,920,830	13,911,413	14,957,608	69,974	286,130	306,395	926,370
Southeast	13,761,346	18,839,621	24,699,909	25,227,877	357,330	675,846	1,038,608	1,607,375
South	4,826,030	6,598,962	8,509,284	8,904,120	30,077	73,325	110,411	170,054
Midwest	1,812,176	2,657,621	3,791,248	4,349,562	10,493	11,257	16,808	57,286
Brazil	29,655,851	41,393,641	54,267,618	57,427,999	480,595	1,144,318	1,650,548	3,224,529

Source: National Censuses 1980, 1991, 2000 and 2010.

Table 5.4: Proportion of Favela Households per Region in Brazil, 1980–2010

Region	1980	1991	2000	2010
North	1.04%	4.11%	5.32%	11.62%
Northeast	0.87%	2.62%	2.20%	6.19%
Southeast	2.60%	3.59%	4.20%	6.37%
South	0.62%	1.11%	1.30%	1.91%
Midwest	0.58%	0.42%	0.44%	1.32%
Brazil	1.62%	2.76%	3.04%	5.61%

Source: National Censuses 1980, 1991, 2000 and 2010.

Table 5.5: Geometric Growth Rates per Region in Brazil of Total and Favela Households

Region	Total Households			Favela Households		
	1980–1991	1991–2000	2000–2010	1980–1991	1991–2000	2000–2010
North	6.25%	3.90%	1.75%	20.37%	6.91%	10.02%
Northeast	2.83%	2.73%	0.73%	13.66%	0.76%	11.70%
Southeast	2.90%	3.06%	0.21%	5.96%	4.89%	4.46%
South	2.89%	2.87%	0.45%	8.44%	4.65%	4.41%
Midwest	3.54%	4.03%	1.38%	0.64%	4.55%	13.05%
Brazil	3.08%	3.05%	0.57%	8.21%	4.15%	6.93%

Source: National Censuses 1980, 1991, 2000 and 2010.

living in favelas in these nine metropolitan areas reached 87.15 per cent (National Censuses 1980, 1991, 2000 and 2010). In 2010, it was still high, with these areas accounting for 71.10 per cent of total favela residents. Data from 2010 show a type of inversion of this trend: although predominantly a metropolitan phenomenon, today favelas are also found in other towns—26 per cent of the favela population in 2000 were located in municipalities with between 100,000 and 500,000 residents (ibid.).

The São Paulo metropolitan region has the highest concentration of favelas in Brazil, with 1,703 agglomerates (27 per cent of total favelas in Brazil) with a population of more than two million people (19 per cent of total favela residents in Brazil) (IBGE 2010). The cities of São Paulo, Guarulhos, Osasco and Diadema alone accounted for 938 favelas in 2000—approximately one-fourth of the total number of favelas in the country, according to the demographic census (ibid.). In 2010, these four municipalities had 1,348 agglomerates, 21 per cent of the Brazilian favelas. In 2010, the total number of favela houses in the metropolis reached 596,479 (ibid.). The proportion of favela households in the metropolis has been increasing since 1991. As such, 5.72 per cent in 1991 grew to 8.14 per cent in 2000, reaching 9.29 per cent of household units in 2005 and 10.37 per cent in 2010 (ibid.). The housing situation in the São Paulo metropolitan region has deteriorated during the last decades.

This fact represents a trend of poverty expanding towards the peripheral metropolitan areas, evidenced here by the territorial expansion of precarious housing. To precarious houses, we can add other important factors that contribute to the precariousness of these dwellers: longer commutes to work, long distance to access jobs and high transport prices. In greater São Paulo, the total favela population reached 2,162,368 residents, with 56.2 per cent of these living in the capital city.

Demographic census figures show that there were 933,000 people living in favelas in 2000, that is, 9 per cent of the São Paulo municipality's total population. This number had increased to 12,802,400 by 2010, accounting for 11.42 per cent of the total population. This means that the favela population has been growing at a faster rate than the population of the city as a whole (4.68 per cent growth rate from 2000–2010, while the total population grew at an annual rate of just 0.73 per cent). Favelas remain a serious issue for the financial capital of the country.

PUBLIC POLICIES REGARDING FAVELAS

Until 1984, the policies on social housing in Brazil, and especially those regarding favelas and tenement houses, were highly centralised at the federal level. There have always been interventions at the local level, but prior to the closing of the National Housing Bank (BNH) in November 1986, these interventions were not as relevant as they later became in 1990. One detailed analysis of the policies at the federal level can be seen in Pasternak-Taschner (1997).

The first favela urbanisation programme in Brazil took place in Rio de Janeiro at the end of the 1960s, and was largely inspired by the ideas of John Turner. However, it was only after the 1980s that this type of intervention was consolidated under the responsibility of local and/or state governments. After the 1988 Federal Constitution, urban policy became a responsibility of the local government. The City Statute approved in 2001 is an important instrument for urban policy, and is used in different ways according to the specificities of each municipality and government.

Pasternak and D'Ottaviano (2015) present a chronology of the public policies related to favelas since the 1960s. Since then, as pointed out by Cardoso (2007), the interventions in precarious settlements can be divided into three basic models: urbanisation, re-urbanisation and removal. Since the closure of BNH in the mid-1980s, there was no major investment policy in Brazil on urban infrastructure such as the one that was seen in recent years—during the Workers' Party government (led by President Luiz Inácio Lula da Silva, and then by his successor, Dilma Rousseff, from 2002–2016). In fact, from the late 1980s and throughout the 1990s, interventions in favelas and even in infrastructure networks depended on the entrepreneurship of municipal administrations, which were given almost no federal funds or support. During this period, some municipalities such as Recife (PREZEIS Programme, 1987), Rio de Janeiro (Favela Bairro Programme, beginning 1993) and São Paulo (Luiza Erundina government, 1989–1993) implemented local intervention policies in favela and irregular settlements. However, many of the projects faced a lack of funds or legal restrictions, such as land tenure.

In the 1990s, urbanisation programmes began to be officially incorporated as an object of public policy in the various spheres of government. Preventive interventions and gradual urbanisation projects predominated.

The 2000s saw two important milestones for Brazilian urban management: the approval of the City Statute in 2001 and the creation of the Ministry of Cities in 2003. With the City Statute, normative issues to guarantee the permanence of the favela population in their homes were regulated. Instruments such as the CUEM (Concessão de Uso Especial para Fins de Moradia/ concession of special use for housing purposes) and urban or collective expropriation represented important advances for the population living in irregular settlements. The Ministry of Cities with its three secretariats–(*i*) Housing; (*ii*) Transportation and Mobility; and (*iii*) Sanitation and Urban Programmes–represented the importance of the urban issue in President Lula's government from its beginning. However, in relation to urban infrastructure and public policies for favelas, the recent event of greatest impact was the federal investment programme launched in 2007: the Growth Acceleration Programme (PAC).

Tables 5.6 and 5.7 provide a quick glimpse into the federal programmes and São Paulo municipality programmes related to favelas.

Table 5.6: Brazilian Federal Policies and Programmes on Favelas

Date	Policies/Programmes/ Projects	Theoretical background	Interventions
2009	My House, My Life Programme (PMCMV—Programa Minha Casa Minha Vida)	Economic anti-crisis programme	Construction of three million new houses
2007	Growth Acceleration Programme (PAC—Programa de Aceleração do Crescimento Urbanização de Assentamentos Precários)	Major infrastructure programme	Upgrading favela neighbourhoods
2001	City Statute (Estatuto da Cidade)	New federal urban law based on the right to the city and social function of the property principles	Intended to be the guideline for urban legislation and growth

Source: Pasternak and D'Ottaviano 2015.

Table 5.7: São Paulo Municipality Policies and Programmes on Favelas

Date	Policies/Programmes/Projects	Interventions
Current	Favela upgrading programme (Urbanização de Favelas)	Upgrading favela neighbourhoods with removal and new housing by PMCMV federal programme
Current	Dam Programme (Programa Mananciais)	Upgrading favela neighbourhoods with infrastructure implementation
Current	Public Areas Land Tenure Programme (Regularização Fundiária de Áreas Públicas)	Land tenure process with some infrastructure implementation
Current	Private Land Upgrading and Land Tenure Programme (Urbanização e Regularizaçãofundiária de loteamentosemáreasparticulares)	Land tenure process with some infrastructure implementation
2005–2012	Land tenure programmes	Land tenure process
	Upgrading favela programme	Continuation of upgrading favela programmes with a different approach (maintenance of the households as much as possible)
	Upgrading programmes in big favelas	Constructions of new housing units: Heliopolis (2,090 units) and Paraisopolis (13,064 units)
	Guarapiranga Project	Focussed on sanitation and regulation of settlements surrounding natural basins.
2001–2004	*Bairro Legal* (legal neighbourhood) Programme	Set of integrated actions in delineated territories occupied by lower-income population, including land tenure and favela upgrading and irregular settlements. This programme differs from the previous administration's as it integrates actions among different municipal agencies.

(Contd)

Table 5.7 (Contd)

Date	Policies/Programmes/Projects	Interventions
	RESOLO (Departamento de Regularização de Loteamentos)—Land Tenure Programme	Land tenure programme
1990s	Cingapura—Favelas Urbanisation and Verticalisation Project (PROVER—Programa de Urbanização e Verticalização de Favelas)	Construction of vertical building in the same place of the invasion by building companies, without popular participation, sponsored by International Development Bank (IDB)
Early 1990s	First favela upgrading projects	Upgrading of the favela by local government, though self-management. Emphasis on popular participation.

Source: Pasternak and D'Ottaviano 2015.

Image 5.4: Favela Jaguaré—City and Housing Complex View from the Favela Hill, São Paulo, Brazil

Photograph: Camila D'Ottaviano.

Nevertheless, the experiments with the virtuous cycle of upgrading favelas, conducted by Brazilian cities since 2002, with federal investment and support to local policies and interventions, ended in 2016 with the political-economic crisis that culminated in President Dilma's impeachment.

Since 2017, although PAC and PMCMV federal programmes formally still exist, there is no more funding for new projects and the ongoing ones are being funded at a slower rhythm.

CONCLUSIONS AND QUESTIONS

As mentioned earlier, according to Cardoso (2007), interventions in precarious settlements can be divided into three different models: urbanisation, re-urbanisation and removal. Urbanisation involves interventions that do not change the structure of the settlement, providing only infrastructure and paving. This type of intervention has been the most prevalent, despite the fact that favelas usually feature urban patterns that do not meet formal regulations. Re-urbanisation consists of interventions that completely redesign the settlement's structure, resettling the families in the same area. This was the case of the model urbanisation of the Brás de Pina Favela in Rio de Janeiro, the first favelas intervention project. Removal implies the total displacement of residents and their relocation in a different area. In practice, many interventions rely to some degree on the three alternatives, re-parcelling parts of the settlement, working on infrastructure wherever possible, and even removing part of the population in very crowded areas, when additional space for roads and infrastructure is required. Such removals usually entail the payment of indemnities (Pasternak and D'Ottaviano 2015).

Interventions in favelas can also be more specific—targeting a part of the settlement or the whole area. Specific interventions have resulted from political motives or emergency needs, such as the reconstruction of areas hit by fire, floods and/or landslides. Total interventions were seen, for example, in programmes like *Favela-Bairro* (Favela-Neighbourhood) in Rio de Janeiro, and *Santo André Mais Igual* (Santo André More Equal), a programme in a municipality of the São Paulo metropolitan area. The focus of both programmes was the integral improvement of a group of smaller favelas. The projects usually took two years to be completed. Huge amounts of resources are required for programmes of this nature, making them infeasible for most local administrations, as funding is very restricted. Both Rio de Janeiro and Santo André relied on foreign resources (European Community and the IDB). As for management models, interventions can be classified as participatory, as in the Recife's Plan of Regularisation for Special Zones of Social Interest (PREZEIS), or authoritarian, such as Cingapura in São Paulo, or *Favela-Bairro* in Rio de Janeiro.

After almost two decades of intense public intervention in favelas and irregular settlement areas, the mega events that occurred in Brazil in 2014 (World Cup) and 2016 (Olympic Games) were responsible for different types of regresses in the public agenda, for favelas especially. The construction of new avenues, parks and public transport lines were responsible for the removal of a large number of houses and entire favelas. Vila Autódromo favela in Rio de Janeiro, located just beside the Olympic Park, is a paradigmatic example (Oliveira et al. 2016, 2017).

The *Operações Urbanas Consorciadas* (Consorted Urban Operations) connected to mobility projects were also responsible for several removals. São Paulo's Água *Espraiada* project is responsible for the complete removal of more than thirty favelas for the construction of a new avenue and a line park (Ferreira 2015; Nobre et al. 2017).

The new federal government, the political and economic crisis and the end of the mega events represent a period of great incertitude about the maintenance of federal and local public policies, not only towards favela improvement programmes, but also for housing for the poor and irregular settlements development.

References

Abreu, Maurício. 1994. 'Reconstruindo uma história esquecida; origem e expansão inicial das *favelas* do Rio'. *Espaço e Debates* 14(37): 34–46.

Cardoso, Adauto. 2007. 'Urbanização de favelas no Brasil: revendoaexperiência e pensandodesafios'. Proceedings of XII Encontro Nacional da Associação Nacional de Pós-graduação e Pesquisaem Planejamento Urbano e Regional - XVII ENANPUR. Belém: ANPUR.

Ferreira, Paulo. 2015. 'Urbanização de Favelas Vs Desfavelamento: Notas Sobreuma Operação Paulistana'. Proceedings of third *CIHEL, Congresso Internacional da Habitação no Espaço Lusófono*, 252–266. São Paulo: FAUUSP.

Guimarães, B. 2000. 'As vilasfavelasem Belo Horizonte. O desafio dos números'. In Queiroz Ribeiro (ed.), *O futuro das metrópoles: Desigualdade e governabilidade*, 351–374. Rio de Janeiro: Revan/FASE.

IBGE (Instituto Brasileiro de Geografia e Estatística). 2010. *2010 Demographic Census*. Rio de Janeiro: IBGE.

______. 2011. *2010 Census Enhanced the Identification of Subnormal Agglomerates*. IBGE, Comunicação Social. Available at http://www.ibge.gov.br (accessed February 2021).

Leeds, Antony and E. Leeds. 1978. *A Sociologia do Brasil Urbano*. Rio de Janeiro: Zahar.

Nobre, E., J. Bassani and C. D'Ottaviano. 2017. 'São Paulo: Sports Mega-Events and the East Zone Local Development'. In E. Nobre (ed.), *Sports Mega-Events and Urban Legacies: The 2014 FIFA World Cup Brazil*, 162–182. London: Palgrave Macmillan.

Oliveira, F., G. Tanaka and R. Bienenstein. 2016. 'A batalha da Vila Autódromo: negociação' e resistência à remoção'. In C. Vainer, A. M. Broudehoux, F. L. de Oliveira and F. Sanchez (eds), *Osmegaeventose a Cidade: Perspectivas Críticas*, 483–512. Rio de Janeiro: Letra Capital.

Oliveira, F., F. Sanchez, G. Tanaka and G. Bienenstein. 2017. 'Social and Urban Impacts of the Maracanã Stadium Renovation'. In E. Nobre (ed.), *Sports Mega-Events and Urban Legacies: The 2014 FIFA World Cup, Brazil*, 117–136. London: Palgrave Macmillan.

Pasternak, S.2006. 'São Paulo e suasfavelas'. *Revista Pós* 19: 176–197.

Pasternak, S. and C. D'Ottaviano. 2015. 'Intervention Policies and Practices Regarding Favelas and Other Precarious Dwellings: Brazil and the City of São Paulo'. In Brian C. Aldrich and Ranvinder S. Sandhu (eds), *Housing for the Urban Poor in Developing Countries*, 190–207. New Delhi: Rawat.

Pasternak-Taschner, Suzana. 1997. *Favelas e cortiços no Brasil: 20 anos de pesquisa e política*, Cadernos de Pesquisado LAP 18. São Paulo: FAU-USP.

São Paulo, Município and Secretariada Habitação e do Desenvolvimento Urbano. 1992. *Urbanização de Favelas em São Paulo: umaexperiência de recuperaçãoambiental*. São Paulo: PMSP.

Zaluar, Alba and M. Alvito (eds). 1998. *Um Século de Favela*. Rio de Janeiro: FGV.

VI

Settlement in a 'Smartening City'

Amita Bhide

INTRODUCTION

Slums and informal settlements have emerged as the most visible forms of urban poverty in India. This phenomenon has been acknowledged and measured, and policy responses have been designed to 'formalise existing slums and prevent new ones'[1] since the 2001 census. In the current policy push towards a global acknowledgement of India as an emerging economy, ready to assume its leadership role in ushering 'smart, sustainable and inclusive urbanisation', slums have no place in the imagination of the future of Indian cities. They are seen as a relic of the past, a 'problem' that has to be 'quickly fixed' and which essentially lies within the domain of housing. A plethora of housing policies and programmes have been initiated since 2005 at the national and state levels towards this objective. The imagination of the slum and meaning of inclusion in these policies can be the subject of an independent critique. The focus of this chapter is on the overall direction of urbanisation and the push towards 'smart' cities that not only poses a threat to the existence of these settlements, but also begins to unravel the very fabric that has enabled the *birth, sustenance, and development of the settlements and offered some opportunities for upward mobility to the inhabitants*. The Smart Cities programme's simultaneous pursuit of infrastructure projects and changes to the governance modes of cities have meant multilevel changes to the socio-cultural, political and institutional fabric of Indian cities, with an enhanced emphasis on disciplining, surveillance and new modes of operation. An analysis of these directions of change, informed by a 'right to city' perspective, reveals that the impact of the current programme is far-reaching and goes beyond the actual implementation of the projects. It enables a consolidation of interests for those at the higher end of the political economy while creating multiple forms of exclusion, marginalisation and displacement for those on the lower end.

SLUMS AND SETTLEMENT IN INDIA

The term 'slum', a European import, is today being widely applied to several forms of settlements in India that do not conform to the idea of 'formal' buildings or structures. It is the predominant mode of urbanisation, whose presence is slowly being recognised by official data in varied scales of cities all over the country. Unlike its recognition in official data and policy, the phenomenon is not new and has been evolving in parallel with the growth of cities. Multiple aspects of this phenomenon have been labelled, analysed, converted into policy targets and perpetuated, and yet the evolving complexity of this form of settlement eludes policy makers and theory-building as well. An attention to the multiple facets of these settlements gives some insight into the multiple forces that intersect here.

P. K. Das, an activist-architect, calls slums a 'bundle of exploitations'. Those systemically excluded in the Indian social order, the Dalits, OBCs (Other Backward Classes) and Muslims, are the predominant inhabitants of slums. It is interesting to note the findings of some of the empirical studies conducted by this author on the Mumbai slums—only one Brahmin household was found amidst an inventory of 120,000 slum households in M(East) ward (TISS 2014). Similarly, a qualitative inquiry in Dharavi identified a group of upper-caste households who had settled in the primarily lower-caste and Muslim neighbourhood only after 1990—a period associated with its emergence as a high value area (Bhide and Spies 2013). While one would not go so far as to call slums *the reproduction of rural spatial exclusions onto the urban landscape*, it is undoubtedly a spatial hub of several social exclusions. The stigma associated with slums is also linked to this dimension.

Slums are also shadow cities that have roots in people's aspirations. They offer an option for poor migrants; they represent footholds for further claim-making. As Maringanti (2007) observes, slums are collective strategies of people to make claims on a city that excludes them, and yet needs their labour. Local histories of settlement reflect this collective dimension in the form of settlement patterns that often reproduce the spatial practices of the village, of interactions that link migrant groups from the same region, cast together and creating new collective actions that help them to consolidate their claims to the city. Consolidation of socio-economic status in the city enables many settlers to build assets in the village such as houses, contribute to the creation of public infrastructure like temples, and to organise as a group. This 'community' dimension of the slum may be changing significantly, but is nonetheless an essential aspect of it.

While slums do represent the struggle of the subaltern, they are also produced through top-down processes. Benjamin (2008) points out the practices of 'occupancy urbanism' that comprise the interstitial spaces of governance and institutional actors acting in alliance with the poor. Maringanti (2007) also asserts that *everyday actions of city state agencies, politicians and labour contractors are critical, besides the people who live in them*. This implies that the availability of a certain operational space for local government actors and other service providers at the lower level, and the thickness of their interactions and overlaps with the poor enable inclusion, albeit on highly unequal terms.

Chatterjee, in his celebrated essay *Politics of the Governed: Reflections on Popular Politics in Most of the World* (2004), elucidates the 'politics of the governed', which comprise attempts to mobilise with appeals to a larger humanitarian sensibility rather than a language of rights. Such mobilisations are then supported through patronage politics. Several others, for example de Wit (2017), have focussed on this link between the urban poor and electoral politics. Vote-bank politics has afforded conditional tolerance of certain settlements while meting out brutal evictions of others, created ungovernable instruments such as date lines, and resulted in a proliferation of schemes that perpetuate dependence on the political service provider and deny the agency of the slum dwellers. It also means that slums are invisible or even absent in all legalistic or statutory decision-making processes such as municipal budgets, development plans and so on. A radical politics that challenges the rule of *ostensibly legal politics of appropriation of the city by middle and elite classes* has not taken root yet in India, despite the increasing proportion of slums in cities.

There have been significant changes in the 'politics of the governed' in the recent past. Chatterjee (2004) questions 'whether Indian cities have become bourgeois'. There are others—Maringanti (2007), Bhide (2009)—who point out the increasing aggression in the anti-slum discourse, the spate of legislative action and some vicious eviction drives. Clearing the city of slums has taken the form of various euphemisms like 'clean city', 'world city', 'slum free city' and now 'smart city'. Each of these euphemisms carries particular import in cities, where it has been deployed by powerful groups within and outside the state to enforce measures to 'discipline' the poor and their increasing presence in the cities. These efforts have been successful in part, but have been countered as well.

Simultaneously, there is another aspect of 'change' that is aspired for and directed by forces from the ground up. Bhan (2017) points out the inter-generationality that characterises several slum settlements in major cities, which have now been embedded in 'making life in city through the slum' for more than two generations; their profiles, connection to the village, aspirations from the city and form of politics are changing. They have also engaged with the state, NGOs and other intervening actors and experienced the potentials and limitations of these, leading to a scepticism vis-à-vis these institutions. The new generation wants to engage with the city further and deepen their claims, and seeks to challenge these older forms of mobilisation. The 'statisation' of the slum has also introduced the presence of 'interested' non-resident parties in slums and created new state-slum forms such as 'resettlement colonies'—a new dynamic.

Finally, the aspect of materiality of slums linked to the status of land, particularities of land owners, recognition and form of tenure, extent and nature of service provision produce a certain texture of everyday life that defines the opportunities and vulnerabilities of the residents. These materialities are extremely situated, localised, and produce a high heterogeneity of lived experience. In Mumbai, which has over 2,959 settlements, there are some settlements where the term 'slum' is a label that defines the glass ceiling and becomes a hindrance to developments such as having individual toilets, or building higher floors and so on, while there are others that strive to be recognised as a 'slum' in order to escape the viciously disabling cycle of frequent demolitions, temporary settlement, denial of basic services and inability to access the opportunities offered by the city due to ever-present insecurity. Similarly, there is also an increasingly visible presence of the 'homeless', who are unable to stake claims to the city even through the 'slum', thereby turning the slum itself into a relatively privileged category of urban poor.

The contemporary slum in India thus has multiple, overlapping and often contrary narratives. The space of the settlement itself is one that is strategic as well as contingent, exclusionary as well as one that offers opportunities for mobility, and represents bottom-up struggles as well as larger politico-economic forces. Settlements come to be and are sustained through a city fabric, which is constituted by the crisscrossing currents and counter-currents comprising economic interests (cheap labour and informal industry), inequality, electoral democracy, pervasive political influence, and an informality endogenous to a rigid regulatory system. Evictions that dotted Indian cities right till the 1980s were instances of disruption in this delicate balance of currents. The subsequent period has seen relatively fewer evictions, the gradual incorporation of a more accepting discourse and attempts to replace slums with formal housing. These too were local efforts and highly constrained by resources, as well as subject to the balance of interests referred to earlier. The new millennium is the key turning point that shifted the discourse around cities and brought in more central government presence in cities. The Jawaharlal Nehru National Urban Renewal Mission (JNNURM) symbolised an attempt to tip the balance in favour of more ordered and formalised cities through an inflow of substantive central government funds. Reviews (Bhide 2015; Kamath 2015; Patel 2013; Venkat and Subadevan 2015) of the programme indicate that while there were indeed substantive disruptions in the lives of several settlements in the 'beneficiary' cities, changes in the governance paradigm were subtle and highly resisted (Bhide 2015; Gadgil et al. 2016). The Smart Cities programme is distinct in its approach; it intensifies the earlier trends and adds new components to governance, disciplining, surveillance and creating acquiescence to authority. The threats represented by these can deeply impact the city fabric and negate the spaces available to the poor to stake their claims to cities and the opportunities they offer.

SMART CITIES–IN THE WORLD AND IN INDIA

The concept of 'smart cities' has risen to the agenda of international urban development in recent years. The rise is reflected in the creation of new cities such as Songdo in North Korea, Masdar in Abu Dhabi, Tianjin in China, HOPE City in Ghana or new initiatives in Barcelona, Singapore and Dubai. The proponents of the smart city are information technology majors such as Cisco, IBM (International Business Machines), etc., who take it for granted that cities aspiring to 'smartness' already stand on a bedrock of basic administrative, infrastructural and informational efficiency in terms of human resource and technical hardware, as well as quality of services and built environment. 'Smartness' is thus a layer added on this foundation to prod cities towards greater 'sustainability' and 'efficiency', taking advantage of the huge leap in smart telephony and big data analytics. Smartness, however, acquires different meanings when applied to an emerging economy like India, where the base conditions are entirely different.

The IT and real estate industry are at the forefront of the proposals being presented, sensing a business opportunity of over Rs 100,000 crore. In addition, various state governments are also expected to add to the opportunity. The Ministry of Urban Development (MoUD) has prepared benchmarks/metrics spanning twelve areas for smart cities. These metrics include transport, spatial planning, water supply, sewage and sanitation, solid waste management, storm water drainage, electricity, telephone connectivity, wi-fi connectivity, fire preparedness, education, healthcare, and a few others. The parameters are defined at a fairly high level in comparison to the UDPFI (Urban Development Plans Formulation and Implementation) guidelines used for planning in Indian cities. Bhide and Burte (2015) point out that even the cities heralded as 'Number 1' on the smart city grid do not achieve these comprehensive benchmarks. These raise questions about their achievability and fund requirements. The list of benchmarks does not define a minimum, critical set of parameters that would entitle cities to be called 'smart'.

The Union Budget 2014 allocated a sum of Rs 6,275 crore (or Rs 62,750 million) towards the smart city programme. However, the quantum of funds that every eligible city would receive is not expected to be very high (about Rs 500 crore at most). The MoUD suggests a pooling of resources from varied schemes and other routes for the smart city project, which requires cities to present a financial plan along with their proposals. These suggestions include–(*i*) user charges; (*ii*) land-based taxation or sale of land; (*iii*) issue of municipal bonds, based on a credit rating system; and (*iv*) using public-private partnerships. With such pooled resources, it is estimated that the smart city project could represent a significant business opportunity.

Documents pertaining to the Smart City Mission emphasise a convergence of all urban development schemes and challenge cities to develop in such a manner that can 'act as light houses' for others. This can be interpreted as smart cities developing trajectories that can be blueprints for other parts of the city and for other Indian cities. It is from this perspective that we study the developments in these 'lighthouses' and their implications for the urban poor and informal settlements in these cities.

Smart City, Indore

Indore, the largest city and the commercial nerve centre of Madhya Pradesh (MP), with a population of 3,272,000 (Census 2011), has a tradition of strong slum mobilisations. The housing rights movement in the country was focussed on Indore in the 1990s.

These mobilisations attempted to expand their claims to the city via the development plan around 1995. This is also a state which has given *pattas* (lease tenure) to the slum dwellers since 1984, based on the MP Nagariyon Kshetra ke Bhumiheen Vyakti (Pattadhruti Adhikaron ka Pradan Kiya Jana) Adhiniyam, 1984, popularly known as the Patta Act. This Act entitles all landless persons occupying less than 50 sq. m. of land on a specified cut-off date to leasehold rights for residential use on the same land or on another site. Madhya Pradesh was also one of the first states to adopt a Housing Policy in 1981 that saw the merits of developing smaller plots for the poor, and enabling housing construction and improvement through the provision of loans.

In Indore, the gap between the overt pro-poor policy stance and actual reality unfolds at many levels. First, the data on number of slums and population in slums itself is highly contested. Table 6.1 illustrates the same.

Table 6.1: Slums and Slum Population in Indore from Multiple Sources

Source	Year	Slum population	Number of slums
Indore Municipal Corporation (IMC)	2005	900,000; 60,752 households	407 declared, 200 undeclared
Census of India	2001	259,577	
NGOs	2004		637
Pocket Poverty Situation Analysis (PPSA)	2005	176,545 households	604 total, 229 declared
Madhya Pradesh Urban Services for the Poor (MPUSP) supported IMC slum census	2009	788,619 population	592

Source: SPA (2013: 25).

Second, Table 6.1 also shows that a significant number of slums are not notified and are thus vulnerable to evictions. In terms of location, most of the slums in Indore have developed in close-to-work locations and along the river bed. Several of them are in close proximity to well-developed areas. The application of the Patta Act has been partial. In addition, Indore also has more than 120 unauthorised colonies in the city area and about 300 in the planning area. Thus, a study of the tenure pattern by the School of Planning and Architecture (SPA), Bhopal (2013) reveals that 18 per cent households have freehold rights, 10 per cent have leasehold rights, 11 per cent have *patta* rights, while over 21 per cent of the slum population have no legal rights. The same study also shows that a majority of the population does not have adequate basic services as well, with over 72 per cent of the population not having access to piped water and with one toilet seat for 520 persons. Significant tenurial security has thus not translated into better basic service provision or entitlements. A study by Participatory Research in Asia (PRIA) in 2014 of slum households in Indore reveals that 68 per cent of the households had a ration card, indicating access to the public distribution system. While 29 per cent households had a bank account and 91 per cent households were indebted, none of them had access to institutional credit.

The shift of policy towards a more market-based approach began in 1995, which retained the talk of pro-poor policy but emphasised the involvement of market-based rehabilitation for slums on high value lands and the optimal development of such lands. This has also meant that there have been successive dilutions of the Patta Act. Further, the *patta* provision has been insufficient to redress the vulnerability of the slum settlements to eviction. In 1999, for example, slums like Priyanka Gandhi Nagar, Rajiv Gandhi Nagar, Rahul Gandhi Nagar, Durgehswari Nagar, Bajrang Nagar and Choittharam Patti, which had *pattas*, were demolished for the construction of a ring road. Some settlements underwent the experience of resettlement more than twice. Further, the operation of relocation failed to follow due process (India People's Tribunal 2000).

The inclusion of Indore as one of the four smart cities in Madhya Pradesh has given a new intensity to the anti-settlement processes. The part of the city proposed for area-based development overlaps in terms of location with nearly 40 per cent of the slums in the city. In this area, several programmes with divergent agendas highly unrelated to that of settlement are converging together in the threats that they pose to settlements. The Swachh Bharat Abhiyan (SBA) is a programme that advocates sanitation in cities. In Indore, several houses in slum settlements that did not have a toilet have been demolished by agencies responsible for the Abhiyan (or movement) through the deployment of bouncers. The pursuit of convergence as a facet of smart governance has also contributed to this intensity. One instance of such convergence is the issue of Samagra cards for the poor. These cards, described as an 'all-inclusive, holistic, proactive and entitlement-based model'[2] for poor households, are instead becoming a means of exclusion. First, all identification documents, from the ration card, to Aadhaar card, to the unorganised sector worker identification card, are expected to be linked to Samagra. Further, officers issuing the cards unilaterally decide which schemes a household can avail of, and remove their names as beneficiaries from other schemes that they could also potentially benefit from. Decisions such as benefitting from the subsidised public distribution system or skill-building or loan subsidy for an enterprise are being made by government officials. Convergence thus means greater legibility of the poor and, in turn, vulnerability to practices of governmentality.

Major road-widening projects are being undertaken for the smart city, and slum settlements along these roads are consequently being cleared. The politics of these road-widening schemes is such that while the homes of people, including houses that have been in existence for nearly 100 years, and slum-cum-shop structures are being cleared, malls and commercial structures belonging to politically influential persons are left intact. More than the evictions per se, the mode and the process of contemporary evictions are of concern. The deployment of bouncers, as was done in the case of evictions linked to SBA, indicates a shift away from the legislative process. In the case of the evictions in Biyabani in the central area of the city, where more than 400 structures have been razed for road-widening, the local courts refused to hear the petition filed by residents. The High Court also shut the door on the possibility of a Public Interest Litigation (PIL). The aggrieved were instead asked to file individual writ petitions, a tedious and costly affair. The court also disposed of six writ applications, asking the litigants to claim compensation from the municipal body, without assigning a time limit for compliance.

> There is no provision for compensation. We are ready to give additional floor-area ratio, and for those who have lost their complete structure, we will construct a new building in Lodha Colony for relocation of families....For the poor who lost livelihood in the demolition drive, we will give a job to one family member in the municipal corporation.–Mayor Malini Gaud (*Hindustan Times* 2016).

None of the local politicians across the board came to the scene of eviction and remained inaccessible to appeals. Two of the conventional modes that have aided the poor settlements–judicial redress and political intervention–have thus signalled their closure in Indore at the current juncture.

Smart City, Bhubaneswar

Bhubaneswar is the capital of Odisha, a state that has a low rate of urbanisation, is rich in mineral resources and is characterised by a high level of migration to the western parts of the country. The city has multiple legacies: (*i*) legacy of ancient culture focussed around the old city; (*ii*) city planned as a new capital created in the aftermath of independence; and (*iii*) neo-city emerging around the eastern axis, with IT companies and private educational institutions. The older parts of the city, such as those around the Lingaraj temple and the Master Canteen, are hubs of informality, with several vendors, small businesses and para-transit operators. The planned city is largely characterised by administrative buildings and residential uses. The roads here are wide (internal roads are more than 40 m.) and are the most serviced part of the city. The rapidly growing peripheries epitomise two kinds of development–slums and informal developments–that have clustered around previous relocations carried out by the city, and new institutional and industrial developments. The low density of the city and the fairly moderate rate of growth have meant that the city has been able to respond to conflicting demands on land through the maintenance of spatial distinction without major conflicts.

The proportion of slums in the city, fairly low to begin with, has increased gradually, and the 1999 super cyclone has been a major contributor to the same. A survey by the Bhubaneswar Municipal Corporation (BMC) after the cyclone identified 190 slums (an increase by nearly two times), of which fifty-nine were located on own land or government land, while 131 were in the nature of encroachments. As per the profile prepared by BMC in 2008, there were 377 slums in the city, of which ninety-nine were authorised (Rout 2008: 60). The proportion of people staying in slums is highly contested. Non-governmental organisations like Ruchika claimed that over 40 per cent of the population stayed in 486 slums (ibid.). The largest slums in the city are Saliyasahi and Dumduma, which have populations of over 20,000. One of the other critical issues in the city is the definition of slum itself. Several of these settlements were small revenue villages where people continue to hold land for generations, and such areas have absorbed the brunt of new migrations by the poor and become large slums. Some include relocations done in the past. In both these situations, a fair number of people actually possess a *patta*. It is the quality of housing, services and overall poverty that qualifies them as 'slums'. USAID (2012) reports that over a third of the slums are not serviced by water, in spite of the fact that the city receives more than double its requirement of water. In the central area of the city, slums resemble 'encroachments' on public lands, but they are usually small in size. The Odisha Municipalities Act 2003 provides for ongoing registration and issue of identity cards to slum dwellers, the provision of basic minimum services as an entitlement to all slum dwellers irrespective of land tenure, the entitlement to schemes of special assistance or welfare, including health, education, financial services, prohibition of child labour, and integration into the master plan. The fact that only ninety-nine slums are authorised is thus reflective of the state government's neglect of these issues, and the level of basic amenities even in these authorised slums is extremely poor.

In spite of the spatial distinction afforded by the large land mass of the city and the low proportions of land under slums, Odisha since 2005 has faithfully followed central government initiatives and has unleashed an agenda of relocation and building *pucca* houses for slum dwellers. Under the JNNURM, the state government undertook drainage and sewage works in the city, which affected slums and relocated some of them in housing projects under the same mission. The transport projects undertaken in the name of public transport adversely impacted auto-rickshaw operators.

The smart city project has only intensified these trends that have been unleashed since 2005. The project for area-based development involves 985 acres around the station area, including the Master Canteen and the Lingaraj temple. The stated objective of this area-based development is 'to create a well-connected, walkable, mixed use area with visible public realm investments, low carbon neutral development through innovations in transport and green infrastructure, child friendly, support pro-business environment' (Bhubaneswar Smart Cities Plan 2011, submitted by Government of Odisha to Ministry of Urban Development). It is evident that these plans do not have place for the small businesses, vendors and slum settlements that crowd the area. Nilmadhav *bustee*, a small slum in the area, has faced the heat; more than 840 houses have been demolished to make way for a 100 ft. road. The families in the slum had been living there for the past fifteen years and been served notices several times. Dwellers of the slums who lost their homes were paid six months' rent for new accommodation. 'We paid Rs 25,000 to each family, which includes Rs 10,000 for buying utensils and blankets and Rs 15,000 house rent for the next six months,' Sumant Mishra, Deputy Commissioner of Bhubaneswar Municipal Corporation, said at the end of the two-day demolition at Nilmadhav *bustee* (*The Indian Express* 2016). This represents a huge change from the earlier practice of providing alternate accommodation. The dwellers, some of whose houses were *pucca* and built through the earlier Rajiv Awas Yojana barely six years ago, were given a promise of alternate accommodation within six months and the compensation mentioned above. But the residents will have to pay 20 per cent of the cost of the new houses. Each of the components of demolition and re-housing thus seems to have been broken up into separate compartments, reduced to a hands-off involvement as much as possible, and separated in time. Uncertainty around home and living and livelihoods has been equated to cash compensation, through which the state government has washed its hands of sticky issues such as transit accommodation, court cases, and so on. Meanwhile, new transit projects such as city buses threaten the livelihood of auto- and cycle-rickshaw operators, while tourism projects threaten the presence of street vendors.

READING THE CONTEMPORARY DIRECTIONS OF CHANGE

Elites in Indian cities have always been opposed to the existence of 'the poor, the dirty, the insanitary', who are lumped together under the labels of 'illegal, unauthorised, encroachers'. There have been periodic drives against slums, vendors, and other segments of the urban poor in several cities. In parallel, a discourse on slums and informal settlements as housing solutions, and human rights around housing and livelihood grew, and spread through electoral and political routes, and increasingly came to define the policy space towards the turn of the millennium. This was in keeping with the evolution of an international discourse as well, and was reflected in the institution of a slum census in 2001 and initiatives that showed some appreciation for the living and working conditions of the urban poor. The unravelling of this emergent progressive strand of discourse has been almost simultaneous.

In Indore and Bhubaneswar, several changes in governmentality can be seen. The first is the enhanced space given to consultants in local governance. Consultants, by becoming a repository of 'how to do things', including writing proposals, making presentations, eliciting central government and private funding, and evaluating are bringing significant changes in the knowledge and skill base of municipal bodies. They are also becoming the key mediators in inter-governmental relationships. Several of these roles were earlier played by political actors. Political space is thus being reduced.

It has been observed that local politics in Indian cities is seeking rents and gains outside the 'system' (de Wit 2017), and often sanctions 'unruliness' (Kabeer 2000). In Indore, local politics applied 'unruliness' against its own clientele by using bouncers for evictions, suggesting a conjunctural convergence of a right-ward tilt in city politics, discretionary exclusions from welfare schemes in the name of convergence and governance outsourced to private agencies. In Bhubaneswar, there is no evidence of unruliness, but it is a state where local political space has been rendered weak over a period (Bhide 2015). Here, too, new 'hands-off' modes of governing slums, such as giving 'cash compensation' or 'rent in advance', are being experimented with, as opposed to the sticky and tricky terrain of resettlement housing. Given that informal settlements have been able to stake claims to the city largely through a political process, these changes have significant implications for their modes of claim-making and prospects.

Deeper changes in the local state-citizen relationship that can be delineated include ideas or visions of cities, conceptualising governance along corporate customer-service relations, privileging a few infrastructure development pathways and projectified thinking. Consultants, by their very nature, also circulate ideas and 'success stories', and themselves play multiple roles in multiple cities and thereby produce a more homogenised field of local governance. The urban question in this condition is muted to a conflict of interest rather than a structural conflict, and is managed accordingly. It is issues such as these that point to a process of constructing a 'smartmentality' that is underway. Vanolo (2014) deploys the term to describe the process by which new docile subjects and a regime of 'post-politics' (Swyngedouw 2007) is sought to be created in Italian cities by diffusing the public-private divide, recasting the concept of citizens and creating a technocratic language of governance. The case of how the smart city agenda is unfolding in Indore and Bhubaneswar reveals an attempt to recast politics, but even more importantly, it seeks to delegitimise 'poor' citizens for staying where they do, for not having toilets or for practising their livelihoods on the street in 'unmanageable' numbers. This is a punitive dimension of the 'smartmentality' that exacerbates other direct and indirect threats that informal settlements face as the Smart Cities Mission (SCM) progresses. Another feature of this delegitimation is the seeming closure of several channels that provided a voice to the informal settlers. The real threat is, however, that the changes underway in smart cities such as Indore and Bhubaneswar could stretch beyond the cities selected by the SCM, expected as they are to be 'lighthouses' for others.

CONCLUSION

The Smart Cities project gave an impression of being ambiguous (Hoelscher 2016) at its inception, its vision of a smart city being splintered. Several critics voiced their apprehensions of exclusions that the programme would generate, for example, its privileging of the technical versus the human (Mehrotra, as quoted in *Live Mint* 2015), inability to work its way around the larger challenge of urbanisation (Bhide and Burte 2015; Roy 2016), the intensification of the already existing spatial segregation (Dupont 2015), and the superficiality of participation (Aijaz and Hoelscher 2015).

A closer examination of the smart cities programme as it unfolds indicates that the changes unleashed are not confined to displacement alone. This chapter argues that the current path of 'smartmentality' comprises a new determination to discipline the 'undisciplined' informal settlements and subalterns through punitive means and a recasting of the political. The reach of changes is much larger and an entire way of life, of settlement and of urbanisation is sought to be changed, posing threats to the sheer modes by which settlements could survive and develop in cities.

END NOTES

1. Such a twin-track path to dealing with the issue of slums has been recommended by Geoffrey Payne (2003).
2. This is the description of the Samagra cards on the Madhya Pradesh government portal. See samagra.gov.in.

References

Aijaz, R. and K. Hoelscher. 2015. 'India's Smart Cities Mission: An Assessment', ORF Issue Brief December (124). New Delhi: Observer Researcher Foundation.

Benjamin, S. 2008. 'Occupancy Urbanism: Radicalizing Politics and Economy beyond Policy and Programmes'. *International Journal of Urban and Regional Research* 32(3): 719–729.

Bhan, G. 2017. 'From the basti to the house: Socio-spatial readings of housing policy in India'. *Current Sociology* 65(2).

Bhide, A. 2009. 'Shifting Terrains of Communities and Community Organization: Reflections on Organizing for Housing Rights in Mumbai'. *Community Development Journal* 44(3): 367–381.

______. 2015. 'Governance and Infrastructure Transformations via JNNURM in Bhubaneswar', Research report. Mumbai: Tata Institute of Social Sciences.

Bhide, A. and H. Burte. 2015. 'Smarter urbanisation, not (just) smart cities', NCAS discussion paper 1. Pune: National Centre for Advocacy Studies.

Bhide, A. and M. Spies. 2013. 'Dharavi ground up: Dweller focused design tool for upgrading living space in Dharavi, Mumbai', Project report 184. Development Commission of Austrian Academy of Sciences.

Chatterjee, P. 2004. *Politics of the Governed: Reflections on Popular Politics in Most of the World*. New Delhi: Permanent Black.

de Wit, J. 2017. *Urban Poverty, Local Governance and Everyday Politics in Mumbai*. New Delhi: Routledge, South Asia edition.

Dupont, V. 2015. 'Secured residential enclaves in the Delhi region: Impact of indigenous and transnational models'. *City, Culture and Society* 7(4).

Gadgil, R., S. Vernekar and A. Madhale. 2016. 'Impact of JNNURM on governance in Pune', Research report. Mumbai: Tata Institute of Social Sciences.

Hindustan Times. 2016. 'Houses go down in Indore to make way for a smart city', 14 April. Available at https://www.hindustantimes.com/indore/houses-go-down-in-indore-to-make-way-for-a-smart-city/story-ks0SiaIeFwVss1jfxvSfXK.html (accessed June 2021).

Hoelscher, K. 2016. 'The evolution of the smart city agenda in India'. *International Area Studies Review* 19(1): 28–44.

India People's Tribunal. 2000. 'Hunted, hounded and homeless in Indore: A report on large scale forced evictions'. Mumbai: Indian People's Tribunal on Environment and Human Rights.

Live Mint. 2015. 'I have no idea what a smart city means: Rahul Mehrotra', 22 August. Available at http://www.livemint.com/Politics/VFwRPtdqCtg6lyBeacEfZI/I-have-no-idea-what-a-smart-city-means-Rahul-Mehrotra.html (accessed February 2021).

Kabeer, N. 2000. 'Social Exclusion Poverty and Discrimination: An Analytical Framework'. *IDS Bulletin* 31(4): 83–97.

Kamath, L. 2015. 'Narrative report on Impact of Infrastructure and Governance Transformations of JNNURM in large, medium and small cities', Research report. Mumbai: Tata Institute of Social Sciences.

Maringanti, A. 2007. *Neoliberal Inscriptions and Contestations in Hyderabad*. Minneapolis: University of Minnesota Press.

Patel, S. 2013. 'Upgrade, Rehouse or Resettle: An Assessment of the Indian Government's Basic Services for Urban Poor (BSUP) Programme'. *Environment and Urbanisation* 25(1): 177–188.

Payne, G. 2003. 'Getting ahead of the game: A twin track approach to improving existing slums and reducing the need for future slums', Paper presented at Second Urban Research Symposium. Washington D.C.: World Bank.

Participatory Research in Asia (PRIA). 2014. 'Government led Exclusion of the Urban Poor: Indore and Bhopal Study Report'. New Delhi: PRIA.

Rout, N. 2008. 'Slum Growth in Bhubaneswar: Problem or Solution?' *ITPI Journal* 5(4): 59–64.

Roy, S. 2016. 'The Smart City paradigm in India: Issues and challenges of sustainability and inclusiveness'. *Social Scientist* 44(5 and 6): 29–48.

School of Planning and Architecture (SPA). 2013. *Implementing Security of Tenure and Housing Improvement Policies: A Case of Indore and Jaipur*. New Delhi: School of Planning and Architecture.

Swyngedouw, E. 2007. 'Impossible "sustainability" and the postpolitical condition'. In R. Krueger and D. Gibbs (eds), *The Sustainable Development Paradox: Urban Political Economy in the United States and Europe*, 13–40. New York and London: The Guilford Press.

The Indian Express. 2016. 'Demolition deal in Bhubaneswar: monthly rent now, new homes later', 5 January. Available at https://indianexpress.com/article/india/india-news-india/demolition-deal-in-bhubaneswar-monthly-rent-now-new-homes-later/ (accessed June 2021).

Tata Institute of Social Sciences (TISS). 2014. *A Study of Socio-Economic Vulnerabilities in M(East) Ward, Mumbai*. Mumbai: Tata Institute of Social Sciences.

USAID. 2012. *WASH (Water, Sanitation and Hygiene Programme): Facts and Factors*. Bhubaneswar.

Vanolo, A. 2014. 'Smartmentality: The Smart city as disciplinary strategy'. *Urban Studies* 51(5): 883–898.

Venkat, T. and M. Subadevan. 2015. 'Implementation of JNNURM/ BSUP in Chennai', Research Report. Mumbai: Tata Institute of Social Sciences.

VII

Urban-Poor Housing Development in Asia

From Target Group to Negotiating Partner

Somsook Boonyabancha and Thomas Andrew Kerr

INTRODUCTION

During the 1970s and 1980s, when urbanisation was gathering steam in Asia, some very interesting and leading housing development programmes and policies were developed by different governments, such as the public housing programmes in Singapore and Hong Kong, the Kampung Improvement Programme (KIP) in Indonesia, the Million Houses Programme in Sri Lanka, and the Tondo Foreshore Project and Housing Development in the Philippines. Some of these housing development models were on a city-wide and country-wide scale and have immensely influenced the direction of housing development undertaken by governments in many Asian countries. However, from the mid-1980s onwards, in response to economic changes, the role played by the government and public sector in housing has diminished, and an increasing role has been given to the private sector or the market. Meanwhile, more and more people—many of them poor—have been pulled into cities, where they cannot find housing they can afford. The absence of policies and appropriate support systems from the government sector to respond to this influx and the consequent need for housing caused the emergence of a large number of slums, squatter settlements, pavement settlements and cheap small rental rooms—all without proper infrastructure. Many of these low-income settlements also found themselves targeted for eviction. Cities like Mumbai, Jakarta, New Delhi, Dhaka, Manila and Karachi now have 30–60 per cent of their populations living in these informal, illegal settlements.

Housing Development: Still a Large Gap between the Government and the Urban Poor in Asia

Today, Asia's cities are in the midst of a long period of explosive physical and economic growth and urbanisation. But with this growth comes many big problems—problems of poverty, inequality, unaffordable housing, slums, deteriorating urban environments and failure to adapt to the changing climate. The existing formal systems of development are not working, and are unable to keep up with the real substance, scale and pace of change in Asian countries. Many Asian countries have insufficient policies and mechanisms to address these issues, or they address them in the conventional government-led ways, or they just allow the market to deal with housing supply, even though the market does not reach large numbers of the poor and causes more evictions. At the same time, there is insufficient knowledge about people's own survival systems and almost no policies, mechanisms or resources available to poor people on the ground to give them the opportunity to make changes by themselves. Most international development agencies, national government institutions and conventional development agencies operate within a culture of agency-led development with considerable rigidity in the planning process, budget systems and organisational structures. This development culture is at cross-purposes with the realities of the urban poor and the dynamism of our fast-changing societies.

People's Solutions

There is another direction of development, however, and it has long been led by the urban poor themselves, who have built most of Asia's existing housing supply for the poor, and done so on a scale, and in ways that may be imperfect, but are realistic, affordable, appropriate and reasonable. In our changing and democratising world, poor people on the ground should have the same space and opportunities as everyone else to determine what they need and to bring change in their own lives and living environments, so they can live decently, as full citizens.

Even in situations of poverty and illegality, with no land or housing provided for them, most of the poor manage to survive, nourish themselves, build houses, educate and bring up their families, without much support from anyone. The poor are already the creators and builders of the most large-scale solutions to problems of poverty, housing and service delivery in Asian cities. These solutions are a long way from perfect—they are mostly informal and illegal, and can be exploitative, inequitable and substandard. But they represent the best people can do with extremely limited resources, in response to urgent necessities, where no 'legal' alternatives exist.

If these poor communities themselves could be supported to become the key actors in solving problems of poverty, housing and infrastructure, we could reach the real scale of the solution that is needed. The scale of the solutions should emanate from the scale of the problems. This is why the mechanisms by which poor people build housing and create communities need to be understood and promoted, so that this huge people's mechanism can work with better knowledge, strength and organisation, and become a new direction of development. This people's mechanism can not only meet the physical needs of housing and basic services, but can also achieve better social and economic status for the poor in their cities.

The development of people's solutions to poverty and housing problems at scale in Asia has become more noticeable since the 1980s. In the early stages, Asia's housing activism movement mostly focussed on housing rights and dealing with eviction problems. There were some scattered housing projects here and there, which began to show solutions, but most of this early activism was reactive, confrontational, and rights-based or welfare-based. Later on, more and more alternatives in people-driven development were experimented with and developed, alongside a growing understanding of people's processes and the expansion of people's own organisations. Some key organisations that have pioneered some of Asia's people-driven development models since the 1980s are: the Orangi Pilot Project (OPP) in Pakistan, the women's savings programme of the Mahila Milan supported by the Society for the Promotion of Area Resource Centres (SPARC) in India, Women's Bank in Sri Lanka, land sharing and community development funds by the Community Organisations Development Institute (CODI) in Thailand and the Community Mortgage Programme (CMP) in the Philippines.

The large-scale people-led development movements in Asia have emerged and been well-linked due in part to several interventions, including the regular information that has been disseminated since 1986, with emphasis on people's process, by Father Jorge Anzorena and his SELAVIP newsletter, the support from understanding donors such as MISEREOR and the role of the regional network of the Asian Coalition for Housing Rights (ACHR).

The ACHR was established in 1988 to build a regional platform to share knowledge and to support activities among the key active groups working on the issue of urban-poor housing in countries around the Asia region. ACHR's key activities have been its regional Training and Advisory Programme (TAP), community-to-community exchanges, support for the development of community-based organisations, support for the setting up and strengthening of community savings and funds, support for community architects, and the more recent Asian Coalition for Community Action (ACCA) Programme, which has supported a process of city-wide upgrading in 215 cities in Asia since 2009. Since it was set up, ACHR has facilitated an ongoing and intensive programme of exchange visits and knowledge-sharing among community groups, community workers, professionals, city actors and government officers across cities and countries, as well as workshops, trainings and meetings across countries in the region. ACHR has also supported development activities by communities and the transfer of knowledge horizontally to a wide range of groups in the Asia region, and has initiated and supported a range of community-driven development activities. As a result, there has been an energetic interaction between active groups in Asia in a process of joint learning, joint support, joint implementation, transfer of knowledge and policy advocacy across the region.

All this work in Asia has led to a growing body of experience and examples of how Asia's big problems of urban-poor housing can be solved, in different ways and in different contexts. After three decades of growth and support, Asia's urban-poor groups have transformed themselves into large-scale community organisations and networks, have made significant achievements in developing new and creative ways to solve their poverty and housing problems at scale, and have forged new working alliances with their local governments in the process. For example:

1. **Community organisations and networks** are now active in cities and towns in nineteen Asian countries;
2. **Savings groups**: There are 75,000 community-based savings groups in Asia, with 1.5 million members (mostly women) and collective savings of about US$ 200 million;
3. **City Development Funds**: City-based development funds (CDFs) are now active in about 400 cities in fifteen countries, with national CDFs now active in seven countries;
4. **New partnerships and new politics**: Community groups in hundreds of cities have forged close working partnerships with their local governments and other local stakeholders.

CHANGES IN POLITICAL RELATIONSHIP TO BRING CHANGES TO HOUSING SOLUTIONS FOR THE POOR

Housing and poverty are highly political issues. Solving the problems of housing and poverty in our cities requires changes in the political relationships between the poor, the government and the broader systems they exist within. Housing is not just a technical or construction issue, as it is generally considered, with a solution that is technical. Equitable housing development requires:

1. **Availability of land**, but much of the land in Asian cities is controlled by the government, or is too expensive for the poor to buy from the market;

2. **Affordability**, but the poor, whose earnings in the informal economy are low, irregular and insecure, cannot connect to formal finance systems or access loans;
3. **Building standards**, regulations and procedures exist, but they place housing beyond the reach of the poor;
4. **Acceptance of the urban poor as legitimate citizens in their cities**, with registration and legal status, which the majority of the urban poor lack.

Most of the problems being faced by the poor today are the direct product of the powerful underlying structures which produce poverty and inequity in our societies in the first place: the structures which determine land ownership and land use, the financial structures, the governance structures, the economic development and resource allocation structures. These serious problems in the larger system are bringing more and more people into poverty, in both urban and rural areas. So, if the poor are powerless, invisible, illegal, fragmented and totally under the control of the formal system, it will be difficult and beyond their means to make these structural issues work in their favour. Therefore, housing development for the poor will only be possible if there is a change in power to negotiate and to shift the political relationship between the powerless poor and the powerful formal system and the market.

We can understand why the people's process is important only if we understand these power relationships. Otherwise, we will see the people's process in the shallowest way—only as people's participation in somebody else's programme, something predetermined by the development plan, which obliges the poor to follow the plans and accept them obediently. But it is important to cultivate a sense of changing politics, of how the power of the people, their power and freedom as human beings can be strengthened, and can shift the way the system determines how things happen in our cities.

The following are contributing to this change in power relationships in Asian cities:

1. **Community organisation and networking** breaks the isolation and powerlessness inherent in poverty by linking

the poor to work together as communities and in larger groupings, support each other and develop a stronger negotiating power as a group;

2. **Community-managed finance**: Developing community-managed savings and finance systems is a way to support community-driven housing and livelihood development. This is something quite different from micro-credit, which is a purely technical means of making finance accessible to poor borrowers as individuals. Micro-finance entails no shift in power. But with community savings, there is a shift in power because the community owns the financial resources and has the power to decide how to use them;
3. **Community-driven housing development**: A variety of housing projects that address the enormous needs in different ways, and different land tenure, financing, layout design and construction options are the possible solutions now developing at scale in Asia;
4. **City-wide information**: Getting information from city-wide surveys and mapping in which the poor are the survey leaders, so that they become visible and understand their situation and understand the structural factors that cause their lives and settlements to be considered illegal;
5. **Partnerships**: Issues like housing and land are not something the poor can solve alone, nor can they be solved by the local governments or NGOs in the cities where they live. It takes partnership, co-ordination and co-operation, and building of alliances to do it, and that is happening more and more in Asian cities;
6. **Constant learning and sharing**, through active horizontal experience-sharing, community-to-community visits, network-building and alliance-building;
7. **City-wide scale and country-wide solutions**: Only by working at scale and moving beyond the old emphasis on individual projects and pilots that never scale up can city-wide and country-wide solutions become possible.

SAVINGS AND COMMUNITY FINANCE: TOOLS TO BRING PEOPLE TOGETHER AND BUILD THEIR OWN FINANCIAL RESOURCES

Community savings and credit and development funds are forms of finance that start from the ground, from people's own resources. Even if it starts very modestly, this kind of finance system within poor communities has the power to gather people together and allow them to start doing things, because it is finance that they manage themselves. This is a bottom-up financial development system, and it begins with the simple rituals of collective saving within the communities. The saving amounts might be small, but it means their development has started and that they are part of a collective process, part of a search to find ways to bring about change. Community savings and credit activities gather scattered and vulnerable urban poor together, build their financial management capacity, build their collective social strength and build their belief that they can make changes to their lives together.

More than just Access to Credit

Community savings and funds are mechanisms by which poor communities are developing control over their own internal resources and planning how to match those resources with outside development resources, as a group, not individually, since the poor are weak individually. Saving is the process in which poor community people are the owners: they set the rules, make the decisions about how to use the resources to do what they think is important. *Community savings is democracy in practice.* It is a democracy that ordinary people on the ground can be a part of. For, nothing clearly divides the empowered and the powerless as control over money for their development.

Community savings and credit is the first layer. Then all the community savings groups in a city link together and help build the second layer, which is the larger city development fund (CDF). The job of the CDF is to link and support the small savings groups and to pump additional resources and capacity into the people's finance system (through loans or grants, and with a certain direction), which is now prepared and ready to handle them. This extra-financial resource in the CDF greatly expands people's financial space and capacity to create, to develop and to negotiate. It allows them to speed up and scale up their problem-solving initiatives and to push beyond the limited capacity of their internal savings. Most CDFs are managed by community networks, with some kind of collaboration with local governments and NGOs. CDFs are now active in around 400 cities in about fifteen Asian countries.

Community savings and funds function like financial institutions of the poor. In the absence of appropriate and people-friendly financial mechanisms and services for the poor, a system of community savings groups and funds is extremely important. It can function as a community financial mechanism or bank for the urban poor, which can help bridge the informal urban poor's financial systems with the formal and government systems. When poor communities have access to finance for development, they can solve their various problems quickly, directly, simply and easily. These community funds allow poor communities to expand their financial parameters, which implies a much broader scope and possibilities for development by poor families or communities. When even very small development funds go into the hands of poor communities, those funds can be used flexibly and strategically to finance people's development needs, to leverage external resources and to cultivate partnerships and collaborations that they could never have developed without resources in their hands. The CDF is also an important transitional financial development mechanism that links with the more serious bigger money in the formal system with better negotiated terms and relationships.

Community savings are more than just a convenient source of low-interest credit to the poor. Community-managed savings and credit is a key ingredient in poor people's struggle towards better lives, better incomes, more secure housing, more healthy settlements and greater participation in the city's development. With savings and credit at the core of the process, communities have money, people and power.

Community Savings and Funds Movement in Asia

In the past two decades, the community savings process in Asia has grown from a few scattered experiments into a very large movement that now has a life of its own. Community savings and funds are a kind of revolution among poor people, who are eager to bring about a change in their lives and settlements, and view control over finance as a way to own that change process and start it right away.

In Sri Lanka, the Women's Coop (formerly called Women's Bank) links community savings groups all over the country and supports a variety of community development activities, including housing, from the basic unit of the small savings group of fifteen–twenty women to the branch, the city, the regional and the national level. Women's Coop is similar to the Women's Savings Co-operative movement in Nepal, which has developed at the community, city and national levels. The groups in these two countries have found ways to formalise their community savings and funds as registered cooperatives, which provide them with an accepted legal structure that allows them to function legally, like a community bank. In Thailand, however, where community savings and city development funds have developed throughout the country in more than 300 cities, this community finance movement is accepted, but there is still no strict legal structure to formalise it. A similar situation exists in Cambodia, the Philippines, Lao PDR and Mongolia, where community-driven finance systems and development projects now cover many cities, but these people's systems are still without any formal legal structure.

Once these people-managed financial structures start developing within communities and within networks of communities in a city, a little external finance can be an important tool to allow the people to think bigger. The small, flexible finance support from the ACCA programme in city-wide upgrading, given directly to communities, helps groups to do this by allowing community upgrading activities in a city to start right away. If communities and their support organisations manage those small funds wisely, they can not only fund the first round of upgrading projects, but can also seed and grow new alternative financial systems to finance more community projects and become magnets for funds from other sources. The ACCA programme's support for the first housing project in the city channels the finance in such a way that it seeds the city CDF, which then gives loans to that first housing project. As a result, more than 150 community housing projects have been implemented and more than 150 city development funds have been set up. And the seed funds from ACCA have increased to more than six times the size of original grants.

In the city-wide and nation-wide community upgrading being supported in Thailand by the CODI, through its Baan Mankong (Secure Housing) programme, city development funds have been used as a key community-driven development tool and mechanism in some 100 cities. In Thailand, all urban poor communities are encouraged to organise community savings and fund activities. And if they want to access housing and land loans from CODI, community savings is compulsory: 'no savings, no housing'. These community-managed financial mechanisms, which function at both community and city levels, help to prepare urban poor communities for their housing development projects. Grants and loans from the Baan Mankong programme can then be channelled to this community finance mechanism for their collective housing development. The key to making it possible for the urban poor to make large-scale change themselves is to develop the financial management capacity of urban-poor community organisations, and to channel financial resources, either as grants or loans, directly to those collective mechanisms.

CHANGING FROM THE INVISIBLE POOR TO AN ACTIVE MAJORITY

Most national and city governments do not have information about the poor, and as a result, the poor are routinely excluded from many aspects of development in cities. It is important to reach out to all the poor in the city by conducting city-wide surveys, to understand the scale and quality of problems. Later, a more comprehensive socio-economic enumeration of all the individual settlements can be organised.

Reaching Out to all the Poor by Gathering City-wide Information

In many cities, the surveyed slums have all been mapped. Some surveys have also gathered land ownership information about potential land for housing, and about formal development plans which may affect existing informal communities in the future. A city-wide survey will generate information which links all the poor in the city and puts them on the city map, so that all the urban poor groups—who had been invisible and informal—will appear, will be numbered and each household will be counted. Community survey and mapping is, in fact, a simple way to register all the poor, to make every poor person in a city visible and to start to link all of them into a joint community development process.

Mapping works as a catalysing process. The city-wide slum mapping process does not only mean marking the existing houses and settlement boundaries. It should also be a process which gets all the people in those communities to come together to participate, to start talking about their communities and what they need to fix, and to start their upgrading plans.

Building Community Organisations and Networking

Community organisations can be built through the implementation of all sorts of development activities: community savings, community planning, land negotiations, youth groups, elderly groups, education and day care activities. Any issue can be the subject of discussion among concerned people, groups can be formed to work together to deal with that issue and to link it to the larger community organisation. Community organisation is a basic platform that links all the poor and scattered groups to meet, discuss, plan and work together. No development can be possible without community organisation.

The next step is bringing these scattered communities in a city together to form networks, as well as alliances of existing community federations and associations, to build a platform for sharing and supporting each other and setting a common city-wide development agenda for the poor. A community network is the key development mechanism to enable invisible, marginalised groups of the urban poor to become part of a big collection of communities, which in turn can become a major active citizen group. There can be many dimensions to community networks, which can link communities living in the same area, or around issues common to a group of communities (like eviction or a common landlord or tenure situation), or on the basis of particular joint activities (like housing projects or urban farming). Several community networks can then even link and grow into a bigger network, as national or international networks or federations.

Why networks? As a platform for large-scale development which involves a synergy of learning, experience-sharing, morale-boosting and mutual inspiration, community networks have given Asia's poor people's movements enormous confidence and created a large development mechanism which belongs to them.

1. Networks build collective capacities at scale in poor communities, and enable them to deal with many of the big structural issues which make them poor and marginalised in the first place.
2. Networks are learning platforms which allow people to learn from each other and to transform the experience of a few communities into learning for hundreds, based on real action and in a shared belief in community-driven processes for structural change.
3. Networks open up community processes by creating more space for more people from more places, with different kinds of skills, to involve themselves in varied activities.
4. Networks are horizontal support systems for people's processes, exchange of ideas and mutual help. Networks also bolster an individual community's negotiating power.
5. Networks work as bridges with the formal system, helping poor communities to work with their cities and other stakeholders and initiate collaborations in city, province and country-wide development projects that affect the poor.

6. Networks work as a horizontal checks-and-balances mechanism in the people's movement to resolve problems and conflicts and sustain a balanced outcome, to monitor and to provide scrutiny. It becomes a vital mechanism of balance, diffusing tensions and resolving problem situations.

Community networking is the glue that holds together Asia's community movement: In most development work, different groups work individually, and different communities have no links with each other, only with the NGOs or the governments who manage these issues vertically. When people are scattered like that, they have no voice or strength. It is a question of micro- and macro-scales. A network can negotiate on a macro-scale, on behalf of a community, for benefits that an individual community may be unable to obtain. And when the big numbers that come with a community network are backed up with finance and support, that network can begin negotiating with the stakeholders in the city and bring their development ideas to the bargaining table–whether that involves cleaning a canal, relocating a slum or solving the city's garbage problems.

In the network model, individual communities are the smallest structural unit and represent the most local constituency. But once they link together into networks at city, provincial, regional or national levels, they become a people's political force. Networks are a powerful mechanism for dealing with housing issues at more structural layers. For example, hundreds of informal communities on State Railway Authority land in Thailand have formed a national network of railway communities, and this national network has successfully negotiated alternatives to eviction, secured long-term leases for many railway settlements and developed a productive working relationship with the railway authorities.

City-wide Thinking, City-wide Action

It is necessary to make community upgrading a proactive part of city politics. The best way to do that is to work on a city-wide scale. That is the scale necessary to bring about changes in the deeper political and structural problems that lead to poverty, eviction and social exclusion. It is important to link development projects and initiatives into a city-wide whole, so that people can view their communities and their reality in a larger city context, and in relation to the city's larger structures. Once the whole picture is put together, people understand where they fit into that overall picture of their city. They will gradually understand the broader situation of poverty and the reasons behind it. This more structural understanding of their city helps poor community people to break out of their isolation and powerlessness, and to see their problems as being related to other communities in the city. Their problems are not isolated at all, but interlinked and related with the city development structures as a whole.

It is important to pull people slightly out of themselves, to understand the scale and causes of things they are involved in. While they can still concentrate and work on their own problems, they will also understand the relationship of their problems with others in the city. With this understanding, they then realise the need for friends, allies, helpers and partners. Each community is a representative of a particular structural problem of the whole city. This understanding enhances their struggle and elevates it to the level of a more structural problem of the city. Suddenly, it brings some dignity into their fight, something grander than 'my personal needs and my community'.

BUILDING LOCAL PARTNERSHIPS FOR COLLABORATIVE HOUSING AND CITY DEVELOPMENT

When large-scale community processes become active and take off with various development possibilities, it is important for the communities to be more involved in regular decision-making and co-ordination. With city-wide upgrading at scale in action led by communities, it is natural and easy to play a more proactive and constructive politics of building local partnerships with city government agencies and other local development actors.

Building Partnerships and Getting City Acceptance and Support as Development Partners

This changes the status of the poor in a city and makes them a more equal stakeholder: a part of the city process as partners in development. This transformation from victims of urban development to full partners in such development has been the high point of strategic change in the past decade in Asia's urban-poor housing movement. It also represents a big change from the past, when housing projects were few and scattered, when upgrading was done on a project-by-project basis, and each eviction was dealt with on an *ad hoc* basis. The direction and politics have changed, and that change has happened mostly in places where the poor have become key participants in their cities' development, and where their organisations and projects have earned them legitimacy and improved status as full citizens.

The problems of land, housing and poverty are far too big for city or national governments to solve alone. But if all the stakeholders in a city can become active development partners and work together as unified, problem-solving teams, these big problems can be solved. Joint city development committees are being set up, and these partnerships and joint committees are becoming important new structural platforms that allow poor communities to work with their local governments and other urban partners. The process of jointly planning and implementing real projects together is the most immediate way to begin changing power relations in a city.

Every city can solve its own city-wide housing development problems if it works together with the people. City governments invariably complain that they do not have enough power, land, budget or the right policies, and it is not their job anyway. But most city governments do have funds and scattered programmes and activities. In fact, it is possible for cities to solve these problems within their own constituency with the power and resources they already have; if they work with the people, development agencies and private sectors, large-scale implementation is possible and doable. Land can be sought out and negotiated; the city plan can be organised to help open up new land and to better negotiate;

infrastructure can be developed; a livelihood programme can be organised; and rights to all citizens can be granted. Large-scale comprehensive solutions can be effectively organised at the city level, city-by-city, with the help of the new joint process between cities and the urban poor on a city-wide scale.

CONCRETE ACTION BY COMMUNITIES TO LEAD CHANGE

Instead of being the victims of development or waiting passively for someone else to do something for them, poor communities are showing that they can take concrete action to solve their problems, especially if there is direct funding support for them. When people start doing things themselves, moving forward and determining what they need and what they can do to address those needs, they are shedding that passivity and changing the way things work in their cities. And if many activities are taking place at the same time, not in just one community but in several, there is a new learning and a new political vibrancy. As a result, governments cannot avoid coming to a new positive perception of the poor and engaging with them. When people begin showing their local governments that community-led change is possible, then little by little, they begin to unlock resources that are lying in their cities and bring those resources into an active process. This is the people-led politics of change.

Turning People Who Wait into People Who Do

In these ways, besides solving some immediate problems, communities are woken up and activated through the projects they plan and implement themselves, no matter what the size. These projects change communities: from being groups that wait for someone else to bring them development, they become people who deliver benefits themselves, determine their own needs and resolve them right away. Once a community builds a walkway or a communal toilet, they invariably start thinking–What next? The implementation of small upgrading projects also acts as a chess piece in a community's negotiation with their cities and with the larger development forces. Many communities may prefer to plan and construct their small improvement projects without asking for anybody's permission, and use the project as part of their negotiation strategy. For example, when the Matina Crossing community in Davao (Philippines) decided to build a bamboo bridge over the tidal creek which separates their settlement from the city, they were facing eviction, but decided to go ahead and build their bridge, to physically bolster their negotiations to stay. Once communities finish their projects, they often organise a festival and invite the mayor to cut the ribbon, see their achievement and offer words of encouragement: 'Now that we have a very good walkway,' the people can then ask their smiling District Chief, 'How about municipal water supply? What about land?' With this soft link and a positive relationship established, it is a short step from small projects to negotiations for land and larger development needs.

Yet it is a strange quirk of development funding these days that while it is quite easy to get 'software' funding to train poor people and pay for various 'capacity-building' activities, it is not so easy to get 'hardware' funding to allow communities to make immediate, tangible, physical improvements in their slum communities. In fact, the best capacity-building happens when communities take concrete action to tackle the problems, and learn how to solve those problems collectively.

What Action Projects Can Do: The Experience of the ACCA City-wide Upgrading Programme

1. **Getting people into an active, collective process:** The small upgrading projects in the ACCA programme are a tool to bring community people into an active process of understanding their needs and then taking action to resolve them. After deciding on what they want to do and planning their project, most communities use the small project funds to buy materials, and contribute by putting in all the labour

themselves, adding cash, food or additional materials. The action projects help to activate and rejuvenate communities, and from this point onwards, they usually will remain active.

2. **Building a bridge between communities and their city governments:** Most local authorities tend to pay serious attention to any 'hardware' projects that communities undertake, like streets or drains or walkways, especially if they have not been authorised. Such public goods are usually supposed to be provided by government authorities. Communities use the small project implementation as an opportunity to open a dialogue with the concerned local government agencies. If people really need these improvements, the authorities usually agree, and most even contribute to the project budgets.
3. **'Warming up the machine':** If all the small changes and development projects can be linked, this will create a positive development momentum. This is a concept that appears in both Buddhist philosophy and physics, and it is a profound aspect of the way communities learn and how good ideas become popular and spread wider. We can see this when communities in a city use their savings to start surveys, networking and small improvement projects. When those activities are conceived and carried out in concert on a city-wide scale, that flurry of activity can reach a momentum that is enough to make the city take notice. And in most cases, it draws the city into this community action and keeps it moving along with itself. It is akin to warming up the machine of city-wide action and collaboration.
4. **Leveraging other funds and support:** If community people negotiate well, they can often get help from the local authority in some form: a funding contribution, building materials, technical assistance or access to construction equipment. In many of the small projects, community groups have been able to use the modest ACCA funds to leverage significant additional support in cash, labour and materials from their local governments, local development

organisations, and from within their own communities (especially in Cambodia, Vietnam and Nepal).

5. **A step towards getting land:** With this soft link established, it is a short step to land negotiations. The implementation of these small projects may not bear directly on the issue of land security, but already in several cases, communities have been able to use the momentum from the small projects to go on to negotiate for land (for example, Bharatpur in Nepal, several Cambodian cities, and Nuwara Eliya in Sri Lanka).

CONCLUSION

Scaling up urban-poor housing development is possible today, as large numbers of urban-poor communities have become very active and are moving forward in these more open, democratic times. With an understanding of some key conditions and potentials, it is possible for development interventions to be planned and support programmes to be built which open up possibilities for a new, large-scale *development by people* at scale. A good example of this kind of intervention is the ACCA programme, which was strategically designed to support large-scale transformation by people, offered tools that allowed Asia's forgotten, invisible urban-poor groups to become active, and recognised city development partners in 215 cities around Asia.

Our most important questions today are about development knowledge and development interventions. Significant development processes by poor communities on the ground have already taken off in cities all over Asia. This shows us clearly that *development by people*, at scale and in collaboration with their cities, is something that is possible, and which leads quite naturally into many other related urban development changes and governance. However, it seems that the formal institutions shepherding the development of our cities do not seem to change much in their direction, their understanding, or their way of doing things. We still see, again and again, the same rigid, conventional project design, top-down planning, strict selection of target groups, sectoral isolation and free-standing projects in which there is no relation to a given context. Sadly, this is still the way most development is practised, with no active revision and no sense of regret when it keeps failing to address the problems. The absence of flexible finance for the poor to unlock their creativity to make their most urgently needed changes remains another major challenge.

References

ACHR. 2015. '215 Cities in Asia: Fifth Yearly Report of the Asian Coalition for Community Action Program'. Bangkok: Asian Coalition for Housing Rights.

______. 2017. 'Community Finance in Five Asian Countries'. Bangkok: Asian Coalition for Housing Rights.

Archer, D. 2012a. 'Finance as the key to unlocking community potential: savings, funds and the ACCA programme'. *Environment and Urbanization* 24(2): 423–440.

______. 2012b. 'Baan Mankong participatory slum upgrading in Bangkok, Thailand: Community perceptions of outcomes and security of tenure'. *Habitat International* 36(1): 178–184.

Boonyabancha, S. 2009. 'Land for housing the poor—by the poor: Experiences from the Baan Mankong nation-wide slum upgrading programme in Thailand'. *Environment and Urbanization* 21(2): 309–330.

Boonyabancha, S., F. N. Carcellar and T. Kerr. 2012. 'How poor communities are paving their own pathways to freedom'. *Environment and Urbanisation* 24(2): 441–462.

Boonyabancha, S. and D. Mitlin. 2012. 'Urban poverty reduction: Learning by doing in Asia'. *Environment and Urbanisation* 24(2): 403–422.

Boonyabancha, S. and T. Kerr. 2015. 'How urban poor community leaders define and measure poverty'. *Environment and Urbanisation* 27(2): 637–656.

Mitlin, D. 2011. 'Shelter finance in the age of neoliberalism'. *Urban Studies* 48(6): 1217–1234.

Patel, S. and C. d'Cruz. 1993. 'The Mahila Milan Crisis credit scheme: From a seed to a tree'. *Environment and Urbanisation* 5(1): 9–17.

Patel, S., A. Viccajee and J. Arputham. 2017. 'Taking money to making money: SPARC, NSDF and Mahila Milan transform low-income shelter options in India', Working paper. London: International Institute for Environment and Development.

Satterthwaite, D. and D. Mitlin. 2014. *Reducing Urban Poverty in the Global South*. London and New York: Routledge.

Part 3

Informal Housing and Right to the City

VIII

The Politics of Poverty and Property in Indian Metros

The Case of Kathputli Colony in New Delhi

Bhuvaneswari Raman

INTRODUCTION

In 2009, the Government of India introduced a poverty alleviation programme called the Rajiv Awas Yojana (RAY) with the aim of creating slum-free cities (Dupont 2011; MHUPA 2006). The programme adopted a two-pronged strategy to provide housing for squatters, namely in-situ redevelopment of their settlements or relocation in tenements outside the city (Dupont 2008, 2011; MHUPA 2006, 2013). In 2011, The Ministry of Housing and Urban Poverty Alleviation (MHUPA) rolled out pilot projects in the country's capital city, Delhi. RAY and its predecessor BSUP (Basic Services for the Urban Poor) departed from the earlier approaches of the national and regional governments. When these programmes were introduced, there was euphoria about the programme as a tool for strengthening the legal rights of the poor to land and housing. Prior to the programme, particularly in Delhi between 2000 and 2006, eviction and resettlement of squatters in tenement housing on the outskirts were widely promoted by different institutions (Benjamin and Raman 2011; Bhan 2009; Dupont 2011; Ramanathan 2004). This chapter traces the experience of RAY's implementation at Kathputli colony (KC), a squatter settlement in west Delhi.

The Kathputli colony is home to nearly 3,500 households from diverse regional, caste and religious backgrounds. It was one of the three squatter settlements identified by the Delhi Development

Authority (DDA) for piloting in-situ redevelopment. This in-situ redevelopment involved the construction of housing units along with provision of infrastructure on the same site. The Kathputli redevelopment plan under RAY was inaugurated in 2009 by the then Minister for Housing and Urban Poverty Alleviation, Mr Ajay Maken, and was implemented under a PPP (Public-Private Partnership) involving the DDA, the developer–Raheja Builders–and the community. Besides which, there were non-governmental organisations (NGOs) working with the community. The project was originally designed to be completed in two years, that is, in 2011, but was extended by a further two years. The project implementation resulted in a prolonged ongoing conflict between the planning authority, namely the DDA, NGOs, the private developer and the colony residents. Till the end of 2016, the project had not progressed beyond a spiral web of surveys, plans of the settlement layout and house design, and negotiations over contracts and documentation. These conflicts manifested discursively in different domains–the colony, the courts and the public domain–and also affected intra-community relations.

Several research articles portraying the colony residents' struggle have subsequently been published, which have tended to conceptualise and treat the residents' struggles to secure their location mainly as a technical matter reflecting, for example, shortfalls in project implementation in terms of community participation and involvement (Banda et al. 2012; Dupont 2011; Dupont et al. 2014; Raman 2015; Sheikh and Banda 2015). This chapter focusses on three other questions: Why did KC residents oppose the project? How did they respond to state interventions? What space do squatters have to rework projects that are likely to affect them adversely? These questions are explored through ethnographic research conducted at the settlement between 2012 and 2016.

Ethnographic studies have illustrated how the poor creatively use overt and subtle forms of subversion to avert eviction and hold on to their places (Benjamin 2004; Raman 2010; Weinstein 2014). Unlike in the context of settlements facing eviction, KC was planned as an in-situ development. Further, residents have on earlier occasions lobbied state institutions for housing. Despite this, why did they oppose the project? The residents' struggle was precisely over the norms for redevelopment, which includes the area of land they can hold and the number of people that can be accommodated in the project. In order to understand this, it will be useful to review the KC residents' interests, the interpretation of housing and the official proposal. The residents' interests, discussed in the fourth section titled 'Residents' Responses to DDA Design', lie in securing housing at the same location they are currently occupying and, preferably, to have a greater share in KC's land in the form of plots. Although over time residents compromised on their demand for a plot, a majority of residents wanted to remain at the same site.

Developers are attracted to the land of squatter settlements such as Kathputli colony because of their location and vast stretches suited (or amenable) to commercial development, as can be inferred from the developers' design. Under the PPP arrangement, private developers are incentivised to capture a substantial part of land value gains. This is facilitated through the planning instruments of land share and the Transfer of Development Rights (TDR). The land share arrangements affect the area of land available to squatters such as the KC residents, and which in turn affects two aspects, namely the number of households that can be accommodated and the share of land for each household. These aspects, viz., who, how many, and the form of housing, were at the heart of the struggle between the colony residents and state institutions. Their norms are prescribed by the Master Plan, which is a legal document. Hence, squatters have very little say over the extent of land share or the TDR. Thus, while residents strove to bargain for more land, the developer and the DDA sought to restrict the number of squatter households who have to be accommodated under the scheme.

The PPP with arrangements for TDR and land share is seen by the Government of India (GoI) as a key model for squatter redevelopment throughout the country. Their norms are tilted in favour of developers and reinforced legally through the Master Plan. Further, the dominant policy interpretation of housing for squatters has been access to a built structure at any location in the city. The reduction of housing issues to one of access to a built structure allows for building a justification for eviction and resettlement as the only option. Poor households' interest in location is overlooked. A poor household's interest in land, particularly location, is linked to several aspects, including place identity, opportunities for jobs and social networks outside the community that facilitate such access (Benjamin and Raman 2001). Interestingly, in-situ development under RAY is limited to squatter settlements in established neighbourhoods, on land commanding high value, while a majority of other squatter settlements are demolished and their inhabitants relocated to the outskirts. Land held by squatters in a location/ localities commanding high value are thus gold mines waiting to be tapped. It is for this reason that we argue for a specific focus on land issues as it affects poor households in the contemporary political-economic context.

Weinstein (2014) argues that even though squatters may fight back against the state, the latter returns with more powerful instruments to evict them. Raman's (2010) work on Chennai evokes a similar sentiment. As will be discussed in the last two sections, KC residents sought to influence the norms and design of the project at the time of implementation. The DDA had outsourced the contract of the project design, which included the preparation of a detailed project report and surveys for enumerating the households. The KC residents had little information at the formulation stage. It was only when the DDA attempted to shift the residents to the transit camp and hand over the land to the developer that KC residents started to fight back. The early stages of their struggle involved mobilisation politics (protests and collective lobbying) and participatory mapping and enumeration. A significant part of the residents' struggle post 2011 involved quiet and continuous negotiation to rework the language in government orders such as the demolition slip, transfer orders and final agreement, and modifying the rules for identifying the list of eligible households. Despite the use of new instruments, the takeover of land occupied by squatters was not easy. At the same time, KC residents had limited success in influencing the DDA to reframe the project. This is because the legal framework, including the Master Plan and the Court order, constrained the extent to which DDA's original design could be altered. When there was no clear win, both state institutions and residents adjusted their interests and expectations from the project.

The rest of the chapter is organised under three sections. A brief background of the settlement is outlined in the next section. This is followed by the sections engaging with two themes, namely residents' interest and official plans, followed by people's responses and the outcomes. The concluding section identifies some key issues that have implications for policy and further research.

HISTORY OF KC

The colony's history goes back to the mid-1950s when a group of seasonal migrant artisans from the state of Rajasthan began to occupy a vacant marshland, which was then on the city's fringes. Until the 1970s, they remained itinerant. These original settlers were later joined by tribals from Andhra Pradesh in southern India, whose speciality is to prepare and trade herbal medicines. Households from twelve other artisan communities settled in the colony in the 1970s, an expansion facilitated by Rajiv Sethi, a well-known artist in the city. The artisan community residing in the colony today includes puppeteers, musicians, magicians, jewellers, carpenters, jugglers, metal workers, acrobats, balladeers, storytellers, singers, dancers and snake charmers from Rajasthan, Andhra Pradesh, Uttar Pradesh, Haryana, Punjab and Maharashtra. Over time, members of other communities from Maharashtra, Kerala and Bihar, mostly labourers in nearby factories, came to stay as well. Today, thirteen different communities live in the colony, but the artisans form the dominant group, constituting nearly 50 per cent of the colony's population, and these households (over 1,500 of them) trace their roots to thirteen clans living in the settlement. Estimates of the number of households residing in the colony vary, but range from a minimum of 2,800 to a maximum of 4,000. The number has become more fluid with the community's renegotiation with DDA in November/December 2016.

The colony has an identity as an artisan colony, 'Kathputli' meaning wooden dolls. It features a mixed use of land, including residential and work spaces. With the exception of the houses along the main road, access to the interior parts of the settlement is difficult and the colony suffers due to inadequate basic facilities, including water supply, storm water drainage and sewage. Whilst the main road leading to the settlement is paved, side lanes are neither paved nor provided with drainage. Even moderate rainfall leads to flooding sewers, and during the rainy seasons access to houses in the side lanes becomes increasingly difficult.

The colony residents' struggle to consolidate their claims to Kathputli land has a long history, starting in 1976 (*Hindustan* 1978). They were allotted plots in a resettlement site outside Delhi, but many households returned to Kathputli colony. With the help of an NGO, Saarth, the residents formed a co-operative called the Bhule Bisre Kalakar Co-operative (BBKC) in 1978. The BBKC embarked on a dream project—an artisan village named 'Anandgram' (1982), which was designed as a residential and work space for artisans. The plan provided for accommodating 1,500 artisan households with residential units organised around an open workshop. Each street was designed to showcase a particular craft, and an open-air theatre was planned to educate visitors to the colony about the life of the artisans. Subsequently, in 1989, another plan was prepared, called Nehru Kala Kunj. These plans were drafted after extensive research on the artisans' ways of living and working, and were facilitated by some of the country's leading architects and the Asia Arts Foundation. The colony artisans' dream plan remains a paper plan till today. Besides the BBKC, there are two other societies—Piyush Krotha (leper) society and the Mahila Co-operative Society (MCS), formed by another NGO called the Kalakar Trust.

In 1984, after several rounds of discussion, the then DDA governor formed a committee to implement the Anandgram plan; however, this did not materialise. Subsequently, in 1989, the Housing and Urban Development Corporation (HUDCO) drafted a plan for the redevelopment of KC colony, but the plan involved the relocation of many non-artisan households. The plan fell through, but it led to a fracture in intra-community relations. The DDA tried to demolish the settlement a third time, around the 1990s, but the colony residents managed to ward off the threat. In 1990, under the Janata Dal regime, the then prime minister, V. P. Singh, regularised the occupancy status of all squatter citizens in the city and issued identification tokens. Protection was given against eviction and an occupancy certificate popularly known as the V. P. Singh card was issued to all squatter citizens in the city. However, the problem of demolition and evictions resurfaced in the 2000s in all metro cities, including Delhi, with GoI's policies for restructuring the image of cities to attract foreign direct investments. Subsequently, in 2002, there was a proposal to relocate Kathputli residents to the outskirts of southwest Delhi, which also did not materialise.

In 2009, the DDA announced the redevelopment of KC under the RAY programme via a PPP arrangement. The DDA appointed an architecture-planning organisation called the GPMA (Gian P. Mathur & Associates Pvt. Ltd.) to develop a detailed project report (DPR) and Raheja Builders to redevelop the colony under a PPP arrangement. Two years later, the community, the DDA and the builder entered into a tripartite agreement for implementing the redevelopment project. According to the agreement, the DDA would shift the colony residents to a transit camp, clear the land and hand it over to the builder for reconstruction.[1] Conflict broke out between the three parties when the DDA came to clear the land in November 2011.

What had been a low-key, invisible conflict between the DDA, the private developer and citizens escalated in November 2011. Since then, Kathputli colony has attracted students, activist citizens, NGOs and the developer—each vying to convince citizens of their best interests in land and housing. Among them, an NGO from the city, called the Hazards Centre (HC), played a significant role in the early stages in terms of mobilising the community, negotiating on its behalf, and facilitating participatory surveys and plans. The DDA tried to coerce people to move to a transit camp called Anand Prabat. Cases were foisted on leaders on various grounds. Mobilising a fracture in the settlement, the DDA managed to move 550 households, but a majority of the residents remained at KC. The camp was started after clearing a part of a squatter settlement at that site. Frequent quarrels and lack of access at the transit site, and a fear that developers would not return the land influenced colony residents' decision not to move. This resulted in a prolonged conflict. In 2014, the community took legal recourse to stay the project, but failed. However, the Court offered relief to residents through restraining the DDA and the developer from forcefully evicting residents to the transit camp.

In 2014, cracks began to surface between the community and the NGO, leading to the latter's exit. In March 2015, the DDA announced that the pilot project at Kathputli colony had failed and that they were considering the introduction of a new project. In fact, the project came to a standstill by the end of 2015. After a period of no action lasting ten months, a youth group, with the support of a few community leaders, restarted the negotiation with the DDA. The community compromised on its demand for a greater share of land and agreed to be re-housed in multi-storeyed tenements. However, they wanted the DDA to rework the terms of the contract and its procedures.

COMPETING INTERESTS AND ORIGIN OF THE CONFLICT: RESIDENTS' INTEREST AND DEVELOPER'S DESIGN

Residents' Interest in Land

Throughout the struggle, the KC residents wanted to hold on to their current location. Their first preference was for a plot at the same location. Their interests were not easily discernible in the early stages of the project. When the project was inaugurated in 2009, the KC residents assumed that they would have access to a plot (land), taking the cue from the DDA's earlier approaches to in-situ upgradation. Prior to RAY, some members of the community had developed a plan for their ideal community, which was designed to provide each artisan with a plot of land. First, the artisan families claimed that their work demanded that they be allotted plots, and that their identity as artisans was closely tied to the location of their work and the locality. Second, both artisans and non-artisans felt that a plot would enable them to develop their residences vertically as new households form, that is, when the children of the first generation of settlers get married and move out after forming their own families. In the plans facilitated by the NGOs and prepared by architects and planners, the community opted for a plot at the KC location as a first choice, failing which, they wanted to restrict the number of floors in multi-storeyed apartments at the present location. In the early stages of their collective action, marked by protests, rallies and campaigns (described in the next section), they articulated their interest as one of access to the same location (that is, colony land) and a share of the land.

That said, there were differences between the artisan and non-artisan households in terms of their willingness to compromise on location and type of housing. During the course of the conflict, non-artisan households' articulation of their interest in land and housing altered between access to a plot or access to dwelling space in a multi-storeyed tenement, depending on their threat perception from within the community and outside at any particular time. When the project was announced in 2011, the non-artisan communities decided to settle for housing on DDA's terms, that is, to be re-housed in multi-storeyed tenements. While the artisans preferred to remain in the same location and demanded a plot, non-artisans were willing to move out at one stage as long as they were able to secure a dwelling space in the city. However, when the household list of 2008 excluded several of their community members, the non-artisans decided to align with the artisans.

Leaders from the non-artisan community stated that their decision at that time was influenced by a previous conflict with artisans in 1991 about their claims to Kathputli land. Moreover, the colony is identified by outsiders as an artisans' colony. The place identity was an important factor for the influential citizens of the city supporting the KC residents' struggle. Although at first the artisan community was unwilling to compromise on plot options, they shifted their position, recognising the importance of non-artisan households' support to fight the DDA and the Court case. At one time, they even considered the option of moving to a location within 5 kms of the settlement to ensure that both artisan and non-artisan households would be accommodated in the same place. The alliances between artisans and non-artisans were strengthened when the DDA tried to relocate colony residents at the transfer camp. Subsequently, with other options closing, both communities considered the possibility of multi-storeyed apartments at their present location, limiting the height of such apartment blocks to a maximum of four to five floors or a height of 13–17m.

Official Project Design: The DDA and the Developers' Design for the Project

Although the RAY project was publicly announced in 2009, the planning of in-situ development for Kathputli colony started in 2007. As mentioned, the DDA had outsourced the process of household enumeration and preparation of DPR to the GPMA, and the construction of houses to Raheja Builders, respectively. The GPMA rolled out surveys but prepared the DPR prior to the completion of surveys, which is discussed further in the next section.

The DDA rolled out household surveys in 2008, signalling the start of the project. The DDA's contractor, GPMA, conducted the first survey in 2008 and identified 2,704 households. The chief architect of the DDA approved the survey findings in September 2008 and published the findings in 2009.[2] However, the GPMA mentioned another number of 2,800 households in the final report submitted to the DDA, which appears in the DDA's official oral and written communications since 2009 (Banda et al. 2012).[3] A second survey[4] was organised by the DDA when the community contested the GPMA numbers. The DDA surveyed for the third time in 2009, as part of a city-wide survey of squatter settlements, and counted 3,100 households.[5] After a period of no activity, in 2011, the DDA requested another parastatal agency, the Delhi Urban Slum Improvement Board (DUSIB), to undertake biometric mapping in selected squatter settlements, one of which was Kathputli. This plan was abandoned midway due to the lack of necessary infrastructure at the DDA and the DUSIB.[6] In our interviews at the DDA in December 2012, the chief engineer mentioned that the DDA had decided to use the biometric cards issued to all citizens, including squatters, under a national programme called the Aadhaar. The depth of information collected under the household surveys was also scaled down. Subsequently, in August 2013, the DDA recruited a private agency to videograph and register each household, which was completed for 2,300 households (ibid.). Another re-survey was organised by the DDA in July 2014 to implement a Court order issued on 25 March 2014. The DDA again counted all households living in a plot as one. Subsequently, the DDA Chairman declared in a public meeting held at the Colony that numbers will be frozen at 2,800.

The GPMA relied on one of the findings of its household survey conducted in 2008 while preparing the DPR for the colony. Their DPR followed the norms outlined in the Delhi Master Plan 2021, which stipulates a land share of 60 per cent for the redevelopment of squatter housing and 40 per cent for the private developer. Besides, developers are provided with favourable land use control and development norms, such as mixed land use and higher floor space index to facilitate the capture of real-estate value gains. The logic of arriving at the ratio of 60:40 for land share is unclear, but the DDA claims that it is required to incentivise big developers to participate in squatter redevelopment projects.

Raheja Builders are one of the few big developers operating across different Indian cities, with a record of projects like shopping malls, IT parks, Special Economic Zones and high-income luxury housing. Based in Mumbai, the builders have specialised in PPP projects, whereby land for their projects is transferred by the state. Their interest in Kathputli land is explained by the strategic location of the colony, which abuts a main road and is close to a metro station. Land prices are expected to rise further due to a transport corridor plan along the main road abutting the colony. Further, the colony sprawls over 5.22 hectares of land. The Raheja Builders' plan for commercial development on the 40 per cent land boasted of the world's largest high-income residential complex of fifty-two storeys, or roughly 60 m. high, along with a mall and a convention centre on their 40 per cent share abutting the main road. The squatters were to be re-housed in eleven towers with a height of fifteen storeys in the 60 per cent share of land, which are to be screened off from the view of the main road. As the Chairman and MD of Raheja Developers Ltd. said, 'Nobody wants poor people to be their neighbour' (*The Wall Street Journal* 2012). Their commercial project abutting the main road, 'Raheja Phoneix', comprising of luxury housing complexes and a mall with a plaza and a pool, will be sited on the colony land abutting the main road.

The builder planned to develop the commercial component on Kathputli colony land in collaboration with Arabtec Constructions, the builders of the Burj Khalifa, the tallest building in the world, located in Dubai (Ramnani 2011). The builders had to revise their redevelopment plans to conform to the norms of the Ministries of Environment and Civil Aviation. Their initial plan for housing the colony residents was modified by reducing the height by 30 ft. or 10 m. This meant a reduction in the overall number of houses proposed to be built for the colony residents. While the interest of the builders and the DDA is to limit the number of eligible residents to fit them in the 60 per cent of land, residents fought to secure property rights in land and greater space for their dwellings. This manifested as rambling conflicts over listing, share of land taken by the developer and the housing design.

The DDA's reasons for selecting the GPMA for designing the DPR and Raheja Builders for implementing it are unclear. Conversations with the director of GPMA suggest that the DDA approached them for preparing the DPR. They acceded to the request as DDA is one of their important clients and they were aware, as early as 2009, that the construction contract would be awarded to Raheja Builders.[7] While the DDA claims that only Raheja Builders submitted a tender for KC redevelopment, the rumour is that the terms of the tender process were organised favourably for them. An internal audit report of the DDA also criticised the organisation for the terms of the awarding of contract and transferring land to the developer.

Origin of the Conflict

At the time of the inauguration, the DDA enlisted oral consent from the residents, but did not reveal any other detail. The DPR was prepared before the contestations over the number of households were settled. While the DDA refused to alter their list, the community also did not want to compromise on the number.

Disagreement over the number escalated over time into a prolonged conflict. In the midst of this conflict, in 2011, on the suggestion of the developer, the DDA entered into a tripartite agreement with the developer and the community. According to the contract signed by the DDA and Raheja Builders, 5.22 hectares of land along with Rs 6.11 crore were transferred to the builder and the DDA was to clear the land and relocate the colony residents to a transit camp for constructing the houses.[8] The residents alleged that although they were forced to sign the tripartite agreement, they were not given any information on the redevelopment plan.

In early 2014, the DDA tried to move the residents to a transit colony 5 kms away from the KC site. By this time, the community had lost its trust in both the DDA and the builder. They feared that once they vacated the land, there was no guarantee that the builders would allot the housing to them in the same location, and they would be forced to accept resettlement elsewhere. The DDA responded forcefully by organising periodic eviction raids and foisting criminal cases against the colony leaders and the youth of their families. The conflict intensified when the DDA organised another eviction and demolition drive to clear the colony and transfer the land to Raheja Builders. The DDA officials, along with the developer, managed to secure the signatures of 574 families, of whom around 400 remained at the transit camp as on May 2014. This situation continued till October 2016. Some of these households still maintain their houses both at the colony and the transit camp. The majority of residents continue to stay at the colony.

From Land Share to TDR

In March 2015, the DDA announced that they planned to adopt the Mumbai model of slum rehabilitation, which promotes the Transfer of Development Rights (TDR). Under the TDR, the state will repay the private sector for constructing housing units, not in cash, but with transferable development rights (Nainan 2008). The development right is defined as the permissible floor area in a particular plot, also known as the Floor Space Index (FSI).

The TDR instrument separates the land from development rights. Therefore, it allows developers to transfer the development rights from one location to another. The Mumbai experience shows that TDR provisions allow for developers to appropriate land held by squatters in neighbourhoods commanding higher value, and to relocate the residents to locations of relatively low real-estate value.[9] The higher-value land appropriated from squatters is then redeveloped for commercial or luxury residential apartments. After securing the consent of a certain proportion of squatters for redevelopment, a developer can request the state to acquire the land from squatters and transfer it to them for redevelopment. The practice of developers in Mumbai is to form co-operatives enrolling not necessarily the squatters, but their potential clients from lower-middle income or middle-income households, together with the use of force, to secure the consent of squatters.

The TDR is now a regularly traded commodity in Mumbai like any other asset, with rates varying according to neigbourhood (Mehta 1996). The TDRs based on squatter redevelopment projects are also allotted to non-governmental agencies, conflating their role as a representative of the community with that of real-estate developers. The large NGOs with significant power and connections in the national and international policy arena have managed to secure TDR contracts for slum rehabilitation in Mumbai. Thus, the new instruments of land development such as land sharing, the PPP for land development, the TDR, together with the proliferation of surveying and mapping of squatter settlements, generate incentives for all actors to push for large-scale housing projects, apart from the squatters, whose interest is in land and location as much as in housing.

RESIDENTS' RESPONSES TO DDA DESIGN

In this section, I discuss the colony residents' actions to influence the project design. When the DDA attempted to move residents forcefully to a transit camp, the conflict came into the open. As residents started to get information about the project, they came together to oppose the project design proposed by DDA. Their collective action encompassed a repertoire of actions, including protests, participatory surveys and design, legal action and sustained negotiation with DDA. Their struggles were punctured by long periods of no action, followed by coercive threats by DDA. There were occasions when it appeared that the colony would be evicted. Their actions and the outcome are described below.

Collective Action to Secure Colony Land and Housing

Disagreement over the number of households residing at the settlement catalysed different groups in the colony to come together for collective action. Until December 2016, the disagreement over the number remained. The colony was surveyed eight times between 2008 and April 2015, five times by different state institutions[10] including the DDA and DUSIB, and thrice by the community on their own or along with an NGO. Despite several rounds of surveys, information on the total number of households in the colony remained unsettled.

By early 2013, an NGO called Hazards Centre (HC) had mobilised the community and offered to support their fight to secure land rights. HC campaigned for squatters' rights to the land and housing in the city. They organised regular weekly meetings at the colony. The discussions and songs sung at the weekly meetings echoed the demand for their land. HC mobilised colony residents to participate in protests and rallies against the eviction of different communities in the city. With the entry of HC, the community articulated its demand explicitly over their rights to the colony land. In the initial stages, the NGO negotiated directly with concerned government agencies. Every time there was a threat of eviction or conflict between police and the community, the NGO intervened, mobilising their contacts. HC often engaged directly with the DDA Chairman, who was a government appointee, and informed the community leaders. On some occasions, they took a few representatives to official meetings where HC set the agenda and steered the discussion.

The HC worked closely with the leaders of the artisan community, who then mobilised the non-artisan community. They initiated a community-led survey, arguing that it is important to contest the DDA survey results and their housing design in the Court. The NGO, together with independent activists in the colony, recruited students from a leading university in the city and the colony's youth for the 'participatory' survey exercise in November 2013. The *pradhans* (or the leaders) played a significant role in enumerating the households from their own communities. The level of organisation differed between the various communities in the colony, which affected the time it took to complete the survey. The artisan community was highly organised and had maintained a list of households, changes in family structure, etc., rigorously. They had to just update the records. This was not the case with migrant communities, which had limited experience with the state agencies in the city. HC centralised the survey data at their office, supposedly for ease of data analysis. Although the rationale for the community survey was to feed into the legal process, the NGO did not complete the analysis as late as February 2014, when it led the community to file a case at the Delhi High Court. During this time, HC's count of households roughly estimated a number between 3,200–3,400. Residents were still waiting for the findings even a year after the survey was completed. This aspect fed into the conflict between HC and the residents at a later date.

Right to Information

Residents, with the help of an architect researching the settlement in 2013 and an artist who had come to work as an apprentice with one of the puppeteers in the area (both of whom were part of the Friends of Kathputli group, which brought together several professionals), secured information on the project by utilising the provision of the Right to Information Act. Until they secured the DPR, they were under the impression that the project would provide them access to plots (land titles) with houses. The initial consent from the community was enlisted orally by the DDA from the *pradhans*, in the presence of the then Chief Minister, Sheila Dixit, and the then Union Minister for Housing and Urban Poverty Alleviation, Ajay Maken. However, many community members were unaware of the proceedings of this meeting. They also claimed that neither the builder nor the DDA shared the DPR with them. The DDA and the builder, on the other hand, maintain that they moved ahead with the project only after the community consented to the housing component. The DDA rationale for not involving the community in the preparation of the DPR is that it requires technical expertise. When the residents managed to secure a copy of the DPR through a PhD scholar, they were unhappy with the arrangements for land sharing and the proposal to accommodate the colony residents in multi-storeyed apartments. They started raising questions about the DDA's decision to allot 60 per cent of the land to the developer.

Legal Action against DDA

Newspaper articles (*Hindustan Times* 2013; *The Hindu* 2013) on the Kathputli colony project, together with DDA's city-wide survey of encroached land for digitisation in early 2013, stoked the colony residents' fears of eviction. The colony residents interpreted the survey as a step towards their eviction, and this galvanised action once again. The NGO motivated the residents to file a case in the Delhi High Court to contest the DDA grid (Master Plan and the Detailed Development Plan).

When the community filed the legal petition, their demand was for the allocation of plots or for an individual share in land. They were confident about organising their own house construction. The colony residents, on the advice of HC, filed a petition in the Delhi High Court to stay the construction project. The petition was filed under the name of the Bhule Bisre Artisan Co-operative, along with twenty-eight other petitioners and two NGOs. The directors of the two NGOs, HC and Sethi, led the process, including the appointment of lawyers and framing of the case. At a meeting held at the DDA head office on 22 February 2014, as the

Court proceeding was in progress, the artisans pleaded with the DDA Chairman to allot them a plot or to transfer the land to the community for implementing the project.

The Court heard the case thrice. During the first hearing, the colony residents pleaded to stay the construction of houses on their site, arguing that several of the community's members had been excluded by DDA. The DDA lawyer informed the Court that only 2,641 houses will be allotted new flats under their list. The Court granted time to the colony residents to produce evidence disputing the DDA's list. The first hearing dampened the community as the Court refused to stay eviction, but gave additional time to the community to represent their case.

It was in the second hearing that DDA revealed the plan to accommodate all families in eight towers with a capacity for housing 2,800 households. Further, the agency stated that they could accommodate an additional 160 flats to genuine households left out in their survey. The lawyers representing the community argued that DDA's list was incomplete, and that there are 3,200 households. The hearing ended with the Court instructing the DDA to resurvey the colony and the community to submit their plans for redevelopment. At the third hearing on 19 March 2014, the Delhi High Court dismissed the community's petition for staying the redevelopment project. However, it provided relief to the residents by prohibiting Raheja Builders and DDA from coercively shifting them to the transit camp without meeting the community's demands. The Court also directed a team of five representatives from the colony to survey the transit camp and to submit their list of facilities required at the site.

Between these hearings, there were continuous raids on residents and *pradhans*, and many were arrested and booked on charges of petty crime. On the day of the third hearing, while the case of Kathputli residents v. DDA was being heard at the High Court, many *pradhans* had to be present in the district court to face a hearing on petty crimes.

Participatory Design

The participatory planning efforts started as an offshoot of the Court proceedings. When the Court was hearing the case, the Hazards Centre (HC) encouraged the community to develop layout plans. Though described by HC as 'participatory design', the NGO and Friends of Kathputli mobilised architects and planners in the city to prepare alternative plans. Three NGOs were involved in this process, namely HC, National Alliance of People's Movement, and Indo Global Social Service. The HC requested three architects to prepare a plan each. One was prepared by a university faculty member, the second by a well-known architect from Delhi, and the third by an architect from Mumbai, who was involved in the design and implementation of R&R (Resettlement and Rehabilitation) projects in the city. When the community was shown these plans, they chose three to present to the Court. Except at this stage, the residents' involvement was minimal in the design.

The KC residents opted as their first preference a plot that allowed them flexibility to develop vertically. The second preference was for G+3 (a four-storeyed building comprising a ground floor, and three additional floors) and the last option was to go for six to seven storeys. All these options meant that the residents required more land, and this led to their questioning the land share arrangement and demanding that the Raheja Builders plan be stayed. However, the Court order constrained the residents' demand for more land or staying Raheja's plan, as explained earlier. This influenced residents to take a pragmatic stand, compromising on their demand. With HC arguing with the community not to compromise, fractures began to surface, leading to the NGO's exit by the end of 2015.

After the Court Case: Exit of NGO and Hiatus in the Struggle

Immediately after receiving the Court order, the NGO, HC, mobilised researchers and planners to document the life histories of colony residents and their everyday use of space, arguing that the community should now be prepared with their participatory plans to negotiate with the DDA. By July 2014, the move to transit camp seemed certain. The community resisted it—with the women blocking the entry of DDA officials and the police. The NGO organised another meeting with the developer, Raheja Builders, in January 2015, which deepened the simmering conflict between itself and the colony leaders. By now, the community was wary of both the official surveys and the so-called participatory surveys. The intentions of these surveys were unclear to them as HC, like DDA, never shared the survey findings. The Sunday meeting organised by the NGO activists had become a regular ritual in the community, with the NGO elaborating on the need for the survey and planning. Several residents, with the exception of a few leaders close to the NGO, started to perceive these meetings as a burden with no outcomes. Some leaders, facing pressure from the community, started to question the NGO's intention.

Amidst these conflicts, the representatives of Raheja Builders regularly visited the colony to convince each household of the dream house they could own if they vacated the land and allowed the builder to start construction. The developer attempted to pay the leaders to mobilise residents to move to the transit camp. The delay in the project, conflict with the NGO, together with rumours that some leaders were bought off by the developer snowballed into intra-community conflict. By then, the youth leaders had taken over. The settlement had been surveyed for the second time in 2009 by DDA as part of a city-wide survey of squatter settlements, and had counted 3,100 households. In December 2016, the DDA surveyed the settlement again, following an agreement with the community to accommodate all households in the redevelopment scheme.

Elections to the local government of Delhi and the national government provided a respite to the residents. Residents hoped that with the election of the Aam Aadmi Party (AAP) in December 2014 and re-election again in February 2015, there would be space for negotiation.

By the beginning of May 2014, the previously mentioned independent artist-apprentice, who had moved to work with a famous puppeteer in the colony, Puran Bhat, decided to take a different approach. While the NGOs preferred to publicise the issue around the land question, the artist decided to work on supporting the livelihoods of the residents, as by now the lobbying, meeting and court cases had affected the income of *pradhan* households. More than direct eviction, there was everyday harassment from the police, fearing which men chose to remain in their houses. DDA, along with police officials, frequently visited the site and forcibly handed over the *parchis* (tokens) for moving households to the transit site.

Towards the first week of May 2014, nearly 400 of the over 3,000 households moved to transit camp, but 100 of them came back. The remaining households, predominantly from the artisan community, were still adamant on the location. Even within their narrative, there is ambiguity in their interest with respect to location, heritage village and house. Despite Raheja Builders' best efforts, the project came to a halt. There was a lull in the negotiation after the NGO's exit and till October 2015, there was no move on the part of the different actors.

Renegotiation with the DDA

With the exit of the NGO, HC, the community, led by a group of youth leaders, decided to renegotiate with the DDA. The community regrouped once again and decided to sideline the leaders working closely with HC, choosing to draw on the support of a network of professionals and NGOs rather than letting an external NGO lead the struggle. In their renegotiation with the DDA, they argued that their interest is housing and they are willing to compromise on the provision of multi-storeyed houses. Some residents were willing to move out of the community. One example was the community of leprosy patients, who felt that their integration with the dominant group of KC residents was nearly impossible. However, residents argued with DDA that the contract for housing and relocation to the transit site must be reworked. This phase of their struggle was focussed on lobbying for reworking the terms of government procedures and contracts.

Space for Manoeuvre

As can be inferred from the above discussion, there was no clear-cut win for either the DDA–developer alliance or the community. Despite mobilising the law and police power, the DDA–developer alliance could not take away the land easily from the community. The delay in the start of the project, in the words of Raheja Builders representatives, affected the company. The Raheja representatives held a meeting with the community to discuss the conflict over the numbers list. They argued that they have invested Rs 760 crore in the project, and it is up to DDA to create conditions for construction. The DDA's response was that since it was a tripartite agreement (among the DDA, Raheja Builders, and the slum dwellers, represented by each household in the colony), it was Raheja's obligation to fulfil the contract. At this meeting, the builders threatened to file a petition against DDA in the Court because of the loss incurred to them since the start of the project. This remains a verbal threat till now. The builders are now negotiating directly with the community in the hope of reclaiming the land.

The community, on the other hand, could not entirely alter the project design. The Master Plan as well as the Court, while providing some relief, constrained their actions. Residents pragmatically adjusted their interest in a share of land to a permanent house in a multi-storeyed building at the same location. The fact that the DDA had been forced to rework the contracts for relocation and house-ownership was considered a success for the residents, as was their ability to influence the DDA on four aspects, namely:

1. Forcing DDA to adopt the DUSIB policy (with reference to identifying households);
2. Reworking the requirements for identity card (on spot verification and agreement, rather than ration card, voter card);
3. Reworking the wording of the demolition slip (to relocation for construction of permanent shelter);
4. Ownership agreement after ten years.

CONCLUSION

This chapter has explored the KC residents' experience with the implementation of a RAY project. The project promised the residents access to land and housing at the same location. First, the chapter illustrated the manner in which new instruments, such as PPP with land share and TDR promoted for slum redevelopment, pose the threat of dispossessing squatter residents from access to land in established localities. The PPP model is to be scaled to other regions. Despite a standoff of eighteen months, developers are still holding on to the project and striving hard to make it a success. While contestation from the ground made it difficult for builders to implement the plan as they had visualised, the fact that PPP and land share arrangements are enshrined in the Master Plan, which is a legal document, compelled the DDA to transfer the land. It is for this reason that I have argued that a specific focus on land issues as it affects poor households is important, rather than subsuming land issues under housing. Second, the colony residents enacted a variety of actions, as described in this chapter. Whilst they were not completely able to alter the project design, they succeeded in forcing the DDA to rework the contracts and the terms of the project, particularly the number of households to be accommodated under the project.

End Notes

1. Interview with Sahil, ex-DDA planner, dated 23 June 2014.
2. Available at http://www.pudr.org/?q=content/kathputli-colony-receiving-end.
3. Interview with GPMA, 14 November 2012; correspondence between Executive Engineer, DDA WD 5 (West Division), Commissioner (LM [Land Management]); and letter dated 7 May 2011 from Raheja Developers to Executive Engineer, DDA WD 5, Commissioner (LM).
4. Interview with the Director, Hazards Centre, dated 12 April 2014. RTI documents and interviews with the Chief Organiser of Friends of Kathputli colony.

5. Interview with community leaders and archives maintained by the community.

6. Interview with GPMA, 14 November 2012; correspondence between Executive Engineer, DDA WD 5, Commissioner (LM); and letter dated 7 May 2011 from Raheja Developers to Executive Engineer, DDA WD 5, Commissioner (LM).

7. Interview with chief architect and team leader at GPMA, November 2013.

8. Interview with Sahil, ex-DDA planner, dated 23 June 2014.

9. See Nainan (2008) for a discussion on the TDR experience in Mumbai.

10. The conflicts around the DDA-organised surveys have been documented by Banda et al. (2012). This section builds on this work. The details of the four official surveys are as follows: survey undertaken by GPMA, contracted by the DDA in 2008; household enumeration survey by the DDA between April 2010 to August 2010; DUSIB survey as requested by the DDA for videography documentation of households between June–August 2011; and DDA resurvey in August 2013.

References

Banda, S., Y. Vaidya and D. Adler. 2012. 'The Case of Kathputli Colony Mapping Delhi's First In-Situ Rehabilitation Project', Working Paper. New Delhi: Centre for Policy Studies.

Benjamin, S. 2004. 'Urban land transformation for pro-poor economies'. *Geoforum* 35(2): 177–187. Available at 10.1016/j.geoforum.2003.08.004 (accessed June 2021).

Benjamin, S. and B. Raman. 2001. 'Inclusive and Pro-poor Urban Governance in Bangalore', Working Paper no. 26. Birmingham: International Development Department, University of Birmingham.

______. 2011. 'Claiming Land, Contestations and the Urban Poor in Globalizing Times'. In Zerah et al. (eds), *Urban Policies and the Right to the City in India: Rights, Responsibilities and Citizenship*. New Delhi: UNESCO-CSH.

Bhan, G. 2009. '"This is no longer the city I once knew". Evictions, the urban poor and the right to the city in millennial Delhi'. *Environment and Urbanisation* 21(1): 127–142.

Dupont, V. 2008. 'Slum Demolitions in Delhi since the 1990s: An Appraisal'. *Economic and Political Weekly* 43(28): 79–87.

Dupont, V. 2011. 'Infrastructure project, beautification and forced evictions in Delhi—The exemplary story of a cluster of slum dwellers rendered homeless'. Paper presented at the DSA and EADI conference on Rethinking Development in an Age of Scarcity and Uncertainity, New Values, Voices, Alliances for Increased Resilience. York: University of York.

Dupont, V., S. Banda, Y. Vaidya and M. M. Gowda. 2014. 'Unpacking Participation in Kathputli Colony. Delhi's First Slum Redevelopment Project, Act I'. *Economic and Political Weekly* 49(24).

The Hindu. 2013. 'A question of survival', 11 September. Available at https://www.thehindu.com/features/metroplus/society/a-question-of-survival/article5115593.ece (accessed June 2021).

Hindustan. 1978. 'Bhoole Bisre kalakaron ke sangharsh ki saalgirah', 2 June.

Hindustan Times. 2013. 'DDA starts relocation of Kathputli slum dwellers', 22 August. Available at https://www.hindustantimes.com/delhi/dda-starts-relocation-of-kathputli-slum-dwellers/story-Ko5FNCq3FuBr1R1FvvoDDK.htm/ (accessed June 2021).

Mehta, J. B. 1996. 'TDR: A Vital Instrument of Town Planning'. *Journal of the Indian Institute of Architects* August: 3.

MHUPA. 2006. *Rajiv Awas Yojana: Guidelines for Slum-Free City Planning*. New Delhi: Government of India.

______. 2013. *Rajiv Awas Yojana 2013–2022*. New Delhi: Government of India

Nainan, N. 2008. 'Building Boomers and Fragmentation of Space in Mumbai'. *Economic and Political Weekly* 43(21): 29–34.

Raman, B. 2010. 'Street Traders, Place and Politics. A Case Study of Bangalore, India'. Unpublished PhD dissertation. London: London School of Economics, UK.

______. 2015. 'The Practice of Urban Poverty Policies in India: Citizens Participation in Public-Private Partnership Projects'. In K. Goymen and O. Lewis (eds), *Public Policy Making in a Globalised World*. Istanbul: Istanbul Policy Centre.

Ramanathan, U. 2004. 'Illegality and Exclusion: Law in the Lives of Slum Dwellers', Working Paper 2. Geneva: International Environmental Law Resource Centre.

Ramnani, V. 2011. 'Delhi set to go higher, taller'. *Hindustan Times*, 24 December.

Sheikh, S. and S. Banda. 2015. 'Surveying Slums: Process of Survey and Use of Data'.*Economic and Political Weekly* 50(22): 72–79.

The Wall Street Journal. 2012. 'From Slum to Skyscraper', 17 February.

Weinstein, L. 2014. *The Durable Slum: Dharavi and the Right to Stay Put in Globalizing Mumbai*. Minnesota: University of Minnesota Press.

IX

Approaches to Informal Settlements and Livelihood-building Processes in Durban

Tara Saharan

INTRODUCTION

Space played an important role in apartheid and continues to shape the post-apartheid development of cities in South Africa, albeit with a different focus. After 1994, the discourse of spatial segregation was replaced by the alternative vision of an integrated society, both socially and spatially (Harrison et al. 2008; Pieterse 2006; Seekings 2000; Todes 2000; Watson 2002), with the aim of eradicating the legacy of inequitable access to urban services and housing of the black majority. Despite these noble intentions, the reality of urban life for the majority of black South Africans, many of whom live in informal settlements, remains one of poverty and an ongoing struggle for access to housing and services. Statistics show that the South African government has delivered 3.7 million houses and serviced sites during the past two decades (NDHS 2014). However, according to the latest census, 13.5 per cent of the population still lives in informal structures (Statistics South Africa 2011), and the housing backlog has escalated from 1.5 million units in 1994 (Department of Housing 1994) to 2.3 million in 2014 (Presence 2014). The housing policy has been criticised for limited participation, peripheral location and segregated spatial legacy (Bradlow et al. 2011; Huchzermeyer 2014). In addition, political meddling through the bureaucratic waiting list process has also shaped housing allocation, which is increasingly turning into a question of access to resources rather than the needs of the beneficiaries (Tissington et al. 2013: 8).

Informal settlements existed in South African cityscapes long before the arrival of democracy in 1994. Despite several decades of planning and policy interventions, the precarious settlements continue to exist, thrive and grow. In this chapter, this disjuncture in planned and lived spaces is explored by questioning the rationalities of the state and its interaction with the lives of residents in informal settlements. An examination of the national, city and household levels by Charlton (2009) revealed the constraints that hold back South Africa's housing reforms, highlighting the range of different rationalities in the objectives and outcomes of the housing programme at different scales. This clash of rationalities is rooted in the technocratic and managerial systems of administration and service provision to the marginalised urban populations, which live largely under informal arrangements (Watson 2009: 2267). Similarly, Massey (2013) explored the differences in the rationalities between Cape Town's in-situ upgrading process and the efforts of residents living in two informal settlements of the city. Since urban planning has been a dominant state strategy of governance in South Africa, this research seeks to understand the cleavages between the policy and planning interventions vis-à-vis the households' processes of building livelihoods. It brings together the rationality of governance and urban planning, articulated through approaches to informal settlements that emphasise spatial integration of the urban form, and the logic of survival based on urban livelihoods at settlement and household scales of informal settlements in Durban,[1] South Africa.

The chapter is organised as follows. The next section presents debates related to urban livelihoods and governance, in particular the urban planning perspectives in the global South. This is followed by a discussion of the research methodology. The subsequent section provides details on the changing context of eThekwini, South Africa. The state's approaches to informal settlements are examined through spatial planning documents and programmes for housing the urban poor. Also, the households' livelihood-building strategies in one of the inner-city informal settlements are contrasted with the approaches elaborated earlier. The final section examines the differences and similarities in the rationalities of the state and the residents in informal settlements.

URBAN GOVERNANCE, PLANNING AND LIVELIHOODS IN INFORMAL SETTLEMENTS

Urban governance relates to 'a particular way of understanding the complexities of steering urban development' in cities (Haferburg and Huchzermeyer 2015: 4). These complexities are born out of power negotiations that underlie the processes of interaction between several state and non-state actors (Baud and de Wit 2009; Devas 2005). City governance operates under two sets of constraints: (*i*) external, the complex multi-scalar environments in which the cities operate; and (*ii*) internal, relating to the nature of cities (Paddison 2016). With regard to the external constraints, informal settlements form a node–involving actors and arrangements at multiple scales beyond city institutions–in which the framework and norms for policy interventions are set (Milbert 2006; Sutherland et al. 2016). For instance, the Cities Alliance's slogan of 'cities without slums' was the basis of the UN's Millennium Development Goal 7, Target 11 that dealt with the 'improvement in lives of 100 million slum dwellers worldwide by 2020'. Nevertheless, the discourse of 'improvement' was undermined and dominated by the idea of 'slum-free cities', which legitimised a direct and often repressive approach to informal settlement eradication (Gilbert 2007; Huchzermeyer 2010). The international discourses generated by the Cities Alliance and the United Nations have strongly influenced national and local government approaches towards slums.

The internal constraints in relation to informal settlements are associated with two debates, namely 'right to the city' and the geography of their location. The debate of right to the city highlights issues related to social justice from a critical spatial perspective and underlying processes that contribute to the production of uneven geographies (Soja 2009). It confronts both the state's approaches to informal settlement eradication and the struggles that underline these processes (Huchzermeyer 2011; Kudva 2009). While the rationality of the state's approach centres on effectuating the desired change by drawing on expert knowledge (Dean 2010; Li 2007), it is often challenged by a distinct 'politics of informality' produced in the segregated spaces of informal settlements (Benjamin 2004, 2008). These strategies are not limited to 'quiet' encroachment (Bayat 2010) but also include elections as a negotiating tool (Benjamin 2004, 2008), as well as protest and mobilisations as mechanisms for negotiating services (Mottiar and Bond 2012). Additionally, the significance of the location of informal settlements brings out the inequalities in power and resource allocation on the one hand, and overlapping patterns of residents living and working together on the other (Kudva 2009; Nijman 2010). Furthermore, understanding the capability of local government is a prerequisite for analysing urban planning (Haferburg and Huchzermeyer 2015; Pierre 1999).

Planning is understood as an important tool through which a government manages the territories and residents of informal settlements (Watson 2009). In urban planning, informal settlements are viewed as 'grey spaces' that lie between the 'white' formal areas of the city and the 'blackness' of eviction (Yiftachel 2009). These 'grey spaces' of informality are often tolerated and even encouraged because their existence is unimaginable without the effective facilitation of the state (Nijman 2008; Roy 2009; Yiftachel 2009). However, it has been argued that formal and informal spaces do not have a dichotomous relationship in different territories, but rather share a continuum (Kudva 2009; McFarlane 2012; Nijman 2008; Roy 2009).

The planning rationalities of the state are linked with power relations that are context-dependent (Flyvbjerg 1998). With evolving contexts, the power structures that sustain these rationalities are constantly being reproduced (ibid.). The growing technical expertise in the private sector is increasing its power over local government, thereby redefining power relations (Baud et al. 2014). In this chapter, the governance and planning of informal settlements are configured through a combination of (*i*) policies and practices of eThekwini Municipality; (*ii*) planning discourses; and (*iii*) political coalitions emerging from the dynamic power struggle of democratic South Africa.

On the other hand, formal planning interventions often result in unintended outcomes because of the conflict between the rationalities of governing and administration and the logic of survival of the poor and marginalised (Watson 2009). This logic of survival of the marginalised populations is visible in the strategic choices made by households for building livelihoods (Moser 1998; Rakodi 2002). The process of building livelihoods in cities of the global South differs considerably, depending on the status of the settlement (formal or informal). The livelihoods approach used here draws upon the assets and vulnerability framework by Moser (1998, 2009), which provides a multi-dimensional (financial, human, social and physical assets) and holistic way to understand poverty and inequality, in contrast to the income and consumption analysis approach (De Haan and Zoomers 2005; Moser 1998; Rakodi 2002). Despite its advantages, the livelihoods approach has been criticised for several shortcomings. To begin with, multi-dimensionality needs to be approached relationally. For example, in her empirical work on moving out of poverty and accumulating assets, Moser (2009) reports that sectoral interventions have to be strategically mapped in terms of their impact on the accumulation of other assets. Also, Parizeau (2015) argues that conceptually, assets and vulnerability cannot be treated separately, nor does the increase in one dimension result in the depreciation of the other. The mere existence of an asset is an insufficient measure—asset quality is the crucial determinant for poverty alleviation. Second, the approach has been criticised for inadequately addressing the role of power and politics (De Haan and Zoomers 2005; Devas 2002; Hendriks 2011; Scoones 2009) and for placing too much emphasis on the agency of the poor, rather than on the structural constraints they face (De Haan 2012; De Haan and Zoomers 2005; Gough et al. 2007; Scoones 2009). Therefore, it is important to include the extent to which governance relations may act as constraints or opportunities to secure livelihoods over time. This is done by analysing the planning strategies and practices of the Municipality in relation to the way households build up their livelihoods at a household scale and the history of the informal settlement where they are located.

METHODOLOGY

This chapter explores the rationality embedded in the governance processes in eThekwini Municipality and the livelihoods of households living in informal settlements. eThekwini Municipality was selected as the empirical case for this research, given its long legacy of spatial planning and growth of informal settlements and the possibility of gaining access through a larger research programme (chance2sustain.eu). The methodology section elaborates on the research context of eThekwini Municipality, followed by the data collection and analysis section.

eThekwini Municipality is the third largest city in South Africa, spanning an area of 2,297 sq. km. (Statistics South Africa 2011). It is located on the east coast of the country in the province of KwaZulu-Natal. Demographically, the population of Durban grew from 2.7 million in 1996 to 3.4 million in 2011, in two distinct phases. Despite the increase in population, the growth rate in 1996–2001 of 2.3 per cent has since sharply declined to 1.1 per cent for 2001–2011 (ibid.). The initial growth of Durban can be linked to the development of food processing and petrochemical industries, coupled with proximity to the port that facilitated import and export operations (Marx and Charlton 2003). In contrast, the 2011 Census recorded 73 per cent of employment in the tertiary sector, followed by the secondary sector with 26 per cent and the primary sector with up to 1 per cent (Urban Econ 2012). Robbins (2010: 534) notes that though new jobs have been created and the absolute level of the formally employed has increased over past years, this growth has been overshadowed by a substantial increase in the numbers of the unemployed and the growing number of people resorting to informal-sector work.

The city is characterised by high levels of poverty and inequality. As per the Census of 2011, 21 per cent of the metropolitan population is living in informal structures (Statistics South Africa 2011). Of this 21 per cent, 12 per cent live in shacks not located in backyards, 4 per cent live in shacks in backyards, 4 per cent in traditional dwellings and 1 per cent other (ibid.). This data is limited to enumeration areas with 100–250 households and does not take into account smaller informal settlements (Housing Development Agency 2013). In contrast to the Census data, the Housing Sector Plan prepared for the Integrated Development Plan (IDP) of eThekwini Municipality states that 30 per cent of households live in informal settlements, 5 per cent in informal backyards, and 12 per cent in shacks not in backyards (eThekwini Municipality 2012: 46). The definitions of informal structures in the statistics of South Africa and eThekwini Municipality also differ. While the former focusses on legal norms and structures, the latter also takes into account the level of services available. Therefore, depending on data sources and definitions, between 12 and 31 per cent of the population reside in informal settlements in eThekwini municipality (Sutherland 2016). The population living informally is spread over 520 informal settlements, clustered along the peripheral areas and in the inner-city marginal lands (ibid.). Since the peripheral settlements have a distinctly rural character and the focus of this chapter was limited to inner-city informal settlements,[2] River Side[3] located in the central zone of eThekwini Metropolitan Area was selected as the case study (see Figure 9.1).

Taking into account the multi-scalar dimension of this research, data was collected at the city, settlement and household scales in two periods: during one month in 2012 and four months in 2015. At first, to better understand the city's policy discourses and approaches to informal settlements, a review of the eThekwini Municipality's Spatial Development Framework (SDF) and Housing Sector Plan was carried out.

In addition, twenty-three semi-structured interviews with municipal officials, researchers, councillors, NGO staff, ward committee members, architects and activists were conducted. Second, the historical development of the settlement was mapped through two focus group discussions and five semi-structured interviews with key informants such as settlement leaders, residents, local councillors and neighbours. Third, a survey of 100 households was administered in the settlement to analyse livelihood-building processes. The focus group discussions, interviews and surveys were complemented with participant observations and informal discussions with settlement residents. The data was collected in the isiZulu language by research

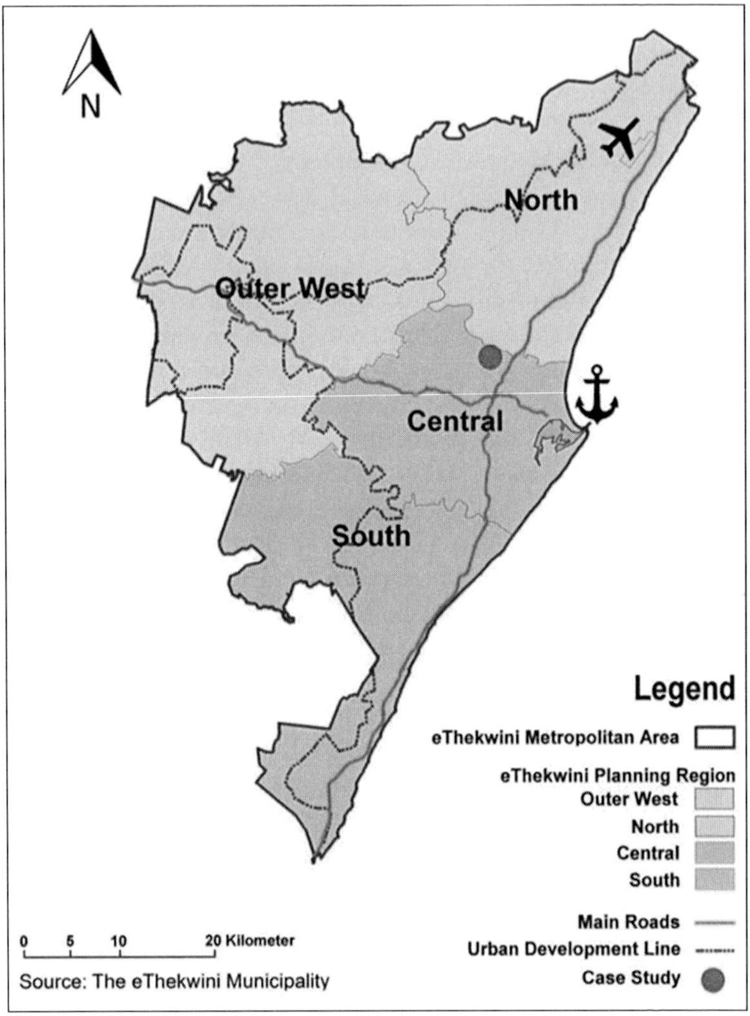

Figure 9.1: Location of Case Study Area in the Metropolitan Context of eThekwini

Source: Author, based on data from eThekwini Municipality (2013).

assistants. Quota sampling was used by selecting equal numbers of households from each of the four clusters that made up River Side, namely KwaMamsuthu, Monpondweni, Mcondo I and Mcondo II.

The qualitative and quantitative data were analysed simultaneously. Thematic qualitative analysis of interview notes, transcripts and planning documents for understanding the approaches to informal settlements in eThekwini Municipality was carried out. The settlement history was mapped using data collected from interviews and focus group discussions and complemented with visual image interpretation of aerial photographs (before 2001), collected from eThekwini Municipality and Google Earth images (after 2001). Descriptive statistical analysis was applied to the data collected through household surveys.

GOVERNANCE PROCESSES AND URBAN LIVELIHOODS IN INFORMAL SETTLEMENTS

This section demonstrates how urban governance processes in eThekwini Municipality influence opportunities for and constraints on building livelihoods by households in River Side. It starts with the macroeconomic and political contexts of eThekwini Municipality and a discussion on its approaches to informal settlements. This is followed by the development history of the settlement and a discussion on urban livelihoods at the household scale. The analysis brings out how the governance and planning approaches towards informal settlements differ from households' livelihoods by elaborating on two relations between the household, settlement and city scales.

Governance of Informal Settlements in eThekwini Municipality

The post-apartheid period marked a crucial transition in policy and governance in South Africa. Previously fragmented and racially divided local authorities were fused into very large local government units, incorporating both wealthy and poor areas (Todes 2014). Two-tier structures, initially put in place in metropolitan areas in 1996, were consolidated into unitary metropolitan municipalities in 2000. Moreover, the local governments had to adapt from a traditional role of 'regulation and administration' to a greater emphasis on urban development. eThekwini Municipality's housing division, renamed the Human Settlements Unit, is the nodal department for informal settlements within the local government. Over the last two decades (since 1994), the eThekwini Municipality has delivered a staggering record of 160,000 formal dwelling units; however, the demand backlog has also increased, from 240,000 units in 1994 to 412,000 in 2016 (eThekwini Municipality 2012: 27). Since 1994, eThekwini Municipality's strategy has been to provide Redevelopment Project (RDP) housing[4] through basic services and top-structures[5] in greenfield sites located on the periphery of the city (Sutherland 2016). The high cost of more accessible, centrally located land, coupled with a rigid housing policy, has contributed to the peripheralisation of the urban poor, with resulting high-bulk infrastructure costs in the short term as well as high operating costs in the long term (Breetzke 2008). The Breaking New Ground (BNG) policy was introduced in 2004, with a change in rhetoric from focussing on housing to integrated development approaches, inclusive of in-situ upgrades and participatory measures. Despite the policy shift from delivery of houses to a focus on the settlement scale, an element of continuity in state practices towards informal settlements was maintained, as stated below:

> There is no such thing as BNG. It is just words on paper and it does not really exist as a policy. Some experts on the country would say that the concept should be banned because the concept of sustainable human settlements is an oxymoron, and it is over-ambitious for the government to try to do that because they cannot do that. All they can do is to try and intervene in the least damaging way possible with the maximum kind of benefit. But certainly the very lofty aspiration of sustainable human settlement strategies of the housing department has not been fulfilled (NGO Official,[6] June 2012).

Moreover, both the RDP and BNG are national government programmes. Post-2010, eThekwini Municipality has undertaken short- and long-term approaches simultaneously (eThekwini Municipality 2012). In contrast to the long-term full upgrade of

RDP, the Interim Service programme is a short-term initiative that allows for the provision of basic services without tenure, until additional interventions can take place. In addition, the Emergency Service programme was also part of an interim approach that included measures such as provisions of corrugated galvanised iron sheets for the construction of temporary accommodation in case of fire or flood. While the discourse of upgrade (whether short- or long-term) is the dominant practice of the Human Settlement Unit of the Municipality, the Land Invasion Unit is actively involved in removing 'new' shacks under legal mandates of the court, and seeks to curb the growth of informal settlements in the city (Sutherland 2016).

In terms of planning, the concept of compact cities has been influential in South African policy discourses and has informed the Spatial Development Frameworks (SDF) formulated in the 1990s (Todes 2000). The SDF served as a spatial planning tool to steer future economic growth and development within the frame of Integrated Development Plans (IDPs) (Musvoto et al. 2016). The first SDF for Durban Metropolitan Area was formally adopted in 1998, with a focus on spatial restructuring to promote a 'compact, integrated and efficient urban form'. Although the political representatives of the poorer and spatially peripheral communities actively promoted development in the outlying areas, this effort supported dispersal rather than the compaction and integration outlined in the SDF (Breetzke 2008). In contrast to the informal settlements in the 1990s, which were mainly located on spatially marginalised areas in close proximity to the townships (Durban Metropolitan Area 1998), at present many informal settlements in Durban are scattered across the city, including in areas of least needs[7] (eThekwini Municipality 2016). The existence of inner-city informal settlements reveals spatial advantages for the households to access employment, combined with the possibilities of receiving less resource allocation because they are less visible from a helicopter view (Martínez et al. 2016).

The latest review of the SDF discusses a model-based decision-making process for housing delivery, which would select those informal settlements that are least costly to implement from a bulk infrastructure perspective and with favourable locations (eThekwini Municipality 2016). This rationale is also reflected in the Housing Sector Plan. Compiled by consultants (Anton Aiello Consultancy and McIntosh Xaba Associates), the plan was funded by the KwaZulu-Natal (KZN) Department of Human Settlements with the Housing Department of the Municipality as a client. The plan outlines informal settlements as the 'largest challenge', with a call for integration to overcome 'spatial, social and economic exclusion' (eThekwini Municipality 2012: 46). Drawing on GIS-based maps, the analysis under the Housing Sector Plan refers to several models and plans: (*i*) Consolidated Infrastructure Plan, (*ii*) Cost Surface Model, (*iii*) Access Model, (*iv*) Integrated Transport Plan, and (*v*) Spatial Development Frameworks and Plans. Depending on the location, the plan advocates a dual approach of short-term interim provision of housing along with long-term RDP upgrades through the 'prioritisation model'. The model prioritises projects based on accessibility of bulk infrastructure, social services, travel cost, employment opportunities and the urban development line (ibid.). These criteria are spatially mapped to assign the development response based on planning standards in the form of a four-tier classification system: A) Full Upgrade, B1) Interim Services initially, B2) Emergency Services, and C) Relocation. Even though full upgrade is stated to be the largest programme implemented in eThekwini Municipality, it also includes the rural projects; and interim and emergency services apply to most informal settlements in the Municipality. For the model, planning standards, service availability, land tenure and funding possibilities are taken into consideration for the classification of different development options. The Housing Plan thus attempts to depoliticise the development of informal settlements by engaging in discussions driven by advanced technology, sophisticated models and funding mechanisms.

The development of Durban is closely linked to the politics of KwaZulu-Natal province, and its history of political violence. Since the early 1980s, tensions between the African National Congress (ANC) and the Inkatha Freedom Party (IFP) escalated to the level of a low-intensity civil war, with high incidences of violence. The IFP had a traditional and rural support base compared to ANC's more urbanised constituency. ANC has been the leading national party since the first free elections in South Africa in 1994. At the provincial level, the IFP marginally won control of KwaZulu-Natal in the elections of 1994 and 1999; however, since 2003, ANC has secured majority votes at provincial as well as national levels. The national-level dominance of ANC since 1994 has blurred the line between the party and the state in South Africa (Southall 2014). The post-apartheid housing politics in South Africa was shaped by a supply-based discourse of standardised housing delivery (Huchzermeyer 2010). This led to large-scale housing construction, which prioritised physical assets while overlooking other dimensions of well-being of households living in informal settlements. One respondent reflected on the impact of this policy focus:

> It is not like if you get a house, you will get a job. But the thing is that people have got a roof on their head and they have a property in their name. And the city has the rates applicable to these properties (Government official,[8] March 2015).

Livelihood-building Processes in River Side

River Side is located in the central zone of eThekwini Municipality (see Figure 9.1). The exact historical origin of the settlement could not be established. Many respondents argued that the settlement has existed since the 1970s; however, the same could not be corroborated from the aerial photographs of the neighbourhood present in the archival records of eThekwini Municipality. This disjuncture could be related to the regular evictions during the apartheid era. The initial settlers had rented the land from the private owner at very low prices as the land was devoid of basic services (Focus Group Discussion,[9] January 2015). The settlement grew in size like other informal settlements in the 1980s due to social movements and economic transformations in Durban (Maharaj 2002: 172). The river bifurcated the settlement into two sections, which were further divided by a private fenced area and auto garage, producing four physically distinct yet socially connected clusters (Figure 9.2). Three of these clusters were named after the first settlers of each—KwaMamsuthu, Monpondweni and Mcondo (Focus Group

Discussion, January 2015). The settlement grew incrementally with KwaMamsuthu as the first cluster, followed by Monpondweni and Mcondo I and II (ibid.). KwaMamsuthu and Monpondweni are located on privately owned land, while Mcondo I and Mcondo II are situated on public land belonging to the Municipality.

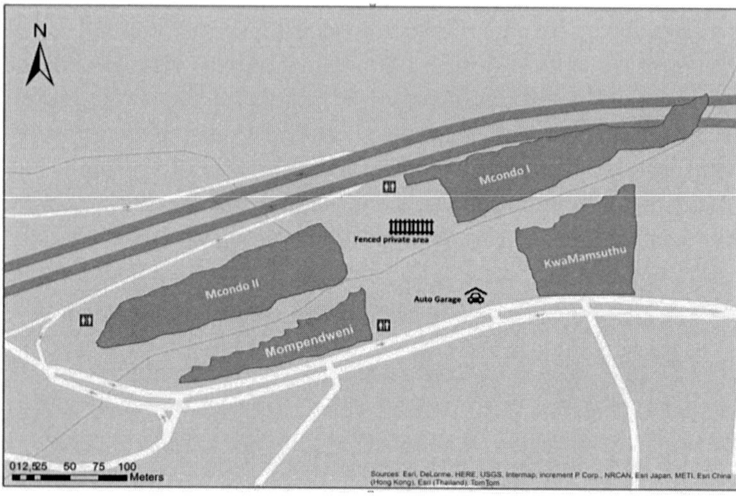

Figure 9.2: Settlement Map for River Side

Source: Author, based on Basemap: ArcGIS online (https://www.arcgis.com/index.html).

As a part of the RDP intervention, the residents of Mcondo I were relocated to a greenfield project in Verulum, 25 kms away in 2004. Within two years, Mcondo I was sprawling again with a mix of new arrivals and returnees from the greenfield project. After the floods of 2012, the residents expanded the settlement into Mcondo II (Focus Group Discussion, February 2015). The expansions in 2006 and 2012 ran parallel to the councillor elections. The local councillor's support for expansion and reoccupation of the territory was closely related to vote-bank politics in the area. Moreover, the local councillor was a crucial interface between the Municipality and the households, as residents turned to him for help during incidents of fire and floods in the settlement. Like other settlements in Durban, residents of River Side have resorted to protest by stalling traffic and marching to the councillor's office in their pursuit of access to services in the past. More than half of the surveyed households participated in the area committee meetings, which theoretically served as a civic association, but in practice was a derivative of the ANC and represented its power structures at local levels. The political and civil arm of the ANC was left unchallenged due to a lack of civil society in the settlement.

The total number of households in River Side was difficult to estimate. The official estimate of eThekwini Municipality was 542 households while residents reported more than 1,500 households (Focus Group Discussion, January 2015). More than half of the surveyed households were female-headed, with two or more people living together. Among male-headed households, the majority were one-person households. While the majority of households came from the Eastern Cape province, the settlement also attracted a fair share of population from Malawi, Mozambique and Zimbabwe (ibid.). Regarding the period of migration, most of the surveyed households had migrated to River Side after 1994 (see Table 9.1). A few households reported to have migrated before 1994, revealing the process of internal movements in the different clusters of the settlement. The settlement served as a 'gated community' with a high level of social control, and prospective residents had to rely on their social networks prior to migration. These networks also proved crucial for risk-mitigating strategies for those whose houses were destroyed in floods or shack fires, as they turned to their friends and relatives for shelter until they found a stable alternative, as mentioned below:

> In case of floods, the Municipality provides people with the poor material of blanket and actually those blankets are for covering the furniture. They also provide 250 grams of movite (porridge) and some people receive vouchers from the Municipality to buy food. The people who are at risk leave their houses and stay with their friends or relatives but within the settlement (ibid.).

Table 9.1: Distribution of Assets in River Side (in percentage)

Asset	Dimension	Indicator	Households (%)
Financial	Access to Stokvels	Households with Stokvels membership	33
	Commodities	Relative luxuries	42
		Basic durables	58
Human	Skill	Unemployed	29
		Low-skilled	44
		Semi-skilled	12
		Vocational	15
		Soft-skilled	0
	Education	No or limited school experience	7
		Primary education	25
		Pre-matric school	17
		Matric education	30
		Higher secondary	20
		Tertiary or university education	1
	Health	Households reporting communicable disease	41
Social/ Political Asset	Local area committee	Households participating in area committee meeting	52
	Period of migration	Before 1994	13
		1994–2004	43
		2005–2012	36
		2013 onwards	8
Physical	Adequacy	Adequate house	20
	Ownership	Renter	15
		Structure Owner	84
		Home/land owner	0
	Sanitation	Open defecation	2
		Pit latrines	3
		Public Toilet	95
		Private Toilet	0

Note: Missing data is not indicated here.

Source: Original data from 2015 household survey by author, with N=100.

Spatial location, accessibility and proximity influence how population groups can build up their livelihoods (Meikle 2002; Verrest and Post 2007). The central location of River Side enabled residents to work in the neighbouring middle-class areas and access transport easily to visit family and friends in their home towns/villages (Focus Group Discussion, February 2015). Additionally, living merely 7 kms from the central business district of Durban provided a unique spatial benefit for accessing employment opportunities. Most residents worked in the informal sector, according to the household survey data, and the prospect of employment (albeit informal) lured many new arrivals from poverty-stricken rural areas. Collective funds in the form of Stokvels[10] (a form of ROSCA, or Rotating Savings and Credit Association) supplement income, guarantee access to credit when needed and provide start-up capital for new informal enterprises, run mainly by women (Verhoef 2001). About one-third of households in the settlement were Stokvel members. While less than half of surveyed households possessed one or more items of relative luxury (such as a refrigerator, sofa or car), more than half reported ownership of basic durables such as bed, television and mobile phone. The settlement is located in a least needs area as per the Needs Index[11] mapped by eThekwini Municipality. However, inequality at the ward-level was evident in the dismal levels of sanitation. Also, the use of a large, slippery sewage pipe as a walking bridge between two clusters of the settlement confronted residents with the irony of infrastructural deficits, exposing them to other forms of risks such as falling into the river while crossing (see Image 9.1).

Illness and health problems are some of the most significant reasons for the perpetuation of poverty, due to the associated loss of income (Krishna 2010). Poor socio-economic conditions in Durban's informal settlements were related to the high prevalence of tuberculosis (TB), asthma and diarrhoea (Cunnan and Maharaj 2000). Because of the sensitivity associated with sexually transmitted diseases, it was not possible to discuss these with all the respondents. The data revealed poor levels of health among the residents, indicating that more than half of the surveyed households visit clinics one or more times per month. The most

Image 9.1: Sewage Pipe as a Walking Bridge in River Side

Photograph: Tara Saharan, March 2015.

prevalent healthcare strategy was accessing free healthcare in the neighbourhood. Similarly, most school-going children were enrolled in the neighbourhood. In terms of employment, about one-third of the surveyed households had no employed members (see Table 9.1). Most residents were engaged in low- or semi-skilled informal employment, as domestic workers, taxi drivers, truck assistants, street vendors, grass-cutters (see Table 9.1). The precarious informal employment further exacerbated household vulnerability, characterised by insecurity, low wages and poor benefits, without much institutional support from the state (Skinner 2006).

Moser (2009) argues that physical assets in terms of basic shelter are a 'prerequisite' for building other assets in informal settlements. If we look at this dimension, we see that River Side is marked by different housing types, closely linked to its location and settlement history. Except for a few permanent structures made of brick and concrete, the houses in the settlement are temporary and built using a range of materials. The majority of houses in KwaMamsuthu were made from corrugated iron, whereas wooden walls and plastic sheet roofs were common in Mcondo II.

Both Mcondo I and Monpondweni had a mix of corrugated iron as well as wood and plastic dwellings. This difference could be best explained by past shack fires, after which residents received corrugated iron sheets from the Municipality to reconstruct their structures. While the land in River Side was partly owned by the Municipality, there was always the risk that the state might decide to remove the residents. Nevertheless, those who had been staying longer were structure owners and had invested more compared to recent arrivals. Looking at basic services, water and sanitation were provided through standpipes, and three ablution blocks in the settlement were installed as part of the Interim Services programme in 2013. While the ablution blocks were insufficient for the large number of people living in the settlement, the majority used it for sanitation purposes. Due to the unattended waste along the river, the settlement was termed 'dirty' by many residents (Focus Group Discussion, February 2015), although many of their houses were often immaculately clean and arranged in an orderly fashion. The lack of legal electricity connections was a major concern. Tapping exposed electrical wires along the walking paths was a common practice, with frequent electrocutions, especially during the rainy season, as a tragic consequence (ibid.).

DISCUSSION AND CONCLUSIONS

The main research question raised in this chapter is how governance and planning approaches intersect with the livelihood-building processes of households living in informal settlements. The approaches towards informal settlements were explored as a combination of (*i*) policy and practices of eThekwini Municipality, (*ii*) planning discourses, and (*iii*) political coalitions. The provision of housing has dominated the political discourse of post-apartheid South African governments, with their central goal of addressing the history of spatial inequality. While urban planning in post-apartheid South Africa is based on the developmental discourse of spatial integration, it has not yet succeeded in reducing the spatial legacy of apartheid (Musvoto et al. 2016). The lack of substantial progress can be linked to the different priorities of the diverse units of municipal governments at the level of the city. The practices of the Human Settlement Unit are not aligned with the planning norms suggested in the Spatial Development Frameworks: the former argues for spatial integration and compactness, which contrasts with the dispersed and peripheral housing development practices of the latter. In addition, the Land Invasion Unit actively seeks to curb the growth of informal settlements in the Municipality. The Planning Department relies on rational planning approaches, underpinned by sophisticated models and technologies. In the Human Settlement section, policies are implemented through political assent, while the Land Invasion Unit takes a legal route wherever possible. Interventions are 'rendered technical' in planning documents by highlighting the use of expert knowledge that depoliticises housing (Li 2007).

This chapter shows that the technocratic approach of the Municipality is limited to the physical environment, and does not cater to the complex social reality of informal settlements. Moreover, the Municipality's proposal for housing and integrated development depoliticises the development of informal settlements. This is in direct contrast to the political agenda of the actors concerned. The land invasions of 2006 in Mcondo I and of 2012 in Mcondo II were closely linked to the councillor elections, and against the Municipality's policy of curbing the growth of informal settlements. Despite not being able to directly change the discourse, residents have successfully negotiated their 'right to the city' by staking claims to the land in question.

Processes of building urban livelihoods show a clear spatial strategy by households and the precarious nature of the assets that they build over time. First, at the household level, the research revealed the residents' spatial strategy for building livelihoods. Living in River Side gave residents improved access to jobs, which was the primary reason for migration among the surveyed households. Other than employment, proximity to health and education institutions was a crucial factor for residents. The settlement is deprived of basic services such as electricity, drainage and adequate sanitation, despite being located in the central zone of eThekwini Municipality, a ward with the lowest needs requirement.

Although the settlement has grown over the last couple of decades, the precariousness of assets has contributed to higher risks for residents. For instance, the long delay in securing fire- and rain-proof housing from the state had disastrous results, leading to loss of life and assets. Continuous threats of eviction and disasters such as floods and fires discouraged residents from investing in physical assets. These findings suggest that residents aligned their strategies to build assets with the approaches of the state (Moser 2009). However, the focus of the state has been limited to interventions related to the physical environment, be they services or structures.

Overall, the findings indicate that analysing governance and planning approaches towards informal settlements in relation to the urban livelihoods of households not only reveals a 'conflict of rationalities' between the marginalised population and the managerial state (Watson 2003, 2009), but also reveals ambiguities among the different institutions and their diverse approaches. Furthermore, the two relations explored in the chapter were crucial for revealing these different rationalities. While the argument presented in this chapter is limited to an inner-city informal settlement of eThekwini Municipality, further research can explore the survival logic of residents living in peripheral settlements in order to explore if this conflict of rationalities differs across the entire range of informal settlements, or whether intervention policies need to take into account the specificity of different settlement types. From a policy perspective, it can be concluded that the city needs a combined approach for planning and practice towards informal settlements, which needs to be integrated with the survival logic of the urban poor. Otherwise, the goal of addressing spatial inequalities in the post-apartheid period will remain an unrealised dream.

End Notes

Acknowledgements: This research was carried out in the context of the EU-FP7 project Chance2Sustain: Urban Chances, City Growth and the Sustainability Challenge, with EADI as the lead partner of the project. I gratefully acknowledge several rounds of comments by Isa Baud and Karin

Pfeffer. I would also like to express thanks to Catherine Sutherland, Glen Robbins and Eric Chu for comments on an earlier draft of this chapter. I am very thankful to Marcel Heemskerk for making the GIS maps. I am also thankful to Catherine Sutherland, Dianne Scott, Glen Robbins and other staff members of UKZN for their support and co-operation during my stay in South Africa. I am very grateful to my research assistants–Sibongile Buthelezi, Ma Dudu Khumalo and Sibonelo Gumede–for tirelessly working in the scorching summer heat of February and March. I am also indebted to all the respondents in Durban for their valuable time and insightful discussions. The residents of River Side deserve a special mention for their participation in the surveys and discussions; without their valuable input, this research would not have been possible.

1. The city of Durban and its surrounding municipalities were renamed as eThekwini Municipality during the post-apartheid transition. However, Durban refers to the city more generally. In this chapter, I will use Durban interchangeably with eThekwini Municipality in order to represent the same city.

2. The data presented here is part of a wider research project focussing on informal settlements, which includes the case of Chennai in India. Because of the comparability of eThekwini and Chennai, the research was limited to inner-city informal settlements.

3. The name of the settlement used in the chapter is fictitious, in order to safeguard the confidentiality of all research participants.

4. Houses under RDP include services and top-structures for sites that are viable for redevelopment with tenure security. The 1994 White Paper on housing policy for RDP aimed to collate government and private-sector effort in relation to housing delivery for the poor.

5. 'Top-structure' is a common term used in South African planning and housing literature and signifies 'a house added on top of land'. To ensure broad access to housing and rapid delivery in the post-apartheid period, housing subsidies were introduced in the form of top-structures in serviced sites.

6. This interview is part of the author's own fieldwork. The identity of research participants cannot be revealed to maintain confidentiality.

7. The 'areas of least needs' is based on the 'Needs Index', explained in end note 11. The index was mapped spatially along the wards in eThekwini. So, the areas of least needs include many such wards where the Needs Index was reported to be low.

8. This interview is part of the author's own fieldwork. The identity of research participants cannot be revealed to maintain confidentiality.

9. This Focus Group Discussion is part of the author's own fieldwork. The identity of research participants cannot be revealed to maintain confidentiality. This holds true for all Focus Group Discussions excerpted in the chapter.

10. Stokvels are savings clubs with twelve or more members, where each member contributes a certain amount each month. This can be anything from R50 to R1,000, depending on individual income. Each month, a different member receives the money.

11. The Needs Index is a zone-wide plan of eThekwini composed of unemployment, average income at ward-level, ward GDP, and physical and social infrastructure backlogs.

References

Baud, I. S. A. and J. de Wit (eds). 2009. *New Forms of Urban Governance in India: Shifts, Models, Networks and Contestations*. New Delhi: SAGE Publications.

Baud, I. S. A., D. Scott, K. Pfeffer, J. Sydenstricker-Neto and E. Denis. 2014. 'Digital and spatial knowledge management in urban governance: Emerging issues in India, Brazil, South Africa, and Peru'. *Habitat International* 44: 501–509.

Bayat, A. 2010. *Life as Politics: How Ordinary People Change the Middle East*. Amsterdam: Amsterdam University Press.

Benjamin, S. 2004. 'Urban land transformation for pro-poor economies'. *Geoforum* 35(2): 177–187.

______. 2008. 'Occupancy urbanism: Radicalizing politics and economy beyond policy and programmes'. *International Journal of Urban and Regional Research* 32(3): 719–729.

Bradlow, B., J. Bolnick and C. Shearing. 2011. 'Housing, institutions, money: The failures and promise of human settlements policy and practice in South Africa'. *Environment and Urbanization* 23(1): 267–275.

Breetzke, K. 2008. 'From conceptual frameworks to quantitative models: Spatial planning in the Durban metropolitan area, South Africa – the link to housing and infrastructure planning'. Case study prepared for Planning Sustainable Cities: Global Report on Human Settlements 2009. UN-Habitat. Available at https://mirror.unhabitat.org/downloads/docs/GRHS2009CaseStudyChapter08Durban.pdf (accessed June 2021).

Charlton, S. 2009. 'Housing for the nation, the city and the household: Competing rationalities as a constraint to reform?' *Development Southern Africa* 26(2): 301–315.

Cunnan, P. and B. Maharaj. 2000. 'Against the odds: Healthcare in an informal settlement in Durban'. *Development Southern Africa* 17(5): 667–686.

De Haan, L. 2012. 'The livelihood approach: A critical exploration'. *Erdkunde* 66(4): 345–357.

De Haan, L. and A. Zoomers. 2005. 'Exploring the frontier of livelihoods research'. *Development and Change* 36(1): 27–47.

Dean, M. 2010. *Governmentality: Power and Rule in Modern Society*. Los Angeles: SAGE Publications.

Department of Housing. 1994. 'White Paper: A new housing policy and strategy for South Africa'. Pretoria: Department of Housing.

Devas, N. 2002. 'Urban livelihoods–Issues for urban governance and management'. In C. Rakodi and T. Lloyd-Jones (eds), *Urban Livelihoods: A People-Centred Approach to Reducing Poverty*, 205–221. London: Earthscan Publications Limited.

______. 2005. 'Metropolitan governance and urban poverty'. *Public Administration and Development* 25(4): 351–361.

Durban Metropolitan Area. 1998. *Spatial development framework–Spatial development plan*. Durban: Durban Metropolitan Area. Available at http://www.durban.gov.za/Documents/City_Government/IDP_Policy/18%20SDF(original).pdf (accessed June 2021).

eThekwini Municipality. 2012. 'eThekwini housing sector plan–the housing chapter of IDP'. eThekwini: eThekwini Housing.

______. 2013. 'Spatial development framework (SDF) report 2013/14'. eThekwini: eThekwini Municipality.

______. 2016. 'Spatial development framework–review 2016-2017'. eThekwini: eThekwini Municipality.

Flyvbjerg, B. 1998. 'Rationality and power'. In B. Flyvbjerg (ed.), *Rationality and Power: Democracy in Practice*, 225–236. Chicago: University of Chicago Press.

Gilbert, A. 2007. 'The return of the slum: Does language matter?' *International Journal of Urban and Regional Research* 31(4): 697–713.

Gough, I., J. A. McGregor and L. Camfield. 2007. 'Theorising well-being in international development'. In I. Gough and J. A. McGregor (eds), *Well-being in Developing Countries: From Theory to Research*, 3–43. Cambridge: Cambridge University Press.

Haferburg, C. and M. Huchzermeyer. 2015. 'An introduction to the governing of post-apartheid cities'. In C. Haferburg and M. Huchzermeyer (eds), *Urban Governance in Post-apartheid Cities—Modes of Engagement in South Africa's Metropoles*, 3–14. Pietermaritzburg: University of KwaZulu-Natal Press.

Harrison, P., A. Todes and V. Watson. 2008. *Planning and Transformation: Learning from the Post-Apartheid Experience*. Abingdon: Routledge.

Hendriks, B. 2011. 'Urban livelihoods and institutions: Towards matching institutions for the poor in Nairobi's informal settlements'. *International Development Planning Review* 33(2): 111–146.

Housing Development Agency. 2013. 'KwaZulu-Natal: Informal settlements status (2013)', Research report. Houghton: Housing Development Agency.

Huchzermeyer, M. 2010. 'Pounding at the tip of the iceberg: The dominant politics of informal settlement eradication in South Africa'. *Politikon* 37(1): 129–148.

______. 2011. *Cities with 'Slums': From Informal Settlement Eradication to a Right to the City in Africa*. Claremont: University of Cape Town.

______. 2014. 'Changing housing policy in South Africa'. In J. Bredenoord, P. Van Lindert and P. Smets (eds), *Affordable Housing in the Urban Global South: Seeking Sustainable Solutions*,336–348. London: Routledge.

Krishna, A. 2010. *One Illness Away: Why People Become Poor and How They Escape Poverty*. Oxford: Oxford University Press.

Kudva, N. 2009. 'The everyday and the episodic: The spatial and political impacts of urban informality'. *Environment and Planning* A 41(7): 1614–1628.

Li, T. M. 2007. *The Will to Improve: Governmentality, Development and the Practice of Politics*. Durham and London: Duke University Press.

Maharaj, B. 2002. 'Segregation, desegregation and de-racialisation: Racial politics and the city of Durban'. In B. Fruend and V. Padayachee (eds), *(D)urban Vortex–South African City in Transition*, 171–194. Pietermaritzburg: University of Natal Press.

Martínez, J., K. Pfeffer and I. S. A. Baud. 2016. 'Factors shaping cartographic representations of inequalities: Maps as products and processes'. *Habitat International* 51: 90–102.

Marx, C. and S. Charlton. 2003. 'Urban slums reports: The case of Durban, South Africa'. UN-Habitat. Available at https://www.ucl.ac.uk/dpu-projects/Global_Report/pdfs/Durban.pdf (accessed June 2021).

Massey, R. T. 2013. 'Competing rationalities and informal settlement upgrading in Cape Town, South Africa: A recipe for failure'. *Journal of Housing and the Built Environment* 28(4): 605–613.

McFarlane, C. 2012. 'Rethinking informality: Politics, crisis, and the city'. *Planning Theory & Practice* 13(1): 89–108.

Meikle, S. 2002. 'The urban context and poor people'. In C. Rakodi and T. Lloyd-Jones (eds), *Urban Livelihoods: A People-centred Approach to Reducing Poverty*, 37–51. London: Earthscan.

Milbert, I. 2006. 'Slums, slum dwellers and multi-level governance'. *The European Journal of Development Research* 18(2): 299–318.

Moser, C. O. N. 1998. 'The asset vulnerability framework: Reassessing urban poverty reduction strategies'. *World Development* 26(1): 1–19.

———. 2009. *Ordinary Families, Extraordinary Lives: Assets and Poverty Reduction in Guayaquil, 1978–2004*. Washington, D.C.: Brookings Institution Press.

Mottiar, S. and P. Bond. 2012. 'The politics of discontent and social protest in Durban'. *Politikon* 39(3): 309–330.

Musvoto, G., G. Lincoln and R. Hansmann. 2016. 'The role of spatial development frameworks in transformation of the eThekwini municipality, KwaZulu-Natal, South Africa: Reflecting on 20 years of planning'. *Urban Forum* 27(2): 187–210.

NDHS. 2014. *Celebrating 20 Years of Human Settlement: Bringing the Freedom Charter to Life*. Pretoria: Republic of South Africa.

Nijman, J. 2008. 'Against the odds: Slum rehabilitation in neoliberal Mumbai'. *Cities* 25(2): 73–85.

———. 2010. 'A study of space in Mumbai's slums'. *Tijdschrift Voor Economische En Sociale Geografie* 101(1): 4–17.

Paddison, R. 2016. 'The rise of urban governance'. In O. Nel-lo and R. Mele (eds), *Cities in the 21st Century*, 263–269. New York: Routledge.

Parizeau, K. 2015. 'When assets are vulnerabilities: An assessment of informal recyclers' livelihood strategies in Buenos Aires, Argentina'. *World Development* 67: 161–173.

Pierre, J. 1999. 'Models of urban governance: The institutional dimension of urban politics'. *Urban Affairs Review* 34(3): 372–396.

Pieterse, E. 2006. 'Building with ruins and dreams: Some thoughts on realising integrated urban development in South Africa through crisis'. *Urban Studies* 43(2): 285–304.

Presence, C. 2014. 'SA's "sad story of housing"–Lindiwe Sisulu'. *Mail and Guardian*, 15 July. Available at https://mg.co.za/article/2014-07-15-sas-sad-story-of-housing/ (accessed June 2021).

Rakodi, C. 2002. 'A livelihoods approach—Conceptual issues and definitions'. In C. Rakodi and T. Lloyd-Jones (eds), *Urban Livelihoods: A People-centred Approach to Reducing Poverty*,3–22. London: Earthscan.

Robbins, G. 2010. 'Beyond local economic development? Exploring municipality supported job creation in a South African city'. *Development Southern Africa* 27(4): 531–546.

Roy, A. 2009. 'Why India cannot plan its cities: Informality, insurgence and the idiom of urbanisation'. *Planning Theory* 8(1): 76–87.

Scoones, I. 2009. 'Livelihoods perspectives and rural development'. *The Journal of Peasant Studies* 36(1): 171–196.

Seekings, J. 2000. 'Introduction: Urban studies in South Africa after apartheid'. *International Journal of Urban and Regional Research* 24(4): 832–840.

Skinner, C. 2006. 'Falling though the policy gaps? Evidence from the informal economy in Durban, South Africa'. *Urban Forum* 17(2): 125–148.

Soja, E. 2009. 'The city and spatial justice'. *Justice Spatiale/ Spatial Justice* 1(1): 31–39.

Southall, R. 2014. 'Democracy at risk? Politics and governance under the ANC'. *The Annals of the American Academy of Political and Social Science* 652(1): 48–69.

Statistics South Africa. 2011. eThekwini. Available at http://www.statssa.gov.za/?page_id=1021&id=ethekwini-municipality (accessed February 2021).

Sutherland, C. 2016. 'National and urban contexts of the settlement cases: An overview'. In V. Dupont, D. Jordhus-Lier, C. Sutherland and E. Braathen (eds), *The Politics of Slums in the Global South: Urban Informality in Brazil, India, South Africa and Peru*, 30–48. London and New York: Routledge.

Sutherland, C., E. Braathen, V. Dupont and D. Jordhus-Lier. 2016. 'Policies towards substandard settlements'. In V. Dupont, D. Jordhus-Lier, C. Sutherland and E. Braathen (eds), *The Politics of Slums in the Global South: Urban Informality in Brazil, India, South Africa and Peru*, 49–78. London and New York: Routledge.

Tissington, K., N. Munshi, G.Mirugi-Mukundi and E. Durojaye. 2013. '"Jumping the queue", waiting lists and other myths: Perceptions and practice around housing demand and allocation in South Africa'. Johannesburg: Socio-Economic Rights Institute of South Africa.

Todes, A. 2000. 'Reintegrating the apartheid city? Urban policy and urban restructuring in Durban'. In G. Bridge and S. Watson (eds), *A Companion to the City*, 617–629. Oxford: Blackwell Publishing.

______. 2014. 'New African suburbanisation? Exploring the growth of the northern corridor of eThekwini/ KwaDakuza'. *African Studies* 73(2): 245–270.

Urban Econ. 2012. 'Economic review for the eThekwini municipal region 2010/11'. eThekwini: eThekwini Municipality.

Verhoef, G. 2001. 'Informal financial service institutions for survival: African women and stokvels in urban South Africa, 1930–1998'. *Enterprise and Society* 2(2): 259–296.

Verrest, H. and J. Post. 2007. 'Home-based economic activities, livelihoods and space in Paramaribo, Suriname'. *International Development Planning Review* 29(2): 161–184.

Watson, V. 2002. *Change and Continuity in Spatial Planning: Metropolitan Planning in Cape Town under Political Transition*. London and New York: Routledge.

______. 2003. 'Conflicting rationalities: Implications for planning theory and ethics'. *Planning Theory & Practice* 4(4): 395–407.

______. 2009. 'Seeing from the South: Refocusing urban planning on the Globe's central urban issues'. *Urban Studies* 46(11): 2259–2275.

Yiftachel, O. 2009. 'Theoretical notes on "gray cities": The coming of urban apartheid?' *Planning Theory* 8(1): 88–100.

X

For a Pedagogy of Co-existence in the *Polis*

Fernando Lannes Fernandes, Jailson de Souza e Silva,
Jorge Luiz Barbosa, Eliana Sousa Silva and Tatiana Moura

> *... on that broad, splendid boulevard, on the polished asphalt, in contrast to the rich facade of the tall buildings, in contrast to the parade of carriages and cars, coming across with that old vehicle, in which the drunken devotees howled, gave me the impression of a monstrous anachronism: the resurrection of barbarism–it was a wild age that came back, like a mud from another world, coming to disturb and shame the life of the civilized age.*
>
> (Bilac 1906, cited in Pesavento 2002: 186)[1]

INTRODUCTION

Hate and social indifference have been dominating public debate, political rhetoric and media discourse in contemporary society. The advance of such a paradigm configures a threat to not only democracy and its respect for diversity, but also to very basic aspects of respectful relations that should sustain life in society and, furthermore, to co-existence. Xenophobia, homophobia, Islamophobia and racism are some of the most dominant discourses in politico-ideological agendas in the contemporary world. The intensification of socio-symbolic tensions sustained by narrow socio-political, cultural, religious and ethnic discourses have produced, reinforced and disseminated narratives of disposal and dehumanisation. These discourses emerge in a historical context where the ideal of a democratic state has never been so challenged. Not surprisingly, we may be entering a period, as Santos (2007: 18) holds, in which 'societies are politically democratic and socially fascistic' (ibid.: 20).

Such discourses represent forms of labelling (or the reinforcement of established labels) that can refer not only to individuals and groups, but also to their *territories*: favelas, cortiços, slums, squats, ghettos and other similar settlements that share a lower socio-political and symbolic status in the urban landscape. Their social representation is typically associated with negative labels, reinforcing physical and social features which are below the normative characteristics defined by hegemonic aesthetics and living standards.

In this chapter, we argue that the improvement of livelihoods in those territories is very much dependent on changes in their symbolic capital. These changes, however, are not related to the incorporation of hegemonic aesthetics and living standards, but lie in the recognition of the *inventive power* of peripheral groups, which arises not only from their strategies and forms of interaction and affirmation in the urban space, but also from their genuine and authentic forms of organisation. That means the acknowledgement of other aesthetic and symbolic references that challenge the idea of normalcy, reaffirm the agency of people and reject any form of externalised labelling that ultimately sustains *symbolic violence* (Bourdieu 1998).

We conceptualise the urban space as a *field* where the symbolic capital of neighbourhoods and their residents is accumulated by economic and social status. Following Bourdieu's (1977, 1984, 1998) conceptual framework, we maintain that the accumulation of symbolic capital in the city is central to the accumulation of economic and social capital and, ultimately, to the affirmation of individuals and groups in the public sphere. As such, strategies of social *distinction* operate to reinforce social hierarchies and oppression through *symbolic violence*. This symbolic violence, we argue, bases itself on *pedagogical* processes of a naturalisation of indifference, social disgust and hatred that results from social tensions in the urban space. Such pedagogies result in the public humiliation and dehumanisation of targeted groups, which consists of the *mechanisms of inculcation* that conform to the *social habitus* in the urban space: we learn to hate, to be indifferent to and to ignore the *Other* through the incorporation of a narrative of social disgust (Tyler 2011), disposal (Giroux 2010) and denial (Bauman 2009), which together configure processes of decivilisation (Rodger 2013) of peripheral groups. These *pedagogies of monsterisation* are at the heart of the othering processes that generate and reproduce social tensions which negatively impact co-existence in the city.

The recognition of the *inventive power* of peripheral groups—and widely, of urban *peripheries*[2]—is central, then, for the development of a *paradigm of potency*, where the living style (rather than the living conditions) is acknowledged on its own terms, as a form of accumulated *symbolic capital.* Although this capital is devalued by dominant forces driving hegemonic urban agendas, we acknowledge that progressive urban agendas should challenge symbolic violence. The starting point should be the questioning of its epistemological forms of manifestation, which regards hegemonic forms of knowing, doing and representing. Here, we agree with Santos (2007) on the necessity of claiming an 'ecology of knowledges' in which counter-hegemonic, pluralist and propositive thinking are acknowledged. Santos argues about the incapacity of hegemonic epistemologies to move beyond an abyssal line that is rooted in colonial divide, where the 'colonial zone' (or, in our own interpretation, the 'peripheral zones') 'is *par excellence*, the realm of incomprehensive beliefs and behaviours which in no way can be considered knowledge, whether true or false' (ibid.: 8).

If we take this claim into account, it will be necessary to consider these 'peripheral epistemologies' as a necessary component for any urban agenda. This means not only giving room to a different thinking, but also establishing a sense of *ignorance* that is the 'result of the forgetting or unlearning implicit in the reciprocal learning process' (Santos 2007: 30). In other words, we claim that *ignorance*, as a means to forget or 'unlearn' dominant/hegemonic systems of knowing and doing, is the only way to acknowledge the inventive power of peripheries and peripheral groups. Furthermore, those peripheral neighbourhoods and their people should be appreciated as 'urban makers' and positive contributors to urban life, rather than as neighbourhoods of disposal where deprivation and other negative representations operate as symbolic forces that lower their status and reputation in the public sphere. As such, the simple ideas sustained by a binary 'right' versus 'wrong', 'acceptable' versus 'unacceptable' and 'normal' versus 'abnormal' need to be forgotten, in order to give way to forms of acknowledgement of 'peripheral epistemologies'. Peripheral groups develop systems of understanding that are not always captured or understood. Instead, they are valued and represented as 'non-conforming to acceptable standards' and, by doing so, are defined as 'abnormal' in the first place. Our claim does not suggest a romantic notion that people should live according to their established living standards, simply because such standards are, in most cases, a result of oppressive mechanisms—for example, 'poor sanitisation'. However, the responses given to these conditions, as well as the 'solution before the solution' (non-reactive, but simply embedded in traditional forms of doing) tend to be either co-opted (in a tokenistic way) or ignored (because of the scientific arrogance that sustains the discourse of 'evidence-based policy'). What we see, then, is a hegemonic system of representation that 'filters' divergent epistemologies to sustain dominant models of knowing and doing. Not surprisingly, we observe that many public claims to address 'participation' tends to be co-opted by those groups that are better positioned in the social space, or in other words, those who have more symbolic capital (some illustrative examples can be found in Flint and Rowlands 2003; Hastings and Matthews 2015; Locock et al. 2016).

What is proposed is the development of 'pedagogies of co-existence' in line with the idea of 'ecology of knowledges' proposed by Santos (2007). Our point, however, goes beyond the epistemological element, and sustains the idea that such 'pedagogies' constitute learning processes that will fundamentally challenge all forms of othering that fabricate urban 'monsters': the practices, aesthetics and living strategies of stigmatised groups need to be acknowledged, incorporated and embedded into the development of responses to social issues. Here, we consider the need to give voice to the people and increase spheres of participation and the expansion of democracy in the city. We also observe the need to incorporate the symbolic dimensions, aesthetics and social practices that are usually ignored by the hegemonic parameters that define policy, practice and rights in the city.

This conceptual framework will be further considered through empirical references from Brazilian favelas, most specifically, in Rio de Janeiro city. Rio's example will help to illustrate the processes of social tension and 'monsterisation' of groups (as well as their practices and their epistemologies) that to some extent are similarly reproduced in other places across the world. With this, we expect to provide some references that can be used to reflect upon the 'pedagogies of monsterisation' that operate in the dehumanising processes of othering. Moreover, we also hope to provide references for the identification of the *potencies* in each specific context, and the conditions for the development of 'pedagogies of co-existence' in the city and beyond.

FAVELA AS THE URBAN EXPRESSION OF CORPOREAL-TERRITORIAL DISTINCTION OF RIGHTS

It is widely accepted that urban settlements with limited access to infrastructure and public services, and with a low social status profile (lower levels of education, higher levels of unemployment and precarious jobs, prevalence of poor health outcomes and so on) are fundamentally classified as 'deprived', 'disadvantaged', 'underprivileged', 'impoverished' and 'needy'. These 'adjectivations' sustain the universe of discourses to which the *doxa* (Bourdieu 1977) of urban thinking conforms. Such doxa has been widely adopted by policy documents, mass media and the dispersed narratives (jokes, gossips, talks) as assumed hegemonic characteristics of those settlements and their people. The recognition that such areas do not meet the expected standards of living (as well as social practices) drives the claims for improvements based on state investments that can secure better living standards, tenancy, as well as 'behaviours' that align individuals and communities to certain policy expectations (one example sits behind the idea of 'health literacy'). This is at the core of housing and urban regeneration policies and is legitimated by research, public opinion and official data that show the lack of resources and *adequate* living conditions.

The acknowledgment of such characteristics is central to the consolidation of minimum standards of living. But this becomes a matter of concern when the emphasis on what those areas *are-not* or *need* obliterates other relevant characteristics that are typically ignored or downplayed—for example, the inventive power translated into creative solutions, strategies of survival, means of co-existence and resolution of conflicts, cultural production and entrepreneurism that were developed under specific living conditions. Here, 'deprivation' means strategies that resulted in the production of specific living arrangements that are delegitimated by the hegemonic social, cultural, political and aesthetic references sustained by the paradigm of deprivation. Fundamentally, these are *social habitus* developed under specific living conditions, which are symbolically depreciated as part of the process of socio-spatial distinction and symbolic violence that takes place in the urban space. Such a depreciative symbolic process is part of a wider dynamic that involves the production of narratives aiming to gain popular support and justify actions that will benefit specific sectors in society, to the detriment of others. These disadvantaging practices are carried out by economic and political elites who use symbolic violence to maintain the *status quo*. Carried out under the questionable tag of 'democratic practices' (framed under the idea of political democracy co-existing with social fascism, as suggested by Santos [2007]), urban interventions are presented as beneficial to a wider parcel of society, who will enjoy the by-products of the elite's capital accumulation.

The joint efforts of peripheral groups to build shelters for themselves and their families were never recognised by society in general, or by the state. Their territorialised constructions have always been seen and treated as illegal, irregular, clandestine, subnormal and precarious, especially for having been built without government approval, thus confronting the hegemonic order of the market, and most evidently, due to their social and racial origins. In contrast, we cannot subscribe to simplistic explanations such as a lack of public resources to meet the social demands of the favelas' residents, offered by governments more or less sensitive to peripheral groups. The incompleteness of access and the precariousness of fundamental public services (education, healthcare and sanitation) are expressions of a territorial distinction of rights, unequivocally showing that citizens of the same city have their rights respected and guaranteed depending on which neighbourhood they live in.

It is necessary to highlight that this is not a 'broken city' issue; it is much more than merely a problem of access to public services and consumer goods. In fact, it is about the non-recognition of citizenship within territories marked and inhabited by those enduring a legitimate struggle towards their right to the city. It is a distinct relation that dictates what is in and what is out of the urban order of rights, creating a territorial hierarchy largely supported by the non-recognition of the rights of some subjects and at the limit, by a perverse indifference towards the Other's life in her unequal conditions (here presented as the different). As Sodré (2002) points out, the signal, conceptual and imagery description of the Other in their subaltern position corresponds to generalised understandings and practices related to the legitimacy or the lack of rights. In this sense, rights distinction operates as an ontological alienation between the hegemonic and the subaltern classes. Such alienation is found in social privileges and territorial hierarchy markers that reproduce social classes and groups in the city. The territorial distinction of rights has explicit ties with racial relations. The myth of 'racial democracy' and *mestiçagem* (mixture of races) as symbols of nationality were always ideological attributes of social hierarchies established by a racial classification of humanity, constantly reproduced in Brazilian society, notably in the racial identity of homicide victims in Brazil's metropolises.

Indeed, Brazilian society is quintessentially interracial if we consider the cultural differences. However, also undeniable is the territorial distinction of rights—with explicit ties to racial relations—defined by corporeal classifications of human superiority and inferiority, with decisive consequences for the territorial order of society. The social composition, dominated by the presence of black and '*pardo*'[3] people (therefore, black people), corresponds to the forms of non-recognition of urban citizenship and the effectiveness of fundamental rights. Therefore, we can say that our cities and metropolises are not only machines for the reproduction of social inequalities, but they are also liquidators of the rights of territorialised social subjects.[4]

THE 'PEDAGOGIES OF MONSTERISATION'

The 'pedagogies of monsterisation' refer to the wider range of inculcation and *learning* processes that are underpinned by stigmatisation and depreciative attitudes towards the *Other*, or as part of the *othering* processes. Essentially, this refers to the systems of belief that are inculcated in the formation of the social habitus (Bourdieu 1984) in relation to *others*, and, in addition, to what is morally and aesthetically accepted as the truth, normal, correct or superior. Such processes conform to social habitus in the urban space. The key feature of the pedagogy of monsterisation is the annihilation of any trace of humanity through diffuse and dispersed narratives that gradually produce truth, or 'regimes of truth' (Foucault 1976) that do not merely conform to mindsets and forms of understanding (in this case, of the *Other*). Such a process has some similarities with the formation of the juridico-moral monstrosity explored by Foucault (2004), but beyond that, also conforms to a system of hierarchical values in the formation of which two parallel processes take place. First, the 'self-fulfilling prophecies', where predictable behaviours that are used as stigma labels reinforce the characteristics and situations in which social disgust, disapproval and hate take shape. In simple words, based on expected behaviours, systems are set up for people to fail, or to 'fit in with' what is expected from them. In Bourdieusian terms, every time the dominated/subaltern habitus comes in contact with the dominant habitus, there is non-conformity in a given social field. One typical example is when social benefit claimants come into contact with services. Policy design is based on certain norms and expectations set by the dominant habitus. If good timekeeping is of value to those inserted in the world of work, working ethics and norms, this is taken as an expected rule. As such, we can observe the case of many benefit claimants who may never have been engaged in stable employment (and furthermore, are outside the hegemonic idea of work ethics) being sanctioned[5] for not fulfilling some rules, such as attending their appointments on time. This rule is chosen because there is a belief that this will 'adjust' behaviour, but also as a clear way to punish the *habitus* of those who will not be able to perform those tasks appropriately, or, in addition, not be articulate enough (in terms of dominant habitus codes, language and posture) to justify any episode that resulted in late or missed appointments,[6] resulting in more punishment (self-fulfilling prophecy). Besides, those street-level bureaucrats (Lipsky 2010) dealing directly with service users also maintain a certain level of class arrogance by imposing on the ones lower down the social ladder the morality of their beliefs. This is a classic example of social fascism in a 'democratic' state.

Second, the process of symbolic annihilation can be so strong that any attempt to produce counter-narratives will face resistance based on 'filters' set by inculcated social representations. This can even naturalise the inferiority of any argument in the face of dominant explanations. In other words, the voice of stigmatised groups is limited to their peer supporters and will face strong resistance in their attempts to convince those who have already made a prejudgment. One example is when stigmatised groups make legitimate claims, such as the Dalits' struggle to access water and sanitation in India (Johns n. d.).

Through monsterisation, humanity is stripped away from the other. This results in the creation of forms of interpretation and representation that conform to social avoidance and the diminishing of any form of co-existence. The consequences of the radicalisation of this attitude can be observed in the ideological discourse emerging from the 'war on terror', which resulted in Islamophobia. In a closer example for us, in Brazil, we can see the increasing indifference to the deaths of youngsters and young adults living in favelas. Their association with criminals and the historical component of race has created conditions for the radicalisation of symbolic violence.

THE MONSTERS FROM FAVELAS

> *And on the muddy ground covered with puddles, in the sultry humidity, a living world, a human community, began to wriggle, to seethe, to grow spontaneously in that quagmire, multiplying like larvae in a dung heap.*
>
> (Azevedo 2000: 12)

Official data from the Brazilian Census 2010 acknowledged the existence of 763 favelas in Rio de Janeiro city, with a total population of almost 1.4 million. This corresponds to approximately one-fourth of the city's population. Unofficial estimates, however, may suggest higher numbers when considering areas with similar socio-spatial arrangements that for land law reasons were not included in the census statistics. This would possibly raise the figures to approximately 30 per cent of the city's population. The numbers, however, do not tell the whole story, and may become secondary when other aspects are considered.

The existence and permanence of favelas in Rio's landscape (and widely in the Brazilian landscape) cannot be seen only as a matter of unequal distribution of wealth and access to land. Favelas represent the power of resistance and survival of highly stigmatised social groups. As such, any consideration of this 'urban phenomenon' should first consider the relevance of favelas as spaces of insurgent citizenship, where the so-called 'illegal invasions' can actually be viewed as acts of survival and class resistance. The matter of 'illegality' is always a matter of who makes the law. Brazil, as a colonised country, has always been an invaded territory taken by arrest, and at different times by the Portuguese, French and Dutch.

The survival of favelas has also to do with the geography of the city. Rio is possibly unique in the world in that the city has a mix of mountains, forests (the biggest urban forest in the world), hills, lagoons and beaches that offer not only a great visual experience, but are also very attractive for real-estate investments. After the 1940s, beaches became key areas for real-estate investments with the expansion of middle- and upper-class neighbourhoods, such as the famous areas of Copacabana, Ipanema and Leblon (Leitão 1999; Velho 2002). During the 1980s and 1990s, the expansion of a new area in the Barra da Tijuca region[7] gained force with the development of high-security gated communities that were explored by the market as a response to the 'violence' and 'insecurity' in the city (Leitão 1999; Souza 2000).

Historically, given the higher transportation costs, the city hills were left behind by market interests, and in most cases, occupied by the poorest. The end of slavery and the expansion of the urban population observed between the end of the 1800s and beginning of the 1900s, in conjunction with the crisis of low-cost housing, are considerations in explaining the expansion of precarious housing (such as the cortiços, or slum tenements) (Abreu 1994; Rocha 1995). This was in a context where critical urban transformations took place in the central areas of the city, with urban reform and new interests in investing in areas previously destined to become precarious housing. As such, people living in the slum tenements were gradually displaced and many found the proximity of hills the best alternative for housing. It was in 1897 that favela agglomerations started to receive attention from the media and public authorities, although the phenomenon had already been taking shape in previous years (Abreu 1988, 1994). The key feature of favelas, in Rio's context, was its closer location to prosperous neighbourhoods, which worked as an economic system in which a cheap, low-skilled workforce was available to the middle and upper classes still accustomed to the culture of slavery.

This system of economic exploitation (Kowarick 1993) worked well for nearly a century. Favelas provided a cheap workforce while the middle classes enjoyed their lifestyle with the provision of babysitters, maids, cleaners, housekeepers and all sorts of odd-job workers at hand.[8] But favelas were not simply a source of an exploited low-cost workforce. The conditions in which favelas historically interacted with the city also provided 'avenues' from which singular class interactions occurred. 'Exploited workforce' also meant opportunities to encounter differences and cultural exchanges that, to some extent, are found in the Samba and widely, in the Carnival. Not only that, those avenues were an opportunity for changes in the social habitus and the possibility of new forms of interaction beyond economic relations. During the 1980s, this system started to collapse with the emergence of drug trafficking in favelas. The imagery of favelas started to acquire a new configuration in the public arena. In this new context, while the social representation of favelas became increasingly connected to the ideas of crime and drug-trafficking, there was also the emergence of counter-narratives such as social movements, the growth of grassroots NGOs, as well as cultural and artistic movements that challenged stigma and created new links with the city. The social, cultural and political influence of favelas in the public sphere then acquired a new shape. Educational organisations started to prepare local people (in particular, youngsters) to access publicly funded universities. Cultural movements connected with other groups in the city, the nation and the world. The favelas started to produce a different voice, more sophisticated, stronger and influential in the public sphere. In spite of this, there are still challenges that relate to the way favelas are perceived and, in some cases, in the way such emerging movements are embraced in the cultural and political scene. There is not always an integrative approach and on many occasions, prejudice and class arrogance still play a relevant role in determining the socio-symbolic and political place of favelas in the city. However, what those movements have achieved is a greater visibility and increased symbolic capital for favelas. Favelas have also become strong enough to position themselves with relative power in the dispute over hegemony in public forums, and to engage in direct dialogue with governments, being able on many occasions to set agendas and lead to transformative projects.

In Brazil, and more specifically in Rio de Janeiro, the historical and social representations of favelas and other peripheral neighbourhoods were central in excluding them from influencing the directions of urban development and wider public policies. The demoralisation of favela dwellers as 'second-class citizens' (or 'non-citizens'), alongside other negative labels, were historically used to contain those populations and their problems within the territory of favelas. The circumscription of favelas as isolated entities in the urban fabric has also been ideologically used to display them as not belonging to the city, but rather as problem areas whose only viable solution would be their physical elimination—as per the idea of an 'urban cancer' (Fernandes 2005). In more recent times, although the idea of elimination ('removal') is still present, greater emphasis has been placed on the necessity of symbolically (and where possible, physically) eliminating its social product: the '*favelado*'. The acknowledgement that favelas are part of the urban fabric (in legal and policy documents) has not entirely prevented the old discourse of 'removal' from enduring. Rather, this has triggered new social processes in which the symbolic attack on territory and people has worsened. The criminalisation of favela-dwellers and the pathological references to criminal behaviour are at the core of this symbolic attack. The emergence of armed criminal groups with control of territories in favelas (drug trafficking factions, militias and paramilitary groups), and the militarised state response have been a matter of great debate in the fields of urban security and human rights (see, for instance, Mourão et al. 2016; Silva 2012; Soares 2006; Souza 2008; Zaluar 2004).[9] On the other hand, the emergence of grassroots movements in the fields of housing, culture and human rights has created new tensions that contest such stigmatised labelling by reaffirming peripheral groups as relevant social agents in the political and symbolic disputes in the city.

However, the emphasis on 'deprivation' and 'immorality' in those neighbourhoods ignores the forces evident not only in new forms of social activism, but also, and most importantly, in the practices of those who are symbolically marginalised. As such, the 'inventive power' is, in other words, translated into *potency*—or the capacity to generate practical and legitimate responses to hegemonic forces that ultimately configure counter-hegemonic forms of living. These counter-hegemonic forms are, however, ignored or given limited understanding when it comes to conceptualising what these neighbourhoods (and their people) are or are not.

The hegemonic symbolic status of favelas and other peripheral neighbourhoods share a common social representation which is sustained by the ideas of 'deprivation' and 'neediness' that conform to what we have called the 'paradigm of absence' (Fernandes et al. 2018). This myth of origin has driven other representations that followed the idea of absence in a wider sense. For example, many social policy interventions and charity projects believe that they are taking 'citizenship' to neighbourhoods where there is no citizenship (or only a 'second-class' citizenship). Another example is the consideration of their inadequacy in contrast to 'normal' neighbourhoods (Silva and Barbosa 2005; Silva et al. 2009a). To that extent, their representation could be portrayed as 'abnormal' as it is still conceptualised by the Brazilian Census (IBGE 2010). 'Abnormality' is contestable, because it focusses on a hegemonic standard based on aesthetics and cultural perspectives that are shaped by the dominant groups. Therefore, it does not recognise social characteristics and forms of use of space of peripheral groups because they are devalued and depreciated by the symbolic power exercised by dominant groups (Silva et al. 2009b).[10]

There are many problems behind these situations, as we are about to see. They, however, take on a layer of complexity when faced with urban violence and its associated side effects: prejudice, discrimination, stigmatisation and indifference. Indeed, the historical processes of the socio-symbolic marginalisation of favelas can be considered violent forms of 'organised forgetting' (Giroux 2014), where the citizen status of favela-dwellers is downplayed in the face of their 'ignorance', 'illiteracy', and other generalisations that have been used as symbolic forces to manipulate, exploit and mute.

The emergence of a public security discourse in which favelas are the main target in order to deter urban violence is another form of 'organised forgetting' in which the voice, rights and agency of peripheral people are played down by a 'state of exception' (Agamben 2004) ruled by an ideology of fear and mistrust (Baierl 2004; Bauman 2009; Batista 2003; Glassner 2003). As such, there is an increasing process of indifference, anger and intolerance mobilising public opinion and state responses to violence. The fabrication of favelas as the *place* of crime, and black male youngsters as the *face* of crime, has resulted in a new social habitus in the city, increasing social divides and intensifying the fragmentation of the urban socio-political and spatial fabric.

CONTEXT OF URBAN VIOLENCE IN BRAZIL AND RIO

One relevant data to measure urban violence is the homicide rate. Brazil has a high number of homicides when compared to international data. Homicide rates in Brazil historically fluctuate at around twenty-five homicides per 100,000 habitants (for 2018, this was 31.6 per 100,000). This is by far beyond 'acceptable' levels of ten per 100,000 according to the World Health Organization (WHO). These figures are even higher when specific groups are taken into consideration. Young people aged 15–29 represent 53.3 per cent of all homicides in the country (60.4 per 100,000). Out of them 94 per cent are male, and 75.7 per cent are black people (Cerqueira et al. 2020). Clearly, Brazilian homicides are marked by age, gender and colour. Although there is no reliable data to map these deaths (police data is inconsistent throughout Brazilian states), it is possible to say that the majority of these deaths occur in areas with high levels of socio-economic deprivation and symbolic marginalisation. The vast majority of these areas are characterised by typical features of urban deprivation, such as non-existence or precarity of public provision[11] of urban infrastructure. Above all, weak state sovereignty and regulation has created a space for the territorialisation of criminal armed groups (Silva et al. 2008), who take advantage of this situation to run illegal activities as well as play a key role in the regulation of social life in those territories.

The problem of homicides in Brazilian urban centres is rooted in a socio-political context, with urban inequalities playing a central role in the distribution and maintenance of economic power. In that context, the historical permanence of lower-class informal settlements was central in creating a political-economic 'black hole' from which a set of suspect practices could bypass the established and legalised system. That is the context in which criminal armed groups were formed, and police and political corruption gained force. As such, the formation and, most importantly, the consolidation of criminal groups was to some extent 'allowed' to enable a complex system of corrupt practices such as the involvement of state agents in criminal activities (for example, by financing and creating the operational conditions for drug-trafficking). This, of course, created a complex criminal network that expands beyond the boundaries of those neighbourhoods. However, what is observed is an emphasis on policing those neighbourhoods. This emphasis deserves another paper, but the key point here is to explain the implications of such emphasis on life in those neighbourhoods as well as the urban experience as a whole.

In this context, favelas and other peripheral neighbourhoods have been the main target of public security interventions, with a strong emphasis on the use of the police apparatus and the militarisation of measures to address the issue (Souza 2008). Favelas are widely portrayed as the core location for drug-trafficking, and local drug dealers are declared 'public enemy number one'. This is observed in the media's approach to the issue, which limits the problems of security to the favelas' boundaries and ignores the complexity of criminal networks at national and international levels. This is reflected in the reinforcement of an ideal model of crime and criminals that is a portrait of favelas' drug dealers—who we have referred to as 'flip-flop bandits' (Fernandes 2009, 2012)—for being at the very bottom of the hierarchy of criminal networks.

There is the use of a military apparatus (for example, the use of heavy weapons in police operations) alongside the adoption of the war metaphor, where criminals are assumed to be 'enemies' and residents are assumed to be a 'civil population' within enemy territory. Following that strategy, armed conflicts were assumed as 'inevitable' and, as a consequence, so were the high number of deaths on all sides (police, criminal groups, dwellers). The death of residents, in that context, is considered a 'side-effect' of the 'war', as they are perceived as 'civilians' in an 'enemy territory'. This has implications for the way favela residents are socially represented, and reinforces the historical stigma associated with those neighbourhoods (Fernandes 2005, 2009, 2014). For example, the high media exposure of local drug dealers as the 'face of crime' has worked to reinforce the prejudice against favelas, and unbalanced and typically unfair practices have resulted in human rights violations and, at the extreme end of the spectrum, in the deaths of many people. The demonisation of drug dealers has no parallel in terms of social representation when contrasted with others involved, such as businessmen, police officers and politicians. 'Black' and 'favela', alongside other generalisations such as 'funk' (music/dressing style), are labels used to typify drug dealers and, by extension, pathologise favelas as places of crime.

The territorialisation of armed criminal groups in favelas and other deprived neighbourhoods is a key matter when considering the dynamics of any urban centre in Brazil, in particular those with bigger populations. Historically, the responses adopted by the state are oriented by direct armed conflict. This has been widely criticised (Machado 2013; Mourão et al. 2016; and Soares 2019, to give a few examples). However, such an approach has strong popular support and is sustained by ideological discourses that reinforce the historical stigmatisation of favelas (Fernandes 2005, 2009).

Historically, the symbolic status of favelas and similar neighbourhoods was one of strong negative perceptions of their dwellers (criminals, scammers, uncivilised) and their behaviours (dirty, lazy, work-shy) (Fernandes 2005). Similarly, the physical space was also viewed as chaotic and unhealthy—an 'urban cancer', in the view of early 1900s urbanists (under the strong influence of sanitarians) (Abreu 1994; Valladares 2000). Ultimately, those neighbourhoods were considered dangerous places where even the police would not go, as portrayed by Rio de Janeiro writer Orestes Barbosa (1993[1923]) in his prose, A *Favela*: '... terrorist neighbourhood where the 8th district police don't go'.

Those symbolic representations endured over time and took new shapes over the years. However, the basic association between 'urban cancer' and 'dangerous place' has become the key representation since the 1980s, when problems of urban security started to take new forms due to the emergence of armed criminal groups engaged in drug-trafficking from those areas. While the 'side-effects' of drug-trafficking were restricted to the favelas' boundaries, favelas' social representations were more attached to a romantic past, where the bucolic imagination of no-go neighbourhoods and local criminals were enclosed in a place from which the only links with the wider city were the Samba and the offer of exploited low-skilled workers who sustained middle-class lifestyles. However, the consolidation of the illegal drug trade in Rio took issues of policing and public security beyond the boundaries of favelas. The expansion of criminal networks and the dispute over territories implied a new configuration of drug-trafficking with the switch from 'marijuana to .38' and 'cocaine to AR-15',[12] an allegory that portrayed the changes in power arrangements within the drug trade (Souza 2000).

While the adoption of heavier fire weapons (such as the AR-15) can be seen as a sign of increased disputes to sustain the control of territories in a highly competitive drug market, this change also revealed a switch in policing and public security. Those weapons were used not only to protect criminal groups from other criminal groups, but also as a resource to protect themselves from the police—who were adopting the same weapons. As such, what was observed during the 1990s was the emergence of a new socio-political and spatial configuration in the city, with the dissemination of violence (in particular, shoot-outs) and the fear of 'drug dealers'. While the shoot-outs were now reaching surrounding neighbourhoods, the fear was spread throughout the city, as the presence of 'undesirable' characters in middle-class neighbourhoods started to become a major problem. That was the period when 'funk' culture gained force in favelas, giving space to the dissemination of favela youth culture as being sexually obscene, defensive of drugs and inciting gang culture and violent behaviour (Cecchetto 1998, 2004; Herschmann 2005; Vianna 2003). Those were labels used to not only criminalise funk, but also to increase social fear of the youth from the favelas and, as a consequence, trigger the use of repressive forces to control their movement in the city. For example, during the Brazilian FIFA World Cup, we learnt that the police dispersed many street-children from tourist areas. After the World Cup, the police also illegally impeded youngsters from taking buses to the beach, on the argument that they did not have enough money to spend on the day out (Rodriguez et al. 2016). In research carried out in 2008, Fernandes (2009) also found youngsters from favelas to have limited contact with prosperous neighbourhoods, as well as cultural venues and even shopping centres. The main reason for this was not the lack of resources, but the fear of being discriminated against or taken by the police. Fear of the police was indeed a major point highlighted in our research, as well as a higher level of exposure to violence (Fernandes 2009, 2012).

The death of youths from the urban peripheries is the most explicit expression of the 'pedagogy of monsterisation' in Brazil. In Rio's favelas, marginalised youth are seen widely as the face of danger, disorder and crime. The association of young males in particular with drug-trafficking poses dangerous repercussions for their futures. The idea of being 'prone to crime' as a pathogenic result of living in a dangerous neighbourhood and raised by 'dysfunctional families' is so strong that there is apparently no way out of a dual destiny: they will either join crime, or be affected by the label and stigma of crime. More than that, they will carry the label of territorial stigma wherever they go, and whatever they do. That is the reason, as we explained before, why we critically adopt the concept of 'socio-spatial stigma' rather than 'territorial stigma' as proposed by Wacquant (1999, 2008). The label of territory is strong enough to be incorporated as habitus. People are not from the favela. They actually are the favela.

The reconceptualisation of favelas, then, is one of the biggest challenges to promoting co-existence in the city. Such a reconceptualisation sits not only in public discourse, but also in the way the favelas' potency is acknowledged as a positive force to drive a project of urbanity. The recognition of favelas' models of operation, social cohesion and neighbourhood life should overcome their labelling as spaces of crime and deprivation. The potency lies in the capacity of such spaces and their people to survive amidst crime, deprivation and stigma. Survival, here, does not mean accommodation or acceptance, or even 'resilience', but the development of symbolic and material forms of existence that challenge from the inside the living conditions, through creative, positive and proactive (rather than simply 'reactive') processes and mindsets which, in our view, needs to be acknowledged with respect to the design of policies and interventions aiming to address the underlying problems affecting those groups. From a symbolic violence perspective, such forms of existence have been historically ignored and pushed down by academic arrogance (architects, engineers, and urban planners, to mention a few examples), combined with class petulance ('we are better than you'; 'we have culture, we appreciate culture, we are educated…') and social disgust ('you are disgusting'; 'the things you do are repugnant'; 'you do not have culture').

What, after all, are the references that should drive the production of the city? How can such references be incorporated into a democratic process in which the potency of favelas and urban peripheries are acknowledged? How can these neighbourhoods be protagonists in the production of the city, rather than the recipients of normative socio-political and symbolic references? Last, but not least, what do the ideas proposed in this chapter have in common with, and how do they differ in relation to, the issues affecting urban peripheries in other countries? These are questions that we wish to reflect on through the proposition of a *pedagogy of co-existence*.

WORKING TOWARDS A PEDAGOGY OF CO-EXISTENCE IN THE *POLIS*

We must not cease to value the fight for equality undertaken by so many social movements, and in particular those that took place in the nineteenth century. Such claims were expressed, singularly, in the questioning of private property and in the defence of a different model of society. Beyond the question of property, though, the point that drove and continues to drive the principal forms of political confrontation is the quest for equality and human dignity. As such, the legacy that we preserve from those periods of social struggle emerges through the unrelenting defence of this value. This notion of dignity is naturally historical, and the result of a permanent social and political dispute. In this case, the acknowledgement of dignity in multiple fields, and the dedication to bringing it about are key concerns for collective agencies in the contemporary world.

Another legacy of particular relevance to our generation is derived from the more intense battles in the twentieth century waged by groups typically labelled as 'minorities' (when, in fact, some of them are often the *majority*[13] in numbers)—women, afro-descendants, LGBT+ people, indigenous people, the mentally and physically disabled, the elderly, the movement for the defence of children and adolescents—all of which were driven by the recognition and legitimation of *difference*. In effect, historically societies, in their various forms, transformed differences into inequalities. Thus, the fact of being a foreigner, a black person, an indigenous person, a homosexual, a woman, a child—the Other—was a marker to be placed in a subordinated condition. This issue is far from being resolved, though we have advanced in many aspects since. This is not to say that we should lose sight of how far we still have to go to reach due recognition and legitimacy.

We have, then, an affirmation of a *polis* marked by the interlacing ties between the fight for equality and the fight for difference. This bond, now inseparable, is the great conceptual, ethical and political challenge for contemporary utopian propositions. This alone is a great advancement. After all, it was common for socialist parties of the past century to claim that the question of difference was secondary, and that all of its expressions could be resolved with the elimination of private property. The tragic experiences of the so-called 'Real Socialism' revealed the reductionism inherent in this argument.

With regard to the proposition of becoming a full human being, as explained by Karl Marx's concept of the 'omnilateral', Antonio Gramsci's notions of 'socialist men and women', and Che Guevara's idea of 'new men and women', this can only materialise into an integrated perspective if affirmed in four inseparable dimensions:

1. **The Subjective/Singular dimension**: In this condition, the being affirms her/his right to authenticity and autonomy, in Rousseau's terms. In this way, we are, in the first place, our 'pre-name' (our own person): we have the right to be free, to make our own choices, to be who we want to be and to live how we wish to, regardless of the demands and pressures from social institutions. This notion of liberty/freedom, however, is unsustainable in the liberal perspective. Within it, the liberty of one competes with the liberty of another, and human beings' core relation becomes one of naturalised

inequality. Therefore, working on the construction of *individuated* beings and not individualised beings, as we will see, is central to the recognition and construction of authenticity.

2. **The Particular/Social dimension**: In this condition, I cannot ignore who I am, in its different dimensions. Thus, I am also my 'surname', my ethnic/racial condition, geographic and scholarly position, my gender, my sexual orientation, my football team, my age range, my status (or not) as a parent, single/married, etc. In this way I construct both my identity with others and my social insertions; I affirm my representations of my social world and my choices in the way I express my life.
3. **The Human/Generic dimension**: This dimension is central to the construction of an effectively democratic and human *polis*. After all, if I recognise only myself and those similar to me—from a narcissistic perspective—I never learn to live alongside the Other, with those different from me, and I end up reproducing situations of intolerance in the function of the differences established between subjects. There is no democracy without co-existence with that person that I do not see as my equal. Thus, it becomes necessary for a full consciousness of differences to be immediately followed by an understanding of equality via our shared condition as a species; through this condition, I am able to see the other as the same as me, beyond his or her specific characteristics. And, in this way, I am able to recognise that we share the same human path and that this identity as a species makes us existential partners.
4. **The Global/Ecological dimension**: Lastly, we must understand that we are only, above all, one other species on the planet. Beyond just being a source of resources, our planet is a source of life for us and for other beings. As such, the condition of being a living thing brings us closer to all other living things on the planet. We must not allow our demand for resources and the right we have to survive interfere with our responsibility to take care of the earth for other species

and for new human beings. With this insight, we call into question all human action that harms the environmental balance.

Within the above perspective, we are called to live as an 'individuated being'. The term 'individuated' is most well known in psychology, owing to the diffusion propagated by Carl Jung, but its origins, in modern terms, lie in the philosophy of Arthur Schopenhauer, and more recently, in Remo Bodei. We are using it in this context in order to distinguish it from the 'individualised' being—a most hegemonic subject, in the imaginary world and in social practices within the *polis*. For this social subject, worldly action has, as a point of departure and arrival, the singular, without any humanised mediation with other beings. For the subject, the Other exists in order to give pleasure, or be at their service, or to compete with in the pursuit of these 'returns'. The individualised being establishes a permanent process of competition for positions of social distinction in relation to other subjects. At most, contact with those who are the same is valued, while the other and the different are transformed into persons to be either dominated and/or oppressed. In this way, in Spinoza's terms, the individualised subject lives in pursuit of that which concedes immediate returns, and acts as a 'presentified' subject, focussed on the here and now.

In individuation, the point of departure is the subjective being. But in order to self-affirm, she recognises and values the Other, the different. The right to singularity and to difference is, in an inseparable form, valued. She self-affirms, however, in the recognition of the Other as similar and not as a rival or subaltern. In this, she attains singularity when she recognises the Other's dimension in herself, and her own within the Other. The individuated being stands for and with the world, and inwardly, is filled with relation/mediation with other human beings, be they similar or different. Thus, she exists for herself and for others, in consonance, in co-existence, and not in the negation of the humanity of the Other. In this sense, she seeks to self-construct through a permanent bond between what is an element of her singularity (the immediate) and what is an element of her relation with others and the world around (the mediate). This happens as part of a spiral that connects time and space, the place of origin being the reference for her agency in the world.

Therefore, a *pedagogy of co-existence*—which, without using the term, we have affirmed historically in our methodology of action at the Observatory of Favelas and the Maria and João Aleixo Institute—draws support from the conceptions of the social world and of subjects established in the previous paragraphs. It is the base for the practices undertaken by the urban being that exists at the curious and fraternal conjunction of the similar and the different.

This must not be a one-off encounter, but rather a daily discovery of what exists in common between different peoples and what differs between peoples who have much in common. It is materialised in the *territory*, is mediated by the *body* and deepened by the *word*. *Body*, *Word* and *Territory* are then the material expressions of this urban pedagogy.[14]

In working with the *word*, we recognise it as a fundamental dimension of social relations, of the construction of subjectivity and of objective relations. In this case, we speak of the word always in its four dimensions: heard, spoken, read and written. We must take special care not to ignore the last two (historically considered the fundamental reasons for the existence of scholarly institutions), but to recognise that people should have the ability to place themselves in institutional spaces, in particular, through the use of the spoken word, breaking, in many cases, with authoritarian or violent power relations. This is especially important because orality is the most expressive way for popular social groups to engage historically. The use of the word, in all of its dimensions, makes it possible for people to co-exist in a social reality to establish new ways of relating to themselves and with the group, developing cognitive abilities, ethical values and the capacity to work with the sensible, the free and the aesthetic dimension of reality.

In the work of the *body*, of which the *word* is an intrinsic part, we seek to recognise beings for more than just their cognition. People are recognised as beings that idealise, that also live in a world of affection, of politics, of relations with his or her own sexuality, physical dimensions, values and habits. It is thus necessary to recognise and to work with the body in all of its component parts—physical, mental, emotional, sexual, ethical and aesthetic.

Lastly, this being of the *word*, which is an integrated *body*, does not live for herself, but in a *territory*, and with different *scales*—from the scale of her body, immediate, to the local scale, her place of daily living, city, country and world. The challenge, then, is for her to perceive the riches of her territory in its unity and its plurality, like a spiral; and to be able to exercise the experience and the reflexive capacity, the feeling of identity and of compassion—the sharing of common humanity with other beings. This means, in this case, going beyond the singular dimension of subjectivity: it means recognising the particular dimension of subjects and at last, the human-generic dimension, its insertion in the same path of humanity in the common effort to give greater meaning to life, feeling part of human reality, all encompassing.

Concerning Rio de Janeiro, our empirical example in this chapter, this means seeking the various possibilities of the city, not only its environmental resources and wealth, but also human value, taking into account their cultural expressions and the creative and diverse ways in which its citizens reinvent the 'everyday' in unique and shared ways.

The three dimensions of pedagogical action come to fruition at the Observatório de Favelas and the Maria and João Aleixo Institute, through our work in cognitive activities, ethical reflections and actions, as well as aesthetic experiments. In this way, through a continuously developing socio-pedagogical network, we seek to affirm life in its diverse dimensions.

The intent of the proposition elaborated thus far is to sustain an educational project based neither in the teaching–learning process nor on educators and students. Rather, the idea is to break with the vision of a 'school' project of training the *polis*' subjects—an error committed not only by schools, but also by the immense majority of organisations that engage in social and socio-cultural projects.

We are discussing, above all, the *formation* of a being who lives the contemporary, who lives the utopia as *an extended present*, and not as a project frozen in the future. In fact, teleological perspectives—ideas of social utopias with deep faith in the future as progress and proclamations of a time without conflict and without challenges to collective living—have run their course. We must construct the idea of a utopia no longer in time, but in current practices, in the everyday, in the permanent affirmation of a being who makes herself fulfilled, especially through economic, symbolic, physical, social and cultural mobility. This is the great challenge of our contemporary time and space. May we learn to confront it with pleasure and happiness, density and levity, safety and curiosity, expectation and serenity, reflection and action, and above all, with wisdom and joy.

End Notes

Acknowledgement: We would like to thank Daniel Stefani for helping us with challenging conceptual translations.

1. Free translation from the original in Portuguese: '... *e naquele amplo boulevard esplêndido, sobre o asfalto polido, contra a fachada rica dos prédios altos, contra as carruagens e carros que desfilavam, o encontro do velho veículo, em que os devotos bêbados urravam, me deu a impressão de um monstruoso anacronismo: era a ressurreição da barbaria – era uma idade selvagem que voltava, como uma lama de outro mundo, vindo perturbar e envergonhar a vida da idade civilizada*' (Bilac 1906).

2. We adopt a broader definition of periphery. It refers not only to geographically peripheral zones, but also to forms of existence, social position, cultural manifestations and symbolic status that are subaltern (or *subalternised*) in society.

3. *Pardo* is a self-definition for skin colour suggested by the Brazilian Census. Although controversial, *pardo* literally means brown or grizzly. In the context of Brazilian society, it can be understood as a form of unacceptance of black skin colour, by using a classification that distinguishes people via stigmatising labelling associated with blackness.

4. This is one reason why it is preferable to refer to the process of 'subalternisation' in consideration to those groups that are excluded—in part or in totality—from institutions, and by extension, from established means of socio-symbolic affirmation. The term is rooted in Gramsci's studies on cultural hegemony (Gramsci 2002) as a means to consider the potency of the history from below, or in other words, the necessity of galvanising alternative forms of subaltern groups' affirmation in society. Gramsci recognised that only a total rupture with the existing dominant

forces is the alternative to the process of subalternisation, proposing a utopian project for the subaltern to conquer hegemony in society. This view, however, may not guarantee the end of subalternisation, as the processes that configure its dynamics, in our view, involve a more complex consideration of the concept of class and, by extension, class struggle.

Nonetheless, we consider that the adoption of Pierre Bourdieu's analysis of social field can be a complementary reference in understanding the dynamics of subalternisation, which necessarily should include an analysis of the mechanisms of symbolic violence operating in the class (as well as intra-class) struggle in the dispute of hegemony—and the inevitable question on the extent of the imposition of new forms of social distinction and symbolic violence, once new hegemonic powers take place. We acknowledge that such an understanding is still limited to the 'what next' consideration, and the need to understand that favelas have suffered a historical process of symbolic denigration that detaches them from the urban fabric as isolated entities, such as the representation of 'urban cancer' (going back to the early 1900s). Not only this, the lack of acknowledgment of favelas' positive forces have historically played down the possibility of considering a project of urbanity, having the favelas as a possible starting point rather than an end point for 'top-down' (or false 'bottom-up') interventions that ignore its potency.

5. The word 'sanction' is formally used in UK policy/legislation to define situations in which a benefit claimant does not fulfil rules and expectations set by the government. See https://www.nidirect.gov.uk/articles/benefit-sanctions.

6. Some examples can be found in Butler (2015).

7. This is the area where most of the Rio 2016 Olympic Games infrastructure was built.

8. This is more complex, and also involves the provision of workers from the most isolated areas as a result of the reallocation of entire favela dwellers to the peripheries during the 1970s. This is well-portrayed in the works of Licia Valladares (1978) and Janice Perlman (2002[1977]).

9. In 2008, a new strategy took place with the creation of Pacifying Police Units (UPP). These units brought a new concept of public security based on the reduction of direct conflict and the introduction of community-policing principles (which were explored a few years earlier with the GEPAE or Grupamento de Policiamento em Áreas Especiais/Special Areas Policing Group). This strategy, however, was located in selected favelas. Even so, the programme has proven very challenging, in particular the necessity to change institutional culture in the police as a

whole (which has great internal resistance). UPP has started to fade over the past years and the change in roles at the public security senior level may result in their end in the years to come. More in-depth views on this can be found in Leite (2014, 2015) and Misse (2014). We have explored the dimensions of youth–police tensions within UPPs in Correa et al. (2016).

10. For example, Rio de Janeiro's state governor, Antony Garotinho (1999–2002), introduced a programme to promote access to cultural venues for low-income populations. The programme consisted of the sale of cinema, theatre and concert hall tickets for the symbolic value of R$ 1 (approximately US$ 0.30). With this measure, it was expected to attract those who historically never (or rarely) accessed those cultural goods. There was also some expectation that people living in the most deprived neighbourhoods with scarce (mostly none) cultural venues could finally enjoy some 'culture' in the city. Not surprisingly, this measure ended up benefiting a limited parcel of the intended public—most of them from deprived neighbourhoods. These, however, were people who already used to enjoy those cultural goods, but with a more restricted access due to the prohibitive costs. Most beneficiaries, however, were the same frequenters from middle-class backgrounds, who could enjoy their expensive habits at a ridiculously low cost.

This illustration shows the inadequacy of public policy when the habitus and the capital (in its different forms) are ignored by 'policy makers'. Providing cheap access to distinctive cultural goods is not the solution to creating habits of cultural consumption (which, on that occasion, were considered 'culture', possibly in contrast to the 'underculture' or 'lack of culture' experienced by marginalised groups). At the extreme, however, it is common to see the famous 'favela kit' social projects, where low-skilled job training as well as 'undercultural' codes are adopted to promote 'citizenship' for those who are typically considered non-citizens of the city.

11. The existence of deregulated infrastructure known as *gato* (cat) is very common in those areas, which are comprised of improvised (most of the time, very precarious), clandestine connections to public electricity cables and water pipes. Sewerage can either consist of unauthorised connections to existing collectors (overloading the system), or be sent straight to the environment without any treatment. In some locations, the provision of illegal cable TV service is also observed, which is in most cases run by criminal groups who take advantage of the lack of state regulation at those locations.

12. .38 and AR-15 are firearms.

13. Members of some groups who are typically labelled as 'minority' are in fact often the majority in numbers. Official census data shows that 54.9 per cent of Brazilians are of black background, and 51.48 per cent are female. It is also possible to say that a high proportion of people live in informal settlements, but there is no reliable data for that.

14. The limit of these emancipatory pedagogies is, in general, the extreme valourisation of the dimension of *consciousness*, ignoring other fundamental expressions of the self. As such, a simplistic interpretation of Paulo Freire's work valourised the term 'conscientization'. This idea became a jargon, sustaining the ideas and practices behind the dissemination of a 'liberation pedagogy'. Furthermore, 'conscientization', or the acquisition of a critical consciousness, inevitably sustains a hierarchy: the *conscious* and the *unconscious*. The practical implementation of such ideas did not contribute to a new understanding of the systems of knowing and doing of popular groups (the *peripheral epistemologies*). Neither did the valourisation of their inventive capacity offer an effective connection with the forms of knowing and doing of popular groups. In fact, the recognition of these peripheral epistemologies requires the valourisation of the body, of the self, in its integrity, and the necessary apprehension of the role of the territory in its constitutive process.

References

Abreu, M. A. 1986. 'Da habitação ao habitat: a questão da habitação popular no Rio de Janeiro e sua evolução'. *Revista Rio de Janeiro* I (2).

______. 1988. *A Evolução Urbana do Rio de Janeiro*. Rio de Janeiro: IPLANRIO/Zahar, 2e.

______. 1994. 'Reconstruindo uma história esquecida: origem e expansão inicial das favelas do Rio de Janeiro'. *Espaço & Debates* 37: 34–46.

______. 1996. 'Pensando a cidade no Brasil do Passado'. In Iná Elias de Castro et al. (eds), *Brasil: Questões Atuais da Reorganização do Território*. Rio de Janeiro: Bertrand Brasil.

______. 1997. 'A apropriação do território no Brasil Colonial'. In Iná Elias de Castro et al. (eds), *Explorações Geográficas: Percursos no Fim do Século*. Rio de Janeiro: Bertrand Brasil.

______. 1993. 'A favela está fazendo 100 anos, Sobre os caminhos tortuosos da construção da cidade'. In *Anais* of the third 'Simpósio Nacional de Geografia Urbana'. Available at https://biblioteca.ibge.gov.br/visualizacao/monografias/GEBIS%20-%20RJ/3simposiogeografiaurbana.pdf (accessed June 2021).

Agamben, G. 2004. *Estado De Exceção*. São Paulo: Boitempo.

Ahnen, R. E. 2007. 'The Politics of Police Violence in Democratic Brazil, Latin America'. *Politics and Society* 49(1): 141–64.

Azevedo, Aloisio. 2000. *The Slum*. USA: Oxford University Press.

Badiou, A. 2012. *In Praise of Love*. London: Serpent's Tail..

Baierl, L. F. 2004. *Medo Social. Da violência visível ao invisível da violência*. São Paulo: Cortez.

Barbosa, O. 1993[1923]. *Bambambã*. Rio de Janeiro: Coleção Biblioteca Carioca.

Batista, V. M. 2003. *O Medo na Cidade do Rio de Janeiro*. Rio de Janeiro: Revan.

Bauman, Z. 2009. *Confiança e Medo na Cidade*. Rio de Janeiro: Zahar.

Bilac, O. 1906. 'Cronica'. *Kosmos* 3(10).

Bourdieu, P. 1977. *Outline of a Theory of Practice*. Cambridge, UK: Cambridge University Press.

———. 1984. *Distinction: A Social Critique of the Judgment of Taste*. London: Routledge.

———. 1989. 'Social Space and Symbolic Power'. *Sociological Theory* 7(1): 14–25.

———. 1998. *Practical Reason*. Cambridge: Polity.

Butler, Patrick. 2015. 'Benefit sanctions: The 10 trivial breaches and administrative errors'. *The Guardian*, 24 March. Available at: https://www.theguardian.com/society/2015/mar/24/benefit-sanctions-trivial-breaches-and-administrative-errors (accessed February 2021).

Caldeira, T. P. R. 2000. *City of Walls: Crime, Segregation, and Citizenship in São Paulo*. London: University of California Press.

Cano, I. 1997. *Letalidade da ação policial no Rio de Janeiro*. Rio de Janeiro: ISER.

Carvalho, L. A. 1995. *Contribuição ao Estudo das Habitações Populares. Rio de Janeiro 1886–1906*. Rio de Janeiro: Coleção Biblioteca Carioca.

Cecchetto, F. R. 1998. 'Galeras *funk* cariocas: Os bailes e a constituição do *ethos* guerreiro'. In A. Zaluar (ed.), *Um Século de Favela*. Rio de Janeiro: FGV Editora.

———. 2004. *Violência e Estilos de Masculinidade*. Rio de Janeiro: Editora FGV.

Cerqueira, D. et al. 2020. 'Atlas da violência 2020'. IPEA. Available at https://www.ipea.gov.br/portal/images/stories/PDFs/relatorio_institucional/200826_ri_atlas_da_violencia.pdf (accessed June 2021).

Correa, J., F. Cecchetto, P. Farias and F. L. Fernandes. 2016. 'Poor youth and "pacification": Dilemmas between discourse and practice from young people's perspective about policing in Rio de Janeiro favelas'. *International Sociology* 31(1): 100–120.

Fernandes, F. L. 2005. 'Os discursos sobre as favelas e os limites afo direito à cidade'. *Cidades* 2(3): 37–62.

———. 2008. 'Um olhar sobre direitos humanos nos territórios populares e o direito à cidade. Boletim Salto para o Futuro'. *Direitos Humanos e Educação* 8(2).

———. 2009. 'Violência, medo e stigma: Efeitos sócio-espaciais da "atualização" do "mito da marginalidade" no Rio de Janeiro', unpublished PhD thesis. Federal University of Rio de Janeiro.

———. 2012. 'Os jovens da favela. Reflexões sobre controle e contenção sócio-espacial dos párias urbanos no Rio de Janeiro'. *Convergencia Revista de Ciencias Sociales* 19(52): 159–186.

———. 2013a. 'Youth Gang Members in Rio de Janeiro: The Face of a "Lost Generation" in an Age of Fear and Mistrust'. *Bulletin of Latin American Studies* 32 (2): 210–223.

———. 2013b. 'The Brazilian "hyperprecariat" and the socio-symbolical condition of the urban outcasts: On favelas, violence and the "lost generation" in Rio de Janeiro'. *Criminal Justice Matters* 93(1): 12–13.

———. 2014. 'The Construction of Socio-Political and Symbolical Marginalization in Brazil: Reflecting the Relation between Socio-Spatial Stigma and Responses to Violence in Rio de Janeiro'. *International Journal of Humanities and Social Science* 4(2): 52–67. Available at http://www.ijhssnet.com/journal/index/2258 (accessed June 2021).

Fernandes, F. L. and A. Rodriguez. 2009. 'Escape Routes: Lessons Learned From the Development of Prevention Methodologies and the Creation of Alternatives for Adolescents and Youngsters Involved in Drug Trafficking'. Brasília; Geneva: Observatório de Favelas; International Labour Organization.

———. 2015. 'The "lost generation" and the challenges in working with marginalised groups. Learnt lessons from Brazilian Favelas'. *Radical Community Work Journal* 1(1).

Fernandes, F. L., K. Edmundo and S. Dacach. 2009. 'Possible Ways. Eight projects for the youth'. Rio de Janeiro: Observatório de Favelas; Ministry of Education.

Fernandes, F. L., J. S. Silva and J. L. Barbosa. 2018. 'The Paradigm of Potency and the Pedagogy of Coexistence'. *Periferias* 1. Available at http://revistaperiferias.org/en/materia/the-paradigm-of-power-and-the-pedagogy-of-coexistence/ (accessed June 2021).

Flint, J. and R. Rowlands. 2003. 'Commodification, normalisation and intervention: Cultural, social and symbolic capital in housing consumption and governance'. *Journal of Housing and the Built Environment* 18(3): 213–232.

Foucault, M. 1976. *The Archaeology of Knowledge*, Alan M. Sheridan Smith (trans.). New York: Harper Colophon.

______. 2004. *Abnormal: Lectures at the College de France 1974–1975*. New York: Picador.

Giroux, H. 2003. 'Racial injustice and disposable youth in the age of zero tolerance'. *International Journal of Qualitative Studies in Education* 16(4): 553–565.

______. 2010. *Youth in a Suspect Society. Democracy or Disposability?* New York: Palgrave Macmillan.

______. 2011. *On Critical Pedagogy*. New York: Continuum.

______. 2012. *The Disposable Youth*. London: Sage.

______. 2014. *The Violence of Organised Forgetting: Thinking beyond America's Disimagination Machine*. San Francisco: City Lights.

Glassner, B. 2003. *Cultura do Medo*. São Paulo: Francis.

Gramsci, A. 2002. *Cadernos do Cárcere*, Vol. 2. Rio de Janeiro: Editora Civilização Brasileira.

Hall, S. et al. 2013. *Representation*. London: Sage.

Hancock, L. and G. Mooney. 2013. 'Beyond the penal state: Advanced marginality, social policy and anti-welfarism'. In P. Squires and J. Lee (eds), *Criminalisation and Advanced Marginality: Critically Exploring the Work of Loïc Wacquant*, 107–128. Bristol: Policy Press.

Harvey, D. 1993. 'Class relations, social justice and the politics of difference'. In Michael Keith and Steve Pile (eds), *Place and the Politics Of Identity*, 41–66. London and New York: Routledge.

______. 2008. 'The Right to the City'. *New Left Review* 53: 23–40.

Hastings, A. and P. Matthews. 2015. 'Bourdieu and the Big Society: Empowering the powerful in public service provision?' *Policy & Politics* 43(4): 545–560.

Herschmann, M. 2005. *O Funk e o Hip-Hop Invadem a Cena*. Rio de Janeiro: Editora UFRJ.

Hollanda, C. B. 2005. *Policia e Direitos Humanos. Política de Segurança Pública no Primeiro Governo Brizola [Rio de Janeiro: 1983-1986]*. Rio de Janeiro: Revan.

IBGE. 2010. *Aglomerados Subnormais. Informações Territoriais*. Available at: http://biblioteca.ibge.gov.br/pt/biblioteca-catalogo?view=detalhes&id=7552 (accessed June 2021).

______. 2010. *Censo demográfico: 2010: Aglomerados subnormais: Informações territoriais*. Rio de Janeiro: IBGE. Available at http://biblioteca.ibge.gov.br/visualizacao/periodicos/552/cd_2010_agsn_if.pdf (accessed February 2021).

Jensen, T. 2014. 'Welfare commonsense, poverty porn and doxosophy'. *Sociological Research Online* 19(3): 3.

Johns, Hannah. n.d. 'Stigmatisation of Dalits in access to water and sanitisation in India. National Campaign on Dalit Human Rights (NCDHR)'. Available at: http://idsn.org/wp-content/uploads/user_folder/pdf/New_files/UN/HRC/Stigmatization_of_dalits_in_access_to_water_sanitation.pdf (accessed June 2021).

Jones, O. 2012. *Chavs. The Demonization of the Working Class*. London. Verso.

Kowarick, L. 1993. *A Espoliação Urbana*. São Paulo: Paz e Terra.

Leitao, G. 1999. *A Construção Do Eldorado Urbano. O Plano Piloto Da Barra Da Tijuca E Baixada De Jacarepaguá – 1970/1988*. Niterói: EdUFF.

Leite, M. P. 2014. 'Entre a "guerra" e a "paz": Unidades de Polícia Pacificadora e gestão dos territórios de favela no Rio de Janeiro'. *DILEMAS: Revista de Estudos de Conflito e Controle Social* 7(4): 625–642.

______. 2015. 'Novos regimes territoriais em favelas cariocas'. In *Annals*, Florianópolis, XXVIII Simpósio Nacional de História. Available at http://www.snh2015.anpuh.org/resources/anais/39/1428368776_ARQUIVO_paperANPUH2015-Marcia-Leite.pdf (accessed February 2021).

Lipsky, M. 2010. *Street-Level Bureaucracy: Dilemmas of the Individual in Public Services*. New York: Russell Sage Foundation.

Locock, L., A. M. Boylan, R. Snow, S. Staniszewska. 2016. 'The power of symbolic capital in patient and public involvement in health research'. *Health Expectations* 20(5): 836–844.

Machado, L. A. 2013. 'O controle do crime violento no Rio de Janeiro'. *Le Monde Diplomatique (Brasil)* 6: 6–7. Available at https://diplomatique.org.br/o-controle-do-crime-violento-no-rio-de-janeiro/ (accessed June 2021).

Misse, D. G. 2014. 'Cinco anos de UPP: Um breve balanço'. *DILEMAS: Revista de Estudos de Conflito e Controle Social* 7(3): 675–700.

Mooney, G. 2011. *Stigmatising Poverty? The 'Broken Society' and Reflections on Anti-welfarism in the UK Today*. Oxford: Oxfam.

Mourão, Barbara, J. Lemgruber, L. Musumeci, S. Ramos. 2016. *Polícia, Justiça e Drogas: Como anda nossa democracia?* Rio de Janeiro: CESeC.

Nayak, A. and M. J. Kehily. 2014. 'Chavs, chavettes and pramface girls': Teenage mothers, marginalised young men and the management of stigma. *Journal of Youth Studies* 17(10): 1330–1345.

Perlman, Janice E. 2002[1977]. *O mito da marginalidade: Favelas e política no Rio de Janeiro*. Rio de Janeiro: Paz e Terra.

Pesavento, Sandra Jatahy. 2002. *O imaginário da cidade. Visões literárias do urbano*. Porto Alegre: Editora da UFRGS.

Ramos, S. 2016. 'Violência e polícia: Três décadas de políticas de segurança no Rio de Janeiro'. *Boletim Segurança e Cidadania* 21: 1–33.

Ramos, S. and J. Lemgruber. 2004. 'Criminalidade e respostas brasileiras à violência'. *Observatório da Cidadania* 4.

Ramos, S. and L. MusumeciI. 2005. *Elemento suspeito: Abordagem policial e discriminação na cidade do Rio de Janeiro*. Rio de Janeiro: Civilização Brasileira.

Ramos, S. and A. Paiva. 2005. 'Mídia e violência – como os jornais retratam a violência e a segurança pública no Brasil'. *Boletim Segurança e Cidadania* 4(10).

______. 2007. *Mídia e violência. Novas tendências na cobertura de criminalidade e segurança no Brasil*. Rio de Janeiro: IUPERJ.

Rocha, O. P. 1995. *A Era das Demolições. Cidade do Rio e Janeiro 1870–1920*. Rio de Janeiro: Coleção Biblioteca Carioca.

Rodger, J. 2008. *Criminalising Social Policy: Anti-social Behaviour and Welfare in a De-Civilising Society*. Cullompton: William-Publishing.

______. 2013. 'Loïc Wacquant and Norbert Elias: Advanced marginality and the theory of the de-civilising process'. In P. Squires and J. Lee (eds), *Criminalisation and Advanced Marginality. Critically Exploring the Work of Loïc Wacquant*, 87–106. Bristol: Policy Press.

Rodriguez, A. 2013. *Labirintos do Trafico: Vidas, práticas e intervenções. Em busca de saídas possíveis*. Rio de Janeiro: 7 Letras.

Rodriguez, A., L. van Blerk, F. Fernandes, J. Mendel, I. Rizzini, P. McEleavy and N. Fyfe. 2016. 'Mega-Sporting Events, Rights and Children's Everyday Lives: Exploring the Impact of the Brazil 2014 FIFA World Cup'. In N. Ansell, N. Klocker and T. Skelton (eds), *Geographies of*

Global Issues: Change and Threat, 1–23. *Geographies of Children and Young People*, Vol. 8. Singapore: Springer. Available at https://doi.org/10.1007/978-981-4585-95-8_27-1 (accessed June 2021).

Santos, Boaventura de Sousa. 2007. 'Para além do Pensamento Abissal: Das linhas globais a uma ecologia de saberes'. *Revista Crítica de Ciências Socials* 78: 3–46. Available at https://doi.org/10.4000/rccs.753 (accessed June 2021).

Silva, J. S. 2002. 'Um espaço em busca de seu lugar: As favelas para além dos estereótipos'. In Programa de Pós-Graduação em Geografia - UFF, Território. Niterói: EdUFF.

———. 2012. 'Para uma pedagogia da convivência na cidade'. In J. S. Silva, J. L. Barbosa, M. V. Faustini et al., *O Novo Carioca*. Rio de Janeiro: Morula.

———. 2016. 'O Direito a convivência pública ou a barbárie'. *Nexos*. Available at http://of.org.br/wp-content/uploads/2016/04/Artigo-para-a-Nexos-Conviv%C3%AAncia-P%C3%BAblica-ou-a-Barb%C3%A1rie.pdf (accessed June 2021).

Silva, J. S. and J. L. Barbosa. 2005. *Favela: Alegria e dor na Cidade*. Rio de Janeiro: SENAC.

Silva, J. S. and H. Silva. 2005. O. *Análise da violência contra a criança e o adolescente segundo o ciclo de vida no Brasil*. São Paulo/Brasília: Global/UNICEF.

Silva, J. S. and A. Urani. 2002. *Children in Drug Traffic: A Rapid Assessment*. Geneva: International Labour Organization; Brazilian Ministry of Labour and Employment.

Silva, J. S., F. L. Fernandes, R. Willadino. 2008. 'Grupos criminosos armados com domínio de teritório. Reflexções sobre a territorialidade do crime na Região Metropolitana do Rio de Janeiro'. In Justiça Global (ed.), *Segurança, tráfico e milícia no Rio de Janeiro*, 16–24. Rio de Janeiro: Heinrich Böll Foundation.

Silva, J. S., Raquel Willadino, Rodrigo Nascimento, Fabio Rodriguez, Fernando Lannes Fernandes. 2009a. 'Escape Routes. A study on adolescents and youths involved in drug trafficking in Rio de Janeiro'. Brasília; Geneva: Observatório de Favelas; International Labour Organization.

Silva, J. S., Jorge Luiz Barbosa, Mariane de Oliveira Biteti, Fernando Lannes Fernandes. 2009b. *O que é a favela, afinal?* Rio de Janeiro: Observatório de Favelas.

Slater, T. 2012. 'The Myth of "Broken Britain": Welfare Reform and the Production of Ignorance'. *Antipode* 46(4): 948–969.

Soares, L. E. 2006. *Seguranca tem Saida.* Rio de Janeiro: Sextante.

______. 2019. *Desmilitarizar: Segurança Pública e Direitos Humanos.* Brazil: Boitempo.

Sodré, Muniz. 2002. *O Terreiro e a Cidade: A Forma Social Negro-Brasileira.* Rio de Janeiro: Imago; Salvador: Fundação Cultural do Estado da Bahia.

Souza, M. L. 2000. *O Desafio Metropolitano: Um estudo sobre a problemática sócio-espacial nas metrópoles brasileira.* Rio de Janeiro: Bertrand Brasil.

______. 2008. *Fobópole. O medo generalizado e a militarização da questão urbana.* Rio de Janeiro: Bertrand Brasil.

______. 2009. 'Social movements in the face of criminal power. The socio-political fragmentation of space and "micro-level warlords" as challenges for emancipative urban struggles'. *City* 13(1): 26–52.

Tyler, Imogen. 2011. *Revolting Subjects: Social Abjection and Resistance in Neoliberal Britain.* London: Zed.

Valladares, L. P. 1978. *Passa-se uma casa: análise do programa de remoção de favelas do Rio de Janeiro.* Rio de Janeiro: Zahar.

______. 2000. 'A gênese da favela carioca. A produção anterior às ciências sociais'. *Revista Brasileira de Ciências Sociais* 15(44): 5–34.

Velho, G. 2002. *A Utopia Urbana.* Rio de Janeiro: Jorge Zahar Editor.

Vianna, H. 2003. *Galeras Cariocas.* Rio de Janeiro: Editora UFRJ.

Wacquant, L. 1999. 'Urban Marginality in the coming millennium'. *Urban Studies* 36(10): 1639–1647.

______. 2001. *Os Condenados da Cidade. Estudos sobre marginalidade avançada.* Rio de Janeiro: Revan.

______. 2008. *Urban Outcasts: A Comparative Sociology of Advanced Marginality.* Cambridge: Polity.

______. 2010. 'Crafting the neoliberal state. Workfare, prisonfare and social insecurity'. *Sociological Forum* 25(2): 197–220.

Zaluar, A. 1990. 'Um debate disperso. Violência e crime no Brasil da redemocratização'. *São Paulo em Perspectiva* 13(3): 3–17.

______. 2004. *Integração perversa: pobreza e tráfico de drogas.* Rio de Janeiro: Editora FGV.

______. 2007. 'Democratização inacabada: Fracasso da segurança pública'. *Estudos avançados* 21(61): 31–49.

Part 4

Environmental Re(Configurations) of Urban Infrastructure, Housing and Livelihoods

XI

The BRICS New Development Bank's False Dawn

Unsustainable Urban Infrastructure Finance in South Africa

Patrick Bond

INTRODUCTION: DASHED EXPECTATIONS OF THE BRICS REPLACING WESTERN BANKING

In 2013 in Durban, at the heads-of-state summit of the Brazil–Russia–India–China–South Africa (BRICS) bloc, a New Development Bank (NDB) and Contingent Reserve Arrangement were agreed to, and they were formally initiated at the 2014 Fortaleza summit (Bond 2016a). The NDB's mandate was 'mobilising resources for infrastructure and sustainable development projects in BRICS and other emerging economies and developing countries, to supplement the existing efforts of multilateral and regional financial institutions for global growth and development' (BRICS 2013). The West's 'Washington Consensus' ideology and neoliberal policy strategy had done enormous damage by forcing the rest of the world to liberalise finance, trade and investment, causing economic, social and ecological destruction, and strengthening multinational corporate power. In their generally overcrowded and often socio-ecologically dangerous, polluted cities, the BRICS have formidable housing, livelihood and environmental needs. Therefore, a new institutional approach to financing these, beyond the standard state subsidies, was warmly welcomed. Two well-known former chief economists of the World Bank were involved in the initial scoping, emphasising the NDB's potential strengths in sustainability lending, as we see below.

South Africa is an appropriate case study of whether these expectations have been realised over the subsequent seven years, during which ten NDB loans were granted in two currencies: $3.2 billion in US dollars and R17.4 billion ($1.2 billion in 2021 terms). The main national leader during this time, Jacob Zuma of the African National Congress (ANC), was one of the most vocal critics of the Bretton Woods institutions, the World Bank (WB) and the International Monetary Fund (IMF). In 2016–2017, on several occasions, Zuma claimed that because he had brought South Africa into the BRICS, the West wanted him out of power, even murdered.[1] At the 2015 Ufa BRICS leaders' summit, Zuma expressed the need for an alternative to the Washington banks in a *Russia Today* (2015) interview: 'They want to dictate what you should do. You can't utilise that kind of assistance the way you want. So, in a sense, it has conditions that will keep you dependent all the time. That's what we're trying to take ourselves out of.' Zuma held power from 2009–2018. His successor, Cyril Ramaphosa (2018), told the United Nations that the IMF and other multilateral institutions 'need to be reshaped and enhanced so that they may more effectively meet the challenges of the contemporary world and better serve the interests of the poor and marginalised.'

Unfortunately, the subsequent lack of multilateral financial reform—in part due to the BRICS' own assimilation strategy, and willing co-optation by World Bank and IMF leaders—became obvious soon enough.[2] Although this chapter considers the major site of lending, South Durban, as a case study of urban infrastructure sustainability, there are problems already evident in the NDB that reflect similar grievances against the World Bank: a systematic lack of consultation, widespread corruption, reversion to inappropriate hard-currency lending, and the projects' overall dubious illogic (Bond 2019a). All these problems deserve much more critical enquiry than has happened to date, notwithstanding protests against the NDB in mid-2018 on the day before the BRICS Sandton heads-of-state summit, and again at the April 2019 NDB Annual General Meeting in Cape Town. The ten loans granted in South Africa during 2016–2021 are not yet fully transparent, as a result of ongoing fraud investigations (typically termed 'state capture') against the NDB's highest-profile borrowers (the central state and major parastatal institutions), opaque lending agreements, and the NDB's failure to conduct due diligence. Requests made by civil society activists for loan documentation and corruption accountability were ignored.

These ten loans are, in chronological order:

1. $180 million for Eskom renewable energy and a major township's restructuring granted in 2016, which was stalled due to confessed corruption (Wright 2019) but then reactivated in 2018;
2. $200 million for Transnet's Durban port expansion in mid-2018;
3. $300 million for renewable municipal electricity via the Development Bank of Southern Africa in mid-2018 (although the on-lending financier has not announced any particular use of the NDB funding);
4. $480 million to Eskom for de-sulfurisation equipment for the 'Medupi' coal-fired power plant, that on the one hand ameliorates local pollution (certainly a positive, necessary component for the host town of Lephalale), but also facilitates the extension of the world's largest coal-fired power plant currently under construction, at 4,800 MW;
5. $220 million to the Trans-Caledon Tunnel Authority (TCTA) to support the Lesotho Highlands Water Project's next dam, which pumps water across a catchment to South Africa's main cities in Gauteng Province;
6. R1.15 billion ($82 million) to the Industrial Development Corporation for 'clean' energy;
7. R7 billion ($500 million) to the SA National Roads Agency for toll road 'strengthening';
8. $1 billion to the national government's initial mid-2020 bolstering of foreign reserves for COVID-19;
9. $1 billion to the government's 2021 foreign reserves for 'public health and social security' financing associated with COVID-19;
10. R6 billion ($430 million) for Eskom's battery storage strategy.

Before enquiring into the appropriateness of the main loans, we shall consider the NDB's sustainability mandate, followed by a brief survey of the South African urban infrastructural terrain.

NDB MANDATE RHETORIC: FROM ENVIRONMENTAL TO FINANCIAL SUSTAINABILITY

This volume addresses 'critical research, policy formulation, delivery and grassroots activities' with a focus on urban housing, livelihoods and environment (Introduction, this volume). The NDB's South Africa branch has not yet granted housing loans, nor loans addressing livelihoods. However, there are urban services associated with housing, especially electricity and water, and here, at least four more generalised problems are evident: the NDB's proclivity for corruption (and lack of appropriate supervision), its neoliberal export orientation, its lending in inappropriate currency, and its failure to consult affected communities (Bond 2019a).

Before considering each of the main South African loans with sustainability criteria foremost in mind, it is useful to review the NDB's own original mandate, which stressed on the innovative financing options associated with environment-oriented infrastructure lending. The NDB's roots were complicated by the role played by two Western consultants, London and New York economists Nick Stern and Joseph Stiglitz–both former World Bank senior vice-presidents and chief economists–who in 2010 began advocacy for the BRICS Bank. Indeed, in a 2011 memo commissioned by BRICS leaders, they recommended the following:

> Low-carbon infrastructure and technologies, in particular, are crucial to lay different and more resilient foundations for growth in the next decades. Investments are urgently required to both mitigate the risks and adapt to climate change, generate economic growth, reduce poverty and promote stability and security. These are the great challenges of the 21st century. Failure on one is likely to imply failure on the others (Stern and Stiglitz 2011).

Although these are noble sentiments, they have little hope of ever being realised given the broader BRICS project of high-carbon extractive infrastructure. China, the US and India remain the top three greenhouse gas emitters, all of which continued contributing increasingly to climate change, notwithstanding the increasingly obvious dangers to future generations and species. Brazil is much more rapidly exploiting the earth's vital lung, the Amazon rainforest, for the sake of soy, cattle, timber, mining and oil interests under the right-wing, climate-denialist president Jair Bolsonaro. Russia continues with gas exploitation and transmission (increasingly to China). South Africa is engaged in massive new fracking investments, offshore oil and gas (including Total's drilling of a billion barrel-of-oil [BOE] equivalents), the export of 18 billion tonnes of new coal (mainly to India but from late 2020, to China as well), and coal-fired power generation including two 4,800 MW plants now under construction and a 4,600 MW plant initially promised in a Chinese metallurgical complex (though in 2021, this was scaled down to 1,320 MW). A carbon tax of less than US$ 1/ton (compared to Sweden's US$ 120/ton) was imposed in South Africa after seven years of delay, which mainly affects poor people in the form of regressive petrol and electricity levies.

In this context of systematic unsustainability, environmental injustice and worsening inequality in the BRICS countries, it was reasonable to ask whether their leaders were serious about challenging the Bretton Woods Institutions and other structures of global power, particularly from the standpoint of environmental stewardship. After all, if revolutionising development finance was the objective, there was an alternative already in place they could have supported: the Bank of the South. Founded by the late Venezuelan president Hugo Chavez in 2007 and supported by Argentina, Bolivia, Brazil, Ecuador, Paraguay and Uruguay, the Banco del Sur (Bank of the South) had acquired $7 billion in capital by 2013. It offered a more profound challenge to the Washington Consensus, especially after Ecuadoran radical economists led by Pedro Paez improved the design. Instead, the BRICS appear to favour the stabilisation of the world financial *status quo*, rather than radically changing the most unfair and intrinsically destabilising components.

Ignoring the Bank of the South was possible in part because of claims that the NDB would be dedicated to sustainability, as was often advertised. As Standard & Poor's (2019) remarked in its 2019 AA+ rating (a surprisingly strong 'investment grade' award granted to a 5-year-old multilateral financial institution), 'the NDB's mandate is to mobilise resources for infrastructure and sustainable development projects in BRICS and other emerging economies and developing countries'. Although S&P was impressed that $8 billion had been lent to various infrastructure projects—transportation (29 per cent), energy (26 per cent), water/sanitation/irrigation (22 per cent), social infrastructure (15 per cent), and cleaner production (8 per cent)—the ratings agency noted the bias in country recipients: 'India (40 per cent) and China (25 per cent), which we believe reflects the difficulties in finding viable bankable projects in Russia, Brazil, and South Africa.'

Not only did the latter three (BRS) suffer junk bond ratings from 2015–2017, catalysed by the crash of commodity prices, but in addition, all three had also defaulted on their foreign debt in living memory (South Africa in 1985, Brazil in 1987, and Russia in 1998). This uneven financial terrain is something that the two BRICS NDB theorists would have had at the back of their minds. Indeed, when Stern openly bragged to a 2013 London conference that *he* was the co-instigator of the very idea of a BRICS Bank, he did not stress the written rationale (Stern and Stiglitz 2011), that is, to finance a 'different type of economic growth'. Instead, he emphasised the merits of a bank in facilitating deal-making between states and multinational corporations:

> If you have a development bank that is part of a [major business] deal then it makes it more difficult for governments to be unreliable....What you had was the presence of the European Bank for Reconstruction and Development (EBRD) reducing the potential for government-induced policy risk, and the presence of the EBRD in the deal making the government of the host country more confident about accepting that investment. *And that is why Meles Zenawi, Joe Stiglitz and myself, nearly three years ago now, started the idea. And are there any press here, by the way? Ok, so this bit's off the record.*

> *We started to move the idea of a BRICS-led development bank* for those two reasons (Stern 2013; emphasis mine).

This attempt to crowd in corporate investment needs under the rubric of sustainability is cynical. South Africa's own NDB design stage was equally inconsistent when it came to environmental values. While in this chapter there is insufficient scope to explore all the NDB experiences within the BRICS countries, at least an overview of South Africa's borrowing from the local NDB Africa Regional Centre is feasible, focussing on the Stern-Sitglitz (2011) mandate for financing 'low-carbon infrastructure and technologies... [to] mitigate the risks and adapt to climate change, generate economic growth, reduce poverty and promote stability and security'. With these in mind, it is obvious that South Africa faces formidable challenges with regard to urban infrastructure sustainability.

SOUTH AFRICAN URBAN INFRASTRUCTURE IN CONTEXT: THE UNSUSTAINABLE MINERALS-ENERGY COMPLEX

South Africa's housing, livelihoods and environmental problems are immense, and have been for decades (Bond 2002). To illustrate, more than two-thirds of society live below the poverty line of $3.50/day (considered to be the local 'upper bound poverty line'). They suffer a backlog in formal housing of three million units (that is, encompassing more than a fifth of the sixty million residents), and most of the new houses built over more than a quarter-century of post-apartheid democratic state power are much smaller and further away from economic activity than even apartheid-era township houses. The unemployment rate in 2021 has risen to 42 per cent (including people who have formally stopped looking for jobs out of hopelessness), thus generating the world's highest income inequality rate, with a Gini coefficient measured at 0.78 in market terms (prior to state intervention) (World Bank 2014). Johannesburg was measured in late 2017 as the major city with the world's highest Thiel inequality ratio (Razvadauskas 2017). In late 2018, the nitrogen dioxide levels in the area just northeast of

Johannesburg (the city of Emalahleni) were determined to be the highest on earth (Greenpeace 2018).

In this context, urban infrastructure should be the highest priority for state investments, so as to improve basic supplies of housing, water, sanitation (including biogas digestion based on simple, low-flush technology), electricity (featuring decentralised renewable supply), clinics and schools, childcare facilities, tarred roads, public transport, storm water drainage, rainwater harvesting, recreational facilities and well-located settlements. Vast shortcomings in post-apartheid neoliberal urban planning have left such basic needs unmet, or met with tokenistic responses (Bond 2014).

The inevitable problem, however, is that the power relations in the society are skewed away from meeting these basic needs, and towards the satisfaction of corporate priorities. As NDB President K. V. Kamath explained during the 2017 launch of the Bank's Africa Regional Centre in Johannesburg,

> Of particular relevance to the NDB is the National Infrastructure Development Plan which is part of the National Development Plan, which sets out a series of ambitious and far-reaching initiatives in which to start to transform South Africa's economic landscape. We expect that initiatives that NDB supports will form a part of the Strategic Investment Projects (SIPs) identified by the government (Kamath 2017).

If so, the danger arises that the NDB will turn away from providing finance that would solve the genuine needs of urban and rural people, and instead will finance 'extraction'-oriented infrastructure. The central dilemma for any infrastructure bank is that those who have unmet basic needs require subsidisation of both capital and ongoing (operations and maintenance) costs. But a major new bank like the NDB does not subsidise, for it must return profits to its shareholders, especially to retain the AA+ rating won from Western credit ratings agencies (Standard & Poor's 2019). On the one hand, the South African NDP's (National Development Plan) plans certainly include progressive commitments to eradicate shortfalls of basic-needs infrastructure, and of the ten SIPs, several do have potential, *if they are subsidised with grants* (both capital and operating). But on the other hand, as has been repeatedly shown in public policy, it is impossible for a bank to turn a profit so as to ensure that a project has *financial* sustainability, when funding such basic-needs infrastructure.

Moreover, there are also sustainability dangers associated with the four NDB borrowers in South Africa, and specifically with the two largest SIPs in the national infrastructure plan. The second of the SIPs, South Durban port expansion, is already in major trouble due to not only urban unsustainability but also corruption, and yet the NDB holds a 30 per cent financing stake (of $200 million) in the current stage of SIP2. The first SIP is also worth at least brief consideration, since it entails both fossil-dependent energy that in late 2018 brought together the two largest parastatal firms—rail and port manager Transnet and electricity producer Eskom—in a moment of revealing chaos. And the final NDB loan of 2018 went to a local development bank with an appalling record of environmental and financial unsustainability.

To understand South Africa's political-economic-ecological context, in which during apartheid, electricity for poor people was supplied as an afterthought *only after the 1980s*, it requires awareness of the so-called 'Minerals-Energy Complex' that has dominated the economy and ruling class since at least the era of Cecil John Rhodes. The richest man in Africa's history, Rhodes came to prominence 150 years ago in the now-exhausted diamond fields of Kimberley, where he consolidated the De Beers global monopoly. In subsequent years, the Oppenheimer family's Anglo American Corporation (founded in 1917) dominated both mining and urban development in the so-called Highveld of South Africa, including the Bushveld Igneous Complex that reaches up to Zimbabwe's border, and the coal deposits that crisscross the eastern half of South Africa.

As for the affected cities, shown in Figure 11.1, they lie on an arc stretching from the Rustenberg platinum zone on the west in Mogale City and south in Welkom (where gold in the vicinity is still mined), through Johannesburg and Ekurhuleni (whose gold is mostly exhausted), southwards to the Vaal metallurgical complex (home of the major steelworks) and then eastwards to Secunda (where the oil-from-coal extraction site makes it the world's single-largest site of CO_2 emissions), and then north to the Emalahleni coal centre. These cities represent exceptionally unequal sites of pollution and poverty. To be more precise, Johannesburg's historic whites-only centre city and Parktown-Houghton suburbs centralised the mineral wealth during the twentieth century, and after racial desegregation began, the Sandton-Bryanston-Hyde Park strip further north captured surpluses in the twenty-first century, as capital fled its former safety zones for gated communities.

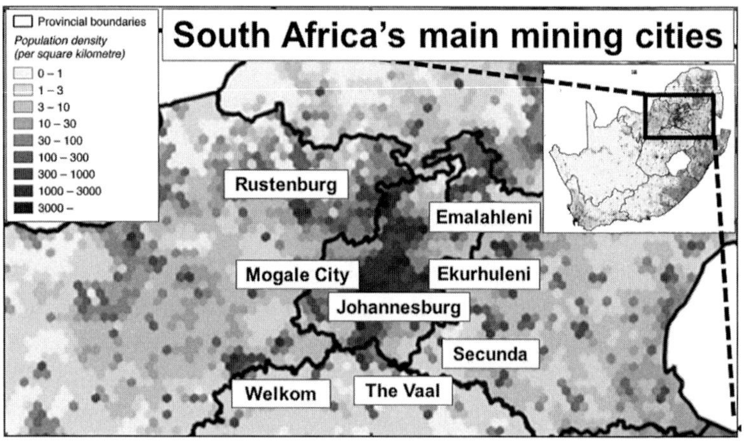

Figure 11.1: South Africa's Main Mining Cities

Source: Created by the author from https://commons.wikimedia.org/wiki/File:South_Africa_2011_population_density_map.svg and https://www.researchgate.net/figure/Distribution-of-human-population-in-South-Africa-in-2011-in-terms-of-density_fig4_269756974.

In all these cities, the working class and poor were–and still are–kept far away from the financial centre and headquarter activities associated with the mining industry. This pattern reflected the needs of mining houses and other industries for cheap labour supplies: workers living in the cities who were termed 'temporary sojourners'. They could reside in the gigantic townships nearby, only so long as they possessed a 'dompas' (pass book that kept black people geographically confined to ethnically-segregated sites), which their employment provided (Bond 2000). After the work was finished, or if the workers became sick or injured, they were expected to return to Bantustan rural areas. The gendered power relations associated with these migrancy relations were another reason—in addition to class and racial power—why workers' inexpensive social reproduction left companies operating in South African cities with profit rates which were among the world's highest (Saul and Bond 2014).[3] The sustainability of these cities was simply not a concern.

After apartheid was dismantled in 1994, urban sustainability degenerated further. The next stage of minerals-sourced accumulation was driven not only by the world's largest mining houses, including BHP Billiton (formerly the South African firm Gencor), Glencore (also with strong South African roots), and Anglo American (from 1999, it was allowed to relist its main financial headquarters in London). By the late 2010s, the largest share in the latter was no longer the Oppenheimer family's, but instead Anil Agarwal's, who owns the Indian firm Vedanta (though he sold much of it during the early 2020s when he could not acquire even a board seat). The massive Iron and Steel Corporation of South Africa foundries of the Vaal—once state-owned—became part of Lakshmi Mittal's Arcelor Mittal empire. Even a Russian, Roman Abramovich, owned Emalahleni's main steel firm, Evraz Highveld, although it was forced into bankruptcy in 2016 due to a wave of cheap Chinese imports, leaving the area's economy in tatters (Bond 2018a). What had been anticipated across the world as the primary site of emerging-market country unity, the BRICS, was now revealed not as a fraternity which would collaborate with each other against the West, but instead as an intensely competitive and sometimes cannibalistic mode of capitalism. The cities suffered enormously (Bond and Garcia 2015).

Also, after 1994, the new black South African tycoons entering mining made the cities even less sustainable. As a result of a greater commitment to extraction (particularly of coal), South Africa suffered even higher levels of particulate pollution, more venal corruption, and a more uneven urban structure, with settlements located even further away from city centres than during apartheid due to the cheaper cost of land there (Bond 2000). The 'Black

Economic Empowerment' and crony corporate elites included Ramaphosa (whose 2012 role in the Lonmin massacre of platinum mine-workers was the most extreme indicator of unsustainability), Patrice Motsepe, Mzi Khumalo, Khulubuse Zuma, and the most notorious: the Gupta brother immigrants (Saul and Bond 2014). To illustrate, the nephew of President Jacob Zuma, Khulubuse, was the main investor in greater Johannesburg's Aurora gold mines, whose steady bankruptcy and asset stripping suddenly amplified a pre-existing 'Acid Mine Drainage' pollution threat. At one point the mine ceased pumping the mine-poisoned water out, thus threatening the region's water table (Bond 2018b).

Perhaps worst of all, the Gupta brothers spent the 2009–2018 period bribing and corrupting the ruling party, but in terms of urban sustainability they were also a formidable negative influence. In 2015–2018 their main mining house Oakbay controlled a massive coal mine (Optimum) that soon went bankrupt. This not only threw the country's electricity supply into question, but compelled Eskom to run much more expensive diesel turbines to supply power. That, in turn, raised tariff costs paid by the urban poor to unaffordable levels. In the decade 2008–2017, the real price of Eskom electricity rose by nearly 300 per cent. Urban poor residents moved from turning on an electricity switch to firing up paraffin, coal and wood energy sources, with corresponding increases in disease (with intra-household gendered and generational implications) (Bond 2016b).

Central to the unsustainable carbon intensity of the South African economy, and facilitating this untenable urbanisation pattern, are the parastatal firms Eskom and Transnet. The former's inability to reduce its reliance upon coal-fired power plants and to replace generation capacity with renewable sources, and likewise the intensity of Transnet's reliance upon coal exports (and lack of concern for a balanced rail transport network), are together reflected in the two largest mega-project investments in the 2012–2030 National Development Plan (Bond 2017).

In the first SIP, the state—led by Transnet and major mining houses—made a $60 billion commitment to the export of 18 billion tons of coal (mostly to India) along new rail lines, using imported locomotives (from China, also financed from China) that can pull

3 kms-long ore-carrying trains. At $60 billion in cost, this is by far the single largest project within the 2011 National Infrastructure Development Plan (the same plan which was enthusiastically endorsed by Kamath in 2017). Eskom relies on coal from the same areas (Limpopo and Mpumalanga provinces) for 90 per cent of its generation capacity. That structural relationship sets Eskom against Transnet and the coal exporters it serves. Competition suddenly emerged over the geographic combustion of the coal, in the competition for domestic (Eskom) or export (Transnet) sales. In 2018, that competition became the source of great national concern due to periodic 'load-shedding' blackouts, in part caused by very low coal supplies at most of Eskom's fifteen power plants.[4]

Another factor was the crash in the price of coal from a high of $170/ton in 2008 to $48/ton in 2015, before recovering to above $90/ton throughout 2018. The 2020 crash caused by COVID-19 pandemic lowered the price to $55/ton, but it soared to $110/ton by mid-2021. Coal price turbulence was one indicator of extremely volatile commodity markets, and although movements in the value of the South African currency compensated such wild fluctuations, it mitigated against planning and investment. Also volatile is the extent to which the average South African emits CO_2 as a result, mainly, of Eskom's coal consumption, used to generate 90 per cent of the country's electricity. Compared to a world average of below 5 tons of CO_2 emissions per person each year, the South African rate has zigzagged between 7.5 and 10 tons (Bond 2016b). But of crucial importance is the skewed consumption, since smelting and mining are vastly over-represented in the South African emissions footprint, and very few poor and working-class people directly benefit (e.g. as workers) from the country's Minerals-Energy Complex. The net negative impact of South African extraction of coal and minerals has been measured by the World Bank (2010) at –9 per cent of national income, a figure arrived at through 'natural capital accounting', by recognising the depletion of society's natural resource wealth by (mostly) multinational mining corporations, whose reinvestment in physical, human and natural capital is net negative (Bond 2018a). All of these represent systematic unsustainability in ecological, financial and also political respects.

The second largest SIP mega-project is the $20 billion expansion of the port-petrochemical complex in Durban, again led by Transnet, as discussed below. It is therefore no surprise that the first two BRICS NDB loans to South Africa also reflect these biases. The 2016 and 2018 credits of $180 million to Eskom and $200 million to Transnet quickly fell into controversy, and in both cases, the projects went into immediate hibernation in part due to the borrowers' systemic corruption, and in part due to the failure of both to properly make their projects sustainable (Bond 2020a).

THE NDB LOANS TO ESKOM: 2016, 2018, 2019

In 2016, the NDB signed up its first South African borrower: the parastatal energy firm Eskom, led by a man who would become notorious due to his links to the Gupta brothers—Brian Molefe. In line with NDB financing in its early stages, the first $180 million in funding was allocated for the transmission of electricity to the grid from several dozen privatised solar and wind 'Independent Power Producers' (IPPs), as well as for restructuring Soweto's electricity supply. In generating solar and wind power, the IPPs' privatisation costs are substantially more than they would be if Eskom had developed its own renewables capacity. The IPPs also require repayment of profits in hard currencies to mainly European producers. Due to these additional costs, such a system has long been opposed by South African progressives who insist on state-supported renewable energy that is self-managed by workers, community-controlled and socially-oriented. A major protest by trade unions from affected sectors was held against Ramaphosa at his Pretoria office in November 2018. Moreover, Soweto residents have an 85 per cent illegal reconnection rate, with more than $1 billion in overdue Eskom accounts, so the NDB's failure to consult with activists ensures continual conflict (Bond 2019a).

Yet at the time, in 2016–2018, neither of the former Eskom leaders who negotiated the loans—Molefe and his successor Matshela Koko (who were both in 2019 subject to prosecution for multiple forms of corruption)—desired renewable energy. They both favoured nuclear instead.[5] 'Energy experts in South Africa believe the NDB is not happy with Eskom because it has earmarked a large chunk of the $180 million loan for projects not related to renewable energy,' according to Peter Fabricius (2017). 'The highly controversial Molefe's indifference to renewable energy suggested to many that he had already signed up to Zuma's dubious nuclear project'—whose cost was estimated at $100 billion—leaving 'great suspicion that Zuma has already promised the construction contract to Russian President Vladimir Putin.' That deal was consummated in mid-2015 at the BRICS summit in Ufa, but reversed in 2017 in the courts when environmentalists challenged the public participation processes.

However, the day before the opening of the Johannesburg NDB branch in 2017, NDB chief executive Kamath revealed that his loan to Eskom was actually 'in abeyance' at Pretoria's request (Cohen 2017). The statement was contradicted by South Africa's NDB vice-president, Lesley Maasdorp, when *Euromoney* (Wright 2019) interviewed him in 2019. He conceded that the Eskom loan was 'saddled with corruption allegations and governance challenges. So that loan was put on ice and never formally concluded.' In fact, it was concluded in mid-2018, with a revival of the loan.

The impression left was that the NDB's role in Eskom is highly inconsistent, and that it has no particular influence over the sustainability of electricity supply required to meet the needs of urban residents. Activists in Soweto, in particular, were militant and well-organised (including during the late 1980s by Ramaphosa himself, a native of the township). Their struggle for Free Basic Electricity, launched by the Soweto Electricity Crisis Committee (SECC) in 2010, was successful within months, for the ANC promised a lifeline supply that Eskom ultimately lowered to 50 kWh per household per month. SECC activists continued to campaign vociferously for double that amount, and for an end to the hated pre-payment meters which represented a self-disconnection system. They pioneered electricity 'commoning' strategies to continue their access to power in spite of Eskom disconnections.

Hence consultation with leading residents' organisations such as the SECC (Ngwane 2003) would be an absolutely critical component of any sound lending strategy. Such consultation was done neither by Eskom nor the NDB. The main grievances associated with non-payment are excessively high prices (and their 300 per cent real increase from 2008–2017), an ungenerously low lifeline supply, intermittent supply, the pre-payment meter system (generally not applicable in rich areas), Eskom's punitive disconnection policy, and systematically inaccurate billing.

The bulk of the US dollar-denominated loan was meant for the transmission of 670MW of solar and wind power, to contribute around 2 per cent more to the national grid (given that money is fungible, it was just as likely that the coal-fired power plant enhancements would benefit from the credit line, as Molefe later was accused of by NDB officials, according to Fabricius [2017]). But if one neglects to factor in the full cost of generating electricity, including non-renewable resource depletion, pollution and climate change (as does Eskom), the IPPs' costs are substantially more (often double the existing per unit costs). Hence, Eskom leadership continually complained that each unit of renewable electricity purchased represented a net loss to their firm.[6] The loan costs are typically much higher if contracted in US dollars—especially if there is a low import content for the project—given that the rand is an extremely volatile currency. In addition, the privatised suppliers are multinational corporations, which require the repayment of profits to mainly European headquarters.

Finally, due to job losses in the coal sector (as renewable energy replaces coal-fired generators), without any retraining or redeployment within Eskom, South Africa's privatised renewable system is regularly criticised by progressives. The major complaints are not only the lack of a 'Just Transition' approach for displaced workers, but the high profit markups that raised prices unreasonably, the foreign currency outflows as profits which are repatriated to the firms' overseas headquarters, and the need to instead build state renewable capacity. These factors all complicate what should have been an obvious trajectory by Eskom to exit coal and adopt renewable energy many years ago.

Insufficient renewable energy had been built, which in turn reflected the neoliberal bias within Eskom *to not build any photovoltaic solar capacity on its own* but instead outsource it to private firms.

However, a more profound reason for Eskom's reluctance was what at the time appeared to be looming overcapacity, what with Medupi's and Kusile's generators coming on-line. The last prior systemic load-shedding had occurred in mid-2015, just before the commodity price crash suddenly lowered demand for electricity from both mining and smelting operations, thus cutting consumption by more than 5 per cent nationally and allowing Eskom a much higher reserve. At this point, lending strategies were being established at the NDB, and Eskom appeared a good borrowing prospect. The NDB's (2016b) loan rationale therefore included this concocted analysis, announced in April 2016:

> Frequent electricity shortages complicate the challenge for the economy from the supply side. According to the country's National Treasury, GDP growth will increase by roughly 2% if the issue of electricity shortage is addressed. Securing energy supply and developing renewable energy are therefore the government's main policy concerns. Coupled with electricity shortage, grid facilities are getting outdated. In Soweto, a township in South Africa, electricity constraint is severe, with aging electricity infrastructure reaching the end of its usage life. Any outage of one circuit can put down the entire electricity network.

There was really no basis for anticipating that relaxing the electricity supply constraint would add 2 per cent to GDP, because the commodity price crash of 2015—the main reason for electricity oversupply (given the curtailment of the mining-smelting sector's immense energy demand) and low GDP growth that year—had already bottomed out by early 2016. The electricity infrastructure in Soweto was not in need of enhancement due primarily to age, but due to the anger of residents against Eskom, since the illegal reconnections degraded the quality of circuit breakers and wiring.

As for the $480 million NDB loan granted in April 2019, in addition to facilitating coal-fired power at Medupi, the credit essentially also endorses Eskom's single largest contract for boiler installation undertaken by the Japanese firm Hitachi (it is the boiler's SO_2 pollution that the de-sulphurisation is required to mitigate). Yet in September 2015, that firm paid the US government (not South Africa) a $19 million fine for Foreign Corrupt Practices Act violations, specifically bribery of the ruling ANC, when Hitachi gifted the party's investment arm a quarter stake in its local subsidiary (Bond 2020a).

The most recent NDB loan to Eskom, in late 2019, was for R6 billion (more than $400 million) worth of battery-based storage systems to enhance a small but growing renewable energy sector, which appears to rely on lithium or lead components. Other energy storage systems have been used by Eskom—including a partially-working pumped hydro storage pilot project (Ingula) and a molten salt storage system serving a Northern Cape solar chimney—that are less invasive and dangerous. The NDB's project proposal lists potential problems: 'leakage of battery electrolyte and soil contamination, potential pollution from waste battery disposal, loss of habitats and potential impacts to protected species at some sites'. Assuming lithium or lead are used (instead of pumped storage and molten salt), there are much greater displacement and disposal dangers. Also, there is again a currency mismatch, for the import cost of lithium and lead are likely to be denominated in dollars, but the loan is granted in local currency.

The NDB-Eskom relationship's various flaws can be identified not only in the Bank's obvious lack of due diligence (as Maasdorp admitted), but also in the climate-insensitive policies of a (corrupt) Eskom management which, until mid-2018, was opposed to using renewable energy, and in the inability to assess how costs could be better matched with revenues, including dollar versus rand currency liabilities. There was, in addition, very little concern for urban sustainability, whether in addressing Soweto customers' willingness and ability to pay for over-priced electricity, or in relation to threats from climate change more generally, given the expansion of Medupi. Similar problems are evident in the NDB's next 2018 loan, to Transnet, for the Durban port's expansion.

THE NDB LOAN TO TRANSNET, 2018

The next loan was in mid-2018, to Transnet, in order to expand the Durban container port. In the same style as Washington bankers, there was no consultation with affected people, especially the South Durban Community Environmental Alliance (SDCEA). Since 1995, SDCEA's members from all races and classes have opposed the ultra-polluting port-petrochemical complex. Container trucks are especially damaging, with one careening off Durban's notorious Field's Hill M13 highway in 2012, killing two dozen black, working-class passengers of minibuses–just one of an annual average of 7,000 truck crashes in Durban. SDCEA is opposed to the massive truck logistics park proposed for the Clairwood Racecourse due to its threat to nearby schoolchildren's safety. Although concessions were belatedly won from Engen, British Petroleum and Shell on long-overdue sulphur scrubbing at the continent's largest refinery complex, it was not long ago that Merebank's Settlers Primary School had a 52 per cent rate of asthma, the highest ever recorded at any school. Leukaemia is still a South Durban pandemic, with rates 24 times the national average (Bond and Desai, forthcoming).

One major objection to Transnet's expansion is that it first built a $1.8 billion pipeline that entails doubling both refining and Durban-Johannesburg oil transport capacity. In addition, four multinational corporations–Italy's ENI, Norway's Statoil, United States of America's ExxonMobil and South Africa's Sasol–are doing exploratory oil and gas drilling 4 kms deep in the dangerous Agulhas Current offshore Durban. This expansion is occurring when not only SDCEA, but also the world, is demanding a local transition away from fossil fuels due to the looming catastrophe of climate change. Evidence is growing ever more obvious, especially in the damage to Transnet's own Durban facilities during the October 2017 superstorm: a ship lost its moorings and blocked the harbour, and overboard containers let loose 49 tons of plastic nurdles, which continue to destroy marine life (Desai and Bond 2019).

Transnet's ability to expand its port-petrochemical operations in a sound manner remains in question. The new oil pipeline was originally budgeted at just $450 million, but its final cost exceeded $2 billion. One reason for the vast cost over-runs was incompetence and 'systematic failings' in mega-project design, as even State Enterprises Minister Malusi Gigaba (2012) confessed:

> Transnet Capital Projects lacked sufficient capacity and depth of experience for the client overview of a megaproject of this complexity. There was an inadequate analysis of risks....Transnet's obligations on the project such as securing authorisations–Environmental Impact Assessments, land acquisition for right of way, water and wetland permits–were not pursued with sufficient foresight and vigour.

Another reason for massive cost over-runs was the line's rerouting from the white areas of Hillcrest and Kloof to South Durban's black neighbourhoods. Moreover, the University of KwaZulu-Natal Centre for Civil Society and Birdlife, South Africa also challenged Transnet's Environmental Impact Assessments (EIA) for port expansion in 2012–2014 due to historic climate denialism and the harbour's ecological degradation, forcing further delays until Transnet reworked its proposal, but still not to the critics' satisfaction. The likely collapse of the large sandbar near the container terminal will demolish vital bird and marine breeding grounds (Bond 2017).

Livelihoods in South Durban are also at stake due to the continual replacement of workers with machines. The economic justifications for the capital-intensive character of the port expansion are dubious, especially because of 'Fourth Industrial Revolution' robotics: the new mega-ships that carry upwards of 10,000 containers now have fewer than twenty crew. Durban is already one of the world's most expensive ports for container handling, even before a new foreign loan for overpriced infrastructure is factored in. Transnet and the NDB also failed to consider rising world economic volatility, such as US protectionism, which adversely affected South African steel, aluminium and car exports during the late 2010s, and the general downturn in world trade (measured as a share of trade to GDP since the 2007 peak, as noted above). Total South African imports had risen from 18 per cent of GDP in 1994 to 37 per cent of GDP in 2009, but then fell to 29 per cent in 2019 even before COVID-19 pandemic disrupted trade further. (Durban's harbour mainly handles container-based imports, while bulk minerals are exported through other ports.) This is a problem shared by all the BRICS countries aside from Brazil, measured by imports as a share of GDP in 2019: it fell from 68 per cent in 2000 to 45 per cent in Russia; from 31 per cent in 2011 to 23 per cent in India; and from 28 per cent in 2004 to 17 per cent in China (Bond and Desai, forthcoming).

Ultimately, though, the most immediately self-destructive feature of the BRICS Bank loan was Transnet's choice of the contractor to do the port-deepening work: an Italian-led consortium, CMI Emtateni, which included the best-known abuser of Durban's patrimonial procurement system, Shauwn Mpisane. Her company was regularly embroiled in corruption controversies (Bond and Desai, forthcoming), and the CMI Emtateni contract was specifically cancelled due to a whistleblower's November 2018 report on 'fraud, BEE (Black Economic Empowerment) fronting and collusion between the Transnet employees and suppliers', leading to the contract's cancellation in mid-2019 (African News Agency 2019).

THE NDB LOAN TO THE DEVELOPMENT BANK OF SOUTHERN AFRICA, 2018

The third loan the NDB made, also in mid-2018, was to the Development Bank of Southern Africa (DBSA), for projects to be delivered between 2018 and 2033. According to the NDB (2018), 'The objective of the Project is to facilitate investments in renewable energy that will contribute to power generation mix and reduction in CO_2 emissions in South Africa', but there are no specific investments mentioned: 'The proposed NDB loan will be in the form of a two-step loan of up to $300 million to DBSA, which in turn will be on-lent to its identified subprojects, including the wind, solar, and biomass energy sectors.'[7]

The most worrisome aspect of this vague ambition relates to the parameters for greenhouse gas reductions, which include attempts at carbon offsets and trading that were initially (prior to 2012) channelled through the Clean Development Mechanism (CDM) in South Africa. The Bisasar Road landfill's methane-to-electricity gas incineration was the first Durban pilot project, and cost $15 million in capital. However, it encountered not only intense community opposition (Bond 2012), but mainly unsuccessful results in 2007–2016, in spite of promotion by the United Nations Framework Convention on Climate Change (UNFCCC), which held its 2011 annual meeting in Durban. The DBSA firmly supported the strategy of carbon trading (Tyani 2010), and a DBSA training in CDM strategies in 2002 was one of the motivations for Durban municipality to attempt the investment. But by 2014, the South African Local Government Association (2014: 4) monitoring the project found:

> The cost of verification is significantly more than the financial benefit of the credits. This process of registering the CDM project with the UNFCCC Executive Board was felt to be long, tedious and costly—emissions reduction monitoring is onerous and gas emissions data needs to be collected every few seconds using rigorous monitoring methods and expensive software packages....Incorrect equipment, not suitable for Durban's climate, caused the system to overheat continuously and rectifying the problem caused the project costs to increase substantially.

Another factor in the NDB's on-lending to the DBSA is that due to financial 'fungibility' (as mentioned earlier, the ability to take one pot of money allocated to one project and move it around within an institution), the rest of the institution also deserves scrutiny. For example, a major campaign was waged by the climate activist network 350.org against the DBSA on the grounds that it was part of a consortium financing a 1,000 MW coal-fired power plant (Thabametsi). So, funding one part of the DBSA frees up finances for the institution to continue its coal addiction. Although the DBSA's chief executive Patrick Dlamini and the then board chair Mark Swilling denied support for coal power (partly on economic grounds due to the 'stranded asset' problem), the Minister of Mining and Energy, Gwede Mantashe, continued to endorse not only coal but also nuclear energy, and put pressure on its main state bank to finance a new generation of mega-projects. Mantashe was implicated in the 'state capture' process, as his house was provided with free security by the notorious firm Bosasa (second most prolific briber of state officials after the Gupta brothers). The subsequent

DBSA chair, Enoch Godongwana, was a dogmatic supporter of coal financing, threatening to impose prescribed asset requirements on commercial banks (when they were announcing coal boycotts) shortly before his appointment to the DBSA in mid-2019 (Sguazzin 2019). Furthermore, corruption allegations of insider loans never repaid in full (dating to the late 2010s) led to a 2021 parliamentary inquiry about the DBSA after former board members engaged in whistleblowing, which the finance minister and DBSA officials claimed were sour-grape, illegitimate complaints (Gilili 2021).

THE NDB LOAN FOR THE LESOTHO HIGHLANDS WATER PROJECT

A second NDB loan announced in April 2019 (in addition to Medupi) was for the Lesotho Highlands Water Project (LHWP), specifically to fund part of another mega-dam in what is Phase 2 of Africa's largest water-transfer scheme. The project is ecologically damaging and unsustainable insofar as it reroutes the upper stretches of the Orange River into the Vaal River, serving Gauteng's needs instead of the logic of the natural environment. South African water consumers are the main beneficiaries, but the pricing associated with the dam water is biased towards excessive payments by lower-income Johannesburg residents, whereas the main consumers—Eskom for cooling coal-fired power, golf courses, hedonistic households with swimming pools—pay a relatively small amount. As a result, the impact of Phase 1 on Johannesburg pricing contributed to the city's dramatic water wars during the early 2000s (Bond 2002; Bond and Ndlovu 2010).

For more than two decades, the best-known individual associated with the LHWP has been a Lesotho national, Masupha Sole, who was convicted of fraud in association with major construction companies who transferred bribes to his Swiss account: ABB, Impregilo, Sogreah, Lahmeyer International, Hochtief, Bouygues, Keir International, Stirling International, Concor, Group Five, Balfour Beatty, Spie Batignolles, LTA, ED Zublin, Acres, Spie Batignolles, Dumez, ED Zublin and others (Bond 2002). This was the first corruption case that the World Bank took seriously, ultimately 'debarring' (banning) the Canadian firm Acres from future contracts, which led to its bankruptcy. After serving nine years in jail for taking the firms' bribes, in 2011 Sole was controversially reappointed as Lesotho's lead advisor to the project.

THE NDB LOAN TO THE SOUTH AFRICA NATIONAL ROADS AGENCY

In September 2019, another loan was granted by the NDB, this one in local currency for R7 billion (the equivalent of $500 million) to the SA National Roads Agency (SANRAL). It had similar implications for the Gauteng area's maldevelopment as the Lesotho dams, insofar as it encouraged inappropriate, unsustainable infrastructure provided by an agency with a major corruption problem. The commodification of highways in the main industrial and political centres–Johannesburg and Pretoria–had already led to citizens' revolts over high electronic toll payments, charged for driving on the main routes in and around the two important cities.

Not only did the largest trade union federation protest these e-tolls through the 2010s alongside a middle-class civil society advocacy group (Organisation Undoing Tax Abuse, or OUTA), general calls to boycott e-toll payment were successful: fewer than a quarter of road users–mostly in government and rental car fleets–were paying the toll fees by 2019 when the NDB granted the SANRAL loan, a fact missing from the NDB loan project description. The losses on the Gauteng toll roads were mainly paid from other SANRAL toll fees and state grants (in Euros) to an Austrian firm, Kapsch Traffic Com, with a long-term guaranteed contract for monitoring licence plates with sophisticated cameras and sending out bills.

The premise behind SANRAL's tolling of roads was generally of great controversy because it represented a tariff paid disproportionately by working-class people faced with the long distances that apartheid imposed via the migrant labour system, which was in contrast to the SANRAL objective, as stated in the NDB loan project document, 'to reduce transportation costs' (not specifying for which class of users). The NDB finance was specifically for 'rehabilitation of the pavement for the existing toll sections of national roads, construction of additional lanes to widen such roads, and rehabilitation of related infrastructure such as bridges and intersections', and hence not for providing new roads.

Like other parastatal agencies, SANRAL had long been accused of corruption, driving up the cost of the Gauteng and other toll roads to levels unprecedented in the world (according to OUTA). In one notorious case in 2015, SANRAL officials forged affidavits of Eastern Cape community residents so as to promote a toll road specifically meant for new mining (by an Australian firm) along the Wild Coast, according to world-famous activist Nonhle Mbuthuma (2016): 'Save perhaps for certain mining companies, SANRAL must be the most ruthless and dishonest company in South Africa. SANRAL managers and consultants are lying...[and] had to withdraw four forged affidavits from court when fighting against the Amadiba coastal community.'

THE NDB COVID-19 LOANS, 2020–2021

By far the largest NDB lending to South Africa was in 2020–2021, in the form of two $1 billion (hard-currency) COVID-19 emergency loans to the national government. These were rife with corruption, as the Special Investigating Unit announced in mid-2021 that of $9.0 billion spent on COVID-19 emergency relief (not associated with social grant spending), irregular contracts under investigation amounted to $1.0 billion. Even Health Minister Zweli Mkhize was forced to resign in mid-2021 because of humiliating cronyism and nepotism revealed in his $10 million COVID-19 communications budget, and Ramaphosa's presidential spokesperson Khusela Diko was also suspended in 2020 due to her husband's allegedly fraudulent Personal Protective Equipment tender.

But aside from corruption, there was a direct positive impact of these two loans which must be acknowledged: several months' subsidisation of living costs for both urban and rural poor people who, as the largest component of the 2020 fiscal stimulus, received a monthly state grant. For those receiving child support (a top-up of mainly $30/month was given to eleven million heads of household) or elder care, this was of help to low monthly budgets, but was terminated too quickly. There was an additional R350 ($25) monthly emergency relief grant for those who were suddenly left unemployed by the COVID-19 economic lockdown in mid-2020.

In comparison, however, to the fiscal stimulus advertised by Ramaphosa, and provided by governments in comparative situations, these grants continued to be tokenistically small. The monthly emergency unemployment grant of $0.83/day was far below the $3.50/day poverty line. It was also desperately inadequate as a macroeconomic stimulant, given the 7 per cent fall in GDP in 2020. There were also other logical means of financing these local-currency grants, instead of a foreign loan: taxation of corporations and the rich; Quantitative Easing to ensure state fiscal support was available; lowered interest rates achieved through tightening exchange controls for ready borrowing; and a crackdown on procurement fraud and Illicit Financial Flows—all capable of raising not $2 billion (the NDB loans), but a conservatively-estimated $40 billion per year.

Indeed, with South Africa's foreign debt/GDP ratio already above 50 per cent, whether a foreign currency-denominated loan was needed was an important question. To be sure, the South African currency did strengthen after mid-2020 (hence the critique of higher effective real interest rates would not immediately apply), but there was a dramatic decline in imports as South African commodity exports boomed, which relaxed the current account constraint (it was South Africa's first positive balance in eighteen years). Very little of the loan inputs described in the NDB project document were required as imports, most (aside from some PPE, or Personal Protective Equipment) were (or could have been) produced locally by the remnants of South Africa's clothing industry.

And hence this again raises a concern—one Maasdorp (2020) himself agreed was valid—about inappropriate currency alignment:

> Given the Covid-19 crisis in the world we're in today, it reinforces the need to ensure that there's debt sustainability

> when a country—or a state-owned enterprise—has debt in a hard currency like US dollars or Euros. As their currency depreciates their cost increases. In other words, their overall indebtedness increases as they have to pay back more in their local currency and also as you know, many infrastructure loans, the actual infrastructure, the revenues are generated typically in local currency so you always have this foreign exchange mismatch which borrower countries have grappled with over the years.

This warning was particularly apposite not in relation to infrastructure (which sometimes does have a large import content), but to something as simple as budgetary support for the South African Treasury, which had no need for more foreign-exchange borrowing in 2020–2021, which even its own officials have agreed with (Bond 2020b).

CONCLUSION

The pages above appeal to the reader to pay more attention to details—especially with respect to sustainability, whether environmental, financial, political or social—than has been achieved by most, regarding the NDB and its partners to date. NGOs, journalists and even sophisticated academics often take the NDB's green intentions for granted, in a context where good governance normally means, simply, less corruption. This is understandable, perhaps, because in the immediate vicinity of the NDB's Africa Regional Centre in Sandton, the headquarter offices of South African corporations invariably rank as the world leaders in bribery, corruption and various other forms of fraud measured by PricewaterhouseCoopers biannually (PwC 2018). With the initial NDB president K. V. Kamath and the second NDB chair, Paulo Guedes, both accused of pre-NDB financial malpractice (in bank lending and pension fund management, respectively), the question of corruption was an ever-present concern, especially given the lax approach taken by the NDB Compliance Officer.

Setting those limited understandings of governance aside, there is also a need to pay more attention to a wide range of urban infrastructure sustainability problems. The BRICS NDB in South Africa has, in just its first few loans, provided many signs of danger. One glaring problem is that policy and project decisions were taken from above, without community consultation, much less ownership. In the case of the Stern-Stiglitz intervention, the rationale for the NDB's role was very different from the sustainability reasons stated. The NDB's renewable energy and climate rhetoric appears designed to beguile, what with the Transnet port-petrochemical complex looming as a major investment, once the corruption-idled project resumes. As in the case of Eskom's renewable electricity, the privatised supply of services is common, in spite of the fact that the broader socio-ecological public goods that such infrastructure should contribute to are not within the ambit of a private firm's profitability (and often stand against such self-interest).

In short, based on South Africa's urban infrastructure financing to date, the NDB does not yet appear as an alternative to a system of Washington-centric development finance that is rife with problems. Instead, it appears from the South African case that the ingredients exist for the NDB to *amplify* uneven development through financing some of the country's most notoriously corrupt institutions, for projects which are themselves highly dubious.

As a result of adverse power relations implied by these projects, the hope for insider processes of engagement and persuasion—including a BRICS NGO Working Group and 'Civil BRICS' networks which met with NDB officials, and more than a dozen letters to the NDB Compliance Officer (Srinivas Yanamandra) from SDCEA and allied scholars—had no impact. The delegitimisation of the NDB would become a 'BRICS from below' strategy instead (van der Merwe et al. 2019). For example, the NDB's Africa Regional Centre was the target of a protest of more than 100 activists led by four African Goldman (environmental justice) Prize winners' organisations in July 2018, namely Earthlife Africa, groundWork, Oil Change International, and the South Durban Community Environmental Alliance (SDCEA), just at the start of the BRICS summit (see Image 11.1) (Moosa 2018). Again, in April 2019, a picket line was held at the NDB's Cape Town Annual General Meeting, also arranged by Earthlife Africa and SDCEA. These were the first of what will be many more protests against the NDB, it is safe to say, unless it shifts away from the projects and policies that are doing so much harm to people and planet.

Image 11.1: Activists Protest before the Start of BRICS Summit in Johannesburg, July 2018

Photograph: Patrick Bond.

End notes

1. In 2016, Zuma told ANC activists about the BRICS: 'It is a small group but very powerful. [The West] did not like BRICS. China is going to be number one economy leader... [Western countries] want to dismantle this BRICS. We have had seven votes of no confidence in South Africa. In Brazil, the president was removed' (Zuma 2016). Zuma reiterated the point at his party's mid-2017 policy conference: 'The ANC is part of the global anti-imperialist movement. We are historically connected with the countries of the South and therefore South-South cooperation such as BRICS is primary for our movement.' A few weeks later, he announced to followers, 'I was poisoned and almost died just because South Africa joined BRICS under my leadership' (Matiwane 2017). His poisoning was actually carried out by his fourth wife, who his confidant Gayton Mckenzie (2017) argued was in league with the US Central Intelligence Agency to halt the progress of the BRICS. However, no one has produced any proof.

2. In 2016, the NDB (2016a) leadership adopted a five-year strategy document which includes a commitment 'to undertake joint projects and knowledge exchanges with the World Bank... to make the most of their decades of experience.' Similar memos of understanding exist with other multilateral institutions, including the IMF.

3. To be sure, there are other standpoints in this debate, for example those that view townships through the lens of collective consumption (McCarthy and Smit 1984), through the urban accumulation of capital (Bond 2000), with attention to administrative and spatial power (Robinson 1995), or with concerns about improving urban efficiency (Urban Foundation 1990).Townships also give rise to debates about South African race and class (Wolpe 1980), activist political agency (Mayekiso 1996) and gender relations (Bozzoli 1983).

4. In December 2018, sabotage of the export rail line by unknown persons compelled a redirection of coal to Eskom. Expanding high-volume coal transport by upgrading Transnet's rail lines and adding more than 1,000 new locomotives capable of carrying 3 kms-long sets of wagons was meant to benefit not only exporters to Richards Bay, but also Eskom's two massive new coal-fired plants, Medupi and Kusile (to the extent that rail lines are built from new Limpopo Waterberg mines to the generators). However, the failure to build the 'forty new coal mines' promised by Eskom officials when borrowing from the World Bank in 2010 means the Waterberg has not yet been developed.

5. In spite of the BRICS NDB loan in 2016, Molefe announced in 2017 that he would no longer buy renewable electricity, as for long-term baseload supply, especially to serve mining houses and smelters, Eskom would focus instead on nuclear energy. In mid-2015, NDB director (and later finance minister) Tito Mboweni had told Bloomberg news that the proposed $100 billion South African nuclear deal with Russia, 'falls squarely within the mandate of the NDB'. This was in spite of enormous local controversy surrounding Zuma's corruption-prone deal-making regarding not only Putin but the Gupta family, whose firm Oakbay would have been the main uranium supplier.

6. At no time did either Eskom or the NDB attempt a full-cost analysis of the coal-fired electricity that would be displaced by the renewable energy coming on-line, including the natural capital accounts that would incorporate Eskom's use of non-renewable resources (Bond 2018a).

7. A flimsy NDB (2018) public statement reports,

> The Project will bring significant developmental impacts through the subprojects, particularly related to environmental and social benefits from reduction in carbon dioxide emissions, increase in generation capacity from renewable energy sources, and increase in the efficiency of the overall energy sector in South Africa. The Project is also expected to have impacts of unlocking private sector investment, and increasing availability of long-term funds for projects in the energy sector in South Africa.

References

African News Agency. 2019. 'Transnet, CMI Emtateni Terminate Controversial R4.2bn Port Expansion Contract'. *Business Report*, 29 May. Available at https://www.iol.co.za/business-report/companies/transnet-cmi-emtateni-terminate-controversial-r42bn-port-expansion-contract-23697589 (accessed July 2021).

Bond, Patrick. 2000. *Cities of Gold, Townships of Coal: Essays on South Africa's New Urban Crisis*. Trenton, NJ: Africa World Press.

______. 2002. *Unsustainable South Africa*. London: Merlin Press.

______. 2012. *Politics of Climate Justice*. Pietermaritzburg: University of KwaZulu-Natal Press.

______. 2014. *Elite Transition*. London: Pluto Press.

______. 2016a. 'BRICS Banking and the Debate over Subimperialism'. *Third World Quarterly* 37(4): 611–629.

______. 2016b. 'South Africa's Next Revolt: Eco-Socialist Opportunities'. In L. Panitch and S. Gindin (eds), *Socialist Register 2017*, 161–185. New York: Monthly Review Press, 2016.

______. 2017. 'Red-Green Alliance-Building against Durban's Port-Petrochemical Complex Expansion'. In L. Horowitz and M. Watts (eds), *Grassroots Environmental Governance: Community Engagements with Industry*, 161–185. London: Routledge.

______. 2018a. 'Ecological-Economic Narratives for Resisting Extractive Industries in Africa'. *Research in Political Economy* 33: 73–110.

______. 2018b. 'Sub-imperial Ecosystem Management in Africa'. In R. Holifield, J. Chakraborty and G. Walker (eds), *Handbook of Environmental Justice*. New York: Routledge.

______. 2019a. 'The BRICS New Development Bank as an institutional alternative to the World Bank: Rhetoric, reality and challenges for China'. In J. Puppim de Oliveira and Y. Jing (eds), *International Development Assistance, China and the BRICS*. London: Palgrave Macmillan.

______. 2019b. 'Interview: Der Klimaterror muss Blockiert Werden'. *Analyse & Kritik (Analysis and Critique)* 648: 26–26.

______. 2020a. 'Subimperial BRICS enter the Bolsonaro-Putin-Modi-Xi-Ramaphosa Era'. In V. Satgar (ed.), *BRICS in the 2020s*. Johannesburg: Wits University Press.

______. 2020b. 'Should South Africa Follow the Law of the Jungle ... or the Doctrine of Odious Debt?' *Counter Punch*, 1 May. Available at https://www.counterpunch.org/2020/05/01/should-south-africa-follow-the-law-of-the-jungle-or-the-doctrine-of-odious-debt/ (accessed July 2021).

Bond, Patrick and Ashwin Desai. Forthcoming. *A City of Rascals: The Uneven Development of Durban*. Johannesburg: Jacana Media.

Bond, Patrick and Ana Garcia (eds). 2015. *BRICS*. New Delhi: Aakar Press.

Bond, Patrick and Molefi Ndlovu. 2010. 'When Mega Projects Crowd out Development: Coega and Lesotho Dams'. In B. Freund and H. Witt (eds), *Development Dilemmas in Post-Apartheid South Africa*. Pietermaritzburg: University of KwaZulu-Natal Press.

Bozzoli, Belinda. 1983. 'Marxism, Feminism and South African Studies'. *Journal of Southern African Studies* 9(2): 139–171.

BRICS. 2013. Fifth BRICS Summit Declaration and Action Plan. Available at http://www.brics5.co.za/fifth-brics-summit-declaration-and-action-plan/ (accessed July 2021).

Cohen, Tim. 2017. 'More Eskom bosses have been suspended, say sources'. *Business Day*, 16 August. Available at https://www.businesslive.co.za/bd/companies/energy/2017-08-16-exclusive-more-eskom-bosses-have-been-suspended-say-sources/ (accessed July 2021).

Desai, A. and P. Bond. 2019. 'Speculators and Scoundrels in South Africa's Secondary Circuit of Capital: A Turbulent Investment Climate at Durban's Point Waterfront'. *Socialism and Democracy* 33(2): 108–141.

Euromonitor. 2017. 'Income inequality ranking of the world's major cities', 31 October. Available at https://blog.euromonitor.com/income-inequality-ranking-worlds-major-cities/ (accessed July 2021).

Fabricius, Peter. 2017. 'Why no Lift-off for Africa's Branch of the BRICS Bank?' Institute for Security Studies, Pretoria, 25 May. Available at https://issafrica.org/iss-today/why-no-lift-off-for-africas-branch-of-the-brics-bank (accessed July 2021).

Gigaba, M. 2012. 'Statement by Minister Gigaba on NMPP Review'. Cape Town, 29 November. Available at http://www.polity.org.za/article/sa-statement-by-transnet-south-african-rail-port-and-pipeline-company-on-celebrating-progress-in-the-development-of-transnets-new-multi-product-pipeline-29112012-2012-11-29 (accessed July 2021).

Gilili, Chris. 2021. 'Scopa to Investigate Claims of Mismanagement at DBSA'. *Mail&Guardian*, 2 June. Available at https://mg.co.za/news/2021-06-02-scopa-to-investigate-claims-of-mismanagement-at-dbsa/ (accessed July 2021).

Greenpeace. 2018. 'Mapped: Nitrogen Dioxide Pollution around the World'. Amsterdam, 29 October. Available at https://unearthed.greenpeace.org/2018/10/29/nitrogen-dioxide-no2-pollution-world-map/ (accessed July 2021).

Kamath, K. V. 2017. 'Speech of President K. V. Kamath at the Opening Ceremony of the Africa Regional Centre of the New Development Bank, Johannesburg, South Africa'. Shanghai, BRICS New Development Bank, 17 August. Available at https://www.ndb.int/president_desk/speech-mr-k-v-kamath-opening-ceremony-africa-regional-centre-new-development-bank-johannesburg-south-africa/ (accessed July 2021).

Maasdorp, Leslie. 2020. 'The New Development Bank: What Washington Should Know About the Newest Multilateral Development Bank'. Center for Global Development YouTube channel, 21 October. Available at https://www.youtube.com/channel/UCWC4mmS_a-0K6JX6QX0hL8w (accessed July 2021).

Matiwane, Z. 2017. 'I was poisoned and almost died when SA joined BRICS, says Zuma'. *Independent Online,* 14 August. Available at: https://www.iol.co.za/news/politics/i-was-poisoned-and-almost-died-when-sa-joined-brics-says-zuma-10782354 (accessed July 2021).

Mayekiso, Mzwanele. 1996. *Township Politics: Civic Struggles for a New South Africa.* New York: Monthly Review Press.

Mbuthuma, Nonhle. 2016. 'Re-emergence of The White Man's Burden: SANRAL's criminal culture of deception and fraud'. *News24,* 4 November. Available at https://www.news24.com/news24/MyNews24/re-emergence-of-the-white-mans-burden-sanrals-criminal-culture-of-deception-and-fraud-by-nonhl-20161104 (accessed July 2021).

McCarthy, Jeffrey J. and Daniel P. Smit. 1984. *South African City: Theory in Analysis and Planning.* Cape Town, South Africa: Juta.

Mckenzie, Gayton. 2017. *Kill Zuma by Any Means Necessary.* Johannesburg.

Moosa, Fatima. 2018. 'Activists Raise their Voices against BRICS'. *Daily Vox,* 25 July. Available at http://www.thedailyvox.co.za/activists-raise-their-voices-against-brics-fatima-moosa/ (accessed July 2021).

New Development Bank. 2016a. 'General Strategy: 2017–2021'. Shanghai. Available at http://www.ndb.int/wp-content/uploads/2017/07/NDB-Strategy-Final.pdf (accessed July 2021).

———. 2016b. 'Project Finance Facility for Eskom'. Shanghai. Available at https://www.ndb.int/eskom-south-africa/ (accessed July 2021).

New Development Bank. 2018. 'Greenhouse Gas Emissions Reduction and Energy Sector Development Project'. Shanghai. Available at https://www.ndb.int/dbsa-south-africa-2/ (accessed July 2021).

Ngwane, Trevor. 2003. 'Sparks in the Township'. *New Left Review* 22 July–August.

PwC. 2018. 'Global Economic Crime and Fraud Survey 2018'. Johannesburg. Available at https://www.pwc.co.za/en/assets/pdf/gecs-2018.pdf (accessed July 2021).

Ramaphosa, Cyril. 2018. 'Address by the President of South Africa to the UN General Assembly, United Nations, New York, USA', 25 September. Available at http://www.thepresidency.gov.za/speeches/address-president-south-africa%2C-h.e.-mr-cyril-ramaphosa%2C-un-general-assembly%2C-united?page=4#!slide (accessed July 2021).

Razvadauskas, Fransua. 2017. 'Income Inequality Ranking of the World's Major Cities'. *EuroMonitor International*, 31 October. Available at https://blog.euromonitor.com/income-inequality-ranking-worlds-major-cities/ (accessed November 2021).

Robinson, Jennifer. 1995. *The Power of Apartheid*. Oxford, UK and Boston: Butterworth-Heinemann.

Russia Today. 2015. 'South African president: BRICS carries the future for our world'. Interview, 6 July.

Saul, John and Patrick Bond. 2014. *South Africa: The Present as History*. Oxford: James Currey.

Sguazzin, Antony. 2019. 'ANC wants to Force Banks to Invest in New Coal Mines'. *Business Day*, 6 May. Available at https://www.businesslive.co.za/bd/national/2019-05-06-anc-wants-to-force-banks-to-invest-in-new-coal-mines/ (accessed July 2021).

South African Local Government Association. 2014. 'Municipal Landfill Gas to Electricity'. Johannesburg. Available at http://www.cityenergy.org.za/uploads/resource_340.pdf (accessed July 2021).

Standard & Poor's. 2019. 'New Development Bank AA+ Ratings Affirmed On Criteria Revision; Outlook Stable'. Singapore: S&P Global Ratings, 27 February. Available at https://www.ademcetinkaya.com/2019/02/new-development-bank-aa-ratings.html (accessed July 2021).

Stern, Nicolas. 2013. 'Emerging Powers as Emerging Economies'. Statement at the British Academy's Emerging Powers Going Global Conference, London, 8–9 October. Available at https://www.youtube.com/watch?v=4ZKQ6wQ-29w (accessed July 2021).

Stern, Nicolas and Joseph Stiglitz. 2011. 'An International Development Bank for Fostering South-South Investment: Promoting the New Industrial Revolution, Managing Risk and Rebalancing Global Savings'. Unpublished paper written for the BRICS Heads of State, London and New York, September.

Tyani, Lwazi. 2010. 'DBSA involvement in Climate Change and CDM'. Presentation, Pretoria, Department of Energy, 16 September. Available at http://www.energy.gov.za/files/esources/kyoto/Web%20info/Carbon%20finance%20workshop/DBSA%20CDM%20project%20financing%20opportunities.pdf (accessed July 2021).

Urban Foundation. 1990. 'Regional Development Reconsidered'. *Policies for a New Urban Future* 3. Johannesburg, South Africa: Urban Foundation and the Private Sector Council.

van der Merwe, Justin, Patrick Bond and Nicole Dodd (eds). 2019. *BRICS and Resistance in Africa*. London: Zed Books.

Wolpe, Harold (ed.). 1980. *The Articulation of Modes of Production: Essays from Economy and Society*. London: Routledge and Kegan Paul.

World Bank. 2010. *The Changing Wealth of Nations*. Washington, DC: World Bank Group. Available at http://documents.worldbank.org/curated/en/630181468339656734/The-changing-wealth-of-nations-measuring-sustainable-development-in-the-new-millennium (accessed July 2021).

______. 2014. *Fiscal Policy and Redistribution in an Unequal Society. South Africa Economic Update* 6. Washington, D.C.: World Bank Group, 1 November. Available at http://documents.worldbank.org/curated/en/2014/11/20339043/south-africa-economic-update-fiscal-policyredistribution-unequal-society (accessed July 2021).

Wright, Chris. 2019. 'NDB: The Brics Bank takes Shape'. *Euromoney*, 9 May. Available at https://www.euromoney.com/article/b1f9vf7w1cf3d8/ndb-the-brics-bank-takes-shape?copyrightInfo=true (accessed March 2021).

Zuma, Jacob. 2016. 'I Know Who are the Witches at Work'. Speech at Pietermaritzburg African National Congress Meeting. *Politicsweb*, 19 November. Available at https://www.politicsweb.co.za/news-and-analysis/i-know-who-are-the-witches-at-work--jacob-zuma (accessed July 2021).

XII

Location, Livelihoods and Environment in Contemporary Delhi

Awadhendra Sharan

INTRODUCTION

Delhi, as any other major city in India, is spatially, economically and socially layered, with different geographies jostling to be recognised as legitimate, and varied social groups contending for their respective claims to livelihood opportunities and decent living conditions. For the majority of the residents of Indian cities, such claims are realised only incrementally, and equally, can be snatched away rather arbitrarily, either through the exercise of brutal power or through the more gentle persuasions of plans and policies. In contemporary Delhi, there are two important features of these opportunities that come accompanied with significant vulnerabilities. (*i*) Much of the transformation that has occurred in the city over the past two decades has been through the rhetoric of 'environmental good', promising ambient air, potable water, green landscapes and a clean river to the people of the city. A decent environment, in other words, seems to have replaced the social welfare rhetoric of earlier times, social costs notwithstanding. (*ii*) In doing so, there is a new emphasis on spatial legality/illegality, with the courts playing a major role in elaborating on the democratic possibilities in our times. In particular, they have done so through an elaboration of Article 21 of the Indian Constitution–the Right to Life–and through a reworking of the legal mechanism that creates the possibility of 'citizen representatives' to seek remedies for what are perceived to be urban deficits. This second feature, the making of the legal/illegal binary, I suggest, is an important reworking of the formal/informal binary of an earlier urban discourse, representing what several scholars have referred to as the judicialisation of governance (see, for instance, Bhan 2016). Together, these two characteristics have marked out a new relationship of location, livelihoods and environment which I hope to speak to in this chapter. However, to appreciate the nature of this change, it would be useful to briefly consider how these issues came to be linked historically, first in the colonial city and then in the wake of comprehensive and regional planning in post-independent India.

CONGESTION AND POLLUTION IN COLONIAL DELHI

Beginning in the 1930s, Delhi officially started addressing what would come to be referred to as the problem of 'congestion' in Indian cities, the estimate being that there was an excess population of 233,000 persons in Delhi, for whom housing would have to be provided over a fifteen-year period from 1931–1946, through schemes of city expansion and town planning (Hume 1936: 21). The congestion was not spatially even, being for the most part confined to the old city of narrow lanes, 'little more than tunnels', 'dark, ill-ventilated and overcrowded' houses, gratings of iron bars, with 'fetid odour from overflowing drains' (ibid.). Slum clearance and town extension schemes were proposed, with the poorest among those displaced proposed to be re-housed along the lines of a 'Model Basti Scheme' as was operational in Calcutta.[1] Not much success was achieved, though, and in the two decades or so between the setting up of an Improvement Trust in Delhi and the end of imperial rule, the poor, the dispossessed and the marginal sections of the population were relegated to new slums, in less desirable locations and less visible to the well-to-do, in spaces that were often cramped and inadequately serviced, such that overcrowding in one location was exchanged for a deteriorated environment in another (Hosagrahar 2005).

In other instances, attention was drawn to congestion on account of the presence of industries and industrial workers within the city. The Government of India proposed that the task of providing housing to workers was not for the individual employer; instead, the responsibility was vested in the local bodies. The municipal authorities begged to differ, arguing that given the large profits, it was for the owners to provide housing for their employees. And as the matter oscillated back and forth between the different authorities and chambers of commerce, it began to acquire a greater urgency from around the 1930s, with a considerable increase in the size of the working population, but with no corresponding improvements in their living conditions. Housing was available only to a limited extent, only at the larger factories and in government establishments. Taken together with the fact that most workers in Delhi were not employed in larger factories but were instead engaged in the many cottage industries that were characteristic of Delhi's industrial landscape, it was evident that pressure on workers' housing was now immense. A note on 'Housing Problem in Delhi City'[2] duly observed: 'If we are able to take out of the city as many as possible of the existing factories and plant these and the new factories in the new industrial area, we would have solved one-third of the problem of congestion in the city' (Sharan 2014: 172). Workers and their factories were to go together somewhere on the margins of the city, or indeed, outside it. As with slums, though, success was hard to come by, with few factories choosing to relocate to the site earmarked by the government.

The site proposed was on the western edge of the city, consisting partly of uncultivated land and partly of groves, well served by rail and road connections and with a drain in the vicinity that could provide for drainage. However, significant other issues remained, especially regarding the nuisances caused by the different industries. These included both hazards and risks, the former through the prospect of explosion and fire, and the latter relating to gases and fumes, smoke, decaying organic matter, obnoxious odours, and mineral and metallic dusts. The prevailing wind in Delhi being from west to east, it was felt that the likelihood of these nuisances reaching the neighbouring residential districts was a distinct possibility. Not much heed was paid to this yet, with the Improvement Trust arguing that such risks would attach to any possible site chosen to function as an industrial area. In this, Delhi was possibly decades behind the other large cities of India, especially Calcutta and Bombay, where smoke nuisance had been dealt with under municipal law since 1862–1863, and statutory smoke nuisance commissions had been set up in 1905 and 1912, respectively. This is not the place to recount the history of these initiatives, except to highlight two aspects of it. First, efforts towards dealing with industrial pollution in colonial cities were firmly anchored in an engineering perspective that viewed efficiency as the necessary and sufficient answer to the nuisance of industrial pollution. Solving pollution was considered a function of good engineering, to be aided by advice from government experts, without taking recourse to binding regulations or the setting up of environmental standards, with success likely to be achieved rather quickly through productive gains (Sharan 2020).[3] Dealing with pollution, in other words, was a matter of utilitarian conservation of resources and not the development of an environmental ethic.

River pollution was dealt with somewhat differently. Towards the closing years of the nineteenth century, when wells began to fail as sources of drinking water, the Yamuna river emerged as the chief source of water for domestic purposes.[4] Since much of this water that flowed into the city also had to find an outlet somewhere, either on land or in a water body, the river also served as the city's sink. The first important requirement, therefore, was to ensure that no native habitations surrounded the point of intake and those that did so were to be evacuated, even if this required the use of force. Cleanliness of source was backed by municipal laws that stipulated fines for those found fouling the waters of wells, public water tanks and the Yamuna by bathing or washing, throwing animal carcasses, or rubbish or filth, or by allowing the water of a sink, sewer, drain, steam engine or boiler to drain into these.[5] The emphasis was on preserving the cleanliness of water as a source of supply for drinking purposes, and on the possible health risks posed to those who may have to take recourse to the river water for drinking, bathing or agriculture. But there was a confidence too that once suitably treated, wastewater itself could be a resource, to be used by farmers for cultivation purposes. As for industrial waste, there was some caution expressed regarding the desirability, or otherwise, of draining these into drains/rivers without suitable treatment, only to be reassured by the engineers of the public works department that trade wastes constituted merely olfactory nuisance, rather than being a bacteriological danger. At most, these could be suitably diluted prior to their discharge.[6] Little risk, it would seem, was felt to be attached to the life of the river itself, and not surprisingly, no standards were developed as regards river water quality.

In brief, there were three legacies that the colonial city left behind—(*i*) how to house the poor in decent surroundings, keeping in mind the varied economic activities that were carried out in these neighbourhoods; (*ii*) how to locate industry appropriately so as to cause minimal environmental nuisance and pollution of air and water; and (*iii*) how to deal with the pollution that was caused by everyday practices, which could not be as easily regulated.[7] In all this, the focus was on an abstract urban space/public, and not on the particular locations and sections of people that were differentially exposed to environmental harms. Post-independence planning would respond to all of these issues through new technical approaches, but perhaps with as little success.

POSTCOLONIAL PLANNING

Planning in Delhi took off in a major way in the 1950s and the nationalist leadership was acutely aware that much still needed to be done regarding housing of the poor. This was as yet a view about the *bustee*, not a view from it,[8] but even as a discourse of national/civilisational progress, it did promise to secure at least a minimum decent living condition for all. As the committee set up to enquire into the functioning of the Improvement Trust duly noted:

> Bad environment affects us all alike; we are choked, each one of us....by the meanness and squalor which stretch their tentacles upwards from the lives of our less fortunate fellow citizens. The slums hold us back; while they exist the roots of our civilization are rotten and our corporate existence as a people diseased (Government of India 1951: 13).

It was also recognised that the problem of encroachment must be considered 'more social than legal'; while some force may be used, evictions should be carried out in a humane manner and people should be *induced* to leave (Delhi Improvement Trust 1951). On the other hand, planners were conscious of the fact that while in Western countries, the 'social conscience' that demanded slum elimination had emerged after a large build-up of capital and resources, in India, the moral, social and political pressure for the same preceded the build-up of the necessary resources. Under the circumstances, a three-pronged strategy was proposed: areas that already had a 'healthy, organic pattern' would be conserved by protecting them from 'encroachment of undesirable and conflicting land use' (DDA 1962: 8); certain other areas would be rehabilitated by improving environmental hygiene and reconstruction of the deteriorated pockets; and finally, unusable buildings would be demolished and improved layouts made in the redevelopment areas. The choices were carefully deliberated, with planners deciding to focus on such areas where slums were entirely in the form of *bustees*, which could be easily eliminated and the people placed in transit camps while the area was being rebuilt. Plans were also drawn up for redevelopment of other areas, including areas of 'unauthorised land use' which included, on the one hand, spaces occupied by beggars, vagabonds, and squatters, and on the other, open markets and small vendors. *Bustee* dwellers, the Master Plan of 1962 recommended, would be accommodated in tenements, in suitable areas not too far away from major work centres. Reasonably sized areas were also to be earmarked in each residential zone for low-income migrants, where they would be permitted to construct cheap houses on regular layouts, with necessary reservation of sites and minimum public services provided by public agencies. Normatively, thus, the Plan seemed to be speaking a language of inclusiveness. But differences of other kinds would matter. Thus, while on the one hand the poor and the squatter seemed to find some place in the planning imagination, there was also an underlying idea that the 'rural' would no longer be the ideal resident. This took many forms and in the context of the argument being presented here, one of these would be of some significance, viz., the desirability or otherwise of 'village industries' in Delhi, assessed through an understanding of the economic value of urban land. Industries such as tannery, pottery, handloom weaving, artistic metal works, etc., it was argued, were located in the heart of the residential areas, intensifying slum conditions, and their relocation would therefore mean the release of 'valuable land' and 'weeding out of those uses not required in the urban core' (DDA 1962: 188).[9]

As regards other industries, the Master Plan being premised on the idea of a strict separation of residential, commercial and industrial areas, several different types of industrial establishments were proposed. First among these were flatted factories—multi-storeyed buildings with high density employment ratios, which could house many of the small industries in the city. Next, located in more outlying areas, would be industrial-cum-work centres with household industries that did not cause nuisance, each of the permitted units being subject to performance standards related to noise, vibration, smoke, dust, effluent and general nuisance. Then came the category of light and service industries—small-scale, non-nuisance industries that could operate near built-up areas, with strict enforcement of factory regulations but with exception for smoke on account of prevailing wind conditions. Finally, there was an area earmarked for extensive industries with huge water and waste facility requirements, which would also house the noxious industries hitherto located in residential areas. As for river pollution, the answer would not be so much spatial as technocratic, with the first Master Plan stipulating that proposals to discontinue sewage overflow into the Yamuna would have to be executed soon, and proceeding to earmark spaces for the same in different parts of the city.

To cut a long story short, the Plan failed abysmally. The necessary housing for the urban poor was never built on the scale required, such that by the turn of the century, barely a quarter of Delhi's population lived in what the Master Plan refers to as planned colonies.[10] And as for industries, their numbers went up from 8,000 to 26,000 between 1962 and 1971, and then from there to over 100,000 by the 1990s, many of them continuing to be located in residential areas. Smoke and toxic gases continued to be regularly released into the air, trade effluents were being discharged into the river and other water bodies without treatment, and dust and smoke from stone-crushing units in the southern part of the city engulfed the entire area. Factories dealing in glass, metal, lead, chemicals, asbestos, etc., were reported to be releasing great quantities of sulphur dioxide and particulate matter. This then set the stage for Delhi's contemporary transformation, guided by the perceived need for obtaining clean air and water for its residents, preserving the river, while demolishing 'illegal' settlements and relocating some of their residents to the urban periphery. Slums, economic activity, air and water pollution were once again conjoined, but this time with a strong emphasis on their (il)legality rather than on the poverty of their residents.

TRANSFORMING CONTEMPORARY DELHI

Contemporary legal practice in India bears the deep imprint of an innovation that was first made in the wake of the Emergency in the 1970s in the form of public interest litigations (PILs). There are several noteworthy features of these PILs that have been discussed at length by legal and urban scholars. Three of these are of special significance for our purposes.

1. As initially conceived, PILs allowed for individuals to represent others who, on account of poverty or other disability, could not approach the court on their own (representative standing). In time, it also permitted those wishing to enforce the performance of public duties to appear before the court directly (citizen standing). A consequence of the latter, Anuj Bhuwania explains, is that the petitioner sues not as a representative of others but in his own right—as a member of the citizenry to whom a public duty is owed (Bhuwania 2017: 34). In extreme cases, the court itself can take up a public cause *suo moto*.
2. Courts have acquired the power to extend the deliberations beyond the specific problem in a specific part of the city to cover the particular problem all over the city. The consequence of this, as Bhuwania again points out, is the emergence of omnibus PILs that continue over several

decades and cover much beyond the original petition (Bhuwania 2017: 9). Indeed, in many cases it is entirely possible that people who stand to be affected by the orders of the courts have little to no idea that they were party to the case (Bhan 2016)!

3. Finally, the courts not only adjudicate, but also take over the micro-management of issues through the appointment of special committees and commissioners, who must report to the courts on a regular basis regarding the progress with respect to the orders of the courts. The consequence is that governance is shared between elected representatives and the judges, and those subject to the court's orders have to find new strategies to deal with 'authority', going beyond the political arrangements that were routinely possible in earlier times.[11]

It is against this background that the question of being 'out of place' has become central to the way an image of 'the city in crisis' was first produced in the Supreme Court of India and, subsequently, in the Delhi High Court, and orders that have been passed have created even greater vulnerabilities for the already marginalised sections of the people. Indeed, the figure of the migrant, slum-dwelling poor as the illegal and polluting presence in the city of Delhi has become central to the transition from walled city to world city, as imagined by some of its elites. Much has been written about these issues, specifically about slum demolition/relocation and about the relocation of industrial units. Here, I take up the case of river pollution and how this question has come to be entangled with the issue of housing, location and work.

By the 1990s, it had become clear that not all was well with the river, and its imminent death was much anticipated, affected as it was by practices that were both local and regional. Pesticide run-offs from fields in the neighbouring state of Haryana, upstream of Delhi, were an issue of contention between the two state governments. In Delhi itself, there was the untreated domestic waste of residents living in the formal city or in informal slums, which found its outfall into the river. The city's industries, though largely situated away from the river, with the exception of a major power plant, also used the river as a major outfall for their effluents, treated or otherwise. And in addition, the immersion of the idols of gods and goddesses, once made of clay and natural colours but now increasingly of dyes and chemicals, began to pose a new threat to the future of the river. And thus the Yamuna, which for much of human history had been viewed as a nurturing and life-enhancing goddess, increasingly came to be identified as a goddess of death, the sister of Yama (Haberman 2006). There were thus both old and new risks for the river itself, for those who lived alongside it, and also for communities downstream, who increasingly began to bring their concerns to the protest sites of Delhi.

The Supreme Court observed in 1995,

> Apart from air-pollution, the waters of river Yamuna are wholly contaminated. It is a paradox that the Delhiites—despite river Yamuna being the primary source of water supply—are discharging almost totality of untreated sewage into the river [....] The water quality of Yamuna, in Delhi stretch, is neither fit for drinking nor for bathing.[12]

In response, it suggested that the treatment of sewage was of utmost importance for health and for the supply of pure water to the citizens of Delhi. Any delay in this respect would be a health hazard and therefore could not be tolerated. The project was not only of great public importance, but indeed also of national importance.[13] Not all were convinced. The potential dispossessed, those whose lands had been earmarked for being taken over for the construction of sewage plants, went to the Delhi High Court and obtained a stay order demanding compensation on current prices, only for it to be vacated by the Supreme Court. Villagers whose lands were set to be acquired for the purpose of setting up of pumping station/ sewage treatment plants (STPs) pointed out to the Court that the land in dispute was shown as agricultural green in the Master Plan and Zonal Development Plan, even as it was being acquired for the purpose of setting up the STP. The acquisition they argued, therefore, was contrary to these plans. But the Plans could not be an effective deterrent, the Supreme Court observing that whatever may have been the use of the land under the Master Plan and the Zonal Development Plan, the state could always acquire the same for public purposes, and the building of sewage treatment plants was exactly such an urgent public purpose. In any case, the object and purpose of constructing the STPs, it ruled, were to protect the environment, control pollution and, in the process, maintain and develop the agricultural green.[14]

Alongside the issue of requisite infrastructure, a different narrative of dirt/waste/pollution of the river and the fate of the people residing adjacent to it also began to unfold in the 1990s. Since the building of the first embankments on the Yamuna in 1955–1956, several new embankments had been built in Delhi. Equally, the lands between the river and these embankments had gradually become sites for informal housing, consequent upon the massive flows of migrant labour into Delhi, especially in the wake of the construction requirements for the Asian Games of 1982. Little to no formal housing being available for these migrants, it was but natural for them to seek more informal living spaces. As an instance of this, Bhan notes the filling in of the vacant marshy embankment on the eastern bank, considered 'too soft' to be built upon, with leftover sand and brick from construction sites, thereby slowly turning it into a habitable settlement.[15] To no one's surprise, such auto-construction, which has been a characteristic feature of most Southern cities, including Delhi, did not merit any sanction of an authorised Plan. From time to time, several of these had been demolished, too, but what was new in the 1990s was the intensity of such demolition, with the Supreme Court referring to its sense of anguish at Delhi having become one of the most polluted cities in the world.[16] Even more damningly, it had gone on to observe that the establishment of slums appeared to be well-organised and a good business, leading to their multiplication by geometrical proportions. Large areas of public land had thus been usurped for private use, free of cost. Under the circumstances, the Court reasoned, rewarding an encroacher on public land with a free alternate site would be like giving a reward to a pickpocket, thereby setting the scene for a new round of displacements of the urban poor.[17] A couple of years later, it was the turn of the

Delhi High Court, which in March 2003 ordered the different governments in Delhi to clear the banks of the Yamuna, as the issue of encroachment became entangled with the question of pollution. Electroplating units, dye units and dairies, together with the seemingly unending flow of human excrement, came together to present a picture of a cluster of twenty-two slums (called the Yamuna Pushta, the largest slum cluster in Delhi) as being the major spoiler of the river (*The Hindu* 2004). Activists begged to differ. According to one such study, around 3,600 million litres of wastewater generated in Delhi went into the Yamuna every day. Of this, less than 1 per cent of the wastewater was the contribution of the slum dwellers (Hazard Centre 2004)! Notwithstanding this, government authorities persisted in their views, with the committee of the Ministry of Urban Development for Yamuna Action Plan (2004) being of the view that the flow of untreated sewage from the slum clusters was an important contributory factor for the polluted condition of the river (Dupont 2008: 10). The consequence was that while 51,461 houses had been demolished in Delhi between 1990 and 2003 under 'slum clearance' schemes, as many as 45,000 homes were demolished between 2004 and 2007 alone, while eviction notices were served on at least three other large settlements towards the end of 2007 (Bhan 2009).

The courts, I suggest, have gone a particular way with the fact of river pollution—an aggressive stance against the illegal poor coupled with highly capital-intensive, even if largely ineffective, technological solutions. Environmentalists, especially those associated with the Yamuna Jiye Abhiyan (Keep Yamuna Alive Campaign), have gone another way, making a plea for understanding the river as an ecosystem, of which riverbeds and floodplains are an integral part (Colopy 2012). Their arguments are based both on moral and economic grounds. For millions of years, during the monsoons, they suggest, the Yamuna had been bringing sand from the mountains and depositing them on its path, thus forming the floodplains. This sandy layer was both porous and had negligible salt content, making it an ideal water recharge zone and freshwater reservoir. By contrast, rooftop rainwater harvesting had a much lower potential, the costs of undertaking water recycling in the event of the loss of the floodplains was prohibitive, and the expense and risks of bringing water from distant sources productive of even more risks (Soni 2003). Thus, in the summer of 2007, the Yamuna Jiye Abhiyan, along with several others, decided to launch a *satyagraha* against the ongoing encroachments on the river. They took their case to the Prime Minister's Technical Committee on the Yamuna River Rejuvenation, before approaching the High Court with the plea that the ongoing constructions for the Commonwealth Games be stopped and the ecology of the river restored.[18] The High Court responded by issuing directions for the setting up of a committee to enquire whether the Games Village site complex was situated on the Yamuna 'riverbed' or 'floodplain'. It did not stay the construction, though it did observe that any construction made or third-party rights created were at the peril and risk of the organisers/government.

The High Court's orders left the government aggrieved and the activists dissatisfied, and the matter now reached the Supreme Court. Two issues figured in the debate. One was the matter of delay, the time lag between the original proposals to undertake developments on the riverfront (1989), the decision to construct the Games Village on the present site (2003) and the filing of the Writ Petition (2007), with the Court observing that such delays after much construction had already taken place were against national interest, and contrary to the established principles of law.[19] The second concerned the assessment of potential damage to the riverside environment. Technical assessments regarding this, petitioners submitted, had shown great variance over time, with only the final report permitting construction of the Games Village complex. They also submitted that inasmuch as the city of Delhi was wholly dependent on the Yamuna river, its riverbed and floodplains had to be protected. They also referred to the ecological principles of 'polluter pays' and the 'precautionary principle'. Their arguments, however, failed to convince the Court, which pointed instead to the initiation of the Yamuna River Front as a Development Area as early as 1989, followed by a public notice changing the area from 'Agricultural and Water Body' to 'Public and Semi Public Facilities', which was then followed by a notification to the same effect in 1999, after which the Master Plan was suitably modified and the Yamuna River Development Authority set up in 2007—all this to suggest that 'at every stage, ecological integrity of the river, the concept of "river bed", "floodplain" and "river zone" were duly considered'.[20] Most interestingly, on the discrepancies of various technical reports, the Court went by the argument that while the previous reports had considered the boundaries of the Yamuna river as demarcated by the east bank and west bank bunds, this was no longer the case since 2002, when a new bund had been constructed for the Akshardham temple, such that the area under consideration was no longer a floodplain, leave alone a riverbed.[21] The irony of a court-mandated division of areas into floodplains and riverbeds, safe from all natural hazards, however, was evident in Delhi's flooding that very year, including of the Games Village site, permitted by the Court to be built as a permanent structure.

CONCLUDING REMARKS

There was nothing natural or inevitable about these transformations. Instead, one may ask: Could the Court have taken another route? The precautionary principle cited by the activists had been formalised in the 1992 Rio Declaration on Environment and Development,[22] among other international conventions:

> In order to protect the environment, the precautionary approach shall be widely applied by States according to their capabilities. Where there are threats of serious or irreversible damage, lack of full scientific certainty shall not be used as a reason for postponing cost-effective measures to prevent environmental degradation.

Since then, the statement had been open to differing interpretations, though this did not detract from its increasing citation to justify the implementation of vigorous policies to tackle issues as diverse as river contamination, acid rain, global warming and North Sea pollution, among others. In India, too, the Supreme Court had on several occasions observed that the 'precautionary' and 'polluter pays' principles were both a necessary component of ecologically sustainable development and within the ambit of Indian laws. What this implied was that the government and statutory authorities were expected to anticipate and prevent the causes of environmental degradation, especially in cases of serious and irreversible damage, with the onus of proof of no harm being on the developer/builder rather than the persons claiming harm.[23] The weight of irreversibility in environmental law was spelt out at length, too, with the Court observing that the precautionary principle was based on the theory that it was better to err on the side of caution to prevent environmental harm, which ran the risk of becoming irreversible. Environmental protection, moreover, they observed, should not only aim at protecting health, property and economic interest, but also protect the environment for its own sake.[24] In light of these observations, and in light of the fact that such irreversible damage regarding the Yamuna had been at the centre of the petitioners' concerns, hopes could be entertained that the Court would bypass traditional demands of 'irrefutable' evidence and 'sound' policy. Indeed, such had been the case in the matter of air pollution in Delhi, wherein the Court had marshalled health-based evidence in conjunction with the precautionary principle to insist that all public transport be run on a single clean fuel (Mathur 2003). In the case of the Yamuna, however, the innovative policy/legal possibility failed to be realised as the Supreme Court chose to go by the weight of evidence produced by official experts that assured minimal harm. 'The decision of expert and autonomous bodies,' it observed, 'supported by materials placed by other [expert] bodies, the same cannot be lightly interfered with by the Court without adequate contra materials.'[25]

Delhi and Yamuna were thus at a crossroads, and have been since then. The Akshardham temple paved the way for the Games Village and the metro stations, which in turn paved the way for Delhi Metro Corporation's staff quarters, even as the Delhi Urban Arts Commission, Yamuna Jiye Abhiyan and others pointed to the violations of the Master Plan and the continued vulnerability of any construction on the Yamuna riverbed. The Yamuna Expressway, a four-lane highway built to speed up traffic at the time of the Commonwealth Games, came in the place of the displaced settlements, bringing one more feature of 'world class' Delhi to the Yamuna bank (Baviskar 2011). Several other structures, public and private, have also begun to find space, including Delhi's largest depot for its public bus service and, as a supreme irony, the office of the Delhi government itself, which remains housed in the building constructed on the riverbed to accommodate players at the time of the Asian Games in 1982. Follman (2015), drawing upon Roy (2009), rightly notes that much of this has been possible by making 'exceptions'—the informality that is inherent in practices of the state, following a style of 'development' that empowers it to permit some large-scale structures (metro and bus depots), while aggressively denying others (slums). Equally, we may add, none of this has gone uncontested, as those adversely affected—the farmers who were once permitted to cultivate on the floodplains of the river and the slum dwellers who had constructed their homes with much difficulty—have periodically joined hands with civic organisations to protest the taking over of their spaces.

End Notes

1. In this scheme, the Improvement Trust acquired land of cheap quality or tanks that they filled in, provided essential services to, and then sold at market value, in lieu of providing alternative accommodation. There were also those who argued that land must be made available at concessional rates, if it was to be within the paying capacity of the poor.

2. Delhi State Archives (DSA), File No. 1293, LSG, Local Bodies, CC Office, 1938.

3. For the use of similar logic elsewhere, see Norman 2001.

4. DSA, *Water Supply Delhi*, Box No. 51/70, W2, Commissioner's Office, 1894.

5. DSA, File No. 263, B, education, 1913.

6. DSA, File No. 1 (24), LSG, Local Bodies, Chief Commissioner Office, 1941.

7. Emissions from non-point sources such as automobiles also came to the notice of authorities, especially in Bombay, but were not deemed important.

8. This is an interesting difference that has been elaborated in Bhan (2016).

9. Noxious industries, that is, those associated with stench, smoke, fumes, etc., were also to be located outside the urban limits.

10. To be sure, it is not only the poor who live in the unplanned areas, but there is little denying that for the most part, the 'informal'/'illegal' settlements are those of the urban poor.

11. Partha Chatterjee has referred to these earlier political negotiations through a distinction between a civil society, managed through law, and a political society, managed through exceptions. See Chatterjee (2004).

12. SCI, 1995, *Jai Narain and Others vs. Union of India*, 29 November 1996, SCC (1) 9.

13. Ibid.

14. Ibid. Notwithstanding the continued faith in these technological processes, as evident in various rulings of the Court, it has since been argued that capital-intensive infrastructure projects have been far from effective, necessitating alternative approaches that are more sensitive to community needs and local participation. See Centre for Science and Environment (2006).

15. See Bhan (2009). According to one estimate, by 2004, almost 350,000 poor squatters lived along the Yamuna in Delhi (Baviskar 2011).

16. SCI, *Dr B. L. Wadehra vs. Union of India & Ors*, 1 March 1996, SCC (2) 594.

17. SCI, *Almitra Patel vs. Union of India and Others*, 15 February 2000.

18. SCI, *DDA vs. Rajendra Singh and Others*, 30 July 2009.

19. Ibid.

20. Ibid.

21. Ibid.

22. This is a short document produced at the 1992 UN Conference on Environment and Development, which was held at Rio de Janeiro. Available at https://www.un.org/en/development/desa/population/migration/generalassembly/docs/globalcompact/A_CONF.151_26_Vol.I_Declaration.pdf (accessed June 2021).

23. SCI, 1999, *A. P. Pollution Control Board vs. Prof. M. V. Nayudu*, 27 January, 2 SCC 718.

24. Ibid.

25. Ibid.

References

Baviskar, Amita. 2011. 'What the Eye Does Not See: The Yamuna in the Imagination of Delhi'. *Economic and Political Weekly* 46(50): 45–53.

Bhan, G. 2009. '"This is no longer the city I once knew". Evictions, the Urban Poor and the Right to the City in Millennial Delhi'. *Environment and Urbanization* 21(1): 127–142.

______. 2016. *In the Public's Interest: Evictions, Citizenship and Inequality in Contemporary Delhi*. New Delhi: Orient BlackSwan.

Bhuwania, Anuj. 2017. *Courting the People: Public Interest Litigation in Post-Emergency India*. New Delhi: Cambridge University Press.

Centre for Science and Environment (CSE). 2006. *Sewage Canal: How to Clean the Yamuna*. New Delhi: CSE.

Chatterjee, Partha. 2004. *Politics of the Governed: Reflections on Popular Politics in Most of the World*. New Delhi: Permanent Black.

Colopy, C. 2012. *Dirty, Sacred Rivers: Confronting South Asia's Water Crisis*. USA: Oxford University Press.

Delhi Development Authority (DDA). 1962. Master Plan of Delhi, 1962, Work Studies, Vol. 1.

Delhi Improvement Trust. 1951. 'Administration Report for 1950-51', 4, 17–18.

Dupont, V. 2008. 'Slum Demolition in Delhi since the 1990s: An Appraisal'. *Economic and Political Weekly* July: 79–87.

Follman, A. 2015. 'Urban mega-projects for a "world-class" riverfront – The interplay of informality, flexibility and exceptionality along the Yamuna in Delhi, India'. *Habitat International* 45(3): 213–222.

Government of India. 1951. 'Report of the Delhi Improvement Trust Enquiry Committee, Vol. 1'. Delhi: Government of India Press.

Haberman, D. L. 2006. *River of Love in an Age of Pollution: The Yamuna River of Northern India*. Berkeley: University of California Press.

Hazard Centre. 2004. 'A Report on Pollution of the Yamuna at the Pushta in Delhi'. New Delhi: Hazard Centre.

The Hindu. 2004. 'Yamuna Pushta dwellers willing to shift: Jagmohan', 23 January. Available at http://www.hindu.com/2004/01/23/stories/2004012311030300.htm (accessed June 2011).

Hosagrahar, Jyoti. 2005. *Indigenous Modernities: Negotiating Architecture and Urbanism*. London: Routledge.

Hume, A. P. 1936. 'Report on the Relief of Congestion in Delhi, vol. 1'. Simla: Government of India Press.

Mathur, K. 2003. 'Battling for Clean Environment. Supreme Court, Technocrats & Populist Politics in Delhi', Working paper 03-01, Centre for the Study of Law and Governance. New Delhi: Jawaharlal Nehru University.

Norman, Hugh. 2001. *Redefining Efficiency: Pollution Concerns, Regulatory Mechanisms, and Technological Change in the U.S. Petroleum Industry*. Akron, Ohio: University of Akron Press.

Roy, A. 2009. 'Why India Cannot Plan its Cities: Informality, Insurgence and the Idiom of Urbanization'. *Planning Theory* 8(1): 76–87.

Sharan, Awadhendra. 2014. *In the City, Out of Place: Nuisance, Pollution and Dwelling in Delhi, c.1850–2000*. New Delhi: Oxford University Press.

______. 2020. *Dust & Smoke: Air Pollution and Colonial Urbanism, India, c.1860–c.1940*. New Delhi: Orient BlackSwan.

Soni, V. 2003. 'Water and Carrying Capacity of a City: Delhi'. *Economic and Political Weekly* November: 4745–4749.

XIII

The Role of Small Towns in Mediating Rapid Urbanisation

Insights from Northeast China

Yanhong Ma and Xi Chen

INTRODUCTION

China has witnessed two major phases of urbanisation since 1949. The urban population grew slowly, from 10.6 per cent to 17.9 per cent between 1949–1978, and then in 1978 entered a phase of rapid growth, increasing by about 1.0 per cent per year to 56.1 per cent in 2015 (National Bureau of Statistics of China 2016). Urbanisation has been driven by a number of forces that include economic reforms, the household registration system, land transfer mechanism and regional disparity. State policy has also had a strong influence and policy has shifted from a 'priority to heavy industry' between 1949 and 1977 to market-oriented reform starting from 1979. Market reform has been accompanied by the aim of 'strictly controlling the size of large cities and rationally developing medium-sized cities and small cities', as per Article 4 of Urban Planning Law in 1989, and from 2012, 'co-ordinating development between land urbanization and population urbanization', guided by the three principles of 'fair sharing, intensive and efficient, sustainable' growth as per the National New-type Urbanization Plan (2014–2020) of 2014. Although there is a strong body of research on how the process of urbanisation has been shaped by the wider policy environment (Chan 2010; Hsing 2010; Shin 2015) and economic forces (Fujita and Hu 2001; Guo et al. 2002; Lennon et al. 2013), particularly those related to the emergence of the country's mega-cities and their living conditions (Jiao 2015; Qi 2015; Qin 2012), less emphasis has been placed on the role of smaller settlements in driving the urbanisation process and how these have shaped the migration choices of would-be urban migrants. This chapter aims to address this gap by exploring the results of extensive surveys (from 1,200 households) in Northeast China, which examined how residents of twelve small towns view their quality of life and the way this shapes their decisions to migrate to larger urban areas.

The chapter first provides an overview of the wider historical and geographic context of Chinese urbanisation, emphasising the role and development path of small towns. It then introduces the methodological approach, including a description of a small-town residents-centred questionnaire design for survey. The context for the case study is then explained, followed by a description of the survey results. Finally, the implications of the survey findings are discussed in the context of the role of small towns in the current and future pattern of urbanisation in China.

DIFFERENT URBANISATION IN DIFFERENT COUNTRIES

Urbanisation of Other Countries

Urbanisation in developing and in developed countries occurred under different historical conditions. Urbanisation in Western countries mainly occurred in the second half of the eighteenth and in the nineteenth century, alongside the development of industrialisation (Bairoch and Goertz 1986). At that time, they had extensive colonies which provided all the resources needed for industrialisation and urbanisation. The surplus population could also be transferred to the colonies: the colonial and semi-colonial urban systems almost exclusively served the industrialisation and urbanisation of the Western countries. Therefore, although their urbanisation has also experienced problems such as poverty, unemployment and environmental pollution, they have overcome these problems in a relatively short period of time by virtue of their dominant position in the world. Nowadays, the degree of urbanisation in developed countries is quite mature and tends to be stable as well. It might be argued that, for many other countries, industrialisation and urbanisation were taking place within the pattern of the world economic system, with Western countries at its core. This pattern determines that these countries are, to greater or lesser degrees, economically dependent on the Western countries, and their cities, as the main carriers of economic development, can only be in a subservient position. At the same time, industrialisation and urbanisation in developing countries can only derive most of the necessary resources from their rural areas, including the labour force, while their cities, having established dominance over the countryside, seem to have reconstructed, on a relatively small scale, the same equation of a 'core' and a 'dependent' relationship (Yu 2011).

As early as 2003, urban population shares in countries like the United States, Germany, France, Canada, Japan and the United Kingdom had reached 78 per cent, 88 per cent, 76 per cent, 79 per cent, 79 per cent and 90 per cent, respectively (World Bank 2005). But in Latin America and the Caribbean, in 2003, the overall degree of urbanisation had reached 77 per cent, and in some countries the share had even surpassed that of the developed countries, with Venezuela at 88 per cent, Uruguay at 93 per cent, Argentina at 89 per cent and Chile at 87 per cent (ibid.). In fact, in contrast to China, other developing countries like India, Brazil, Argentina and Chile more or less adopted a non-interventionist policy with regard to the process of urbanisation, and a large number of people from small towns or rural areas freely flooded into cities (Cherunilam 1984; Davis 2007; Henderson 1988).

Take India as an example. By the end of 2010, 14 per cent of the Indian urban population resided in the three mega-cities of Delhi, Mumbai and Kolkata and the urban population was estimated to be around 360 million (Chaplin 2011). The same year, the Ministry of Housing and Urban Poverty Alleviation of India predicted that the slum population would be around 93.06 million by 2011 (MHUPA 2010). Clearly, the level of urbanisation is never the only measure of a country's or region's level of socio-economic development, and it only shows the proportion of people living in cities out of the total population, instead of accurately reflecting their working conditions and quality of life (Remi and Dietrich 2015). In the face of the problems emerging due to urbanisation, many developing countries have been trying to find ways to overcome them. For example, some Latin American countries adopted 'decentralisation' strategies and India launched its five-year economic plans in 1951 (Gwynne 1985). However, the main problems have not been fundamentally resolved–the number of peasants who are without land or with a small amount of farmland has continued to rise; industry is prioritised while the development of agriculture is ignored, and the inputs into rural areas of both labour and capital have continued to fall. To a large extent, these two aspects have both enhanced the difficulty of peasants to survive in rural areas and pushed them to migrate to the city for other opportunities (Varshney 1995; World Economic Forum 2015).

Urbanisation and Small Towns in China

For much of its history, China was a predominantly agrarian society in which agriculture was the productive sector (Wang and Hu 1999). Chinese small towns have played a major role in the country's settlement hierarchy and economic development since the Tang dynasty (AD 618–907) (Zhong 2014). Small towns in China have always acted as the connectors and transfer stations between the cities and the countryside. There are plenty of them spread all over the country. However, the population sizes of towns are usually small. The average population of small towns in China was about 6,000–8,600 people in built-up areas. And they are also characterised by the dominance of a single economic activity, a weak economy and poor financial situation, lack of authority for self-governance and so on (Gu et al. 2015).

With the establishment of New China in 1949, the central government adopted a number of policies to encourage child-bearing. In 1950, China's population was about 552 million (Wang 1988). Then, by 1978, it increased to nearly 963 million, with a rural population of about 790 million (National Statistical

Bureau of China 2016). Despite the 'One Child' policy, there has been substantial net population growth since the 1970s. In terms of China's urbanisation, from 1949 to 1957, the urban population rose steadily from 10.6 per cent to 17.9 per cent. The national adoption of 'priority to heavy industry' in 1977 included a mandatory requirement to comply with the '*hukou* system'.[1] This restricted farmers to their own land to guarantee food supplies for the nation and to support the development of cities. However, this led to farmers having less and less per capita arable land, while restricting labour supply for secondary and tertiary industries (Liu 2005). As a consequence, there was a low level of urbanisation and the vast majority of small towns served merely as local trading centres for farmers from different villages. The economic reforms of 1978 included a shift in China's agricultural production from People's Communes to the Household Contract Responsibility System (Business), resulting in the freeing of rural surplus labour. This led to many rural dwellers moving to pre-existing small towns to engage in commercial activities and services. Others remained in villages and engaged in industrial activity based on local resources such as brick manufacturing, cloth production, wood processing and transport service, etc., with the result that some villages evolved into small towns in their own right.

Since 1979, the Chinese state has regulated and stimulated the development of small towns through measures such as 'Several Opinions of the Central Committee of the Communist Party of China to Accelerate the Rural Development, 1979', which aimed to strengthen small towns; 'Village and Town Planning Principles, 1982', which initiated the planning of villages and towns; and the formation of the first national standard 'Village and Town Planning Principles, 1993'. By the end of 1996, the output value of village and township enterprises had accounted for two-thirds of the total rural social output value (Chang and Wang 1994), and the number of designated towns (a type of small town) had increased from 3,228 in 1985 to 19,000 in 1999. However, since the mid-1990s, with the deepening of market-oriented reform, the manufacturing industry was increasingly exposed to international and internal markets (Che and Qian 1998; Vermeer 1999), slowing the output value of township–village enterprises to only 1.3 per cent of the gross industrial output of the country in 2011 (NBSC 2012). The liberalisation of the Chinese economy has been combined with the emergence of a real estate market which stimulated the flow of rural labour between and within urban and rural areas (Vermeer 1999). Coupled with the establishment of a city-governing county system, the implementation of a tax-sharing fiscal system in 1994 gave urban governments the right of independent financing and control over development. All urban land is owned by the Chinese state, but most land in small towns is rural land collectively owned by farmers. However, the state strictly regulates the development of rural land in order to protect agricultural capacity, and development can only take place through national government purchase, which generally compensates farmers on the basis of agricultural value, not future development value. These factors are important in deterring the nature and rate of growth of large and medium-sized cities and the curtailment of development in small towns.

The rapid urbanisation initiated by China's Ninth Five-Year Plan (1996–2000) resulted in rural depopulation, from 859 million in 1995 to 603 million by the end of 2015 (Liu et al. 2016). Small towns often act as springboards for rural residents who move into urban areas, leading to a range of questions on the role of small towns in Chinese urbanisation. While there are a large number of small towns (in 2010, there were more than 19,600 small towns), only 740 (3.78 per cent) have a population of more than 50,000 and nearly 50 per cent have populations between 10,000–20,000. The dispersed nature of the small towns also means that they struggle to achieve the benefits of economic agglomeration. In the last twenty years, local governments have been implementing a policy of removal and merger of small towns and villages, in order to consolidate urban form and settlement patterns and expand population sizes and economic strength for better competitiveness and attractiveness. Other development challenges have been the environmental damage caused by heavily polluting industries displaced from urban areas, the waste of arable land resulting from the disorderly expansion of small towns, and poor standards of construction due to financial constraints. As a result, some commentators have been negative about the potential of small towns and instead have advocated giving priority to the development of large cities (Cai and Zhou 2002; Jiang et al. 2008; Zhang and Tan 1998), while other scholars and elements of the Chinese state have advocated a 'Small Towns, Big Strategy' approach, believing that small towns should be developed as a 'Population Reservoir' to prevent rural people from flooding into cities, thereby reinforcing both the 'urban–peri-urban–rural' system and a clear pyramid-like settlement hierarchy (Fei 1984; Qin 2008; Zhu 2000).

From 1999 to 2014, the proportion of the number of large cities in China with a population of one million or more increased by 253.13 per cent. In particular, the population of mega-cities such as Beijing, Shanghai and Guangzhou has exceeded ten million, and they have entered the ranks of the world's top ten cities. The rapid expansion of the size of these cities has not only led directly to the widening gap between different urban levels and a regional economic structural imbalance, but also further induced skyrocketing housing prices, traffic congestion, water shortage, environmental degradation and other serious 'urban diseases' (Li 2012). In addition, after the first quarter of 2015, China's GDP growth entered into a 6–7 per cent era. Even worse, there is a huge possibility for further slowdown of the Chinese economy in the future. Clearly, it is no longer feasible to rely on mega-cities, very large cities and big cities to absorb the surplus rural population (Gu et al. 2015).

CASE STUDY: NORTHEAST CHINA

Background

The urbanisation of China has been expressed through regional differences, with the highest number of small towns situated in coastal areas (where a higher level of industrialisation has provided opportunities for local employment) compared to inland areas. Guo et al. (2014) provided a comprehensive evaluation of small-town development, including an analysis of quality of life measures, economic indicators and the potential for development. They found that the level of development of small towns was highest in Eastern China, followed by Western China, Central China and Northeast China,[2] respectively (see Figures 13.1 and 13.2).

Northeast China is composed of three provinces: Liaoning, Jilin and Heilongjiang. The region accounts for 8.42 per cent (80.84×10^4 sq. km.) of the land area of China and borders North Korea (to the southeast) and the Russian Federation (to the north and northwest), as well as neighbouring Inner Mongolia and North China to the west and southwest, respectively. Northeast China became a base of state-owned industry after the founding of New China due to its existing industrial infrastructure and its proximity to the Soviet Union, which supported many of the projects located here; indeed, out of 156 key projects in the First Five-Year Plan, fifty-seven were in this region, which came to be known as 'the Republic's eldest son'. By 1978, the per capita GDP of the three

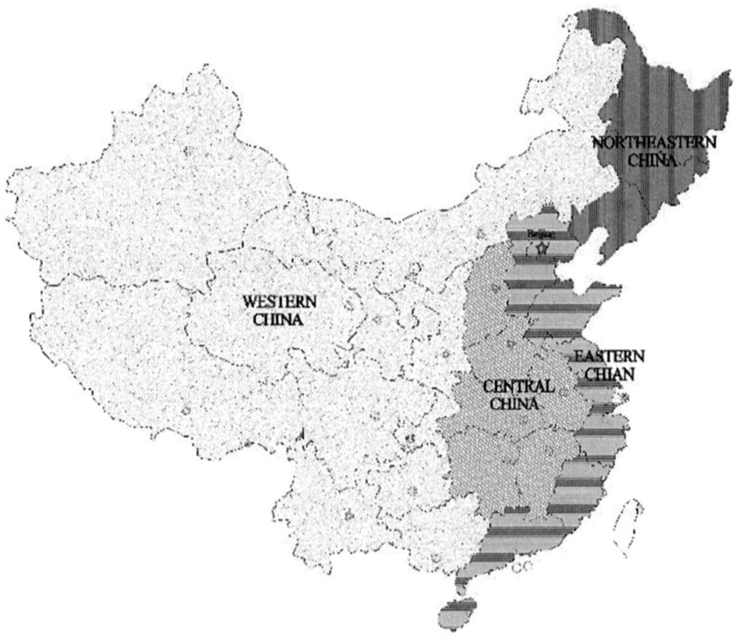

Figure 13.1: Four Major Economic Regions in China

Source: Drawn by the authors.

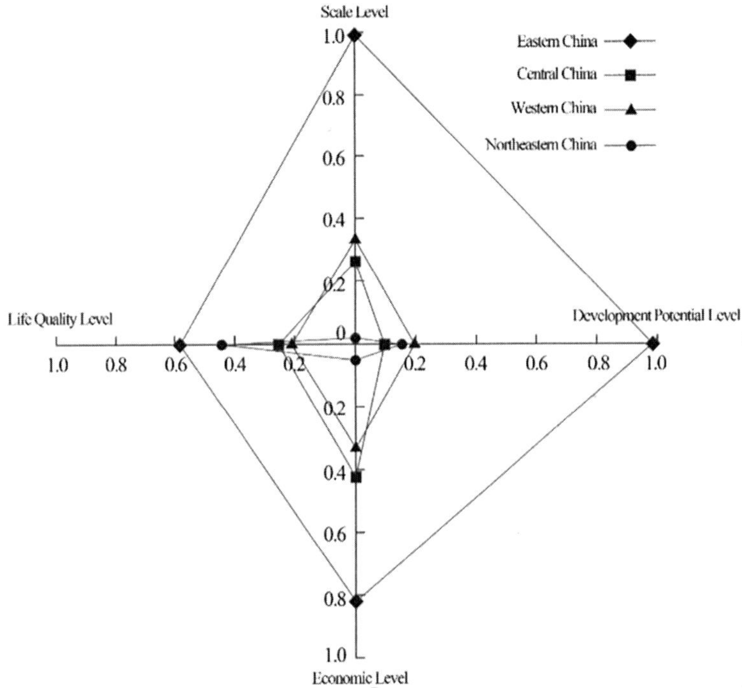

Figure 13.2: The Radar Chart of Regional Guidelines Layer Score for Four Major Economic Regions

Source: Drawn by the authors, based on Guo et al. 2014.

Northeastern provinces was second only to the three municipalities of Beijing, Tianjin and Shanghai, which are directly under the central government. However, the region has not fared as well with the shift to a market economy, at least compared to China's Eastern and coastal regions, because of the domination of large state-owned industries which have restricted the space for the development of private enterprise, R&D (research and development) and private investment (Gamsa 2010; Xie et al. 2016). To address this, in 2003 China launched the 'Northeast Area Revitalisation Plan' (also known as 'Revitalisation of Northeast Old Industry Base'), which included grant funding and preferential policies. Combined with the benefits of a nationwide infrastructure boom, the average annual growth rate of the Northeast region reached 12.7 per cent between 2003 to 2012, but this reduced after 2013 with the slowdown of the overall Chinese economy and the world surplus of steel and other industrial outputs.

In hindsight, the 2003 Revitalisation Plan failed to effectively transform the industrial structure of the Northeast. State-owned industries continue to dominate the regional economy and in 2014, they still contributed up to 80 per cent of the business income of Liaoning Province (Huang and Shi 2016), restricting opportunities for associated economic activity, such that talent, capital and technological innovation have tended to migrate to regions offering more economic opportunities. As a consequence, the 2010 census indicated that there was a net outflow of 2.19 million people from the Northeast during 2009, a large proportion of whom was young. Eighty per cent of emigrants went to the more economically developed Eastern China (Duan et al. 2015). On the other hand, as one of the world's biggest farmlands of black soil, Northeast China's rural areas are the most important and form the traditional commodity grain base for the whole country, while their modernised agricultural sector has been expanding the size of the surplus rural labour force.

The problems of the underlying regional economy have meant that cities in the Northeast have been unable to absorb rural migrants, at least compared to cities in the surrounding regions of Eastern China, Central China and Western China.

Case Study Areas

In July 2016, the Ministry of Housing and Urban-Rural Development of the People's Republic of China (MoHURD) launched a research programme, the 'Detailed Survey of Small Towns in China', aimed at developing an understanding of the development characteristics of small towns in China to provide a sound evidence base for future policy. The results of this policy can provide insights into many of the predicaments facing small towns, particularly in the Northeast region. The survey for Northeast China was based on a sample of four small towns from four different prefectures in each of the three Northeast China provinces, with the authors of this chapter as members of the survey team that actually carried out the survey. The selected towns and sample sizes are shown in Table 13.1.

Table 13.1: Relevant Details for Sample Small Towns of Three Provinces[3]

Province	Name of the small town selected	Prefecture the small town belongs to	Number of registered residents in 2015	Number of registered residents in 2010
Liaoning	Niuzhuang	Anshan	26,629	26,660
	Fuzhoucheng	Dalian	11,877	19,800
	Yangshigang	Shenyang	6,920	7,012
	Dongliang	Fuxin	5,227	5,000
Jilin	Leshan	Changchun	2,592	2,389
	Liaoheyuan	Liaoyuan	6,294	5,331
	Jinchuan	Tonghua	3,742	3,273
	Shixian	Yanbian	19,590	15,080
Heilongjiang	Laohugang	Suihua	1,110	Not Available
	Xianglan	Jiamusi	7,415	7,945
	Hengdaohezi	Mudanjiang	8,960	9,050
	Longxing	Qiqihaer	3,216	3,378

Sources: Liaoning Bureau of Statistics, 2016; Jilin Bureau of Statistics, 2016; Heilongjiang Bureau of Statistics, 2016.

The full Northeast China survey was preceded by a preliminary survey, conducted by telephone, of fifty residents in two small towns in each province (N=300), randomly selected from the list of registered residents provided by the local authorities. The purpose of this was to ensure that the full survey effectively reflected the living concerns of current residents and those factors that most influenced their decision to stay or relocate. This led to the identification of the key survey variables, according to the frequency of answers from high to low,[4] as shown in Table 13.2.

Table 13.2: Key Concerns of Residents of Sample Small Towns

Key survey variables according to the frequency of answers of residents from high to low	Frequency (n=900)	Proportion (%)
1. Disposable income per month	232	25.78
2. Children's education place	169	18.78
3. Medical treatment	102	11.33
4. Travel convenience	82	9.11
5. Housing	75	8.32
6. Sense of belonging	70	7.78
7. Provision for the aged	61	6.78
8. Shopping place	59	6.56
9. Time patterns of work	50	5.56

Source: Preliminary survey designed and conducted by authors.

The resulting survey instrument was then executed in the twelve sample small towns shown in Table 13.3, using face-to-face, random sampling of registered residents until 100 valid responses were gathered in each town. The primary interviewees were household heads, with other adults who were familiar with the situation of the household as substitutes when the heads were unavailable. A total of 1,200 valid questionnaires were collected.

Table 13.3: Variable Assignment and Description (n=1,200)

Variable		Variable	Variable description	Assignment/Categories
Dependent variable		Y	Willingness to continue living	Yes=1; No=0
Independent variables	Basic items	X_1	Gender	Male=1; Female=0
		X_2	Age	18–59 years old=1; 60 years old or above=2
		X_3	Educational background	Without a high school diploma=1; With a high school diploma or above=2

(Contd)

Table 13.3 (Contd)

Variable		Variable	Variable description	Assignment/Categories
Independent variables	Basic items	X_4	Occupation	Civil servant=1; Enterprise staff=2; Being engaged in business=3; Taking odd jobs=4; Farming=5; Attending school=6; Jobless=7; In retirement=8; Other=9
Independent variables	Main items	X_5	Disposable income per month	Below 1,000 RMB=1; 1,000–2,000 RMB=2; 2,000–3,000 RMB=3; 3,000–5,000 RMB=4; 5,000–8,000 RMB=5; 8,000 RMB or more=6
		X_6	Children's education place	The township=1; Other townships=2; The county=3; One city=4; The capital city of the Province=5
		$X_{7\text{-}1}$	Medical treatment place for minor illness	Health clinic of the town=1; County hospital=2; City hospital=3; Provincial hospital or above=4; Private clinic=5
		$X_{7\text{-}2}$	Medical treatment place for serious illness	Health clinic of the town=1; County hospital=2; City hospital=3; Provincial hospital or above=4; Private clinic=5
		$X_{8\text{-}1}$	Travel convenience—Is there a bus stop near your house?	No=0; Yes=1;

(Contd)

Table 13.3 (Contd)

Variable		Variable	Variable description	Assignment/Categories
Independent variables	Main items	$X_{8\text{-}2}$	Travel convenience—going to the county or the surrounding area	Very convenient=1; Convenient=2; Fair=3; A little inconvenient=4; Inconvenient=5;
		$X_{9\text{-}1}$	Type of House	Self-built house=1; Commodity house =2; Affordable house =3; Rental housing=4; Other=5
		$X_{9\text{-}2}$	Housing satisfaction	Very satisfied=1; Satisfied=2; Fair=3; Not satisfied=4; Very dissatisfied=5;
		X_{10}	Sense of belonging	Yes=1; No=0;
		X_{11}	Provision for the aged	Home-based care for the aged=1; Nursing-home-based care for the aged=2
		X_{12}	Shopping place for most of daily foods and necessities	Bazaar on the market day of the town=1; Small shops, stores or supermarkets of the town=2; Hypermarket in county or city=3; Online=4; Others =5
		X_{13}	Hours of work	Nine-to-five job=1; Freestyle work=2; Early to late with continuous working long hours=3; Not at work=4

Source: Full survey by authors.

MODEL SELECTION AND FINDINGS

A binary logistic regression model was used to analyse the questionnaires. Variable assignment and description of dependent and independent variables are shown in Table 13.3. 'Willingness to continue living (represented by the solicited question: "Do you want to stay where you are currently living?")' is designated to reflect the overall willingness of residents to migrate. It is a binary variable (if the interviewee says 'yes', the dependent variable is assigned a value of '1', otherwise, a value of '0'). Basic items X_1–X_4 and main items X_5–X_{13} are all independent variables (some binary, others as unordered categorical variables or ordinal categorical variables). In the course of statistical analysis of data, if the probability of 'like living in this town' is P (Y=1), then the probability of 'dislike living in this town' is 1–P (Y=0). This probability can be calculated using a logistic function, and its expression is:

$$P = \frac{\exp(\beta_0 + \beta_1 x_1 + \beta_2 x_2 + \ldots + \beta_k x_k)}{1 + \exp(\beta_0 + \beta_1 x_1 + \beta_2 x_2 + \ldots + \beta_k x_k)}$$

$$1 - P = \frac{1}{1 + \exp(\beta_0 + \beta_1 x_1 + \beta_2 x_2 + \ldots + \beta_k x_k)}$$

This logistic function is a non-linear function of covariance, with the resulting logit transformation[5] yielding a linear formula:

$$\text{Logit}(P) = \ln\left[\frac{P}{1-P}\right] = \beta_0 + \beta_1 x_1 + \beta_2 x_2 + \ldots + \beta_k x_k$$

In this formula, P is the probability of 'like living in this town'; $\frac{P}{1-P}$ is the ratio of the probability of occurrence of a result to the probability of non-occurrence ('odds'). β_0 is a constant term; x_1, x_2, …, x_k are the factors that affect the 'Willingness to continue living' of interviewees; β_k is the regression coefficient of influencing factors, which indicates the change in the natural logarithm of odds when x_k increases by one unit, with values of the other independent variables remaining constant. Through the logarithmic conversion of the probability *P*, it is consistent with the general linear regression model to explain the range of values of the variables, and is also more in line with the conventional interpretation.

The stepwise screening of independent variables is processed with eleven steps, and the regression result of the model, in step 11, is shown in Table 13.4: *B* is the estimated value of the regression coefficient in the equation; *S.E.* is the standard error of the regression coefficient; the Wald statistic is a test of the regression coefficient used to determine whether a variable should be included in the equation; *df* is the degree of freedom; *Sig.* is the corresponding significance level; and Exp (B) represents the odds ratio of the corresponding variable. And the overall model achieves a significant level (Sig.<0.001). At a cutting point of 0.5, the overall recognition accuracy of the model reached is 82.4 per cent. In terms of correlation coefficient strength, the values of Cox & Snell R^2 (0.434) and Nagelkerke R^2 (0.583) show that the independent variables have a moderate correlation with the dependent variable. Also, the Chi-square value of Hosmer and Lemeshow Test is 5.517 and the Sig. is 0.701, which is much larger than 0.05 and does not reach a significant level. Therefore, it is shown that the fitness of the whole regression model is good and that the independent variables can effectively predict the dependent variable.

From the results of the logistic regression, six of the thirteen independent variables have been kept in the model. None of the four basic items, namely gender, age, educational background and occupation of the respondents, is included. It suggests that the effects of these four factors on 'Willingness to continue living' are all not significant. In contrast, the following factors were found to be significant at 5 per cent and 1 per cent levels and in this order of significance (based on value of Wald): 'X_6–children's education place'; 'X_{10}–sense of belonging'; 'X_{13}–hours of work'; '$X_{9\text{-}2}$–housing satisfaction'; 'X_5–disposable income a month'; and '$X_{8\text{-}2}$–travel convenience–going to the county or the surrounding area'.

Fifty-eight per cent of the respondents chose to say 'No' to the question on 'Willingness to continue living'. An explanation of the relationships between the independent variables provides a further insight into this statistic. Exp (B) values (or the odds ratios) shown

Table 13.4: Results of the Logistic Regression (n=1,200)

Variable	*B*	*S.E.*	Wald	*Df*	*Sig.*	Exp (B) or Odds ratio
X_5 reference			17.447	5	.004**	
$X_{5(1)}$	.182	.232	.620	1	.431	1.200
$X_{5(2)}$	.783	.249	9.918	1	.002**	2.189
$X_{5(3)}$	.855	.269	10.102	1	.001**	2.351
$X_{5(4)}$	.980	.397	6.110	1	.013*	2.665
$X_{5(5)}$	.531	.500	1.128	1	.288	1.701
X_6 reference			311.465	4	.000***	
$X_{6(1)}$	.948	.264	12.917	1	.000***	2.581
$X_{6(2)}$	2.874	.214	180.237	1	.000***	17.715
$X_{6(3)}$	4.377	.313	195.950	1	.000***	79.588
$X_{6(4)}$	2.768	.323	73.282	1	.000***	15.923
X_{8-2} reference			10.235	4	.037*	
$X_{8-2(1)}$	–.013	.239	.003	1	.958	.987
$X_{8-2(2)}$	.507	.217	5.485	1	.019*	1.661
$X_{8-2(3)}$	.206	.288	.511	1	.475	1.228
$X_{8-2(4)}$	.865	.369	5.483	1	.019*	2.374
X_{9-2} reference			21.570	4	.000***	
$X_{9-2(1)}$	–.126	.253	.248	1	.618	.882
$X_{9-2(2)}$	.742	.265	7.828	1	.005**	2.099
$X_{9-2(3)}$	.394	.302	1.706	1	.192	1.483
$X_{9-2(4)}$	1.077	.412	6.817	1	.009**	2.934
$X_{10(1)}$	1.127	.173	42.237	1	.000***	3.088
X_{13} reference			36.202	3	.000***	
$X_{13(1)}$	–.396	.241	2.694	1	.101	.673
$X_{13(2)}$	.999	.258	15.052	1	.000***	2.717
$X_{13(3)}$	–.078	.254	.096	1	.757	.925
Constant	–2.996	.358	70.004	1	.000***	.050
Omnibus Tests of Model Coefficients			Chi-square = 682.426; Sig. = 0.000			
Model Summary			Cox & Snell R^2 = 0.434; Nagelkerke R^2 = 0.583			
Hosmer and Lemeshow Test			Chi-square (X^2) = 5.517; Sig. = 0.701			

Note: *, ** and ***, respectively, indicate that the variables are significant at the 5%, 1% and .01% levels.

Source: Authors.

in Table 13.4 were used to explore the following: 'X_5—disposable income a month' is an ordinal categorical variable, and we see that the categories $X_{5(2)}$ (disposable monthly income of 2,000–3,000 RMB), $X_{5(3)}$ (disposable monthly income of 3,000–5,000 RMB) and $X_{5(4)}$ (disposable monthly income of 5,000–8,000 RMB), are all significant, indicating a willingness to move away from the township 2.189, 2.351, 2.665 times when compared to the category $X_{5(1)}$ (disposable monthly income of below 1,000 RMB). It means the higher the disposable income of the interviewee, the lower the likelihood that s/he will continue to live in the township.

'X_6—children's education place' is the independent variable with top significance (Wald=311.465). It is also an ordinal categorical variable. Compared with the category 'Children's education place—the township', for willingness to move, categories $X_{6(1)}$ (Other townships), $X_{6(2)}$ (The county), $X_{6(3)}$ (One city) and $X_{6(4)}$ (The capital city of the Province) are 2.581, 17.715, 79.588 and 15.923 times higher, respectively. This suggests that once the respondents find education for their children in places other than the small town in which they live, they will have a very high possibility and strong intention to move away.

Variables '$X_{8\text{-}2}$—travel convenience-going to the county or the surrounding area' and '$X_{9\text{-}2}$—Housing satisfaction' are also ordinal categorical independent variables and both have two categories at significance level. Willingness to move away with travel convenience assessments as 'Fair' and 'Inconvenient' is 1.661 and 2.374 times, respectively, of the control assessment 'Very convenient'. A similar situation happens with $X_{9\text{-}2}$, with 'Fair' and 'Dissatisfied' being 2.099 and 2.934 times of 'Very satisfied', respectively. Considering that not all of the categories of these two independent variables are statistically significant, we assume that to some extent $X_{8\text{-}2}$ and $X_{9\text{-}2}$ show that when respondents' assessment on travel convenience or housing satisfaction goes from positive to negative, the 'Willingness to move' goes the same way. 'X_{10}—sense of belonging' is a binary categorical independent variable and the second most contributing factor influencing migration choice. 'Willingness to move' from respondents without a sense of belonging to the township is 3.088 times higher than that of respondents with such a sense.

For 'X_{13}–Time patterns of work' (the third most influencing factor), with 'Nine-to-five job' as a control category, only category $X_{13(2)}$ (work early to late with continuous working long hours) is statistically significant, with 'Willingness to move' being 2.717 times the former.

The above analysis indicates a number of clear influences that determine whether small-town residents in Northeast China are likely to remain in the settlement they currently live in, or choose future migration, possibly to one of the major urban centres. This suggests that the most significant independent factor influencing respondents' migration choice is a concern for their children's education, reflecting the fact that, particularly in traditional rural regions, parents see this as the key option changing the fate of their children or grandchildren. Only 37.3 per cent of respondents chose to have their children educated in the small town in which they are currently living, suggesting that perhaps they have low confidence in the local education facilities, and are aware of the significance of the resources gap in education between small towns and large urban areas. This in turn reflects how official policy has tended to favour cities over rural areas and small towns, leading to a further deepening of the uneven distribution of resources between urban and rural areas.

RECOMMENDATIONS AND CONCLUSION

From an urban perspective, rapid growth has placed huge pressure on resources and the environment, leading to the major problems of air pollution, traffic congestion, overvalued housing prices, resource shortage, etc. These are related to a range of social problems, such as reduced quality of life and impacts on health. In this context, small towns offer opportunities for a higher quality of life for China's middle and upper classes. This could be a key factor in stimulating small towns' development and, in so doing, offer a range of solutions to the array of urbanisation problems faced by China. In order to strengthen this, the following initiatives are suggested.

First of all, funds, especially public development and construction funds and self-development funds such as for hardware, are an essential resource for advancing the development of small towns. However, on the one hand, according to China's current tax system, local taxation is invariably handed over to provincial and national authorities and then redistributed as a whole from the central government level to the local government level. And under the hierarchical administrative system, it means that the higher the administrative level, the more the resources, so small towns cannot get the corresponding funds they need. Hence, hierarchical administrative resource flow, represented by funds, also objectively determines the basic pattern of population movements and gatherings. In such a situation, to get more returns, market-oriented resources are gradually concentrated in large cities or administrative areas of a higher level. On the other hand, land conversion in small towns, as in rural areas, is totally different from the way it occurs in cities. Earnings from the conversion of collective land belonging to the small town government need to be handed over to the upper level of government, and earnings from the land belonging to residents themselves are rarely compensated at market price.

Therefore, from the perspective of public funding, there is a critical need to give preferential measures to small towns, like special national development grants and investment, tax exemption policy, affordable welfare policy and so on. Considering that the rural and peri-urban regions have been feeding city areas for so many years, it is time for the state and cities to compensate or benefit small towns and the countryside. And in the meantime, for the small town itself, in addition to being given some development autonomy, especially with economic autonomy (economic income dominance) as a premise, it also needs to pay attention to opening up its own resources to significantly improve both fiscal revenue and personal income. Among all of the measures and in keeping with the description above, for small town residents, land, which often plays the role of the most trusted source of dependence and security, should be given first priority.

Therefore, in terms of land transfer, there are two key aspects that need to be changed: (*i*) Due to construction needs, if it is indeed necessary for the arable land or farmland belonging to residents of small towns to be converted to construction land, residents should be reasonably compensated in accordance with the estimated earnings to be made after the expropriation of the land, rather than as per the agricultural income before expropriation. (*ii*) Since the founding of New China, residents in small towns and rural areas have only owned the right to use but have had no property rights to their housing, which is not allowed to be freely traded in the market. So, if given complete homestead property rights and allowed to enter the market to achieve free trade, mortgage and transfer, the largest properties (homesteads) of residents in small towns can be taken as operating capital, allowing them to start enjoying the land-value added opportunities. The break-up of the existing moribund system can not only optimise the rationality of the distribution of land resources in the development of small towns, but also provide the possibility and catalyst for further aggregation, resulting in the accumulation of economic benefits. It would also serve as an effective approach to reduce the gap between urban centres and small towns by improving the income of residents.

Second, planned and prospective guidance, as software, is the other most important necessity for small towns' future development. It is well known that China has a large territory and a large number of small towns as well. On the one hand, small towns need huge funds for development. And even if the central government and urban governments at all levels give a hand via financial assistance to the small towns, it is impossible to cover all of them. On the other hand, due to historical administrative needs, a considerable number of small towns actually have only administrative functions, and with a small population size and poor resource endowment, do not have the potential for further development. Therefore, it is necessary to choose a number of small towns with a better foundation, strength and greater potential, to focus on nurturing.

Third, small town public-service personnel should be adequately aware of the advantages or unique resources of small towns, like clean water and air, idyllic environment and neighbourhood, low price and high level of safety, organic fruits and vegetables, etc., and keep them fully displayed and advertised to attract and draw urban residents. These efforts could be especially targeted at the urban middle class and upper class, some of whom have been or would be tired of the worsening urban living environment. Such urban residents moving into small towns can not only inject a certain amount of capital into small-town market circulation, but their high needs for quality education, convenient infrastructure and other services can also act as a stimulus to prompt the development of small towns. In addition, small towns should consciously and gradually nurture their own characteristic industries, relying on local advantages. However, small towns must not be a sanctuary for enterprises that have been eliminated from the larger urban area due to environmentally unfriendly production methods, and the land for them made available from the ashes of pre-existing uses. There is no doubt that, in the long run, the ecological and liveable dwelling environment in small towns is bound to become increasingly valuable, with a competitive advantage over that of the larger urban centres. Therefore, industry should be limited to environment-friendly types like handicraft manufacturing, service industry, eco-agricultural park, agricultural products processing, hi-tech industries, etc.

Fourth, the competitive advantage for rural surplus labour migration should be stressed, which is also one important criterion for population agglomeration. The employment costs for rural labour force transfer, including opportunity costs, cost of living, transportation costs and psychological costs (risks and social adaptation and other aspects of the cost), are much lower when compared with the urban. Also, for the integration and adaptation of rural surplus labour, small towns can allow some psychological security by enabling them to live closer to where they were and sharing some local commons. All of these are built-in advantages. But they are not enough.

For most Chinese, secure tenure and prospects for home ownership are primary concerns. Members of the rural surplus labour force face particular challenges in buying a dwelling in the private housing market. For a long time until now, the homesteads of rural residents have not been allowed to enter into market circulation, as mentioned above. But as the exit mechanism in the current homestead system is not perfect, there are no clearly defined or standard procedures for compensation and other aspects of homestead recovery. In fact, and in practice, very few homesteads are recovered. Keeping in mind that cultivated land is scarce in China and the vast majority of rural homesteads are built on cultivated land, unused homesteads are urgently needed to be reclaimed or better used for forestation/cultivation. So, what kind of innovation can be done in this respect? Just imagine if we could create a relevant mechanism or system which enables the exchange of small-town houses for rural homesteads. In such a system, those who voluntarily give up their homesteads can be compensated with housing, along with full ownership in small towns. This must certainly be supported and dominated by the government, which also takes the responsibility for land consolidation arising from unused homesteads, and putting them into extending cultivated land, or forest or grassland.

End Notes

Acknowledgements: We would like to thank every member involved in the survey for Northeast China. This work was funded by China Postdoctoral Science Foundation (Grant No. 2020M673144) and Postdoctoral Science Foundation Project of Chongqing Natural Science Foundation (Grant No. cstc2020jcyj-bshX0031).

1. The *hukou* system, or 'The Household Register System of People's Republic of China', was established in 1958 to regulate the free movement of people, and for the first time explicitly divided rural and urban residential areas into 'agricultural residence registration' and 'non-agricultural residence registration', respectively, in effect abolishing the provisions of the 1954 Constitution on freedom of movement between the urban and the rural.

2. According to the natural conditions, the economic base, the level of development and opening up, China is divided into Eastern China, Central China, Western China and Northeastern China: four major economic regions (see Figure 13.2).

3. The number of registered residents refers to the population of one small town.

4. In the preliminary survey, every randomly selected respondent was given the question: 'What are the three most important factors influencing your living in this town?', and a total of 900 answers were collected.

5. The ratio of the probability of occurrence of a result to the probability of non-occurrence is called odds (odds = $P/1-P$). Its logarithm, taken as ln(odds) is called logit transformation.

References

Bairoch, P. and G. Goertz. 1986. 'Factors of urbanization in the nineteenth century developed countries: A descriptive and econometric analysis'. *Urban Studies* 23(4): 285–305.

Cai, J. and B. Zhou. 2002. 'Small Town or Metropolis: The Choice of China's Urbanization'. *Shanghai Journal of Economics* 10: 22–29.

Chan, K. M. 2010. 'Fundamentals of China's urbanization and policy'. *The China Review* 10: 63–94.

Chang, C. and Y. Wang. 1994. 'The nature of the township-village enterprise'. *Journal of Comparative Economics* 19: 434–452.

Chaplin S. E. 2011. 'Indian cities, sanitation and the state: The politics of the failure to provide'. *Environment and Urbanization* 23(1): 57–70.

Che, J. and Y. Y. Qian. 1998. 'Insecure property rights and government ownership of firms'. *Quarterly Journal of Economics* 113(2): 467–496.

Cherunilam, Francis. 1984. *Urbanization in Developing Countries: A Socio-Economic and Demographic Analysis*. Bombay: Himalaya Publishing House.

Davis, Mike, 2007. *Planet of Slums*. London: Verso Books.

Duan, C., L. Lv and M. Qin. 2015. 'Revitalization of Northeast China and Cracking Population Dilemma'. *Chinese Cadres Tribune* 7: 64–67.

Farhana, N., Graham Currie and David Logan. 2016. 'Exploring the impacts of factors contributing to tram-involved serious injury crashes on Melbourne tram routes'. *Accident Analysis and Prevention* 94: 238–244.

Fei, X. 1984. 'Complementary Balance between Industry and Agriculture: Develop Small Towns'. *Jianghuai Tribune* 6: 1–4.

Fujita, M. and D. Hu. 2001. 'Regional disparity in China 1985-1994: The effects of globalization and economic liberalization'. *The Annals of Regional Science* 35: 3–37.

Gamsa, M. 2010. 'Harbin in comparative perspective'. *Urban History* 37: 136–149.

Gu, C., Y. Li and S. H. Sun. 2015. 'Development and transition of small towns in rural China'. *Habitat International* 50: 110–159.

Guo, X. X., X. L. Xia, X. L. Zhang and C. Feng. 2014. 'Comprehensive Evaluation Analysis of Small Towns Development Level in China's Different Regions'. *Areal Research and Development* 33(5): 50–54.

Guo, T. Y., D. D. Lu and G. H. Gan. 2002. 'China's regional development policy and its sound effects on the economic development of coastal zones and central & western areas over the past two decades'. *Geographical Research* 21: 504–509.

Gwynne, Robert N. 1985. *Industrialization and Urbanization in Latin America*. London and Sydney: Croom Helm.

Heilongjiang Bureau of Statistics. 2016. *Statistical Yearbook of Heilongjiang Province, 2015*. Beijing: China Statistics Press.

Henderson, J. Vernon. 1988. *Urban Development: Theory, Fact, and Illusion*. New York: Oxford University Press.

Hsing, You-tien. 2010. *The Great Urban Transformation: Politics of Land and Property in China*. New York: Oxford University Press.

Huang, Q. and Y. Shi. 2016. 'Causal Analysis and Countermeasures of Industrial Economic Downturn in the Three Provinces in Northeast China'. *Study & Exploration* 7: 100–112.

Jilin Bureau of Statistics. 2016. *Statistical Yearbook of Jilin Province, 2015*. Beijing: China Statistics Press.

Jiang, Y., J. Fan and Z. Song. 2008. 'The New Strategies of Urbanization in China'. *Reformation & Strategy* 24(4): 32–34.

Jiao, X. 2015. 'Urban Problems in Urbanization Process: The Connotation, Types and Governance Mechanism'. *On Economic Problems* 7: 7–12.

Jieming, Zhua and Li Tianb. 2017. 'Editorial: Inclusive urbanization in the 21st century China'. *Cities* 60: 415–419.

Lennon, H. T. Choy, Yani Lai and Waiming Lok. 2013. 'Economic performance of industrial development on collective land in the urbanization process in China: Empirical evidence from Shenzhen'. *Habitat International* 40: 184–193.

Leung, C. K. 1996. 'Foreign manufacturing investment and regional industrial growth in Guangdong Province, China'. *Environment and Planning* A 28: 513–536.

Liaoning Bureau of Statistics.2016. *Statistical Yearbook of Liaoning Province, 2015*. Beijing: China Statistics Press.

Liu, Y., H. Long, Y. Chen, J. Wang, L. Yurui, Y. Li, Y. Yang and Y. Zhou. 2016. 'Progress of research on urban-rural transformation and rural development in China'. *Journal of Geographical Sciences* 26(8): 1117–1132.

Liu, Z. 2005. 'Institution and inequality: The hukou system in China'. *Journal of Comparative Economics* 33: 133–157.

Li, Yuzhu. 2012. 'A Summary of the Symposium on "Reflection and Innovation of China 's Urbanization"'. *Chinese Journal of Population Science* 3: 106–110.

Liu, Y. and R. Yang. 2015. 'The spatial pattern measure of urban-rural development transformation in the Bohai Rim region in China'. *Acta Geographica Sinica* 70: 248–256.

Lu, Z. and S. Song. 2006. 'Rural–urban migration and wage determination: The case of Tianjin, China'. *China Economic Review* 17(3): 337–345.

Ma, L. J. C. 2002. 'Urban transformation in China, 1949–2000: A review and research agenda'. *Environment and Planning* A 34: 1545–1569.

Ministry of Housing and Urban Poverty Alleviation (MHUPA). 2010. 'Final Report of the Committee to look into Various Aspects of Slum Statistics/Census and Guide Count of Slum Census 2011'. New Delhi: Press Information Bureau, Government of India. Available at http://pibmumbai.gov.in/scripts/detail.asp?releaseId=E2010PR1660 (accessed March 2021).

National Bureau of Statistics of China (NBSC). 2012. *China Statistical Yearbook 2012*. Beijing: State Council of the People's Republic of China.

———. 2016. *China Statistical Yearbook 2016*. Beijing: State Council of the People's Republic of China.

Qi, X. 2015. 'The Comprehensive Evaluation and Horizontal Analysis on Urban Problem in Beijing'. *Modern Urban Research* 12: 71–75.

Qin, D. 2008. 'The path of urbanization with Chinese characteristics: Giving full play to the role of small towns'. *Urban Development Studies* 15(3): 96–99.

Qin, J. 2012. 'Research of Urban Disease in China: Origin, Present and Future'. *Modern Urban Research* 5: 58–64.

Qian, J., D. Feng and H. Zhu. 2012. 'Tourism-driven urbanization in China's small town development: A case study of Zhapo Town, 1986-2003'. *Habitat International* 36: 152–160.

Remi, J. and V. Dietrich. 2015. 'Urbanization without growth in historical perspective'. *Explorations in Economic History* 58: 1–21.

Shin, H. B. 2015. 'Urbanization in China'. In J. D. Wright (ed.), *International Encyclopedia of the Social and Behavioral Sciences*, 973–979. Amsterdam: Elsevier, 2e.

Tan, K. C., 1993. 'China's Small Town Urbanization Program: Criticism and Adaptation'. *Geo Journal* 29(2): 155–162.

Tan, Y., H. Xu and X. Zhang. 2016. 'Sustainable urbanization in China: A comprehensive literature review'. *Cities* 55: 82–93.

Varshney, Ashutosh. 1995. *Democracy, Development, and the Countryside: Urban-Rural Struggles in India*. Cambridge: Cambridge University Press.

Vermeer, E. B. 1999. 'Shareholding cooperatives: a property rights analysis'. In J. C. Oi and A. G. Walder (eds), *Property Rights and Economic Reform in China*, 123–144. Stanford, CA: Stanford University Press.

Wang, X. M. 1988. 'The impact of human migration and flow on the process of human urbanization'. *Population & Economics* 2: 19-24, 51.

Wang, G. T. and X. Hu. 1999. 'Small town development and rural urbanization in China'. *Journal of Contemporary Asia* 29(1): 76–94.

Wang, H. and R. Ji. 2006. 'Small-Medium Sized Enterprise Clusters and the Path of Small Town's Economic Development in China'. *Human Geography* 20(3): 96–98.

World Bank. 2005. 'The Dynamics of Global Urban Expansion'. Washington D.C.: Transport and Urban Development Department. Available at https://documents1.worldbank.org/curated/en/138671468161635731/pdf/355630Global0urban0sept200501PUBLIC1.pdf (accessed June 2021).

World Economic Forum. 2015. 'Global Risks 2015, Part 2: Risks in Focus, 2.3 City Limits: The Risks of Rapid and Unplanned Urbanization in Developing Countries'. Available at http://reports.weforum.org/global-risks-2015/part-2-risks-in-focus/2-3-city-limits-the-risks-of-rapid-and-unplanned-urbanization-in-developing-countries/ (accessed March 2021).

Xie, L., Z. Yang, J. Cai., Z. Cheng, T. Wen and T. Song. 2016. 'Harbin: A rust belt city revival from its strategic position'. *Cities* 58: 26–38.

Xisheng H., Chengzhen Wu, Wei Hong, et al. 2014. 'Forest cover change and its drivers in the upstream area of the Minjiang River, China'. *Ecological Indicators* 46: 121–128.

Yu, J. 2011. 'Reflection on the Urbanization of Developing Countries in the 20th Century'. *World History* 3: 4–23.

Zhang, Z. and X. Tan. 1998. 'Small Towns Cannot Bear the "Protagonist" of Urbanization'. *China Soft Science* 8: 14–19.

Zhong, Y. 2014. *Local Government and Politics in China: Challenges from Below*. London and New York: Routledge.

Zhu, X. 2000. 'Analysis on Advantages and Disadvantages of Small Town Construction under Urbanization'. *Journal of Socialist Theory Guide* 4: 29–32.

XIV

Class and Tenancy Relations in Calcutta, 1914–1926

Ritajyoti Bandyopadhyay and Ujaan Ghosh

INTRODUCTION

This chapter attempts a micro-history of the rental economy of Calcutta during the First World War and its immediate aftermath. In the period under review, an ambitious street scheme of the Calcutta Improvement Trust (CIT) recycled more than 200 acres of prime land of the city, and dis-housed at least 50,000 individuals living in the densely populated neighbourhoods of Surtibagan, Jorabagan and Jorasanko—where an upper-caste Bengali Hindu rentier class population lived with an increasingly prosperous Marwari community, a lower-middle class Bengali constituency, an upcountry Muslim trading community and a huge mass of migrant (male) working-class population working in the Burrabazaar area, mostly as coolies and transport workers. The Central Avenue Scheme of the CIT in this area created a speculative land market and reshuffled the ethnic distribution of property ownership and tenancy. This chapter takes a 'micro-history approach' to study this transformation in Calcutta. The period under review is sandwiched between the nineteenth-century traditions of urbanism (Sengupta 2013) and the twentieth-century narratives of mass political formation in urban centres (Bayly 1971; Chatterjee 1997; Ray 1979), and thus it has remained largely unattended by historians even though the First World War had a significant global impact on the urban land market and tenancy relations (Bhattacharyya 2016; Fogelson 2013; Forsell 2006).

The history of the period under consideration (at least in the colonial metropoles) was dominated by the development of the 'Improvement Trust'. As Prashant Kidambi notes, the Improvement Trusts, both in Britain and in India, were legally empowered to usurp private property rights in the name of 'public interest' (Kidambi 2001). In Indian cities, the Improvement Trusts were essentially executive-driven statutory organisations set up to replan and recycle parts of the city, and to execute suburban developments outside the command of a fast democratising sphere of representative politics of the city Corporation. However, inquiries into the workings of the Improvement Trusts and their role in the urbanisation of the subcontinent have largely been limited to Bombay and, to some extent, Delhi (Legg 2007). In the context of Calcutta, it has not featured significantly in the urban historiography of the city. This is mostly because of the overbearing importance given to the nineteenth century in urban historiography. The few works that briefly mention the formation and workings of the CIT treat it as a culmination of the urban formations of Calcutta, which started from the era of Lord Wellesley (Governor-General of India [1798–1805]) (Datta 2012). In addition, the archives that were hitherto used while writing about CIT were mostly based on the few annual reports that were publicly accessible. The other notable documents of the Trust, like the land committee reports, schemes, valuation documents, and proceedings of the meetings, have all remained out of the public domain until now. Thus, this work attempts to fill this historiographical lacuna by delving into a completely unexplored archive, and builds an argument from within that archive. But in so doing, the chapter seeks to develop a more general understanding of the housing crisis under the capitalist order of things, which inherently privileges resource over refuge and profit over people. What role does ground rent play in this process? The literature on the subject is much developed in the cities of the global North (Madden and Marcuse 2016; Marcuse 1985; Smith 1979; Ward 2006), but there is very little on the colonial and postcolonial contexts. This chapter arrives at a historical understanding of the market economy of urban rent in the Southern context.

THE INFRASTRUCTURAL INHERITANCE OF THE CIT

In 1803, Lord Wellesley appointed an 'Improvement Committee' to bring 'order' to the city of Calcutta. Among other things, the Committee was entrusted to 'ensure that the irregularity of buildings should be forbidden and that streets and lanes, which have hitherto been formed without attention to the health, convenience or safety of the inhabitants, should henceforth be constructed with order and system' (Richards 1914: 16). The financial supply for the Committee's operation came from the lottery profits. In 1817, the Improvement Committee was incorporated into the Lottery Committee, which continued to be in operation until 1836. The Lottery Committee was responsible for developing a road network in the city. The Committee developed five north-and-south roads known as Cornwallis Street, College Street, Wellington Street, Wellesley Street and Wood Street. Further, it constructed Strand Road along the river bank. It also laid out Free School Street, Kyd Street, Colootolah Street, Amherst Street and Mirzapore Street. The Committee created Cornwallis Square, College Square, Wellington Square and Wellesley Square (ibid.).

The Lottery Committee was abolished in 1836. As historians of the city suggest, for the next couple of decades, nothing significant took place in terms of street construction (Datta 2012). Street development in the city proper began to receive attention only after the city was given a Municipal Corporation in 1856. The city Corporation undertook massive underground drainage and a piped water supply scheme. The covering up of open drains and the laying of the water connection to households enabled the Corporation to open out, widen and stretch several alleyways (Richards 1914). In earlier times, many of these lanes abruptly ended in courtyards of private properties, and as such belonged to adjacent property owners. The inauguration of a new regime of municipal services enabled the colonial government to create lanes and to integrate the existing ones with a larger network of traffic. It was estimated that between 1876 and 1888, the surface area of streets in the city increased by 33 per cent (ibid.). These lanes soon became the veritable means of traffic in the city.

Image 14.1: 'A Typical Development Road in the North of the City'[1]

Photograph: Maden and Shrosbree 1913.

The only significant street building activity between 1856 and 1888 was the construction of a 70-foot wide road, connecting the floating Hooghly Bridge (constructed in 1873–1874) and the Sealdah Railway Station. In 1888, the jurisdiction of the Corporation was extended to incorporate a considerable area of suburbs to the east and south, and the municipal area was almost doubled, from 11,954 acres to 20,547 acres. Since 1888, the Corporation began to pay attention to the city's communication with the recently added areas. But its attention remained confined to the south. Thus, in the 1890s, the Corporation built some of the major streets in the south–Lansdowne Road, Harish Chandra Mukherjee Road and Hazra Road. Still, the Corporation lacked an integrated approach. The developments of street networks in the suburbs, on the other hand, did not follow the ongoing developments in the city proper, which eventually resulted in ruptures in traffic flows between the old city and the extended municipal areas. When CIT came into existence in 1912, it had the burden of integrating the city with its suburban areas, thus dispersing rental concentrations within some of the densely populated pockets of the old city.

When the Trust began its operation in Calcutta in 1912, its chief engineer, E. P. Richards, found it a city 'divided into huge half-mile rectangles by narrow streets', devoid of any 'ordinary relation between width and position', in which 'the maximum density of building and population concurs...with the least provision of roads and streets' (Richards 1914: 19). He recommended the construction of a series of intersecting and parallel roads, along with a series of diagonal thoroughfares like that of Harrison Road to reduce the distance between streets. Such infrastructural initiatives, along with sanitation, electricity and water supply schemes, were bound to increase the divergence between the 'capitalised ground rent' in what Richards called the 'street-less neighbourhoods' and the 'potential ground rent' of the same land, understood as the amount that could be capitalised if the land is put to the best possible alternative use (Ghertner 2014; Smith 1979, 2002).[2] The 'rent gap' thus arrived at created the material conditions for embourgeoisement that unfolded through a significant readjustment of the sociological map of the central parts of the city, where working-class slums and substantial residential buildings shared bleeding boundaries with thriving commercial establishments. In other words, bridging the rent gap presupposed the forced separation of a large section of people from the prevailing land use, in favour of the land's anticipated 'highest and best use'. Known as the principle of recoupment, the street schemes of the Trust acquired land beyond the requirement of laying a thoroughfare and sold the excess land at a much higher price as a set-off to the cost of constructing the street. According to C. H. Bompas, the first Chairman of the Trust, recoupment 'formed a very important feature in the finance of the Improvement Trust', especially in the absence of a major land bank in the city for public work (Bompas 1927).

In this respect, the Improvement Trust's operation in Calcutta differed significantly from its counterparts in other Indian cities, which inherited a major share of land from city corporations. In Calcutta, on the contrary, land ownership rested with numerous

Indian private players, which H. H. Risley attributed to the city's Permanent Settlement lineage, which made civic bodies perennially 'land-anaemic'.[3] Even in the 'white' part of the city, ownership of buildings and prime lands were often in the hands of the rich Indian landlords and merchants, which meant many of the British officials were simultaneously tenants and masters of the landed elite of the city. The process of recoupment involved layered negotiations with the property owners and ratepayers[4] of the city, who had already started gaining a distinct civic voice in the early twentieth century. The Central Avenue Scheme that this chapter considers as an exploratory site of embourgeoisement was arguably the most prominent instance of street-building along some of the city's most densely populated neighbourhoods. In the Central Avenue scheme area, as we will show, closing the rent gap happened in two interconnected layers. In the first instance, the dwelling spaces of the poor were valourised for the richer sections of the society, while the second unfolded in the progressive conversion of dwelling spaces to commercial enclaves. In this chapter, we will first track the life of a street in the archives of the CIT. We will further show how such an exercise offers us an introduction to the rental geography of Calcutta. We will then follow a major war-time initiative of rent control to talk about a possible history of urban tenancy relations, which has so far received less attention in urban historiography.

The CIT developed two approaches to the improvement of the city. First, it had a 'General Improvement Scheme' whereby it sought to improve the public health condition of Calcutta by 'wiping out insanitary areas' (such as slums and bazaars). Second, it undertook a massive street scheme powered by the principle of recoupment, aiming at decongesting a large part of central Calcutta, and connected the city with its immediate suburbs. The method of recoupment organised properties in grids, and in a hierarchy of valuation, which in turn encouraged speculative investment in the recycled land in the inner-city areas. The operation of the Trust improved the infrastructural inheritance of the city, which, as we have already discussed, enhanced the capital value of the property and yielded a more exalted gap between the current land use and what could be considered the most valuable use of the same property, leading to a massive population reshuffle in various pockets of Calcutta, where the Trust extended its operation. Figure 14.1 gives us a brief sketch of the work of the CIT between 1912 and 1947.

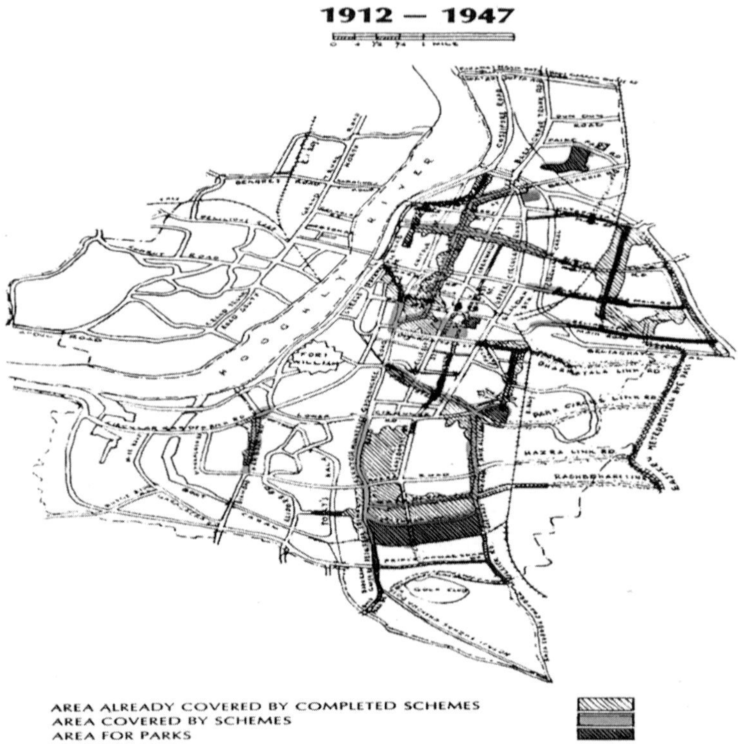

Figure 14.1: Work of the Calcutta Improvement Trust, 1912–1947

Note: The marked areas reflect the work of the CIT between 1912 and 1947.
Source: Datta 2015: 19.

The co-ordinated operation of the Trust, the Corporation, the Port Trust and the PWD in the 1910s and 1920s resulted in a decisive transformation of the material culture of Calcutta. In those two decades, Calcutta received several avenue-style streets paved with asphalt, and with spacious sidewalks. The elevated architectural pattern of these avenues produced new asymmetries between the heights of the low-profile lanes (*gali*) and the high-profile streets (*rajpath*), which impacted the circulation of water in the city. The low-profile lanes became the new sites of waterlogging and diseases. The bright street lamps on the main streets enabled the sprawl of new forms of darkness and new geographies of illegibility in the network of lanes, where thrived the lower-middle class clerkly life. The avenue created a new aesthetic order and diverted civic infrastructural investments towards new zones of concentration. The avenue also created a moral order. A person's elevation from poverty and squalor to enlightenment would involve a spatio-moral journey from the lane to the street (*gali theke rajpath*).[5]

THE CENTRAL AVENUE SCHEME

The idea of a north-south central thoroughfare between the Chitpore Road and Cornwallis Street had been under consideration since at least 1854 when Alderman Clark, the architect of the city's underground sewerage system, projected a thoroughfare linking up Dharmatala and Bagbazaar, roughly along the lines of the map of today's Central Avenue. Finally, in 1914, the CIT took up the 'Central Avenue' project. It began by destroying a host of dwellings and shops in the corner of Dharmatala and Bentinck Street. Chairman Bompas took personal care to ensure that the contrasting grandeur of the Tipu Sultan Mosque and the Ochterlony Monument gained unencumbered visibility within a single photo frame from the cleansed street corner. By 1931, Central Avenue touched Beadon Street in the north. When completed, it covered 201.1 acres of prime land, stretching over 3 miles with a consistent width of 100 feet.

The Central Avenue swallowed smaller bylanes and neighbourhoods and adorned its immediate margins with vertical buildings hosting commercial offices and banks. The adjacent residential quarters were recouped and redeveloped to host commercial establishments, which led to a substantial depopulation in adjoining neighbourhoods. In Colootolah area, for instance, which was in the

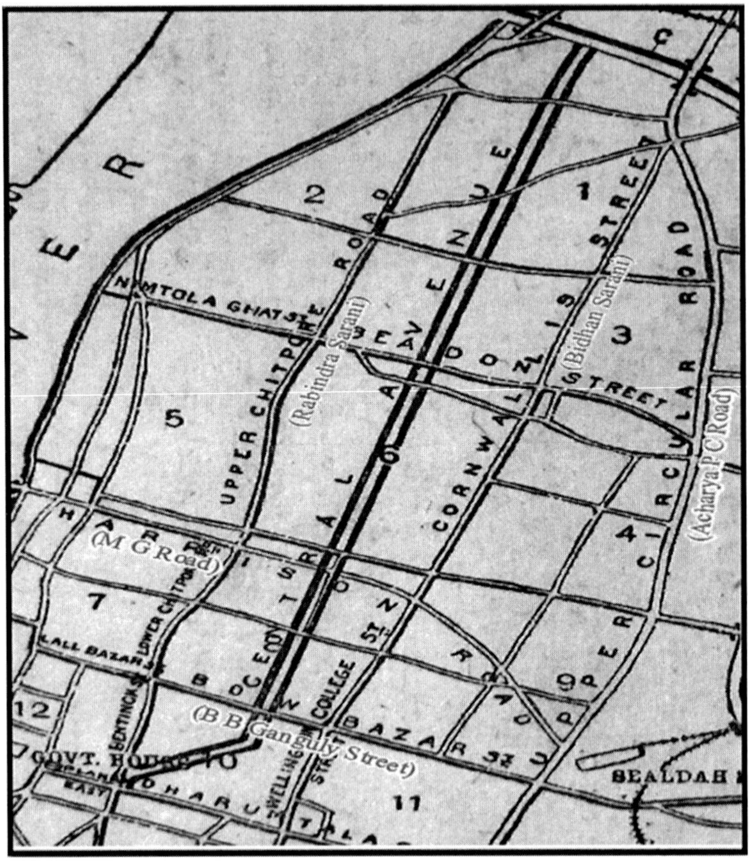

Figure 14.2: Central Avenue, 1914

Note: The present names of some of the major streets have been indicated.
Source: Sinha 1916: 72.

active catchment of the Scheme, population density declined by 32.5 per cent between 1911 and 1921, while Jorasanko witnessed a decline of population density by 3.2 per cent during the same census decade. In these two neighbourhoods alone, the Central Avenue Scheme acquired 33.3 and 22.6 acres of land, respectively (Census of India 1921). In a way, the Central Avenue Scheme carried forward a long process of dis-housing *bustee* populations, comprised mainly of male migrants from Bihar and the United Provinces (modern-day Uttar Pradesh). Already, the Census of 1911 noted that due to the demolition of seventy-five *bustees* in the Colootolah area alone, the population density had come down from 282 per acre in 1901 to 255 in 1911 (Census of India 1911), and to 172 per acre in 1921 (Census of India 1921). The Census of 1911 further registered that in Jorabagan, Jorasanko and Colootolah areas, dwelling houses had increasingly been replaced by commercial quarters (Census of India 1911)—a trend that continues in inner-city areas to this day. We will have more to say on this in the subsequent sections of the chapter.

Let us now present a picture of the Central Avenue Scheme. An estimate of 1918 mentioned that 136 residential properties were being notified for acquisition for the Central Avenue Scheme. Of the 136 properties, twelve were 1 *kottah* in area. These properties were priced at the prevailing market rate between Rs 2,000 (£417) and Rs 5,000 (£1,042), the average being Rs 3,500 (£729). Next, there were fifty-three holdings with an area between 1 and 2 *kottahs* each, with an estimated prevailing market rate between Rs 3,000 and Rs 15,000, the average being Rs 6,000. There were thirty-three holdings between 2 and 3 *kottahs* in area, whose price varied between Rs 5,000 and Rs 18,500, the average being Rs 11,000. The remaining thirty-eight holdings were over 3 *kottahs* in area, of which three properties were priced under Rs 10,000 and nine between Rs 10,000 and Rs 15,000. Many of these properties were partly tenanted, and most of the 136 properties had numerous ownership sub-divisions.[6]

How could the evicted people be re-housed? Bompas summarily excluded the possibility of recognising tenants of the acquired properties. In one of his notes, Bompas clearly mentioned that the overall improvement of the land due to its proximity to the new thoroughfare would make the price of land in this area several times higher than the existing streetless, partitioned mesh of properties. He said, 'It is obviously desirable that building of some size and dignity should front on such a road. It would have been ridiculous for Haussmann when he made the Boulevards of Paris to have allowed them to be lined with small cottages.'[7] Bompas added, 'The only way of re-housing in these cases at a fair expenditure seems to be to compel the people, however reluctant, to move into the suburbs where land is cheaper.'[8] As we progress with this chapter, we will explore why such a vision of dispersal could not materialise in Calcutta in the first couple of decades of the twentieth century. To encourage the affected owners of the Central Avenue Scheme to move to Bhowanipore, the Trust, in September 1918, announced a concession scheme that was 'either 33.3 per cent of the value of the new site or 50 per cent of the value of the old site'.[9]

Table 14.1 illustrates the state of reinstatement of small *bhadralok* owners[10] in 1921.

Table 14.1: State of Reinstatement for Small *Bhadralok* Owners in 1921

Scheme from which displaced	Number of cases	Scheme in which re-housed
I: Surtibagan	1	I: Surtibagan
I: Do	5	V: Bhowanipore Area
IB: Link Road between Chitpore Road and Central Avenue, Surtibagan	1	IB: Link Road between Chitpore Road and Central Avenue, Surtibagan
IC: Surtibagan area	1	IV A: Russa Road Extension
IV: Russa Road Widening	2	V: Bhowanipore Area
IV: Do	1	IV A: Russa Road Extension
IV A: Russa Road Extension	12	IV A: Do
IV A: Do	2	V: Bhowanipore Area
V: Bhowanipore Area	9	IV A: Russa Road Extension
V: Do	12	V: Bhowanipore Area
VII: Central Avenue (between Mechuabazaar Street and Beadon Street)	2	IV A: Russa Road Extension
VII: Do	24	V: Bhowanipore Area
VII: Central Avenue (between Mechuabazaar Street and Beadon Street	3	VII: Central Avenue (between Mechuabazaar Street and Beadon Street

(Contd)

Table 14.1 (Contd)

Scheme from which displaced	Number of cases	Scheme in which re-housed
VII: Do	1	VII B: Central Avenue (between Colootolah Street and Bowbazaar Street)
VII A: Central Avenue (Halliday Street Widening)	2	V: Bhowanipore Area
VII A: Do	3	VII B: Central Avenue (between Colootolah Street and Bowbazaar Street)
VII B: Central Avenue (between Colootolah Street and Bowbazaar Street)	3	V: Bhowanipore Area
VII B: Do	2	VII B: Central Avenue (between Colootolah Street and Bowbazaar Street)
VII C: Maniktola Spur	5	IV A: Russa Road Extension
VII C: Do	6	V: Bhowanipore Area
VII C. S. (Chitpore Spur)	1	XIII: Park Street Widening (between Chowringhee and Wellesley Street)
VII C. S.: Do	4	VII C. S. (Chitpore Spur)
VII C. S. Do	2	VII B: Central Avenue (between Colootolah Street and Bowbazaar Street)
VII C. S. Do	1	IA: Surtibagan
VII D: Central Avenue (between Bowbazaar Street and Princep Street)	1	V: Bhowanipore Area
VII: Central Avenue (between Mechuabazaar Street and Beadon Street	1	V: Bhowanipore Area
R. K. D. S. Square	1	IV A: Russa Road Extension
R. K. D. S. Square	1	V: Bhowanipore Area
Total	109	

Source: *Annual Report on the Operation of the Calcutta Improvement Trust for the Year 1920–1921*. Calcutta: Calcutta Improvement Trust.

Table 14.1 reports that of the total 109 cases of re-housing, sixty-one cases (56 per cent) came from the Central Avenue area, of which fifteen house owners (24.56 per cent) could find an alternative offer within the Central Avenue area. An overwhelming number of displaced owners (thirty-eight of sixty-one, which was 62 per cent) moved to the emerging suburb of Bhowanipore. It is important to add that Table 14.1 provides information on the re-housing of only a tiny section of those displaced during this period. The question of ownership in such old residential buildings tended to be more complex and contested, as each old house being destroyed involved multiple claims to ownership and tenancy. In addition, out of 136 properties notified for acquisition along the emerging Central Avenue, the table gives us an idea of just sixty-one (45 per cent) owners who moved out, which shows a tendency to officially under-report the effect of improvement among the people displaced during the first decade of the Trust's operation.

The re-housing scheme of the Trust for the workmen and dis-housed slum dwellers during the period under review was effectively confined to three three-storeyed tenement buildings with 248 rooms and four shops capable of housing just 1,260 adults.[11] For long, these *chawls* remained vacant. The dis-housed slum dwellers refused to move far away from their places of work, and those who moved refused to be re-housed vertically, against gravitation. After a while, the Trust opened the Scheme to other social classes to recover the cost. Soon, the Trust received an application from one Nirmal Chandra Mitter, who was

> ready to offer Rs 750 a month for the three blocks for a twenty-year lease. Mitter wished to take the two upper floors of the three blocks for the occupation of middle class Bengalis but *only*, it needs emphasis if a gate were put on the staircases and he would then leave the Trust free to lease the ground floors to whomever they liked (*Annual Report on the Operation of the Calcutta Improvement Trust for the Year 1919–1920*).

The fact that the Trust entertained such an application reveals its approach to the housing question as one being couched less in a motive of rehabilitation than perhaps a motive of commerce.

In 1920, the Trust accepted that the 'occupants are not persons of the poorest class', and noticed a 'growing tendency for the buildings to become occupied by clerks and poor students who have not been actually displaced by the operations of the Trust'.[12] Soon, the Trust decided to use parts of the three buildings (Blocks A, B and C) for commercial purposes. Thus, the Annual Report for 1920–1921 shows the 'conversion of two ground floor dwelling rooms in Block "A" into shops and another two rooms on the top flat into restaurants and also a third top flat room in Block "C" into a restaurant'.[13] The Trust's approach to the question of re-housing and compensation led to discontent even within the high circles of the colonial government. In his letters of 31 May 1919, the Secretary to the Government of Bengal wrote:[14]

> I am to add that government are disposed to think that the Board of Trustees have not hitherto made adequate use of the power to execute re-housing schemes conferred on them by the [Calcutta Improvement] Act with the consequence that one of its main objects has not been fulfilled, and I am to suggest for their consideration the desirability of a more active policy in this direction.

The demolition of slums and lower-middle class dwellings from the Central Avenue area enabled the Marwari traders to gradually shift from the alleys of Burrabazaar to the more lucrative frontal sites in Colootolah (Census of India 1921).[15] The spatial movement of the Marwaris received sharp auto-critical responses from the Bengali *bhadralok*, marked by a profound lament for the steady decline of the 'Bengali enterprise'. In 1923, the scientist and public intellectual P. C. Roy reminded his fellow Bengalis that the Marwaris 'will gradually become the owners of most parts of Calcutta', ousting the Bengali. The decayed residential houses of the *bhadralok* would give way to the Marwaris' commercial establishments. Roy anticipated with horror that in the context of the rent bulge in the city, the *Bangali babus* would soon land up as tenants in one or two-roomed flats, 'the size of pigeon holes' (Chatterji 2017). During the debate over the Rent Act—time and again—this wound surfaced. In an evocative contribution, Debjani Bhattacharyya (2016) has shown how the Bengali rentier class arrived at a distinction between the 'legitimate speculation of the earlier generation' (when they controlled the land market) and the 'so-called culturalized [rent] profiteering of the Marwari classes' (ibid.: 467), firmly establishing a 'causal relation between the housing crisis and the entry of new upcountry and Marwari landlords in Calcutta's land market' (ibid.: 472) in the interwar period.

The upgradation of Colootolah also meant that a sizeable section of Muslim petty merchants, traders, shopkeepers, artisans and small moneylenders (*kabulis*) were dislocated from that area. These Muslim groups were fiercely antagonistic to the Marwaris, a factor that fuelled intermittent riots between these two groups in 1912, 1918 and 1926 (Das 1991). Here, it is important to mention that in Bombay, the co-existence of factories and civic life gave birth to an urban material culture in which the Trust could hardly ignore working-class housing issues for too long in its vision of a future city.[16] Calcutta, on the other hand, developed as an administrative centre and a transit hub, with numerous commercial establishments. In the first couple of decades of the twentieth century, only a minor part of the Corporation area had modern industrial enclaves. The working class was predominantly male and was primarily constituted by transport coolies connected to transit centres and warehouses. In the absence of a unified shop floor, classic trade unionism was significantly absent among transit workers. In this city, housing became a political question only in the second half of the twentieth century, during the upper-caste Bengali refugee influx.

As we have already discussed, officials of the Trust anticipated a layered dispersal of the population from the central city with the unfolding of various street schemes. The Census of 1911 gave them an unmistakable sense that population from the central city areas was gradually moving towards suburban wards and municipalities. In fact, the Census of 1911 shows that all the wards outside Circular Road and Sealdah Station experienced an influx of population. In Beniapukur and Ballygunge, for instance, the population plummeted by 53.5 per cent and 28 per cent, respectively. Entally, Beniapukur and Tollygunge registered a steady growth of the female population by 2,000, 5,300 and 2,700, respectively. The increase in the female population in these areas suggested growth in the permanent household population in the suburbs of the city. Thus, when the Trust began to integrate these suburbs with the city proper through an extensive road network, these areas had already begun to witness a land crisis. The population influx in the suburbs coincided with the acquisition of land by various railway and tramway companies in places such as Talla, Belgachia, Paikpara, Ultodingi and Ballygunge.

An area-wise comparison of land prices between London and Calcutta during the First World War revealed that Calcutta's suburban lands were sold at an average price which was twenty times higher than their London counterparts. However, a comparison of land prices in the inner-city areas in Calcutta and London revealed that during the same time, Calcutta's average land price was two to four times cheaper than the land price in central London (Bompas 1927).[17] This means that when the Trust undertook a massive overhaul of the inner-city, land price in the suburbs was already extremely high, and hence the *price differential between the centre and the suburbs was considerably less*. As a result, there was not much scope for the dispersal of rent and decongestion of the inner city by the movement of dispersed/displaced populations to the suburbs, even if the Trust concentrated on developing better communication networks between the city and its suburbs. In these suburbs, the sheer presence of the railway yard created a continuous wall of circulation that obstructed the expansion of the city to the other side of the yard. In fact, in Calcutta, the divide between the two sides of a rail yard was not only spatial, but also civic, moral and cultural. Even in the 1970s, the other side of the track was considered the natural end of urban modernity, where the wagon-breakers and Naxalite insurgents, and poorer and degraded East Bengali refugees would crowd the neighbourhoods—a new frontier to be conquered by flyovers.

THE RENT STORM

Such was the situation when the shiver of the Great War was felt in Calcutta's land market. There had been a considerable hike in house rent in certain parts of the city from 1918 (Bhattacharyya 2016).[18] By the second half of 1919, the land situation had reached a definite crisis of sorts. This could be evinced by the fact that the Maharajadhiraja of Burdwan, Bijoy Chand Mahatab, whose family enjoyed rent-collecting rights in Posta Bazaar and the whole of the Tireta Bazaar on the western margin of the fledging Central Avenue, warned in the provincial legislature in March 1920 that Calcutta was really on the brink of a second Bolshevik Revolution, with rental values more than doubling within a year's time in several cases.[19] On average, the government acknowledged, there was a hike in house rents in Calcutta and its suburbs by 50 per cent between 1917 and 1920. On 30 September 1919, the Provincial Government of Bengal appointed a Committee to gather evidence of the 'abnormal' rise in house rent and property prices in Calcutta. Gathering such evidence in different parts of the city, the Committee recommended an emergency Rent Control Act to monitor and cap the exorbitant rent profiteering by the landlords. The Rent Committee submitted its report to the government on 23 February 1920. One of the contributing factors to the rent storm, according to the Committee, was the slump in building operations during the five years of the War. Further, during the War years, the Trust demolished 643 masonry houses and disposed of 468 *bighas* of land at a much higher margin than the cost of acquisition, and in this process, dis-housed more than 50,000 individuals from the scheme areas.[20]

All this happened at a time when the war-induced commercial and industrial boom attracted more labourers to the city. The jute industry, for instance, expanded from sixty-nine to eighty-five factories between 1914 and 1923, with a 36.8 per cent increase in the workforce in Calcutta and adjacent industrialised municipalities (Bhattacharyya 2016). The presence of a huge presidency secretariat, other government and business headquarters, the mint near Burrabazaar, and an extremely well-propertied University within the limits of the Corporation area meant that a large quantity of prime land was always kept out of circulation in the market, which provided the historical precondition to the crisis.[21]

The available evidence on the rent storm, however, suggests that it affected the central and southern parts of the city more prominently than other areas. The Rent Committee circulated about 1,000 forms asking the landlords and tenants about the current rental situation in the city. The Committee received only around 260 filled-in forms. Given that in 1919–1920, the number of masonry houses in the city was 36,000 (out of which 15,000 houses were occupied by the owners, 17,000 houses by the tenants and 5,000 by commercial establishments and warehouses), the sample collected by the Rent Committee was far from being representative of the situation.[22] A survey of the evidence shows that the majority of responses came from the neighbourhoods of Central Avenue, Bowbazaar and Park Street[23]—areas also affected by the work of the Improvement Trust. Thus, in his speech, the Maharaja of Burdwan documented the following:[24]

> In Lower Circular Road, the rent of three rooms has been raised from Rs 100 to Rs 175; in Elliot Road, the rent of a house with seven rooms has been increased from Rs 220 to Rs 400; in Zakaria Street the rent of one room was Rs 18, it is now Rs 35; in Boloram De Street Rs 80 was demanded for a house let for Rs 40 in the year 1916 and the rents of many flats south of Park Street have been raised from Rs 200 or thereabout to Rs 400.

A further comparison of properties between the Street Directories for the years 1918 (Thacker's Indian Directory 1918) and 1933 (Thacker's Indian Directory 1933) further reveals some major readjustment of properties near the intersection of Central Avenue and Balaram De Street, for instance. A *bustee* land at 49 Balaram De Street, to take an example, appears to have been recycled into a solicitors' firm sometime between 1918 and 1933. The property at No. 50 Balaram De Street, which Naran Dassi and Naran Moti Devi (prostitutes) inhabited in 1918, found no reference in the 1933 Street Directory. By 1933, at least three commercial properties were added to No. 52 Balaram De Street, which had no existence in 1918. In the adjacent Central Avenue, all the property names in the 1933 Directory appeared to be of a non-residential commercial nature—thus, we have Kaviraj Promotho Nath Sen and Joshi and Co. at No. 14 Central Avenue, where Central Avenue intersected Balaram De Street, and the famous Merzapore Building at P-18-B Central Avenue that hosted a number of commercial addresses, including the New Bengal Motor Works and Store Enamelling House. Similarly, 28-B Central Avenue was occupied by the Presidency Electric Co. in 1933.

Equally, in Zachariah Street, the work of the Improvement Trust changed the texture of the neighbourhood 'beyond recognition'. In the 1918 Street Directory, for instance, only three properties have been named, while in the 1933 Street Directory, there are references to fifty-four properties along Zachariah Street. Of the fifty-four properties, the first thirty-five names between Lower Chitpore Road and Surtibagan Lane refer to commercial establishments owned/occupied by people bearing Muslim names. As the street proceeded to the Surtibagan area (where the Improvement Trust had launched its first Scheme), the remaining properties (predominantly commercial in nature) had owners/occupants with Bengali-Hindu (upper-caste) and Marwari surnames. What follows from this evidence is that the work of the Improvement Trust in the central part of the city decisively facilitated the conversion of dwelling spaces into commercial establishments. The steady conversion of properties in these areas led to the erasure of slums and prostitution from the newly created and valourised 'frontage properties'.

In Calcutta, the short-lived prosperity—coupled with the political loss of capital to Delhi, the virtual non-existence of a credible banking network, and the loss of credibility of government bonds during the War—caused a competitive anxiety among those who had made quick money during the war years. In the absence of a credible investment destination, they began to identify the rent gap in the inner city, caused by the aggressive improvement work of the Trust, as a veritable investment destination. They chose to hoard land for an indefinite period of time, and found it more profitable to keep land out of building activities to avoid a rather protracted turnover period that would otherwise have resulted in an enhanced supply of houses in the rental market.

The exceptional rental situation became the pretext for a newly invigorated municipal war to throw some of the thriving trading activities of this area to the ever-mobile margins of the city. The Colootolah-Tireta bazaar area was also the largest transit centre for India's thriving hide trade. A large number of hide warehouses were located along and between Phears Lane, Harinbari Lane and Canning Street (west). Already in 1914—when the Central Avenue project was kicked off—the Corporation mandated the 'removal from residential areas of tanneries, knacker's yards, and blood, offal and gut factories' into the 'outlying areas' east of the railway tracks of Sealdah.[25] In the same year, the Corporation transferred a substantial 'Mohamedan slaughter House' on Halliday Street to the far-off Tangra area. As a result, the Corporation incurred a 'corresponding fall in the receipt from slaughtering fees (Rs 65,130 against Rs 71,713)' during 1914–1915. Needless to say, such ejectments impacted heavily on the working class associated with such trades, who came predominantly from the Muslim, Anglo-Indian and Chinese communities.[26]

No wonder, then, that the work of the Improvement Trust received applause from European visitors to the city. One such visitor (Macmillan 1928: 46–47) was to record the following in 1928:

> Since the formation of the Calcutta Improvement Trust in 1913, the changes made by it in the city have greatly contributed to the more expeditious movement of the vehicular traffic, have driven wide thoroughfares through crowded and unsavoury quarters, and *altered even the centre of the city*...The Central Avenue is 100 feet wide, and already shows signs of what a great artery it will be in the future. *Huge structures of four, five and six storeys, are already flanking it*. No Tram-cars run there, and the public vehicular traffic is confined to motor buses, of which, owing to the Trust's provision of wide roads, there is now a great number (emphases ours).

Note how, in the eye of the European visitor, the work of the Improvement Trust to inject a British architectural and planning ethos into the core of the native city appeared to be a heroic act.

Already in 1920, a citizen-motorist of Bombay wrote to the Editor of *The Times of India* the following (*The Times of India* 1920):

> I have lately returned from paying a visit to Calcutta. Up to the time, of this visit, I have always backed up the claims of Bombay as being ahead of Calcutta, but this is no longer possible...The streets are cleaner. There is an almost total absence of the filthy clouds of dust which get into the eyes, noses and throats of the Bombayite. The roads are for the most part in good condition, and *it is quite possible to get a real motor joy ride even in the erstwhile congested central parts of the city*. Motor traffic is much heavier than in Bombay, and the accidents do not seem to be so numerous either....Sidewalks in Calcutta are made to walk upon, consequently people do not walk any extent in the centre of the roads.... (emphasis ours).

The Bengali *bhadralok* response to the work of the Improvement Trust was largely cautious and ambivalent, and at the same time, it referred to a decisive and irreversible change in the ways in which they had 'selfed' the city in their childhood, and as they were experiencing the city after the onslaught of improvement. While describing the various modes of navigation in Calcutta, Kshitindranath Tagore—a notable resident of Jorasanko, for instance—traced a decisive rupture in time: *sekaal o ekaal* ('then and now'), marked by the improvement work of the Trust in the central city. Thus, Tagore wrote the following (Tagore 1930, translated in Datta 2015: 21): 'Forget about those who left the city half a century ago, even those residents who went abroad ten or twenty years ago, if they came back now would find parts of Calcutta unrecognisable.'

The *bhadralok* too took pride in the growing visual acclaim of the city. However, their celebration of the city was always restrained by a sense of the decline of 'Bengali enterprise', as the veritable property market of the central city went into the hands of the Marwari merchants of Burrabazaar, who allegedly hoarded land even when a sale would have given them normal profits, thereby augmenting the crisis in the housing market. J. N. Roy, a barrister with strong socialist proclivities, for instance, held 'Marwari speculators and up-country profiteers' (Bhattacharyya 2016: 474) responsible for the rent storm. In the new 'ethnicised' moral economy of the housing market, the (often emotive and sentimentalised) category of the 'lower-middle class' appeared to blur the distinction between the mass of petty landowners and small tenants. Thus, in his speech in the Legislative Assembly, Rai Radha Charan Pal Bahadur (also a municipal commissioner and a member of the Improvement Trust) could arrive at a sharp class distinction between the substantial landlords like the Maharaja of Burdwan, and the small property owners who 'travel in tram-cars and cannot afford to drive in motor cars'.[27]

It is difficult to track the popular responses to the improvement work of the Trust during the early decades. But it can well be surmised that it had severely dislocated the everyday life of the working people. Time and again, the transport-sector workers of the city resisted new traffic rules that considered slow-moving locomotion as a potential obstruction to automobile traffic. In 1930, for instance, the Corporation of Calcutta, in connivance with the Trust, promulgated a new traffic rule to restrict the movement of bullock carts beyond certain hours and boundaries of prominent wholesale market places. This was, of course, itself an effect of newly asphalted roads that for the Corporation described a characteristic geographical distribution of smooth-flowing traffic to which the carters presented an obstruction. But the carters did not take to this lightly. In association with young Communist labour leaders of the time like Abdul Momin, the mostly upcountry carters decided to wage a protest against the Corporation's new traffic rules dividing the organisation into six small zonal committees. On 1 April 1930, the day when the new rule was to come into force, carters started taking away bullocks from the carts at about noontime, dismantled the wheels from the carts and arranged them crosswise. In 1935, an Intelligence Bureau (IB) report noted how the official Communist Press acclaimed the strike as the 'first barricade street fight with the police in India—which indeed it was' (Sarkar 1987: 102–103). The first day's firing left seven carters dead. A procession of about 500,000 people took the carters' bodies to perform the last rites (ibid.).

CONCLUDING REMARKS

In accordance with the recommendations of the Rent Committee, the Calcutta Rent Control Act came into force in May 1920, initially for a period of three years (Law and Mookherjee 1924). As a modified version of the Act was further implemented in 1923 for an additional period of three years ending in 1926, it brought to the surface a layered reality of ownership, lease-holding, tenancy and sub-tenancy. The tenants had the entitlement to relief only insofar as s/he was able to regularly pay the rent. This means the operation of the Rent Act would have dispossessed several tenants and sub-tenants whose landlords were able to take the rental disputes to the rent controller. Anyone who lived in Calcutta in the twentieth century would know that rent collection and payment in due course was a messy affair in the lower-middle class and working-class quarters of the city. In that sense, the Rent Act could hardly make a significant dent in formalising these relationships in the frame of the law.

For a number of years since 1926, the city's rental economy was not governed by any acts as such. The war-led land boom was succeeded by a slump in the land market, but property prices never returned to the mid-war standards. As we have already noticed in the above case, the expansion of business and commercial spaces in dwelling areas had been a matter of much anxiety during and after the First World War. This trend would continue in succeeding decades. The house famine became a continuous feature of the city. The Census of 1931, for instance, recorded sixteen residents per household in the city. By 1941, that average rose to 27.5 persons per household (Mukherjee 2015). Again, during the Second World War, Calcutta came under rent regulation (1942, 1943 and 1946). The impact of the housing famine was severe for the lower-middle class and working-class populations of the city, which became part of the city's cultural archive through the *Kallol*-era literature.

The developments that we have witnessed in this period had strong roots in colonial political economy in the second half of the nineteenth century. In fact, it can be said that during the second half of the nineteenth century, the colonial state's fiscal base began to shift from agrarian and forest revenue to a more diverse range of sources beyond the productive land (Chatterjee 1984). From the late nineteenth century, urban centres became a more prominent sector of the state's revenue base, where proximity and agglomeration displaced productivity in the determination of rent. In 1876, Calcutta Municipality assumed the structure of a giant municipal corporation—an entity mandated more resolutely to bring about an 'overall improvement of the town'. Such a corporation was to rely on its share in rising property prices by translating 'property into a taxable entity' (Bhattacharyya 2016: 468). Under the Improvement Trust, colonial rule further consolidated the authority of the foreign and the native ruling class over the scarce resources of the cities, which manifested in the systematic recycling of *bustee* land and lower-middle class dwellings in some of the prime pockets of Calcutta. Increasingly, working-class housing in such locations became more and more difficult owing to the ground rent that arose out of the limited urban space for competing uses, which accrued benefits from the very fact of agglomeration and concentration.

It appears in hindsight that the CIT experience during the First World War and the subsequent interwar periods anticipated the future course of capitalist development in India in the post-liberalisation era, which is essentially driven by enormous investment in the real estate and infrastructure sectors, the so-called 'secondary circuit of capital', which unfolded in the violent erasure of slums and squatter colonies, and in the aggressive conversion of peri-urban agricultural land to urban (and real estate) plots. In 2005, India undertook a massive urban renewal mission (known as the JNNURM) that prompted the municipal governments to 'open up' and liberalise their real-estate markets, which meant the abolition of a number of late-colonial and postcolonial welfare measures such as rent controls and land-ceiling acts (Ghertner 2014). It encouraged urban governments to create municipal bond markets to assist the Finance Ministry's landmark decision to lift the erstwhile 40 per cent cap on foreign ownership in real property, to turn India into essentially a 'property driven stock market'. No wonder, then, that the real-estate index of the Bombay Stock Exchange doubled in 2006 (ibid.). The subsequent 'Smart City' mission of the current

NDA government in India (formally introduced in June 2015) took such developments to smaller cities and district towns. Already in the last decade, such developments in India's urban field displaced millions. In Delhi alone, as many as a million people were displaced in the 2000s (ibid.).

It is often argued that such developments in India's urban land market were unprecedented in its history. This view often overlooks the history of the long acquaintance that some prime colonial cities had with globally circulating capital, wish-images and ideas. As a result, the opening of the urban land market, when seen against the backdrop of India's postcolonial history, appears to be a moment without precedent and lineages. Writings on contemporary transformations in the urban order of things thus often fail to appreciate the traces of Calcutta's connection with 'imperial globalisation of the nineteenth and early twentieth centuries' (Kidambi 2007: 1). This chapter anticipates a much longer history of continuity and rupture in India's urban developments. In this, the Improvement Trust moment remains an important but much ignored episode.

End Notes

1. J. Maden and A. B. Shrosbree. 1913. *City and Suburban Main Road Project*. The Archives of the Calcutta Improvement Trust, Kolkata. Accessed at the CIT Record Room, Kolkata: 26.

2. See Smith (1979). In subsequent decades, Smith's explication of the rent gap as a 'global urban strategy' engulfed Marxist urban scholarship in the global South (Smith 2002). In a recent review piece, Ghertner (2014) has usefully reminded the Southern urbanists of the Northern historical context of urbanisation in which this particular theory is provincialised, whose generalisation in the colonial and postcolonial contexts makes cultural assumptions that 'maybe inapplicable to societies with very different structures of class and gender relations' (quoted in ibid.: 1555). In fact, the suburbanisation of Indian cities hardly followed the North American experience in the 1960s and 1970s, which was marked by a cycle of 'postindustrial decline, middle class flight [to the suburbs], and lower-class displacement via reinvestment in disinvested neighbourhoods'

(ibid.: 1557). In this chapter, we used the rent gap theory only to mark the distinction between the actual use of the property and its potential use.

3. Home Department [India]. 1904. Pro. No. 34, Calcutta Improvement Scheme, October 1904, 58, Notes, Municipalities–A, October 1904, NoS. 33-36. NAI.

4. 'Ratepayer' is a technical term used by colonial municipal officials. The subject populations also used this term and there were 'ratepayers' associations in various neighbourhoods.

5. Literary works in Bangla developed a distinct urban form in the interwar period. This tradition continued in subsequent decades during and following the Second World War and Partition. Literary works of these decades were especially invested in describing the life of the numerous blighted *galis* of Calcutta. See Mitra (1970 [1952]); also see Ghose (1950) and Kar (1957). For a vivid description of the Rajpath (built by the CIT), see Basu (1977).

6. CIT Proceedings, 4 September 1918. 'Note by Chairman (C. H. Bompas) of the Calcutta Improvement Trust on Re-Instatement in Scheme, No. VII'. Proceedings of the Calcutta Improvement Trust, Meeting No. 307. Accessed at the CIT Archives, CIT Record Room, Kolkata.

7. Ibid.

8. Ibid.

9. Ibid.

10. 'Small *bhadralok* owners' refers to property-owning lower-middle class Bengalis whose presence dotted the area under discussion. Most typically, they would own an ancestral dwelling house shared between many brothers and nephews. It was usually a male line of inheritance.

11. *Annual Report on the Operation of the Calcutta Improvement Trust for the Year 1919–1920*. Calcutta: Calcutta Improvement Trust.

12. Ibid.

13. *Annual Report on the Operation of the Calcutta Improvement Trust for the Year 1920–1921*. Calcutta: Calcutta Improvement Trust: 16.

14. Ibid.: 65 (Appendix B).

15. Such a trend was registered in the Census of 1921.

16. Already by 1917, working-class *chawls* in Bombay covered a total area of 77,354 square yards, and the actual cost of the building was Rs 28,82,879. CIT Proceedings, 29 July 1918. 'C H Bompas' Note on the Bombay Improvement Trust *Chawls*'. Proceedings of the Calcutta Improvement Trust, Meeting No. 301. Accessed at the CIT Record Room, Kolkata.

17. An exchange between Bompas and C. E. Payne, who was Chairman of the Calcutta Corporation in the 1910s and then became a surveyor in London, gives us such a picture of the land market in Calcutta and its suburbs. Bompas informed Payne that during the War, in some schemes the Trust had to acquire land in Calcutta's suburbs for £5,000 per acre. In reply, Payne wrote,

> Suburban land around London, with a good road frontage, main drainage, and all modern conveniences, cost roughly from 5 to 7 pounds per foot frontage, and in especially convenient areas like Wimbledon it cost 10 pounds per foot frontage, and sometimes more. That was roughly equivalent to from 1,000 to 1,500 pounds an acre, rising, perhaps, in certain cases, to 2,000 pounds (Bompas 1927).

18. It was estimated that there was a 38 per cent hike in house rent in 1918 (Bhattacharyya 2016).

19. *The Calcutta Gazette*, 31 March 1920. The Speech of the Hon'ble Maharajadhiraja Bahadur of Burdwan, the Legislative Council, List of Business–Item No. 5, Legislative Business, The Calcutta Rent Bill, 1920, Proceedings of the Bengal Legislative Council on Wednesday, 31 March 1920, Government of Bengal, Part IV-A. Alipore: Superintendent, Government Printing, Bengal Government Press.

20. The passage of the Rent Acts in various cities during and following the First World War was a matter of intense anxiety among liberal policy-makers of the time. Everywhere–from metropolitan cities to the colonial cities–they were all in agreement that any prolongation of such legislation beyond the exceptional years of the War would mean the state's interference in the 'natural process' of the market, which, when left to its own devices, would permit the formation of 'normal prices'. See Bengal (India), 1920, Calcutta Rent Enquiry Committee, 'Report of the Committee Appointed to Enquire into Land Values and Rents in Calcutta, Calcutta'. Accessed at the CIT Record Room, Kolkata.

21. Bengal (India), 1920, Calcutta Rent Enquiry Committee, 'Report of the Committee Appointed to Enquire into Land Values and Rents in Calcutta, Calcutta'. Accessed at the CIT Record Room, Kolkata.

22. Ibid.

23. The vicinity of Park Street up to the Lower Circular Road used to host a sizeable section of British officials and British commercial establishments. Many of the buildings in this area were owned by native landlords. This means that the British voice within the Rent Committee tended to side with the tenants. In his speech at the Bengal Legislative

Assembly, Rai Radha Charan Pal Bahadur pointed out how the composition of the Rent Committee was tilted overwhelmingly towards the tenant side. *The Calcutta Gazette*, 31 March 1920. The Speech of Hon'ble Rai Radha Charan Pal Bahadur, at the Legislative Council, List of Business–Item No. 6 and 6 A, Legislative Business, The Calcutta Rent Bill, 1920, Proceedings of the Bengal Legislative Council on Wednesday, 31 March 1920, Government of Bengal, Legislative Department. Part IV-A. Alipore: Superintendent, Government Printing, Bengal Government Press.

24. *The Calcutta Gazette*, 31 March 1920. The Speech of the Hon'ble the Maharajadhiraja Bahadur of Burdwan, the Legislative Council, List of Business–Item No. 5, Legislative Business, The Calcutta Rent Bill, 1920, Proceedings of the Bengal Legislative Council on Wednesday, 31 March 1920, Government of Bengal, Part IV-A. Alipore: Superintendent, Government Printing, Bengal Government Press.

25. Municipal Administration of Calcutta. *Annual Report*. 1915. *Report on the Municipal Administration of Calcutta for the Year 1914–1915*. Calcutta: Corporation Press: 23.

26. Ibid.: 26.

27. *The Calcutta Gazette*, 31 March 1920. The Speech of Hon'ble Rai Radha Charan Pal Bahadur, at the Legislative Council, List of Business–Item No. 6 and 6 A, Legislative Business, The Calcutta Rent Bill, 1920, Proceedings of the Bengal Legislative Council on Wednesday, 31 March 1920, Government of Bengal, Legislative Department. Part IV-A. Alipore: Superintendent, Government Printing, Bengal Government Press.

References

Basu, B. 1977. *Amar Jauban*. Kolkata: M. C. Sarkar & Sons.

Bayly, C. A. 1971. 'Local Control in Indian Towns–The Case of Allahabad 1880–1920'. *Modern Asian Studies* 5(4): 289–311.

Bhattacharyya, D. 2016. 'Interwar Housing Speculation and Rent Profiteering in Colonial Calcutta'. *Comparative Studies of South Asia, Africa and the Middle East* 36(3): 465–482.

Bompas, C. H. 1927. 'The Work of the Calcutta Improvement Trust'. *Journal of the Royal Society of Arts* 75(3864): 199–219.

Census of India. 1911. 'City of Calcutta, Part I, Report', Vol. VI, 1913. Calcutta: Bengal Secretariat Book Depot.

______. 1921. 'City of Calcutta, Part I, Report', Vol. VI, 1923. Calcutta: Bengal Secretariat Book Depot.

Chatterjee, P. 1984. *Bengal 1920–1947: The Land Question*. Calcutta: K. P. Bagchi.

______. 1997. *The Present History of West Bengal: Essays in Political Criticism*. New Delhi: Oxford University Press.

Chatterji, N. 2017. 'Sacred Calling, Worldly Bargain: Caste, Self-cultivation and Mobilisation in Late Colonial Bengal'. Unpublished PhD Dissertation, New Delhi: Centre for Historical Studies, Jawaharlal Nehru University.

Das, S. 1991. *Communal Riots in Bengal, 1905–1947*. New Delhi: Oxford University Press.

Datta, P. 2012. *Planning the City: Urbanisation and Reform in Calcutta, 1800–1940*. New Delhi: Tulika Books.

______. 2015. 'Calcutta on the Threshold of the 1940s'. In T. Sarkar and S. Bandyopadhyay (eds), *Calcutta: The Stormy Decades*, 18–41. New Delhi: Social Science Press.

Fogelson, R. M. 2013. *The Great Rent Wars: New York, 1917–1929*. New Haven: Yale University Press.

Forsell, H. 2006. *Property, Tenancy and Urban Growth in Stockholm and Berlin, 1860–1920*. Burlington: Ashgate.

Ghertner, D. A. 2014. 'India's Urban Revolution: Geographies of Displacement Beyond Gentrification'. *Environment and Planning A* 46(7): 1554–1571.

Ghose, S. 1950. *Madhubansir Gali*. Kolkata: Mitra o Ghose Publishers.

Kar, B. 1957. *Deoyal*. Kolkata: D. M. Library.

Kidambi, P. 2001. 'Housing the Poor in a Colonial City: The Bombay Improvement Trust'. *Studies in History* 17(1): 57–79.

______. 2007. *The Making of an Indian Metropolis: Colonial Governance and Public Culture in Bombay, 1890–1920*. Burlington: Ashgate.

Law, B. C. and V. L. Mookherjee. 1924. *Rent Acts: Calcutta, Bombay and Rangoon*. Calcutta: R. Cambray & Co.

Legg, S. 2007. *Spaces of Colonialism: Delhi's Urban Govermentalities*. Oxford: Blackwell.

Macmillan, A. 1928. *Seaports of India & Ceylon: Historical and Descriptive, Commercial and Industrial Facts, Figures and Resources*. London: W. H. & L. Collingridge.

Madden, D. and P. Marcuse. 2016. *In Defense of Housing: The Politics of Crisis*. London and New York: Verso.

Marcuse, P. 1985. 'Gentrification, Abandonment and Displacement: Connections, Causes and Policy Responses in New York City'. *Journal of Urban and Contemporary Law* 28: 195–240.

Mitra, B. 1970[1952]. *Sahib Bibi Golam*. Calcutta: New Age.
Mukherjee, J. 2015. *The Hungry Bengal: War, Famine and the End of Empire*. London: Hurst & Company.
Ray, R. K. 1979. *Urban Roots of Indian Nationalism: Pressure Groups and Conflicts in Calcutta City Politics, 1875–1939*. New Delhi: Vikas Publishing House.
Richards, E. P. 1914. *Calcutta Improvement Trust: Report by Request of the Trust on the Condition, Improvement and Town Planning of the City of Calcutta and Contiguous Areas*. Hertfordshire: Jennings.
Sarkar, T. 1987. *Bengal 1928–1934: The Politics of Protest*. New Delhi: Oxford University Press.
Sengupta, K. M. 2013. 'Planned Spaces, Intimate Places: Ordering a City and Creating a Neighbourhood in Colonial Calcutta'. PhD Dissertation, New Delhi: Centre for Historical Studies, Jawaharlal Nehru University.
Sinha, S. N. 1916. 'The Central Avenue: Calcutta's New Thoroughfare'. *Bengal Past and Present* 12/13(1): 71–74.
Smith, N. 1979. 'Toward a theory of gentrification: A back to the city movement by capital, not people'. *Journal of the American Planning Association* 45(4): 538–548.
______. 2002. 'New Globalism, New Urbanism, Gentrification as Global Urban Strategy'. *Antipode* 34(3): 427–450.
Tagore, K. 1930. *Kolikatay Chola-phera: Sekaal o Ekaal*. Kolkata.
Thacker's Indian Directory. 1918. 'Embracing the Whole of the Indian Empire, Calcutta Streets'. Calcutta: Thacker's Press & Directories, Ltd.
______. 1933. 'Embracing the Whole of the Indian Empire, Calcutta Streets'. Calcutta: Thacker's Press & Directories, Ltd.
The Times of India. 1920. 'Calcutta vs Bombay, Letter to the Editor', 21 June.
Ward, K. 2006. '"Policies in Motion", Urban Management and State Restructuring: The Trans-Local Expansion of Business Improvement Districts'. *International Journal of Urban and Regional Research* 30(1): 54–75.

Notes on Contributors

Ritajyoti Bandyopadhyay is Assistant Professor in the Department of Humanities and Social Sciences, Indian Institute of Science Education and Research, Mohali, India.

Jorge Luiz Barbosa is Professor of Geography at Federal Fluminense University, Brazil and Co-Director of UNIperiferias, Brazil.

Rajesh Bhattacharya is Associate Professor in the Public Policy and Management Group, Indian Institute of Management Calcutta, India.

Amita Bhide is Professor and Dean of the School of Habitat Studies, Tata Institute of Social Sciences, Mumbai, India.

Patrick Bond is Honorary Professor in the School of Geography, Archaeology and Environmental Studies, University of Witwatersrand, Johannesburg, South Africa.

Somsook Boonyabancha is Director of the Asian Coalition for Housing Rights (ACHR), Thailand.

Xi Chen is Doctoral Researcher in the School of Architecture, Harbin Institute of Technology, Key Laboratory of Science and Technology of Urban and Rural Living Environment in Cold Region, Ministry of Industry and Information Technology, Harbin, China.

Camila D'Ottaviano is Associate Professor in the School of Architecture and Urbanism, University of Sao Paulo (FAUUSP), Brazil.

Fernando Lannes Fernandes is Reader in the School of Education and Social Work, University of Dundee, Scotland, UK and Co-Director of UNIperiferias, Brazil.

Ujaan Ghosh is Doctoral Researcher in the Department of Art History, University of Wisconsin–Madison, USA.

Sourav Hazra is Executive Director in a global multinational firm in New Delhi, India, specialising in Infrastructure Advisory across Emerging Markets.

Thomas Andrew Kerr is English Language Publications Co-Ordinator at Asian Coalition for Housing Rights (ACHR), Thailand.

Yanhong Ma is Assistant Professor in the School of Architecture and Urban Planning, Chongqing University, Key Laboratory of Mountain Town Construction and New Technology, Ministry of Education, Chongqing, China.

Eduardo Cesar Leão Marques is Professor in the Department of Political Science, University of Sao Paulo and Director of the Center for Metropolitan Studies (CEM), University of São Paulo, Brazil.

Tatiana Moura is Senior Researcher in the Centre for Social Studies, University of Coimbra, Portugal and Co-Director of UNIperiferias, Brazil.

Ekaterina Norkina is a Russian Specialist and Global Events professional based in Moscow, Russia.

Bhuvaneswari Raman is Professor and Associate Dean (Academic Affairs) in the Jindal School of Government and Public Policy, O. P. Jindal Global University, India.

Tara Saharan is Post-Doctoral Researcher in the Water Management Department and Multi-Actor Systems Department, Delft University of Technology (TU Delft), The Netherlands.

Urmi Sengupta is Senior Lecturer in Spatial Planning and Director of Education (PGT Courses) in the School of Natural and Built Environment, Queen's University, Belfast, UK.

Awadhendra Sharan is Director, Centre for the Study of Developing Societies, India.

Annapurna Shaw is Former Professor in the Public Policy and Management Group, Indian Institute of Management Calcutta, India.

Eliana Sousa Silva is Professor and Director at Redes da Maré, Brazil and Co-Director of UNIperiferias, Brazil.

Jailson de Souza e Silva is Funder and Co-Director of UNIperiferias, Brazil.

Index